THE DENT MASTER MUSICIANS

KT-445-893

VERDI

Series edited by Stanley Sadie

B.C.H.E. – LIBRARY

00012172

The Dent Master Musicians

Titles available in paperback

Bach *Malcolm Boyd*
Bartók *Paul Griffiths*
Beethoven *Denis Matthews*
Berlioz *Hugh Macdonald*
Brahms *Malcolm MacDonald*
Britten *Michael Kennedy*
Dufay *David Fallows*
Grieg *John Horton*
Haydn *Rosemary Hughes*
Liszt *Derek Watson*
Mahler *Michael Kennedy*
Mendelssohn *Philip Radcliffe*
Monteverdi *Denis Arnold*

Rossini *Richard Osborne*
Schoenberg *Malcolm MacDonald*
Schubert *John Reed*
Schumann *Joan Chissell*
Sibelius *Robert Layton*
Richard Strauss *Michael Kennedy*
Tchaikovsky *Edward Garden*
Verdi *Julian Budden*
Vivaldi *Michael Talbot*
Wagner *Barry Millington*

Titles available in hardback

Bach *Malcolm Boyd*
Brahms *Malcolm MacDonald*
Liszt *Derek Watson*

Stravinsky *Paul Griffiths*
Vivaldi *Michael Talbot*

In preparation

Elgar *Robert Anderson*
Handel *Donald Burrows*

A list of all Dent books on music is obtainable from the publishers:

J.M. Dent
The Orion Publishing Group
Orion House
5 Upper St Martin's Lane
London WC2H 9EA

THE DENT MASTER MUSICIANS

VERDI

Julian Budden

J. M. DENT, LONDON

BATH COLLEGE
OF
HIGHER EDUCATION
NEWTON PARK
LIBRARY

PD

CLASS 780.92 VER
No.   B

ACC
No.   00012172

© Text, Julian Budden 1985

First published 1985
First paperback edition 1986
Revised 1993

All rights reserved. No part of this publication may be reproduced, stored in a retrieval system, or transmitted, in any form or by any means, electronic, mechanical, photocopying, recording or otherwise, without the prior permission of J.M. Dent

This book if bound as a paperback is subject to the condition that it may not be issued on loan or otherwise except in its original binding

Music examples set by Paul Courtenay

Printed and bound in Great Britain by
Butler & Tanner Ltd, Frome and London
for
J.M. Dent
The Orion Publishing Group
Orion House
5 Upper St Martin's Lane
London WC2H 9EA

British Library Cataloguing-in-Publication Data
A catalogue record for this book is available
from The British Library

ISBN 0 460 86111 5

Preface

Few composers have been as spectacularly revalued over the last fifty years as Verdi, especially in Britain. If certain of our inter-war critics – notably Dent, Blom and Tovey – were never in doubt as to his greatness, for the majority he was the composer of *Il trovatore* who acquired respectability only in *Otello, Falstaff* and the *Requiem*. The pioneering studies of Bonavia and Toye undoubtedly helped to turn the tide in his favour. Yet for many years to come English Verdians would feel themselves to be on the defensive; and a note of apology can be sensed in their writings on the subject. But with the end of the war the Verdi-renaissance that had begun in Germany in the 1920s showed no signs of abating. Operas which had been thought dead beyond recall were unearthed, staged and found to be good. The ominous critical opening, 'It is easy to see why this opera is so seldom revived', was less and less frequently to be encountered. A landmark in the growing appreciation of Verdi's works was the foundation in 1960 of the Istituto di Studi Verdiani at Parma under the presidency of the veteran composer Ildebrando Pizzetti. Over the following years it acted as a focal point for international scholarship. Its sister branch, the American Institute for Verdi Studies in New York, founded in 1975, possesses a unique wealth of archive material. A comparison of Bonavia's 120-page life-and-works of 1930 with Busch's massive monograph on *Aida* of 1978 or the *Macbeth* source-book will give a fair idea of the altered perspective on a composer whose name Wagner could hardly bear to hear mentioned. In the meantime Frank Walker's *The Man Verdi* (1962) set an entirely new standard of biographical accuracy and acumen.

Inevitably, therefore, Dyneley Hussey's admirable study of 1940 in the Master Musicians series falls short of today's needs if only because, like his predecessors, he was forced to pass judgment on operas which he had never seen but which today are staged all over the world. Indeed, it could reasonably be asked whether there is any longer a place for a single volume devoted to the life and works in view of the vast mass of material relevant to both. The answer is that a short study written in the light of the latest scholarly findings without setting them forth in detail can still be useful to the non-specialised musical reader. The present book contains no sensational revelations, offers no radically new perspectives on the music. It is rather a bird's-eye 'Verdi '84', whose purpose is to give information relevant to an assessment of the subject in a compendious and easily accessible form. Inevitably certain lists given in the appendices — notably the *Bibliography* and the *Personalia* have had to be selective. The *Bibliography* is based on that of Andrew Porter following the Verdi entry in *The New Grove Dictionary of Music and Musicians*.

My thanks are due above all to the Istituto di Studi Verdiani in Parma and to its sister organisation, the American Institute of Verdi Studies in New York for making various materials available to me; and also to those friends and colleagues mentioned in the prefaces to my three volumes, *The Operas of Verdi*, who have never ceased to give me valuable help.

1984   J.B.

For the new paperback edition I have taken the opportunity of making a number of minor corrections and of updating the bibliography.

1992   J.B.

Contents

Verdi

Illustrations

Key to sigla

AGV	F. Abbiati	*Giuseppe Verdi* (4 vols Milan, 1959)
AIVS		Newsletters, American Institute for Verdi Studies (New York, 1976–)
AVI	A. Alberti	*Verdi intimo: Carteggio di Giuseppe Verdi con il Conte Opprandino Arrivabene (1861–1886)* (Verona, 1931)
BOV	J. Budden	*The Operas of Verdi* (3 vols London, 1973–81)
BSV	A. Basevi	*Studio sulle opere di Giuseppe Verdi* (Florence, 1959)
BVA	H. Busch	*Verdi's Aida: the History of an Opera in Letters and Documents* (Minneapolis, 1978)
CBM	M. Conati	*La bottega della musica: Verdi e La Fenice* (Milan, 1983)
CI	G. Cenzato	*Itinerari verdiani* (Milan, 1951)
CIIV	M. Conati	*Interviste e Incontri con Verdi* (Parma, 1980)
DFV	R. De Rensis	*Franco Faccio e Verdi: Carteggi e documenti inediti* (Milan, 1934)
GGDC	U. Günther	'La Genèse de *Don Carlos*, opéra en cinq actes de Giuseppe Verdi, représenté pour la première fois à Paris le 11 mars 1867' in *Revue de musicologie* (Paris) 58 (1972) 60 (1974)
GBM	L.A. Garibaldi	*Giuseppe Verdi nelle lettere di Emanuele Muzio ad Antonio Barezzi* (Milan, 1931)
GVIM	G.C. Varesi	'L'interpretazione di Macbeth' in *Nuova Antologia* (Nov.–Dec. 1932) Anno 27 fascicolo 1958. pp. 433–40

HFVO	S. Hughes	*Famous Verdi Operas* (London, 1968)
LCC	A. Luzio & G. Cesari	*I copialettere di Giuseppe Verdi* (Milan, 1913)
LCV	A. Luzio	*Carteggi Verdiani* (4 vols Rome, 1935–47)
LPB	A. Luzio	*Profili biografici e bozzetti storici* (2 vols Milan, 1927)
MCVB	M. Medici & M. Conati	*Carteggio Verdi-Boito* (2 vols, Parma, 1978)
MGV	G. Marchesi	*Giuseppe Verdi, l'uomo, il genio, l'artista* (Milan, 1981)
MV	G. Monaldi	*Verdi (1839–1898)* (4th ed. Milan, 1951)
MVA	G. Monaldi	*Verdi aneddotico* (L'Aquila, 1926)
MVLT	G. Martin	*Verdi, his music, life & times* (London, 1964)
PLVE	J.G. Prod'homme	'Lettres inédites de Giuseppe Verdi à Léon Escudier' in *Rivista Musicale Italiana* (Rome) 35, 1928
PRB	A. Pascolato	*Re Lear e Ballo in Maschera. Lettere di Giuseppe Verdi ad Antonio Somma* (Città di Castello, 1902)
PUVD	J.G. Prod'homme	'Unpublished letters from Verdi to Camille Du Locle' *Musical Quarterly* (New York) 1921, VII
PVAF	A. Pougin	*Vita aneddotica di Giuseppe Verdi con note aggiunte di Folchetto* (Milan 1881)
PVS	A. Porter	'*Les Vêpres Siciliennes*: New letters from Verdi to Scribe' in *Nineteenth Century Music* (Berkeley), 2 no. 2 (1978)
TGV	F. Toye	*Giuseppe Verdi, his life & works* (Milan, 1931)
VBISV		*Verdi: Bollettini dell' Istituto di Studi Verdiani* (Parma, 1960–82)
WMV	F. Walker	*The Man Verdi* (London, 1962)
ZMVS	U. Zoppi	*Angelo Mariani, Giuseppe Verdi e Teresa Stolz* (Milan, 1947)

1

Early life at Busseto

'. . . But alas! Born poor, in a poor village, I hadn't the means of acquiring any education; they put a wretched spinet under my hands and some time after that I started writing notes . . . notes one after the other. That's all . . . And the fact is that now I'm an old man I have great doubts as to the value of those notes . . .'[1] Verdi's own words written to Caterina Pigorini Beri on the eve of his seventy-eighth birthday in a mood of depression have too often been taken by biographers at their face value as a thumbnail sketch of his career. Nor did he himself discourage this. The story of the illiterate peasant boy who rose by his own effort to become his country's tutelary deity had a great appeal for a moralising century – another progress from log-cabin to White House. The truth is less dramatic though not quite as different as certain recent writers would have us believe. Verdi's background was indeed provincial; and because of it he made his way slowly even though from an early age his gifts were never in doubt. No Italian composer of comparable eminence had to wait until the age of twenty-six for his first opera to be staged.

In the previous century such a background would have been no bar to early success. Certainly it was an advantage to have been born into the profession as were Bach, Mozart and Beethoven; but so long as there was a music-loving noble in the vicinity, who would take him into his employ, the boy who showed a talent for music would be given every opportunity for developing it. His patron would send him at his own expense to some well-known musical centre where he could perfect himself in the latest style of composition and in due course do credit to his patron's establishment. But with the decline of private orchestras, the founding of conservatories in which places were competed for, and the general shift of the musical centre of gravity north of the Alps, the picture changed. For one who aspired

[1] CIV, p. 25.

to the heights of artistic accomplishment Verdi was badly placed.

He was born on 9 October 1813 at the hamlet of Le Roncole, three miles from Busseto, a little market town in the province of Parma. Soon to revert to its status as a Duchy, Parma then formed part of Napoleon's Kingdom of Italy – hence the French Christian names, Joseph Fortunin François, entered in the municipal register instead of Giuseppe Fortunio Francesco. His father, Carlo Verdi, came of a family which had once held property in and around Busseto but whose fortunes had of recent years declined. He himself kept the inn at Roncole which also served as the provision store. In 1805 he had married Luigia Uttini, herself an inn-keeper's daughter from the province of Piacenza. Tradespeople, then, not peasants; and though in a report on the family published in Busseto in 1832 both are described as 'illiterati' ('uncultured', rather than 'illiterate', for which the Italian word is 'analfabeto') Carlo was sufficiently educated to act as secretary to the treasury of the church, S. Michele Arcangelo, in Roncole from 1825 to 1840. Several letters have survived written in his own hand; one was even put on display in a theatrical exhibition organised by the Casa Ricordi in 1894. There was never any excuse for the belief that Carlo Verdi could neither read nor write.

Of Verdi's life as a child little survives except legend and some jottings for an unwritten biography made long afterwards by his fellow-Bussetan and fanatical admirer, Giuseppe Demaldé. It is said that when the allied armies swept back in 1814 Luigia was forced to take refuge in the church belfry together with her infant son. Two years later she bore a girl, Giuseppa Francesca. A verbal tradition has it that Giuseppa's brain was damaged as a result of meningitis; but Demaldé, recording her death in 1833, mentions nothing of this, only that she was pleasant, beautiful, kind and well-mannered and that Verdi loved her as himself. Italian families are usually very close; yet there is no evidence that Verdi was ever close to his, though once his fortune was made he took care to set them up in ease and comfort. His contemporaries remembered him as a solemn, reserved boy to whom music meant everything even if it was only the grinding of an itinerant barrel organ. Once, when serving in the church of S.Michele, he was so absorbed in the singing that he forgot to attend to his duties and received a cuff from the enraged priest. 'May God strike you down!' the boy cried as he picked himself up. Never a friend to the cloth, Verdi used to enjoy recounting how the curse was fulfilled. Years later lightning struck the church of Madonna dei Prati, killing the selfsame priest and several members of the congregation including – though he was usually silent about this – one of his own relatives.

The organist of S.Michele was Don Baistrocchi, who also taught at the elementary school. It was he, we are told, who first discovered Giuseppe's musical bent and persuaded Carlo to buy him the 'wretched spinet' which had belonged to a priest of the neighbourhood; and a more tangible relic exists in the form of a card signed by one Stefano Cavalletti, repairer of instruments, declining payment for having put to rights the keyboard mechanism and added pedals, 'seeing the good disposition the young Giuseppe Verdi has for learning to play his instrument'. The date is 1821.

At the age of ten Verdi was sent to the *ginnasio* in Busseto where he lodged with a cobbler known as 'Pugnatta'. On the death of Don Baistrocchi a few months earlier he had been appointed organist in his stead; this meant that on Sundays and holidays he now had to make the three-mile journey on foot from Busseto to Roncole. His organist's fee was nugatory (Walker estimates it as the equivalent of four pounds per annum);[2] the lodgings at Busseto had to be paid for. Though Luigia was by general consent a 'good manager', Carlo never succeeded in making money. Ten years before Giuseppe was born he was convicted of having permitted gambling at his inn, only to be certified to the authorities as being unable to pay the fine. In 1830 he incurred a debt which he only succeeded in settling after fourteen years. One can believe the story that the young Giuseppe used to walk from Busseto to Roncole and back in bare feet in order to save shoe-leather.

It has been said that great art is born on the plains within sight of mountains. The young Beethoven had his horizon bounded by the Siebengebirge and the romantic Drachenfels of Turner's famous painting. Mozart could lift up his eyes to the hills of the Salzkammergut. But the region of Italy where Verdi was born and bred and which he was to make his home must be accounted a very unpromising terrain. The foothills of the Apuan Alps, visible westward from Parma, are nowhere to be seen round Busseto, but only the Bassa Parmense at its most uneventful, enlivened by the occasional line of

2 WMV, p. 4.

poplars and the antique charm of its farmhouses and churches. Little has changed there since Verdi was a boy. A railway branch line runs northward from Fidenza (then Borgo San Donnino) passing Busseto – indeed it was built in Verdi's lifetime and its route plotted so as to avoid his own estates. A modern highway passes within a hundred yards of the Villa Verdi carrying an endless stream of lorries to and from Cremona. But no outcrops of week-end villas spoil the country-side – there is so little to spoil. One can understand why once he had settled at S.Agata Verdi should have created his own romantic landscape within its walls.

However, Busseto in the 1820s was by no means a cultural desert. Its *ginnasio* could boast excellent teachers, eminent in their own sphere of learning, from whom it was possible to obtain a good liberal education. Indeed many emerged from it to attain leading positions as mathematicians, scientists, lawyers and theologians. Its director was Don Pietro Seletti, who also ran the public library and was to found an academy of Greek language and literature. Verdi, who even before entering the school had begun his classical studies under two Franciscans, had lessons in Italian grammar from Seletti himself, and in 'humanity and rhetoric' from Carlo Curotti and Don Giacinto Volpini. In 1825 he entered the music school of Ferdinando Provesi, organist of the church of S.Bartolomeo and municipal music master. Seletti, it appears, was sufficiently impressed by his progress to want to make a priest of him, but soon yielded to evidence of the boy's true vocation. It was during these years that Verdi was taken up by Antonio Barezzi, a well-to-do merchant from whom Carlo bought his provisions. Verdi became one of his household along with his four daughters and two sons. Barezzi was the founder and president of the Philharmonic Society, a miscellaneous band of players that gave concerts in the piazza and sometimes played in church. Their rehearsals were usually held in Barezzi's house, he himself taking part as flautist. A record of 1834 gives an idea of the band's constitution: 6 violins, 1 cello, 1 viola, 2 double-basses, 8 clarinets, 2 oboes, 2 flutes, 5 trumpets, 4 horns, 1 bass drum, 6 other percussion instruments and 'several other small instruments'. So it was that Verdi found himself thrust into the heart of Busseto's musical life. In a document of 1853 he tells of the innumerable pieces that he composed from his thirteenth year onwards – marches and overtures for the Philharmonic Society, variations for piano for himself to play at concerts, arias and cantatas for local singers to perform in church or in the theatre, of which he singles out a *Stabat Mater*. To these Demaldé adds an overture to Rossini's opera *Il barbiere di Siviglia* which 'as everybody knows has no overture(!)'; and a setting of Alfieri's *I deliri di Saul* for baritone – 'a true jewel, a precious stone, something really grand, to which any established composer would not be ashamed to put his name' . . .[3] a judgment whose validity we may respectfully presume to doubt.

For whatever the level of general culture at Busseto, there is no reason to believe that the standard of music would have been anything but modest, to say the least. Philharmonic societies were a trans-Alpine institution (one hears of no Philharmonic societies in Rome or Naples during that time). Mostly they came into being after the Napoleonic Wars in order to replace those private, aristocratic orchestras for whom Haydn and Beethoven wrote their symphonies. The Viennese *Gesellschaft der Musikfreunde* arose in this way, the music-loving nobles pooling their resources with those of the wealthier members of the new bourgeoisie. Verdi himself would encounter another society of the same character in Austrianised Milan – the *Filodrammatici*. But between an organisation capable of performing Haydn oratorios and one that disposes chiefly of wind instruments and for which everything has to be arranged there is a vast gulf. The chief administrator of the States of Parma under Napoleon, Moreau de Saint-Méry, laid stress in a special report on the inhabitants' passion for music; but one shudders to think of the form that music took at the time of Verdi's adolescence. Indeed the concert-bills tell their own story: marches and overtures, variations – of a sub-Paganinian nature we may be sure – by a local virtuoso, the latest vocal 'hit' by Rossini. Nor is it a surprise to see a movement from *I deliri di Saul* arranged as a bassoon solo. The only advantage that Verdi would have derived from such an ambience was that sense of rough-and-ready effectiveness that shows so clearly in his early scores.[4]

In 1829 he applied for the post of organist at the nearby village of Soragna but despite an enthusiastic testimonial from his teacher, Provesi, he was not accepted. With the prospects of profitable

---

[3] AIVS, newsletter no.1 (May 1976), p. 10.
[4] There is a tradition that the banda march from Act IV of *Nabucco* is a composition from Verdi's Busseto days. It has little to recommend it as music.

employment in the vicinity thus closed it was clear as the years passed that Verdi needed more training in his profession than could be accorded at Busseto. He had fallen in love with Barezzi's eldest daughter, Margherita, and wanted to be in a position to marry her. So it was decided that Carlo Verdi should apply for a grant from the local charitable institution, the Monte di Pietà, to send Giuseppe for four years to the Milan Conservatoire as a paying pupil. The application was sympathetically received; but grants for the following two years were already allocated. No matter; Barezzi agreed to advance the necessary money, with the assurance of being reimbursed (in the event he was not to be indemnified without a good deal of trouble). Verdi was accordingly dispatched to Milan in June 1832 to sit for the entrance examination. Such was his reputation in and around Busseto that it was with incredulity that Barezzi and his friends heard the news that he had failed.

It was one of those early setbacks that composers of Verdi's temperament can never forgive or forget. Throughout his life he railed at conservatories, maintaining that they never taught a composer anything worth knowing. But for the most part biographers have long ceased to blame the Milan authorities for their verdict. Basily, the registrar and chief examiner, submitted in his report to the director that

> Signor Angeleri, teacher of the pianforte, found that Verdi would have to change the position of his hands, which, he said, at the age of eighteen would be difficult. As for the compositions which he presented as his own, I am in complete agreement with Signor Piantanida, teacher of counterpoint and vice-registrar, that if he applies himself attentively and patiently to study the rules of counterpoint he will be able to control the genuine imagination he shows himself to possess and thus turn out creditably as a composer.[5]

But the conservatoire was overcrowded; Verdi himself at eighteen was over the required age limit and moreover a foreigner from the Duchy of Parma. There were insufficient grounds for waiving the rules in his case. Among the examiners was Alessandro Rolla, violin professor and former leader of the orchestra at La Scala, to whom Provesi had given Verdi a letter of introduction (the two men had

[5] WMV, p. 9.

known each other when Rolla had led the court orchestra at Parma). He it was who broke the disappointing news. He advised Verdi to study privately in Milan, indicating two likely teachers, of which Verdi chose Vincenzo Lavigna, professor of composition and like Rolla himself a former member of the orchestra at La Scala where he held the post of *maestro al cembalo*. Everything now depended on Barezzi, whose expenses would be more than doubled if he had to maintain Verdi in private lodgings. Fortunately he had set his hand to the plough and did not intend to turn back. It was arranged that during his studies with Lavigna Verdi would lodge with Giuseppe Seletti, nephew of the Busseto headmaster and a personal friend of Barezzi's.

It was not a happy arrangement. Seletti's letters to Busseto are cordial enough to begin with but soon a note of sourness creeps in. Clearly the expenses of life in Milan even for a music student were more than Barezzi had bargained for. There was music paper to be bought, an 'abonnement' for a permanent seat at La Scala, a sub-scription to music dealers for copies of all the latest scores. Besides, Verdi needed to be decently clad if he were not to shame his host. Barezzi never failed to settle the accounts which Seletti sent him. But before two years had passed Seletti made it clear that he no longer wanted Verdi in his house. No specific misdemeanour is mentioned beyond his 'boorish manners' and that 'he is the sort of man I would never have wanted to get to know'. To cap everything Verdi refused to board with the family that Seletti had chosen for him. 'If he were to turn out a thousand times greater than Rossini,' Seletti fumed, 'I will always say that I knew him as ill-educated in his manners, arrogant and – towards me personally – something of a scoundrel'.[6] Dark hints follow about behaviour which he would prefer not to report to Verdi's future father-in-law (had he been over-familiar, one wonders, with Seletti's own daughter?). Soon Verdi received a sharp note from Barezzi pointing out how much he had spent on the young man's needs since his move from the Seletti household. Those who want an explanation of Verdi's later obsession with self-sufficiency need look no further than here. Never can dependence on others have seemed more hateful.

Fortunately the lessons with Lavigna made good progress. The

[6] MGV, pp. 37–8.

professor sent regular reports to the Monte di Pietà, praising his pupil's assiduity, his growing prowess and even his unblemished moral character. Verdi gave his own account of those lessons in a famous letter to Francesco Florimo of 1871:

> Lavigna was very strong on counterpoint and a bit of a pedant, and had no use for any other music than that of Paisiello (his teacher). I remember that in a sinfonia that I wrote he corrected all the scoring in the manner of Paisiello. 'I'd be for it', I said to myself – and from that moment on I did not show him any more of my original compositions and in the three years spent with him I did nothing but canons and fugues, fugues and canons of every kind. Nobody taught me orchestration or how to treat dramatic music.

Taken out of context this sounds reproachful, not to say ungracious. But that was not how Verdi meant it. At a time when young Italians were sitting at the feet of Liszt and Bülow hoping thus to be led to the promised land of transcendental art, the farmer of S.Agata was insisting on the superior virtues of mere technical discipline. No matter that Lavigna was the most minor of composers. Verdi valued him rather as Beethoven valued Albrechtsberger. He concluded his letter: 'He [Lavigna] was learned and I wish all teachers were like him.'[7]

It was Lavigna, too, who introduced Verdi to the Filodrammatici – a Philharmonic Society in which various members of the Milanese nobility took part and which boasted a fine chorus. The director was Pietro Massini, who would soon prove one of Verdi's stoutest supporters. One day during rehearsals for Haydn's *Creation* the three 'maestri' who took it in turns to play the keyboard were all absent. Massini asked Verdi to take their place, adding that he need only play the bass line. Verdi relates how

> I was fresh from my studies and certainly not at all embarrassed by a full score. I therefore accepted and sat down at the piano to begin the rehearsals. I remember very well the ironical smiles of some of the signori dilettanti, and it seems that my youthful figure, thin and not too tidily dressed, was not such as to inspire much confidence. In short the rehearsal began and gradually I began to get worked up and excited and instead of confining myself to

[7] AGV, I, pp. 118–19.

accompanying I began to conduct with my right hand, playing
with my left hand alone. I had a great success – all the greater for
being unexpected.

In the end it was settled that Verdi should direct the performance,
which was given first at the Teatro Filodrammatico (today the
Piccola Scala) and repeated at the Casino de' Nobili before the cream
of Milan society. 'Shortly afterwards', Verdi continues, 'Count
Renato Borromeo engaged me to compose the music of a cantata –
for the marriage of a member of his family, I believe.'[8] In fact it was
in honour of the Emperor Ferdinand – a circumstance which the
musical patriarch of Italy was doubtless only too ready to forget.

The Creation was performed in May 1834. Later that year events
at Busseto put a temporary blight on what seemed to be a promising
career. In the summer of 1833 Provesi had died. No mere village
musician, he was a poet and a teacher of Italian; his sympathies were
liberal, and he was never much in favour with the clergy, several
members of which he had lampooned. Worse still, in his youth he
had been convicted of robbing a church and sentenced to a spell in
prison. To Barezzi and the Philharmonic Society Verdi was his only
possible successor once he had completed his studies in Milan. The
clergy thought otherwise. Their own candidate for the vacant post
was one Giovanni Ferrari from neighbouring Guastalla. He and two
others entered their applications in November 1833. Barezzi did
nothing on Verdi's behalf, having been assured that there would be a
competitive examination. Lavigna wrote to the Monte di Pietà that
his pupil would be ready to take up his duties in a year's time.

For over six months nothing further was done; performances in
church and elsewhere were allowed to drag on under painfully
inferior substitutes, until in July the clergy took matters into their
own hands and appointed Ferrari without the agreed competition.
Verdi was urgently summoned from Milan; he handed in his application only to be told that it was too late. The council of the Monte di
Pietà, under whose foundation the civic duties of the post fell, met
and confirmed Ferrari's appointment. Galluzzi, the deputy mayor,
who had attended the meeting as a supporter of Verdi's cause, had

---

[8] PVAF pp. 40–1. See, however, the document of 1853 (WMV, p. 7) where
the cantata is merely said to have been performed in the house of Count
Borromeo.

the ground cut from under his feet by the intelligence that Margherita Barezzi had been telling all and sundry that her fiancé had not the slightest intention of settling in Busseto; that to do so would be to let down his friends in Milan. Ferrari on the other hand was a married man with a family and needed the emolument. Later the Bishop of the diocese upheld the council's decision, adding that a man of Ferrari's years was more to be trusted than a 'beardless youth' (like Canon Chasuble, he spoke figuratively) 'who had been exposed to the vices of a great and populous city'.[9]

Verdi at once sent a letter of protest to Maria Luigia, the Duchess of Parma; but it was not answered for a year. Meanwhile faction erupted in full force – a miniature war of Guelphs and Ghibellines, or 'codini' and 'coccardini' as they were called. Lampoons were hurled, public insults exchanged; people came to blows in the street. Both sides did their utmost to influence Francesco Cocchi, Maria Luigia's Minister of the Interior. The whole affair was satirised in an epic poem of nine cantos called *Gli uccelli accademici*, by the 'codino' Don Pettorelli, in which the Duchess figures as an eagle, Barezzi and Margherita as blackbirds, Verdi as a parrot, Ferrari as the cuckoo in the nest. Verdi himself remained in Busseto until the end of the year, taking part in the activities of the Philharmonic Society, after which he returned to Milan and his studies with Lavigna. Tradition has it that one day they were visited by Basily, who complained insistently on the low standard of contrapuntal skill shown by recent aspirants to the post of organist of the cathedral of Monza. Lavigna proposed that Verdi should try his hand at the fugue subject set for the competitors; Verdi did so with complete success embellishing it with a double canon of his own ('the subject seemed to me rather thin and I wanted to give it a bit of richness').[10] True or not – and it is hard to see how a fugue subject could be anything else but 'thin' – the post at Monza was still unfilled when Verdi left Milan in July 1835. Meanwhile the government of Parma had come to its decision. In January a compromise was reached whereby Ferrari was allowed to retain his position as organist, but the post of municipal music director was to be thrown open to competition as originally agreed. However due to the continuing strife and intrigues within

[9] AGV, I, p. 141.
[10] PVAF, p. 15, quoted WMV, p. 19.

Busseto itself it was more than a year before the decree was put into effect. No blame to Verdi then if by autumn he was putting out feelers, via Lavigna, in the direction of Monza, and to such good purpose that he was told that he had only to appear before the cathedral authorities to be given the job. But no sooner was his intention of leaving Busseto generally known than the town was in an uproar. The codini crowed over the latest example of their enemies' perfidy. The coccardini rounded on Verdi and Barezzi and threatened to prevent the former from leaving, by force if necessary. All this Verdi explained to Lavigna in a letter of remarkable delicacy and tact. At length the examination took place in Parma in February 1836 under the Court *maestro di cappella*, Giuseppe Alinovi, a man held in the highest esteem by Paganini for his 'musical science and insight'. Alinovi had the highest praise for Verdi's skill in counterpoint, sight reading, composition (he played a set of his own variations) and piano technique – he could, he said, be a maestro in Paris or London rather than in Busseto. His appointment duly followed; Ferrari had not even bothered to compete.

In May Verdi and Margherita Barezzi were married. After a brief honeymoon in Milan, where Giuseppe Seletti swallowed his antipathy to his former lodger sufficiently to allow them to room in his house, Verdi settled down to the life of provincial music master and family man, teaching the piano, directing the Philharmonic Society (though not in church, where an edict from Parma, issued since the recent disturbances, had forbidden the performance of instrumental music). The former round of marches, overtures, vocal pieces, sacred and secular, was resumed, including a *Tantum Ergo* which has survived and a setting of Manzoni's ode *Il Cinque Maggio*, which has not. During all this time Verdi never lost sight of Milan and its glittering prospects; and he was careful to keep in touch with his influential friends in the Lombard capital, especially Massini. Both their names had been mentioned with praise in the theatrical journal *Il Figaro* in connection with a performance of Rossini's *La cenerentola* at the Teatro Filodrammatico in April 1835; some months after Verdi's return to Busseto Massini had conducted the Filodrammatici in the young composer's imperial ode mentioned above. But already a far more ambitious project was in view. In August of the previous year Verdi had written from Busseto to Lavigna asking him to remind Massini about an opera libretto which he had promised to obtain from one Tasca. Over the next three years the opera remains the burden of his correspondence with Massini. Before his departure from Milan Verdi must have received some kind of libretto since at the end of July he expresses the hope 'to have sketched out all the numbers' by his return and would like to know the vocal compass of the singers that Massini has in mind for the performance. There for the moment the matter rested since Verdi was confined to Busseto for the rest of the year. But with his official appointment as municipal director he felt free to plan for the following autumn when he would be granted two months holiday. September came, and still no word from Massini. The opera was now complete 'except for those little passages which will have to be patched up by the poet'. This time Massini replied kindly but without holding out any definite hopes; and once more the project was shelved for the best part of a year until in September 1837 Verdi announced the prospect of a performance at the new Ducal Theatre in Parma. Here for the first time we learn the name of the opera, *Rocester*, and that the poet is no longer Tasca but Piazza who is urged, via Massini, to 'prolong the duet for the two women and make it a really grandiose piece'. In the event the impresario declined to risk a new opera by an unknown composer; and Verdi's thoughts turned once again to a premiere in Milan. Could Massini possibly interest Merelli, impresario of La Scala? 'Tell him first of all that I should like the score to be submitted for examination by musicians of standing, and if their judgment were unfavourable I should not want the opera to be performed.'[11] That Massini did all that was expected of him we know from Verdi's own account given to Giulio Ricordi many years later.

In August 1838 Verdi suffered the first of those tragic bereavements to which one is tempted to ascribe that indelible streak of pessimism that was to mark his character. At the age of seventeen months his first-born, Virginia, died four weeks after the birth of her brother, Icilio (both names culled from the proudest days of the Roman republic, as set forth in the pages of Livy and Alfieri). Verdi and Margherita handed over the surviving infant to the care of a wet-nurse and set out for Milan, Verdi having applied, rather oddly, in writing to his father-in-law for a loan to cover their expenses. It was not, he added, a mere pleasure trip; matters of professional interest were involved; and he begged Barezzi to keep it a secret and to tear up his note. But the secret was soon out; and in a letter of October to an unnamed Bussetan he admitted that he had come to

[11] WMV, pp. 25–7.

Milan in order to negotiate about an opera, though there would be no possibility of a première before the Carnival season at the earliest – 'we're dealing with a new opera by a new composer to be staged at the first theatre in the world . . .'[12]

Evidently three years' absence in provincial Busseto had not been sufficient to cloud Verdi's hopes. That same year the Milanese firm of Giovanni Canti brought out his *Sei romanze* for voice and piano, the first of his compositions to appear in print. In the following spring they would publish two more songs and a *Notturno* for three voices, piano and flute entitled 'Guarda che bianca luna' which earned high praise from the *Gazzetta Privilegiata di Milano*, an official government organ which did not normally review new publications of music. Though nothing had been settled about the opera by the time the young couple returned to Busseto, Verdi now judged the time ripe for him to pull up his roots. He handed in his resignation to the Mayor of Busseto to take effect from 10 May 1839, the date on which his three-year contract was due for renewal. In the event it was on 6 February that he, Margherita and the baby Icilio set out for Milan from which two of them would never return.

[12] AGV, I, p. 249.

2

Success and failure in Milan

In his 'Storia di Milano dal 1836 al 1848' Antonio Ghislanzoni, future librettist of *Aida*, gives a pungent description of the city at the time of Verdi's arrival there. Capital of the Austrian province of Lombardy-Venetia, it had become an Italian Vienna, a walled city of some 150,000 inhabitants marked by hedonism, political torpor and – until the hygienic reforms of 1844–5 – dirt. Bread and circuses were the order of the day. The coronation of the Emperor Ferdinand I in September 1838 had provided the occasion for a round of public entertainments, open-air balls lasting far into the night, equestrian and acrobatic displays – all referred to by Verdi as a 'bordello'. Austrian soldiery was everywhere in evidence; police vigilance unceasing. But in general the lives of ordinary citizens were rarely interfered with. From the safety of exile Mazzini might preach rebellion; the romantically minded might nourish their dreams of Italian unity on the writings of Pellico, Guerrazzi, Tommaso Grossi and Manzoni; intellectuals might glance with envy across the border to the Kingdom of Piedmont where, through the activities of Massimo D'Azeglio, Carlo Alberto had granted a constitution. But, says Ghislanzoni, 'men who chafed at the foreign yoke were few. Most people were not aware that Italy existed'.[1]

Since the Restoration class barriers had been officially re-erected; but, as in Vienna, music proved a good solvent. The Countess Giulia Samoyloff, who is said, like Poppea, to have bathed in asses' milk, numbered among her lovers the Czar Nicholas I, the tenor Antonio Poggi and Bellini's bête-noir, the composer Giovanni Pacini. In salons such as those of the Countesses Appiani and Maffei members of the aristocracy mingled with artists and men of letters. Coffee-houses on the Austrian model had recently been introduced, causing a sensation. Many of the 'jeunesse dorée', the so-called 'young lions'

[1] Cit. WMV, pp. 30–1.

14

of Milanese society aped the manners of France; they drank absinthe and congregated at the Caffé del Duomo where the *Journal des Débats* was available; but Milan remained essentially an Austrian city, its houses furnished in the fashionable Biedermeier style of the period. The artistic quarter lay in and around the square in front of the Teatro alla Scala. Here musicians of all kinds congregated at the publishing houses of Ricordi and Lucca just as they were accustomed to do at the houses of Stein and Diabelli in Vienna.

The most powerful weapon of Austrian rule before 1848 was La Scala, as Massimo D'Azeglio recalls in his memoirs. It was run by Bartolomeo Merelli jointly with the Kärntnerthortheater in Vienna and disposed of the same artists. With singers such as Erminia Frezzolini, Napoleone Moriani, and Giorgio Ronconi, dancers such as Fanny Elssler and the latest circuses and acrobatic displays from America the authorities kept the Milanese enchanted as in the gardens of Armida. Rebellion was a long way off in 1839; and when it arrived nine years later it was as much a result of outside events as of internal pressures.

Such, then, was the city in which Verdi and his family now settled for a period of hopes and set-backs. La Scala was not after all to give the new opera during the Carnival season. A letter to Giuseppe Demaldé in April indicates that Verdi had another theatre in view but had withdrawn the score due to the wretchedness of the proposed cast. Hopes re-surfaced of a performance by the company of La Scala with Giuseppina Strepponi, Adelaide Kemble, Napoleone Moriani and Giorgio Ronconi at one of their charity shows for the benefit of the Pio Istituto. Here was indeed a notable cast. But this plan likewise foundered through the illness of Moriani. However, Merelli promised to take the opera into the autumn season provided Verdi would make changes in the tessitura of the solo parts to suit the new cast (no trifling task, this, since while Strepponi and Kemble were both sopranos, their replacements were respectively a dramatic mezzo soprano and a deep English contralto, and Ronconi's baritone part had to be adapted for a bass); the text would be overhauled by Temistocle Solera, resident librettist and stage director of La Scala; and Merelli suggested the addition of a quartet for the principals to be added to the second act. There folowed a miserable summer of preparation and waiting. Verdi was obliged to apply for further advances from Barezzi 'certainly not in the hope of piling up riches but rather of being someone amongst my fellow

15

men'.[2] At last the opera was scheduled for the autumn season. Rehearsals were already under way when Icilio followed his sister to the grave. However, the opera duly had its première on 17 November 1839. Its title was *Oberto, Conte di San Bonifacio* and the libretto credited exclusively to Solera. In the title role was the bass Ignazio Marini; his erring daughter was played by his wife Antonietta Ranieri-Marini – both to prove loyal friends to the composer. Lorenzo Salvi was the tenor seducer and Mary Shaw the 'other woman'.

Oberto, Verdi said in his account of 1879[3], was not an outstanding success but big enough for Merelli to exceed the number of performances originally advertised. If anything this is too modest an estimate. In fact the opera created a mild sensation. The Milan correspondent of the *Allgemeine Musikalische Zeitung* singled out for special praise the quartet in Act II which with the benefit of hindsight we would call the most obviously Verdian moment in the opera. Giovanni Ricordi bought the vocal score for the considerable sum of 2,000 Austrian lire; and Verdi was contracted for three more operas to be given at La Scala at intervals of eight months. It remains to be established what connection, if any, exists between *Oberto* and *Rocester*.

In the version of events which he dictated to Giulio Ricordi, Giovanni's grandson, Verdi is quite specific: 'Massini, who seems to have had some confidence in the young maestro, proposed that I should write an opera for the Teatro Filodrammatico . . . and handed me a libretto which afterwards, in part modified by Solera, became *Oberto, Conte di San Bonifacio*.' However at more than forty years' distance Verdi had a tendency to conflate events. An earlier letter written to Emilio Seletti, son of Giuseppe, in 1871 confirms that *Oberto* was adapted from an earlier opera, but gives its name as *Lord Hamilton*. More important is the fact that in his letters written at the time Verdi speaks only of one opera, never two. It is true that the published score of *Oberto* contains no duet for the two women, such as Verdi mentions in one of his letters to Massini; but just such a duet will be found in the composer's handwriting in an appendix to the autograph. Also at the start of the quartet the name 'Rocester' is clearly visible, scored out and with 'Riccardo' written over the top – a curious slip of the pen considering that this was the last piece to be

[2] AGV, I, p. 315.
[3] A. Pougin: *Giuseppe Verdi: vita aneddotica* (Milan, 1881), pp. 40–6.

composed, but a very informative one. Riccardo is the heartless seducer; such also was John Wilmot, Earl of Rochester, one of the liveliest poets of the Restoration. *Oberto* takes its title from the bass rather than the tenor. What more likely than that it was at some stage decided to do the same with *Rocester*? And what better name for an avenging father than Hamilton, murderer of the Regent Murray in Mercadante's *Il Reggente*? Finally to assume that *Oberto, Conte di San Bonifacio* and *Rocester* are two different operas is to ignore the generic nature of Italian opera plots of the time and the ease with which names and places could be switched – indeed often *had* to be switched for reasons of censorship – while leaving the essential situations and their music intact, and above all the sheer implausibility of a young composer at the start of his career completing an opera, then shelving it indefinitely and writing an entirely different one. In those days operas were never complete until they were performed. Verdi himself was to stipulate in all his contracts that he would not begin the scoring until the piano rehearsals were under way. The chances of finding a 'lost' opera by Verdi are indeed slim. The most we could expect to discover would be a lost libretto about the famous Restoration rake, the situations of which, we may be sure, would bear more than a passing resemblance to those of *Oberto, Conte di San Bonifacio*.

For his next opera Verdi was to have set a libretto by the veteran Gaetano Rossi (author of Rossini's first international success, *Tancredi*) entitled *Il proscritto*. Then Merelli found that he was short of an opera buffa for the repertory; Verdi looked through a number of libretti and eventually chose one by Felice Romani, *Il finto Stanislao* written for the Austrian composer, Adalbert Gyrowetz in 1818. According to that law of the Italian theatre whereby an old subject must always be given a new name it was decided to rechristen it *Un giorno di regno*. Verdi worked at it with far more difficulty than at *Oberto*. He suffered bouts of throat trouble as he was often to do when composing an opera. Money ran short as in the previous year; at one point Margherita, unknown to her husband, pawned her jewellery in order to pay for their modest lodgings. Then in June 'Through a terrible disease, perhaps unknown to the doctors, there died in my arms in Milan at noon on the day of Corpus Domini, my beloved daughter Margherita in the flower of her years and at the culmination of her good fortune, because married to the excellent youth Giuseppe Verdi, Maestro di

Musica.'[4] So runs an entry in Antonio Barezzi's diary for 1840. Verdi allowed himself to be led home, and over the next few weeks tried to get his contract with Merelli annulled. Merelli refused; and two months later Verdi found himself back in Milan bringing to completion, then rehearsing, an opera buffa. The first night was a fiasco. 'Certainly the music was partly to blame', Verdi admitted in 1879, 'but so too were the performers.' This last is more than likely. The cast had been assembled chiefly for the performance of the season's most successful novelty, *Il Templario*, Nicolai's version of *Ivanhoe*. Apart from the two bassi buffi, Scalese and Rovere, who in the event acquitted themselves with honour, none of the cast had any talent for comedy. It is probable too that critics and public alike had decided that the comic genre was ill-suited to the composer of *Oberto*. None the less both in Venice in 1845 and in Naples in 1859 the opera was revived and played to well-filled houses under the original title of *Il finto Stanislao*, a sure indication that it had eclipsed Gyrowetz' setting as completely as Rossini's *Almaviva* had eclipsed Paisiello's *Barbiere*.

It is at this point that the narrative of 1879 loses all contact with reality: 'I was alone . . . alone . . . In the short space of two months three persons dear to me had gone for ever: my family was destroyed.' A fine feat of telescopic memory. Yet Verdi had long believed it to be true since the same account appears in Michele Lessona's *Volere è potere* of 1869 where it had Verdi's full approval ('. . . that's the true story of my life, absolutely and completely true').[5] So we may be equally sceptical about his claim that he then and there decided to have nothing further to do with music and spent his time reading bad novels. Merelli's reaction to the fiasco of *Un giorno di regno* had been to cancel all further scheduled performances and replace them with *Oberto*. But Mary Shaw, the singer of Cuniza, was no longer on the roster; in her place was Luigia Abbadia, a so-called mezzo soprano, whose range was slightly higher than that of the Leonora. In a performance in Turin earlier in the year she had omitted her duet with Riccardo and imported an aria by Mercadante. For the revival in Milan Verdi provided her with a new cavatina and a new duet with the tenor, both of which can be found in the appendix to the

[4] WMV, p. 33.
[5] AVI, p. 176

autograph along with the duet for the two women. For a revival in Genoa in the Carnival season of 1841 Verdi added fresh music of which only a two-movement duet for Leonora and Oberto survives. This was again performed in a later revival in Naples, in which the title role had to be modified for baritone. In every case the Leonora was the same Antonietta Ranieri-Marini who had created the role; clearly *Oberto* was one of the few operas which suited her range and style of singing. It was to remain Verdi's one valuable asset until the next break-through occurred. The seed, it would seem, had already been sown in the winter of 1840–1. One day Verdi had met Merelli on his way to La Scala. 'It was snowing heavily'[6] . . . Merilli complained that Otto Nicolai, then at the height of his Italian career, had turned down a magnificent libretto by Solera. Verdi at once offered that of *Il proscritto* of which he had not set a note: and Merelli accepted gratefully. He insisted that Verdi should look at Solera's libretto and with some reluctance the composer took it back to his lodging where he

> . . . with an almost violent gesture threw the manuscript on the table . . . The book had opened in falling . . . Without knowing how, I gazed at the page that lay before me, and read the line:
> Va, pensiero, sull'ali dorate.
>
> I ran through the lines that followed and was much moved, all the more because they were almost a paraphrase from the Bible, the reading of which had always delighted me.
>
> I read one passage, then another. Then, resolute in my determination to write no more, I forced myself to close the booklet and went to bed. But it was no use – I couldn't get *Nabucco* out of my head. Unable to sleep, I got up and read the libretto not once, but two or three times, so that by the morning I knew Solera's libretto almost by heart.
>
> . . . That day I returned to the theatre and handed the manuscript back to Merelli.
>
> Isn't it beautiful?' he said to me.
> 'Very beautiful!'
> 'Well then – set it to music!'
> 'I wouldn't dream of it.'
> 'Go on. Set it to music!'

[6] PVAF, cit. WMV, pp. 34–6.

And so saying he took the libretto, thrust it into my overcoat pocket took me by the shoulders and not only pushed me out of the room but locked the door in my face.

What was I to do?

I returned home with *Nabucco* in my pocket. One day one line, another day another, here a note and there a phrase and little by little the opera was composed.

According to Lessona, writing ten years earlier, it was the death of Abigaille ('the part which was later removed') that first caught Verdi's attention; and the 'piano which had remained silent so long' did not begin to sound again until the spring. Whatever the truth of the matter, the bulk of *Nabucco* was clearly written during the spring and summer of 1841, and by autumn it was complete. Once again Verdi was too late for the Carnival season, whose cartello had already been made up. But he was no longer prepared to wait meekly until the following winter for a production. There were protests, arguments, angry letters. Finally he had the satisfaction of seeing *Nabucco* (or *Nabucodonosor* as it was called before a revival at the Teatro Giglio of Corfu established the shorter title) announced for 9 March 1842. The production was makeshift, scenery and costumes having been resurrected from a ballet on the same subject given four years earlier; Giuseppina Strepponi as Abigaille, the soprano lead, was in execrable voice ('Even her Verdi didn't want her in his opera'[7] wrote Donizetti, indicating beyond a doubt that she had been one of his earliest supporters); but the success was immediate and decisive. At one bound Verdi had arrived at the front rank of Italian composers of his generation. Donizetti, whose *Maria Padilla* had been given in the same season, is said to have spent the coach journey to Bologna where he was to direct Rossini's Stabat Mater murmuring to himself 'That *Nabucco* – beautiful, beautiful, beautiful!'. Fashionable society opened its doors to the young composer; in the words of Lessona, 'He found himself suddenly beset by a crowd of friends who needed to tell him how they had always loved him . . . They all wanted to press his hand, to walk arm in arm with him, to address him as 'Tu'.[8] From this period date his friendships with the Countesses Appiani,

[7] Letter to A. Vasselli, 4.3.1842, G. Zavadini, *Donizetti – Vita, Musiche Epistolario* (Bergamo, 1948) p. 579.
[8] M. Lessona, *Volere è potere* (Florence, 1869) pp. 297 ff.

Morosini and Maffei to whom he addressed letters of a somewhat elephantine gallantry. He visited Rossini in Bologna, who received him kindly ('Oh, it is a fine thing to be Rossini!'[9] he wrote to Countess Morosini in one of those cynical tributes to worldly success that will often occur in his correspondence with Milanese high society).

'With *Nabucco* my career can be said to have begun', he wrote years later to Count Arrivabene; 'Since then I have never lacked for commissions'.[10] This was true enough, even if the level of achievement might fluctuate in the years to come. For the moment he rode high on a tide of increasing vitality and self-confidence. His next opera, *I Lombardi alla prima crociata*, again to a libretto by Solera based on Tommaso Grossi's poem of the same name, followed the grandiose path of *Nabucco* though in a more secular vein and with a certain diffusion of incident due to the long time-span of the subject. The critics were again favourable, the public enthusiastic. The chorus of crusaders dying of thirst in the Syrian desert ('O Signore, dal tetto natio') was to equal 'Va, pensiero' in popularity. It was over this opera that Verdi had his first bout with the censorship. Cardinal Gaisruck, Archbishop of Milan, had objected to the massed bands of crusaders, to the baptism of an infidel on stage, and above all to the singing of an aria beginning with the words Ave Maria. Verdi, whose iron will was becoming more and more in evidence (he had locked Solera in a room during the composition of *Nabucco* until he should have completed the text of Zaccaria's 'Prophecy' which Verdi wished to substitute for a love duet in the third act), refused to change anything or even to discuss the matter; and it was left to Solera and Merelli to come to an arrangement with the chief of police, Torresani, whereby the physical act of baptism was not represented and the word 'Ave' changed to 'Salve'. Austrian complaisance was not so surprising as is sometimes implied. Whatever significance *I Lombardi alla prima crociata* took on retrospectively in the light of 1848, its plot is politically anodyne, with villains and heroes fairly distributed on either side. It is her own people at whom Giselda hurls her imprecations, to be cursed in turn by her father; and it is her erstwhile wicked uncle, turned hermit, who effects the reconciliation. Oronte,

---

[9] AGV, I, pp. 422–3.
[10] AVI, loc. cit.

chief representative of the Saracens, is the most sympathetic of juvenile leads. There are far more implications of political subversion in Rossini's *Mosé* and *L'assedio di Corinto*, neither of which encountered any opposition from the censors of Milan. It was without irony, therefore, that Verdi dedicated the score of *I Lombardi* to the Austrian Maria Luigia of Parma, having first obtained permission from the Court Chamberlain.

So far La Scala had been the venue for all of Verdi's operas. Now he decided to venture further afield. He had already been in contact with the authorities of the Teatro La Fenice, Venice, where *Nabucco* had opened the Carnival season of 1842–3. For the occasion he had supplied a new 'preghiera' for the Fenena, Almerinda Granchi. He now accepted a commission for a new opera to be given the following year. La Fenice differed from most opera houses in Italy in that its policy was determined not by the impresario but by a committee of three noblemen. The Presidente agli Spettacoli, Count Alvise Mocenigo, and the secretary, Guglielmo Brenna, were to prove valuable allies to Verdi, doing everything in their power to accommodate his demands which even at that stage of his career were exacting. As to his fee for *I Lombardi*, Verdi had taken the advice of Giuseppina Strepponi and asked for 10,000 Austrian lire, the sum that Bellini had been paid for *Norma*. This he now felt justified in raising to 12,000, the final instalment to be paid after the first night, not after the third performance as had been originally proposed; for what if there were no third performance? As always he refused to supply the full score before the period of piano rehearsals since that was when he liked to complete his orchestration. Over these and kindred matters the management made no difficulty. But then began the long search for a subject and a librettist. With the possible exception of Bellini none of Verdi's predecessors were so particular as to their choice of plots. The correspondence with Mocenigo began during Verdi's visit to Vienna for the Austrian première of *Nabucco* and continued throughout most of the summer. Two considerations prevailed: the desire for a congenial theme and the need to avoid self-repetition. *King Lear* headed the list of possibilities, but was not to be realised then or at any other time. For the present he dismissed it along with Byron's *The corsair* since it required a baritone of the order of Ronconi, creator of Nabucco, and the Fenice theatre had no one suitable. Bulwer Lytton's *Cola di Rienzi* he thought would make a fine subject 'if treated as it should be', but the censorship would undoubtedly prohibit this. Alternatively he might try his hand at a prima donna opera – Byron's *Bride of Abydos* or Dumas' *Catherine Howard* of which he went so far as to draw up a synopsis. Then he changed his mind in favour of Byron's *The two Foscari* – 'a Venetian story which would really grip a Venetian audience, and besides it's full of passion and very easy to set to music . . . to me it's a most telling subject and much more "simpatico" than *Catherine*'.[11] He sent a synopsis to Venice before setting off for Sinigallia in mid-July to take charge of a revival of *I Lombardi*, for which he would supply a new cabaletta for the tenor, Antonio Poggi. While he was there he heard that both *Caterina Howard* and *I due Foscari* had been rejected by the censors, the first because of its cruel streak, the second for fear of giving offence to certain members of the Venetian nobility.

It was at this point that Brenna put forward the name of a young friend of his who had ambitions as a theatrical poet but so far no experience; he was at present writing a libretto about Cromwell and if after seeing a specimen of his verses Verdi approved, he would complete it for him to set to music. His name was Francesco Maria Piave. Verdi was cautiously favourable; and so began one of the most fruitful partnerships in the world of opera. Piave's lack of experience and therefore authority turned out to the advantage of their collaboration; for it meant that Verdi was never overawed by him into accepting a word or a line of which he was not fully convinced. Piave, as Gabriele Baldini and others have pointed out, was in effect Verdi's literary amanuensis. Every line of his librettos was hammered out into the exact form that the composer wanted. It was fortunate, too, that Piave himself proved so malleable; for in those days libretti were available at every performance and, as house lights were never lowered, except for one brief period at La Scala, could be followed as the opera proceeded; and Piave's often congested lines – for Verdi insisted on the maximum significance from the fewest number of words – were regularly held up to ridicule. But he remained steadfast in his obedience to Verdi's wishes; and only a false aesthetic could fault him for this. The poet who made possible such achievements as *Ernani, Macbeth, Rigoletto, La traviata* and *La forza del destino* was not a bungler. Verdi himself, though frequently impatient, sometimes angry with his collaborator, was always ready to spring

[11] CBM, pp. 55–9.

to his defence. In 1861 he so helped to secure for him the post of resident stage director at La Scala – in which, alas, he proved utterly incompetent; nor was it through lack of Verdi's support that his application for the chair of theatrical poetry at the Milan Conservatory was turned down in favour of the young 'scapigliato', Emilio Praga. When at the end of 1867 Piave suffered a stroke which left him paralized for the remaining eight years of his life, Verdi helped to organise an 'album Piave' of songs to which various eminent composers would contribute, himself included, for the benefit of the librettist and his family. In his funeral oration Giulio Ricordi told of Verdi's regular visits to the invalid whenever he came to Milan.

The Cromwell opera on which Piave and Verdi first collaborated was not, as several have guessed, Victor Hugo's drama but an operatic version of Walter Scott's *Woodstock*, with the action transferred to Scotland. Its title was originally *Allan Cameron* until Verdi suggested that it should be changed to *Cromwell* – even though the Lord Protector, like Edward III in Donizetti's *L'assedio di Calais*, did not enter until the final act. The libretto was already complete when Verdi, acting on a random remark thrown out by Mocenigo, suddenly decided on Victor Hugo's *Hernani*, offering to recompense Piave for the useless work he had put in on *Cromwell*. (In fact Piave was able to offer his libretto under its original title to the composer Pacini in 1848.) Piave was dismayed at the time; but once Verdi had made up his mind he was not to be shifted. Likewise it required all the tact and diplomatic skills of Brenna to ensure the kind of cast which the composer was determined to have. During the summer of 1843 he had agreed unconditionally to write a part for one Carolina Vietti, a very popular musico-contralto of the day. In *Ernani* (as the opera was to be called) there was only one part that would suit her – the title role, whom the play describes as a 'beardless youth'. Verdi however made it clear, as he was to do on more than one occasion, that he was totally opposed to the tradition of the trouser role (though he was to make an exception in his ideas for the Fool in *King Lear*). After much argument it was decided that of the three male principals Ernani should be allocated to a tenor, Carlo to a baritone, and Silva, originally intended for Antonio Superchi, the leading baritone on the roster, should be entrusted to a young supporting basso profondo the burden of whose part would have to be correspondingly lightened. But the difficulties did not end there. The season opened with a revival of *I Lombardi* at which Domenico Conti, the proposed Ernani, sang so badly that he was hastily dropped from the roster. Arrangements were made for Verdi to go to Verona to hear another tenor, but he too proved inadequate. Eventually it was decided to await the arrival of Carlo Guasco from Spain. He complained that the new assignment would be too fatiguing, but the management of La Fenice threatened to sue his 'appaltatore' if he refused. All this meant that the première had to be deferred until March. The Venetians, who had received all the previous operas badly, were not in an accommodating mood. 'If I have a failure I shall blow my brains out'[12] Verdi wrote to a friend; but in the event this was not necessary. On the first night Guasco was hoarse and Sofia Loewe, the Elvira, sang out of tune (she had been put out at having to finish the opera with a terzetto instead of the rondò-finale which singers of her calibre expected as their right). The scenery was half finished. No matter. The audience went into raptures. Among them was Verdi's brother-in-law, Giovanni Barezzi, who wrote home enthusiastically to his father about the opera, its reception – and about Piave ('a big, jolly young man like Solera').[13]

If *Nabucco* had established Verdi's pre-eminence throughout the peninsula, it was *Ernani* that made him an international celebrity. With Bellini in his grave, Rossini in virtual retirement, Donizetti about to vanish from the scene, and Mercadante declining into self-repetition, Verdi's voice was recognised as that of contemporary Italy. Audiences, managements and publishers from now on waited eagerly for every fresh creation. Critics, academics and, for the most part, fellow composers were to remain hostile for years to come. At a time when musical opinion started to divide between the Mendelssohnian conservatives and the partisans of the New German School of Liszt and Wagner, Verdi pleased neither the one side nor the other. Germanophiles of all varieties who managed to extend their tolerance to Bellini and the comedies of Donizetti mostly stopped short at the 'coarseness' of Verdi. To Fétis, the most authoritative voice in French criticism, he merely aggravated the ruin of vocal art that had begun with Bellini. In Austria Hanslick, while admitting the superior energy of *Ernani* over all the operas of Verdi's predecessors, would not

---

[12] AGV, I, pp. 481–2.
[13] AGV, I, p. 497.

begin to take the composer seriously until the appearance of *Rigo-letto*. England's two weightiest critics, H.F. Chorley of the *Athenaeum* and J.W. Davison of *The Times*, may have been mutually opposed in their views of Meyerbeer and Berlioz but they were united in their antipathy to Verdi, though Chorley graciously admitted that he was not a nonentity. Both found him lacking in originality. There were frequent complaints that he ruined singers' voices (Bülow in Germany called him the Attila of the throat). Among composers Wagner, who loved the melodies of Bellini, could hardly bear to hear Verdi's name spoken. But his worst detractor at this time was Otto Nicolai, who wrote in his diary: 'the Italian opera composer of today is Verdi . . . But his operas are truly dreadful and utterly degrading for Italy.'[14] Nicolai was hardly an objective witness. With the libretto of *Il proscritto* which he obtained from Verdi in exchange for *Nabucco* he achieved a fiasco as monumental as that of *Un giorno di regno*. It was the end not only of his stormy engagement to the soprano Erminia Frezzolini but of an Italian career which till then had been one of steadily mounting success. True, as conductor of the Vienna State Opera and of the Vienna Philharmonic Orchestra, of which he was one of the founders, he was able to repair his fortunes; but it can have been no pleasure to him to see his rival's operas triumphing in Vienna, his own newly won home territory. Yet Fate was to link once more the lives of Verdi and Nicolai. Both were to compose their last operas, which are also their comic masterpieces, on Shakespeare's *Merry Wives of Windsor*.

[14] O. Nicolai, *Tagebücher, nebst biographischen Ergänzungen von D.* Schröder (Leipzig, 1892), p. 130.

3

The journeyman

'Of medium height; not unprepossessing but not good-looking either; solemn and haughty.'[1] This vignette of 1845 by an anonymous correspondent of the *Allgemeine Musikalische Zeitung* gives a fair idea of the view of himself that Verdi presented to the world, and would continue to present until mellowed by age. Fortunately we have a more sympathetic witness to the real man.

Emanuele Muzio was born at Zibello in the Duchy of Parma in 1821, the son of the village cobbler. As a boy he studied with Verdi's rival, Ferrari; and when Ferrari moved on in 1840 acted as supply organist of the Collegiate Church. During this time he came under the patronage of Antonio Barezzi who in 1843, after he had failed to qualify for the priesthood for which he was intended, obtained from the Monte di Pietà a grant to enable him to study music in Milan either at the Conservatory or, if he were refused entry, under a private teacher. Like Verdi before him, Muzio failed the entrance examination but remained to study with Verdi himself. For the next three years he would play a similar role in Verdi's life to that of Ferdinand Ries in Beethoven's – part pupil, part amanuensis (from 1844 onwards he would be responsible for most of the piano-and-voice reductions of Verdi's operas). If the good Bussetans hoped for another Verdi to enhance the town's artistic reputation, they were to be disappointed. Loyal to his friends and fundamentally good-hearted, Muzio was a mediocrity, poorly educated and hampered by a tactlessness that made him enemies. That he was to make a career in music at all was due partly to the thoroughness of Verdi's teaching and his recommendations, partly to that routine competence that comes with experience. He composed two operas, *Claudia* and *Giovanna la pazza*, both of which reached the stage though neither were to remain there. In 1861 he gave the first American performance

[1] CIIV, p. 12.

of *Un ballo in maschera*. While there he met and married the young singer Lucy Simons, but the marriage broke up after the death of their daughter. In 1869 he conducted the opening season of the new Cairo Opera house and would have given the première of *Aida* there if he had not in the meantime made himself so unpopular with singers and orchestra. He was resident conductor of the Théâtre des Italiens from 1870 until it closed in 1876; and he ended his career as a singing teacher in Paris. Both Patti sisters went to him for coaching.

From the time that he arrived in Milan in mid-April 1844 he regaled his benefactor with a stream of letters which not only testify to Verdi's kindness of heart and the warmth of his companionship but reveal a thousand details of his daily round. Of Verdi the teacher: 'Believe me, he doesn't pass a note, he wants everything perfect. He won't have two hidden consecutive fifths or octaves (open ones are of course excommunicated); he wants all the parts to move like a scale with never a jump. . . . Up to now I have studied harmony and I assure you that if I had been under another teacher. . . . I should have needed almost a year certainly, for Corbellini . . . in the six months that he has been studying has not got half as far as I have in the same subject in such a short time. [Verdi] is so good to me that sometimes I can't hold back my tears; for sometimes to finish a lesson he keeps people waiting no matter who they are . . .'[2] From Muzio we hear of the visitors who daily thronged his ante-room; the Grand Duchess of Tuscany and her Cavalier who merely wished for the honour of his acquaintance; the contralto who wanted him to include a contralto aria in his next opera (she was to be disappointed); the composer who besought him to avoid a subject which he himself had already chosen; the importunities of Giovannina Lucca, wife of the publisher, Ricordi's rival, who begged with tears in her eyes for the rights in just one of Verdi's scores. ('The lady said that when they are in bed they do nothing but sigh; and the Signor Maestro asked if they really did nothing else but sigh; and in that way he makes a joke of it all and gets rid of her.') From Muzio we hear why Verdi felt unable to accept a commission from the Casa de'Nobili to set a cantata by his friend Andrea Maffei. ('It was truly beautiful and sublime; it was the breath of Eternity that created wisdom; but it was decidedly impossible to set to music . . . There was no sense of dialogue; and the Signor

---

[2] GMB, pp. 157 ff. See also WMV, pp. 117–63.

Maestro . . . wanted something dramatic.') We learn too of Verdi's dismay on hearing that Prosper Derivis, creator of Zaccaria in *Nabucco*, wanted to sing Don Carlo in *Ernani* ('Yesterday the Signor Maestro said, "How could he want to sing 'Vieni meco, sol di rose' with that great voice of his?" '). Doubtless it was this consideration that led Verdi to permit a cabaletta for Silva, so turning a comprimario into a principal part and diverting all bassi profondi from a misguided ambition to star in what had been conceived as a high baritone role.

By the time Muzio had completed his studies in 1846 he no longer wished to return to Busseto to compete for the post of organist and municipal music master:

> To tell you the truth I should be extremely sorry to have to abandon the Signor Maestro after he has given me a second life and is always seeking to have me cut a good figure in society . . . . If only you could see us! I don't seem to be his pupil but rather one of his friends. Always together at lunch, at the coffee house, playing together (for one hour only, from twelve to one); in short he goes nowhere without me. At home he has procured a large table and we both write at the same table and I always have the benefit of his advice. It would be absolutely impossible for me to leave him.

A sentiment that does much credit to them both.

At first, however, Verdi preferred to travel alone for the production of new operas. The venue of his next commission was the Teatro Argentina, Rome, where *I due Foscari*, rejected as a subject for Venice, was scheduled for production in November. Its success was somewhat dimmed by the impresario's decision to raise the prices of admission. In a letter to his friend Luigi Toccagni Verdi described it as a 'mezzo-fiasco' – to which Piave added in a postscript that any other composer would have called it a triumph. The lessee of the theatre, the Duke of Torlonia, gave a banquet at which the veteran librettist and 'Arcadian', Jacopo Ferretti (poet of Rossini's *La Cenerentola* and Donizetti's *Torquato Tasso*) recited a sonnet in honour of Italy's youngest musical genius. He and the sculptor Vincenzo Luccardi would be among Verdi's latest friends. Though usually regarded as minor Verdi, *I due Foscari* was to prove an asset over the following decades. With its modest length and requirements, its unusual plot, so far removed from the standard pattern of star-crossed lovers, it became the ideal 'opera di ripiego' – i.e. the opera to fall back on whenever the scheduled novelty of the season was delayed. Moreover the rather studied, careful writing was to earn the composer a critical pat on the back. For the general public *Ernani* remained the favourite. Before the year was out Verdi had been asked by Rossini to provide an extra aria for his protégé the tenor Nicolai Ivanoff to insert into the second act.

By the end of November Verdi was already at work on his next commission: *Giovanna d'Arco* to a libretto by Solera due to be given during the Carnival season at La Scala. The choice of subject appears to have been Solera's and designed to exploit that furrow of proven profitability, the choral-historical fresco, with the added novelty of a prima donna in whom all the dramatic interest is concentrated. It was, he declared in a letter to Ricordi, an entirely original drama bearing no relation to Schiller's *Jungfrau von Orleans* – which was clearly untrue. It is indeed Schiller's drama reduced to its essentials and with a love-interest between Joan and the Dauphin added; but it provided opportunities for certain untried effects, and Verdi set to work on it with much zeal. Each number is reported on as it was written by Muzio who, characteristically, reserves all his enthusiasm for the parts which today strike us as the weakest – the ceremonial march, the choruses of angels and demons. The season opened with *I Lombardi*, Verdi himself assisting with the rehearsals. 'It makes me very sad to see him wearing himself out', Muzio wrote. 'He shouts as if in desperation; he stamps his foot so much that he seems to be playing an organ with pedals; he sweats so much that drops fall on the score.' Evidently he was not well enough to attend the first few performances – the first sign that he was taking on more work than he could comfortably manage. Meanwhile a rumour had reached Busseto that he was being poisoned by a rival composer, as Demaldé wrote to him in great concern. 'For heaven's sake', Verdi replied, 'what century are we supposed to be living in? . . . We don't behave like that nowadays . . .' On a more serious note, he added, 'I am better: the mountain air has helped, and still more the rest; but I'm afraid that I shall again be poorly when I get back to work. Oh how I hope the next three years will pass quickly!'[3]

His health rallied and *Giovanna d'Arco* was as great a success with the public as he could have wished. But there were signs that

[3] LCV, IV, p. 80.

his honeymoon with the Milan critics was over. Several notices complained that he was repeating himself; and that despite some beautiful moments the opera as a whole lacked inspiration. Even the notice in Ricordi's house magazine, the *Gazzetta Musicale di Milano*, contained some wounding qualifications. As always Verdi held the editor personally responsible for the views expressed by his correspondents.

> That the other journalists should speak badly of me is in perfect order; nowadays they have openly declared themselves my enemies. But from you who claim to be my friend I don't much like to read here an article in defence of me which is worse than an adverse criticism, and there an observation that is almost an insult . . . I am not writing this in order to get praise from you but merely to know whether I must count you among my friends or my enemies.[4]

The latter, so it would appear for the moment. 'He is thoroughly disgusted with . . . Ricordi', wrote Muzio, 'and has written to him that he will never let him have another of his scores.' In March we find Verdi treating with Francesco Lucca for an opera to be given in the Carnival season three years hence and also offering him a group of Romanze for voice and piano which the publisher duly brought out the following summer.

But for the next opera there was no question of breaking with Ricordi to whom the publishing rights had already been granted. This was *Alzira*, contracted the previous year for production at the San Carlo Theatre, Naples. Not only was this the third of Italy's leading opera houses along with La Scala, Milan and La Fenice, Venice; it boasted as its resident poet and stage director Salvatore Cammarano who for the last ten years had taken Romani's place as Italy's most prestigious librettist. Born into a family of actors and scene painters and clearly destined for a stage career, Cammarano had been 'discovered' by Donizetti rather as Piave had been discovered by Verdi; and his first libretto, *Lucia di Lammermoor*, already shows the qualities which would make him so much in demand. His verses may lack the chiselled elegance and clarity of Romani's; nor will their meaning always bear close scrutiny; but they are unfailingly 'musicable'. No librettist showed greater flair for

[4] AGV, I, p. 541.

evoking a mood or an atmosphere within the compass of a single line; none was more skilful in reducing the most unlikely of plots to the standard confrontation of soprano, tenor and baritone, or at removing the political or religious barb (there is nothing in the libretto of *Alzira* to suggest that it is based on the work of a notorious sceptic). Often Cammarano's language sounds like a parody of 'librettese'. Yet it can convey information with ease and brevity – qualities which Verdi continually enjoined upon Piave, not always with success. To be fair to the Venetian, however, his collaboration with the composer produced a string of masterpieces; with Cammarano Verdi only achieved one; and it was not *Alzira*.

Again the choice of subject was not Verdi's; however he assured Cammarano that he had read and admired Voltaire's play. He added 'I am often accused of being too fond of noise and of maltreating the voice: take no notice of that; put plenty of passion into it and you will find that I write quite passably.'[5] Work on the opera was once more interrupted by throat trouble, so that Verdi had to ask for the première to be postponed. Flauto, the impresario, was not impressed by the medical certificates he received and replied that tincture of wormwood combined with the 'stimulating air of Vesuvius' would work the necessary cure. Verdi rejoined with some asperity that what he needed was rest, not stimulation; and he took the precaution of applying to the royal chamberlain for confirmation that his certificate had been received and accepted. Possibly Flauto suspected a diplomatic motive; since by delaying the première of the opera by a month Verdi would be certain of having as his prima donna Eugenia Tadolini, the soprano who had created Donizetti's Linda di Chamounix. The alternative was Anna Bishop, runaway wife of Sir Henry Bishop, who had arrived in Italy in a blaze of totally undeserved publicity. ('La Bishop!' Donizetti exclaimed when she had been offered to him, 'Are you joking???.')[6] But, as Muzio makes clear, the illness was genuine enough; 'but we artists', Verdi grumbled to Cammarano, 'are not allowed to be ill'.[7]

Verdi left Milan for Naples at the end of June, was recognised when he appeared at the theatre during a performance of *I due*

[5] LCC, p. 429.
[6] Letter to T. Persico, 14.6.1843 Zavadini, p. 670.
[7] LCC, p. 13.

Foscari and called out onto the stage. He did not lack enemies in Naples, which was the stronghold of his one remaining rival of any consequence, Saverio Mercadante. The journalists were inclined to be ribald; but the public as a whole was eager and interested. As the première approached Verdi's mood was one of cautious optimism. The singers liked their music, and rehearsals were proceeding smoothly. 'I can't give you a definite opinion of the work,' he wrote to Andrea Maffei, 'because I wrote it easily, almost without noticing. Don't worry, it certainly won't be a fiasco.'[8] Nor was it; several numbers were warmly applauded, especially the overture which had been written at the last minute (it replaced a shorter prelude which, if Muzio is to be believed, contained a musical sunrise modelled on that of Félicien David's cantata *Le Désert*, heard and admired by Verdi shortly before he left Milan). *Alzira* did not repeat the furore of *Ernani* or *Giovanna d'Arco*; but 'it will remain in the repertory', Verdi wrote, 'and, what is more important, will go the rounds along with its sister operas'.[9] Here he was mistaken. *Alzira* proved of all his operas the least successful. So completely had it sunk below the horizon by the time of his death that an English obituary article referred to it as *Montezuma*! In due course Verdi himself came to realise, as one disastrous revival followed another, that the trouble lies 'in its vitals';[10] and he made no attempt to reclaim it by revision. Fortunately he had reaped other more lasting benefits from his first experience of the Parthenopean city: the acquaintance of two singers who would serve him well in the future, Filippo Coletti and Gaetano Fraschini, his favourite tenor for the next twenty years; also of the critic Opprandino Arrivabene, one of the few to report favourably on the opera, though with the ominous qualification that 'the beauties of the score were not such as could be taken in at first hearing.'[11] To Arrivabene Verdi would in later years reveal some of his most interesting thoughts on music in general and the current state of Italian opera in particular.

Verdi did not have to wait three years for his first operatic venture with Lucca. After the triumph of *Ernani* another opera for

---

[8] LCC, p. 431.
[9] WMV, p. 138.
[10] LCC, p. 432.
[11] GMB, pp. 217–19.

La Fenice was an obvious desideratum once Verdi should have discharged his other commitments. By the winter of 1844–5 the cast for the following Carnival season had already been fixed; and Verdi was urging Piave to look out for a 'strong' subject suitable to the combined talents of Sofia Loewe, Fraschini, Constantini and Marini. The contract seems to have been arranged not for once with the Presidenza but with the impresario Alessandro Lanari. Then in January 1845 Lanari withdrew, selling his rights to Lucca. 'Now at last', Muzio wrote proudly to Barezzi, 'Lucca will have the pleasure of publishing an opera by the Signor Maestro.'

The history of music publishing in nineteenth century Italy almost merits a chapter in itself. In the northern states permission to print complete operas could be granted only by royal patent. This had been obtained by Giovanni Ricordi of Milan in 1808; the care which he brought to his task in contrast to the slipshod methods of his rivals in Naples soon drew the flower of Italian composers within his orbit. Bellini would have liked to contract with him for the publication of all his future operas but this Ricordi regarded as too great a risk. In 1840 he had helped to negotiate a treaty between Austria and the Kingdom of Sardinia for mutual recognition of copyright within each other's territory. But his monopoly would not remain for long. A similar patent was granted in 1825 to Francesco Lucca, once an engraver in Ricordi's firm. Lucca set up his premises directly opposite those of Ricordi by La Scala theatre; and for the next half century the two firms divided Italian music between them – in the North until 1861 and throughout the peninsula thereafter until the death of Giovanni's son Tito and the arrival on the scene of a far more deadly adversary, Edoardo Sonzogno, induced them to amalgamate, the widow Lucca selling out to Giulio Ricordi. Each firm had its house magazine as an aid in the struggle: Ricordi, the *Gazzetta Musicale di Milano*, Lucca *L'Italia Musicale*. If Ricordi had the advantage of being first in the field, Lucca was the more open to new ideas. He it was who first regularly abandoned the old clefs for soprano and tenor, substituting the G clef for both; likewise he was the first in Italy to bring out his score in the upright format, so much more suitable for playing at the new domestic piano. While Giovanni Ricordi aspired to the status of artist and gentleman for himself and his descendants, Francesco Lucca, childless, was content to be a hard-headed man of business, as Verdi would find to his cost. During the 1860s, when the Italian operatic tradition was beginning to lose its vitality, it was Lucca who had the foresight to buy up the rights in Gounod, Meyerbeer and – a masterstroke – Wagner. His most farseeing innovation, however, had been to initiate a system whereby the composer could contract for an opera directly with the publisher who would in return take the responsibility for placing it in a suitable theatre and relieve the composer of all practical dealings with the management. All three of Verdi's operas published by Lucca came into being in this way; so, at his own suggestion, did two of those subsequently brought out by Ricordi. From *Rigoletto* onwards Verdi reverted to the old system until Giovanni's grandson, Giulio Ricordi, by far the ablest of the dynasty, coaxed him into entrusting everything to the firm. By the 1880s this system obtained throughout Italy; and composers were mostly happy to accept it, especially as they were regularly granted a high proportion of hiring fees. But it put an inordinately powerful weapon into the hands of the publishers, in the course of whose internecine warfare many a false reputation was created and many a genuine one held back – witness the respective cases of Gobatti and Catalani.

No such consequences were foreseen in 1845. In March, soon after the première of *Giovanna d'Arco*, Verdi paid a visit to Venice to assist with a revival of *I due Foscari* (fears that the subject might cause local offence had evidently proved groundless). It was then that he and Piave found the ideal subject, so they thought, for La Fenice the following year: Zacharias Werner's *Attila*. Not only did it show the Scourge of God turned back from the gates of the Holy City; it depicted the grandeur of Rome re-born on the lagoons of Venice. Also it included a number of choruses ready-made. Andrea Maffei would draw up the synopsis and send it to Piave, who should meantime study Madame de Stael's *De l'Allemagne*. But soon there was a change of plan. 'Good, I see you're thoroughly reasonable', Verdi wrote from Naples; 'so let's not think about the opera for Venice but rather about the ones we're going to do for Genoa, Vienna or wherever.'[12] Evidently he had decided that *Attila* would be more suited to the grandiose manner of Solera, now released from his duties at La Scala. It was an unfortunate decision. Before he had completed the libretto Solera followed his wife to Spain, where she was engaged to sing at the Teatro Real, Madrid. The final months of

[12] AGV, I, pp. 563–4.

1845 Verdi passed in alternating moods of hope and weary depression. Of the opera itself he continued to expect great things. The critics might say what they like, he declared, but he had never tackled a finer subject. He sent to the sculptor Luccardi in Rome for details of Raphael's fresco in the Vatican depicting Attila's meeting with St. Leo at the gates of Rome – a foretaste, this, of the insistence on historical accuracy that he would bring to *Macbeth*. He even suggested to his French publisher Escudier an adaptation of *Attila* as a suitable work with which to make his debut at the Paris Opera. But no amount of prodding by letter would obtain from Solera the missing passages from the last act, let alone those routine modifications of lines here and there that inevitably became necessary in the course of composition. Unable to wait any longer Verdi entrusted all this to Piave and sent the result to Solera for his approval. Only then did Solera react, declaring that a fine libretto had been turned into a mockery. 'But *fiat voluntas tua*' he added; 'you are the one person who has been able to convince me that the profession of librettist is not for me.'[13] It was not an encouraging letter to receive a few weeks before opening night.

In the meantime Verdi had become increasingly involved with the firm of Lucca. In October he had confirmed his offer to write for him an opera for Carnival 1848. About the same time he received a visit from Benjamin Lumley, impresario of Her Majesty's Theatre London who had offered a commission for the summer of 1846. Verdi had accepted and once again the casting and other details were left to Lucca (one may conjecture that he and Lumley moved in the same business circles). The subject was first to have been *King Lear* with Lablache in the title role; but, as he would forever be doing in the future, Verdi shrank from fulfilling this life-long ambition. Then Byron's *Corsair* was proposed and temporarily agreed though there was some argument as to who should write the libretto: Verdi insisted that it should be Piave.

The Carnival season at La Fenice of 1845–6 opened with *Giovanna d'Arco*. In the title role was Sofia Loewe for whom Verdi wrote a new cavatina, now, alas, no longer traceable. Then during January he fell ill with gastric fever and it seemed as though he might not be able to complete *Attila* before the end of the season; but

[13] LCV, IV, p. 245.

complete it he did 'virtually on my deathbed'[14] under inexorable pressure from Lucca. This is confirmed by a letter from the tenor Nicolai Ivanoff to Lucca expressing great concern about Verdi's health on behalf of the Italian musical world. The *Allgemeine Musik-alische Zeitung* even carried a notice of his death. Verdi recovered slowly; there was no question of his fulfilling any other commissions that year; and he never forgave Lucca for his ruthlessness.

The success of *Attila* was real but slow to detonate, its popularity increasing as it went the rounds. It is the only opera in which Verdi was asked to provide two alternative arias – one for Napoleone Moriani, the other for Nicolai Ivanoff, once again at Rossini's request. The music has all the force if not the freshness of *Nabucco* or *Ernani*; and the subject of Italo-German confrontation was becoming more topical with every month that passed. For 1846 was the year of the 'liberal' Pope Pius IX's accession, heralding, it was hoped, a new era of freedom for Italy. At a performance of *Ernani* in Bologna the audience chanted 'A Pio Nono sia gloria ed onor' to the strains that greeted Carlo's granting of a general pardon. Never had Verdi's music been so openly associated with the cause of Italian patriotism. One may even detect a trace of nervousness in his request to Solera to tell him the precise meaning of Ezio's words addressed to Attila:

> Avrai tu l'universo
> Resti l'Italia a me

He had to be ready to answer awkward questions. But as in the case of *I Lombardi* the Risorgimentale associations have been exaggerated in the light of later events. Here too the honours and dishonours are distributed evenly and by no means in favour of the Italians. Attila is at least as estimable as any of his opponents. When Lucca demanded an exorbitant hire-fee for the opera from La Scala in the autumn of that year, it was the Austrian police who stepped in and compelled him to lower it – which shows how much danger the authorities apprehended from that quarter.

But if Verdi was still riding on a tide of success, the long illness of those winter months was a warning and the following months of enforced idleness a blessing in disguise. Free for a while from the

---

[14] LCC, p. 108.

Verdi

theatrical mill-race, he was unable to take thought, to re-consider his artistic ideals and so take the road which would lead to the goal of perpetual self renewal.

4

Florence, London and Paris

Throughout the spring of 1846 Verdi allowed himself to be nursed back to health, first by Piave in Venice, 'with a care that was truly fraternal,' then by Muzio in Milan. By June he was fit enough to stand as witness together with Giulio Carcano to the deed of separation between Andrea Maffei and his wife Clarina; then he followed both men to the spa of Recoaro, where he spent the summer in their company. Maffei and Carcano moved in the highest literary circles; both were poets and translators of merit, steeped as they were in foreign literature. His association with them at such a critical time could not fail to broaden Verdi's horizons.

The first hint of re-awakened creative powers comes in a letter to Piave written in August.[1] Now that the London project had been shelved for the time being Piave had asked whether he might offer the book of *Il corsaro* to another composer. Verdi's reply is at first all incredulous indignation. What, give up a work of which he had already begun to sketch one of the duets? Piave should have his head examined. But the tone gradually changes. If Piave would write him another poem with all the loving care that he had brought to the Byronic subject, then he is welcome to take back his original libretto. In the event *Il corsaro* would serve him for a less important occasion. For the present he had larger ideas.

Attila had been one of two operas contracted with the impresario Lanari; the second, subject still unchosen, was now scheduled for the Carnival season of 1847 in Florence. From Muzio we learn that the subjects under consideration were three: Schiller's *Die Räuber*, Grillparzer's *Die Ahnfrau* and Shakespeare's *Macbeth*; and that the last two were the most likely choices. If Fraschini were available he would do *Die Ahnfrau (L'Avola)*; if not, *Macbeth*. A note from Verdi to Lanari confirms this and specifies the opera's genre as

<hr>

[1] BOV, I, pp. 363–4.

'fantastic'. Fraschini, as it turned out, was engaged elsewhere; but that did not mean the end of Verdi's conditions for writing *Macbeth*. There was, he declared, only one baritone capable of sustaining the title role – Felice Varesi; and he did everything in his power to secure his services for the required period. He wrote to him personally, insisting that his negotiations be kept secret from the other leading baritone on the roster. Once engaged, he worked closely with Varesi on the composition of Macbeth's music, offering alternative versions of the same passage and asking for suggestions as to the scoring. He was lavish with instructions about the interpretation. Varesi was to pay more attention to the words than to the music, to serve the poet rather than the musician. The phrase 'in an entirely new manner'[2] continually recurs. He would rehearse both Varesi and his Lady Macbeth, Marianna Barbieri-Nini, to within minutes of the 'prova generale', which was held in public. Pietro Romani, who directed the orchestra, was driven to despair by the composer's inability to make his intentions clear to the players. But the chief sufferer was Piave. On 5 September 1846 Verdi had sent him a synopsis, using as his source Rusconi's translation of 1838. ('This tragedy is one of the greatest creations of the human spirit. If we cannot make something great out of it, let us at least do something out of the ordinary'.)[3] Throughout the autumn and winter of that year the poet was subjected to a barrage of letters asking for more verses and complaining of those already sent; they were too prolix, insufficiently theatrical; they lacked character. The reason, Verdi was sure, was that Piave had taken on too much work and that he himself was suffering for it. It was normal practice for the librettist of a new opera to act as stage director and to supervise the visual side in consultation with the impresario. Even here Piave was found wanting ('Lanari is complaining of you and so am I').[4] When Verdi asked for some lines for a danced chorus, Piave pointed out, reasonably enough, that the opera would be given in Lent when dancing on stage was forbidden. Verdi wrote back in exasperation telling him to do as he was bid and not make needless difficulties. At length he decided to drop Piave from the production altogether and to arrange everything himself directly

---

[2] GVIM, pp. 437–9.
[3] AGV, I, p. 643.
[4] Ibid., p. 656.

with Lanari including the 'phantasmagorical' (i.e. magic lantern) effects. For final adjustments to the witches' chorus in Act III and the sleepwalking scene he turned for help to Maffei. Piave was roundly told: 'Oh certainly you're not in the least to blame except for having neglected the last two acts in an incredible way. . . . If I must speak frankly I couldn't have set them to music . . . Now it has all been put right – by changing practically everything, however.'[5] In fact Maffei's contribution had been trifling, but Piave's name was omitted from the first printed edition even though he himself was paid in full. But the last laugh was his as Verdi ruefully admitted years later; for the lines which provoked most ridicule on the first night were by Maffei.

'The opera was not a fiasco,'[6] Verdi wrote to Clarina Maffei. That was an understatement. Antonio Barezzi, with the aid of Muzio (both men present for the first time at a Verdi première), described to their friends in Busseto the wild enthusiasm, the thirty-eight curtain calls, the crowd that escorted them all to their hotel. Marianna Barbieri-Nini presented to the composer a golden crown inscribed 'from the Florentines to Giuseppe Verdi'. Clearly Verdi had been shrewd in his choice of venue for so novel an opera. Armed with suitable letters of introduction from his friends in Milan, he had been made much of in the high cultural and aristocratic circles of the Italian Athens: the Marchese Capponi, Baron Ricasoli (soon to play a prominent role in the short-lived Tuscan republic) the poets Niccolini and Giusti and the sculptor Dupré all paid him court. True, a few voices suggested that the applause was more for the composer of *Attila*, which had preceded *Macbeth*; and Giusti, while predicting a glorious future for the new opera, cautioned the composer against the lure of the foreign and the exotic and urged him to 'accompany with your noble harmonies that high and solemn sorrow which fills the heart of the Italian nation'.[7] Verdi acknowledged the implied rebuke; he hoped one day to find a dramatic poet capable of devising a truly national type of melodramma; but in fact he was very pleased with *Macbeth*. Years later he was to tell a German journalist that from the start it had represented for him a 'total art work' in the

---

[5] Ibid., pp. 676–7.
[6] *Verdi's Macbeth: a sourcebook*, ed. D. Rosen and A. Porter (London, 1984), p. 57.
[7] LCC, pp. 449–50.

Wagnerian sense.[8] Nor for once did he allow it to be dedicated to a person of high rank. 'For a long time', he wrote to his father-in-law, 'it has been in my mind to dedicate an opera to you, who have been to me a father, a benefactor and a friend. . . . Here now is this *Macbeth*, which is dearer to me than all my other operas, and which therefore I deem more worthy of being presented to you. The heart offers it; may the heart accept it and may it bear witness to my eternal remembrance, and to the gratitude and love of your most affection ate G. Verdi.'[9]

He returned to Milan in late March to begin work on his next commission, the opera for Her Majesty's Theatre, London. This had been a casualty of Verdi's illness of 1846; and all Lumley's glowing accounts of the reception given to *I Lombardi* were powerless to entice him from Italy that summer. But a London première, the first to be accorded to a foreigner since Weber's *Oberon* of 1826, was not to be passed over. Accordingly Verdi resumed negotiations in the winter of 1846, specifying, however, that the opera was no longer to be *Il corsaro*, which he had now begun to find dull and untheatrical, but *I masnadieri (Die Räuber)*, libretto by Andrea Maffei, of which Verdi claimed (an unlikely story!) to have already composed a third. The chief roles were to include Jenny Lind, the Swedish nightingale, and Gaetano Fraschini – on that Verdi was insistent; though on receiving reports that Fraschini had been heard in London and not liked he was content to accept the young Italo Gardoni, not a star, perhaps, but highly praised by as knowledgeable a judge as the baritone Charles Santley. Then, as for the next hundred years, the main opera season in London began in the early summer. Accordingly Verdi left Milan with Muzio in the last week in May and made his way northward over the St. Gotthard and then by steamer down the Rhine to Cologne – possibly to absorb local atmosphere for the German drama, some have conjectured; thence to Brussels and overland to Paris where he remained for a few days, having heard rumours that Jenny Lind would not appear after all. However, Muzio, whom he dispatched in advance, was able to report her presence and Verdi followed. ('It is true', he wrote to Clarina Maffei, 'that the impresario has reason to complain of my behaviour, but if he says one word to me I shall say ten to him and come straight back.')[10]

[8] CIIV, p. 105.   [9] LCC, p. 451.   [10] Ibid., p. 457.

In fact the impresario had rather more on his mind than the caprices of a young composer. Benjamin Lumley, by profession a lawyer, had been called in to sort out the tangled finances of Her Majesty's Theatre in the Haymarket and had stayed on to take over the reins of management. Tough, enterprising and infinitely persuasive, he established a strong and efficient regime during the 1840s, but he made powerful enemies. Shortly before Verdi's arrival he had quarrelled with his chief conductor, Michael Costa, one of the leading figures in the English musical world. Costa had walked out, taking with him three of the stars of the 'Puritani quartet' (second edition) – Giulia Grisi, Giovanni Mario and Antonio Tamburini. Only Luigi Lablache remained loyal. The seceders set up a rival company at Covent Garden under the management of Persiani, husband of Fanny, star and creator of the title role in *Lucia di Lammermoor*. To the afore-mentioned stars could be added Giorgio Ronconi, creator of Nabucco, and the contralto Marietta Alboni whose phenomenally low range enabled her to undertake the role of Don Carlo in *Ernani*. ('In England a baritone and a contralto are the same thing' Muzio commented.) Both companies opened their season with *I due Foscari*. During his stay in London Verdi was careful to hold aloof from the rival camp. He refused Ronconi's request to help him with the role of the Doge; and he wrote a stiff little note to Mario reproaching him for singing an alternative cabaletta for Jacopo Foscari that Verdi had written specially for him but whose receipt he had never bothered to acknowledge. On the other hand he was favourably impressed by Jenny Lind, finding her character refreshingly simple and untheatrical though clearly she was not the singer for him; ('She is inclined to err in using excessive fioriture, turns and trills', wrote Muzio, doubtless relaying his master's voice, 'things which were liked in the last century but not in 1847.')[11] Verdi's impressions of Dickensian London were mixed. He was impressed by the city, the docks, the surrounding countryside with its beautifully clean houses but disliked the climate and the fog – 'like living on a steamer'. Nor did he care much for English manners – 'or rather I should say they do not suit us Italians'. He was, he said, unlikely to return 'though I like the city extraordinarily well'.[12]

[11] GMB, pp. 327–32.
[12] LCC, pp. 458–9.

In the weeks preceding the première Verdi appears to have led a secluded life. He refused an invitation to be presented to the Queen; but he did attend one of Lumley's famous dinner parties at which Louis Bonaparte was present; and at some point he met the patriot Giuseppe Mazzini, whose political ideals he shared. He also paid the resident Italian librettist, Manfredo Maggioni, the compliment of setting one of his poems ('Il poveretto'). The omens for the opera appeared favourable. The cast at Her Majesty's was a strong one, including Lablache and Coletti as well as Lind and Gardoni. Verdi, for the first time in his public career, conducted from the podium with a baton. Muzio's account of the première is predictable in its enthusiasm: 'The maestro was cheered, called on stage alone and with the singers, flowers were thrown at him, nothing was to be heard except 'Viva Verdi! Bietifol ... *The Times*, the *Morning Post* and the *Morning Chronicle* etc. are all very complimentary both about the music and the libretto ...'[13] One can only hope that the savager verdicts were kept from master and pupil: 'the worst opera ever to have been given at Her Majesty's Theatre'[14] (Chorley) ... 'A new opera by Signor Verdi ... the music very noisy and trivial' (Queen Victoria's Diary). Musical England was still the land of Mendelssohn.

Verdi left England for Paris after the first two performances, thereafter handing over the baton to Michael Balfe. Only two more followed. Clearly the opera had done nothing to enhance Verdi's reputation in London. Something of this must have penetrated to Muzio who observed that 'the English are a matter-of-fact and thoughtful people who don't know too much about music and think it ill-bred to make a lot of noise'.[15] Proposals for further engagements were made both by Verdi and Lumley but nothing was concluded (Verdi's claim that Lucca's refusal to release him from his contract of October 1845 prevented him from writing for Her Majesty's the following summer is arrant nonsense). London would never again have a Verdi première apart from the *Inno delle nazioni* of 1862 and the revised Liber Scriptus of the *Requiem* in 1875.

The possibility of adapting *I Lombardi* for the Paris Opéra, had

13 GMB, pp. 344–9.
14 TGV, p. 56.
15 GMB, pp. 351–3.

been mooted as early as November 1845. Now, with Verdi on the spot, it became a reality. The directors of the Opéra were Duponchel and Roqueplan, the poets Royer and Vaëz, authors of Donizetti's *La favorite*, and the publishers Léon and Marie Escudier ('here everyone comes in pairs', Verdi wrote[16]). Although the crusading ambience remained, the characters were altered; so too certain of the situations. The additions included a ballet and a special scene for Gilbert Duprez, star of the Paris Opéra and more surprisingly creator of that most Italianate of tenor roles, Edgardo in *Lucia di Lammermoor*. The opera was given with reasonable success on 26 November, causing one critic to remark that it had granted the composer a patent of French nationality and the Opèra a new masterpiece. Muzio, who had proceeded straight to Milan, confidently expected his master's return after the première of *Jérusalem*. But for one reason or another Verdi kept putting it off. First, he wished to dispose of *Il corsaro* with as little trouble as possible. By February 1848 the opera was complete and Verdi himself ready to go and assist with the production at the Teatro Grande, Trieste; but a feverish chill prevented him. The opera was mounted in his absence by Luigi Ricci, not however before Verdi had sent a letter to Marianna Barbieri-Nini with detailed instructions for the interpretation of the female lead. Despite a strong cast which included Gaetano Fraschini in the title role and Achille De Bassini as the villain, *Il corsaro* was a fiasco. As Donizetti had found more than once, it is always dangerous for a composer not to be present at one of his premières. Critics and public alike are inclined to take it as an affront.

Verdi did return to Italy that year, but only briefly, in order to purchase the Fattoria S.Agata two miles outside Busseto and once a family possession. Here he installed his parents and would later come to live himself. But his home remained Paris until July of the following year. Those for whom all explanations can be found in the principle 'cherchez la femme' would in this case be right.

Composers are not always fortunate in their choice of wives. Anyone familiar with the matrimonial affairs of Haydn, Glinka, Wagner and Puccini – even Mozart – might well conclude that in

[16] LCC, pp. 462–3.

remaining bachelors Beethoven and Brahms had chosen the better part. Of this Verdi's case provides a magnificent refutation. The woman who now began to share his life is one of the most remarkable ever to figure in a composer's biography. Giuseppina Strepponi was born at Lodi in Lombardy in 1815, the daughter of a minor composer and the eldest of four children. At fifteen she was accepted at the Milan Conservatoire where she showed great promise as a pianist and a singer. Two years later her father died; she was granted a bursary so that she might complete her studies. In 1835 she made a successful debut as Adria in Rossini's *Matilda di Shabran*; from then on she became the breadwinner of the family.

At first it seems to have been roses, roses all the way. Giuseppina undoubtedly had star quality; she was equally at home in comedy and tragedy. She had the flexible technique for Donizetti's Lucia, the tragic dignity for his Antonina in *Belisario* and Bellini's Beatrice, the comic sparkle for Adina, the simple pathos for Amina. Donizetti was to write for her the title role of *Adelia* in 1841. But singers' careers were usually short in those days because they began too early; and Giuseppina's was shorter than most. The necessity of accepting an uninterrupted stream of engagements in order to feed her family, a love-life which produced her three illegitimate children in the space of three years undermined her health; and after 1842 she appeared less and less frequently and only at minor theatres, eventually retiring to Paris as a singing teacher, aged only thirty-one.

The more critical moments of her career are illustrated by a number of vivid, sometimes harrowing letters written to the impresario Lanari who from 1838 acted as her manager or 'appaltatore' (a frequent arrangement in those days). From various hints in their correspondence Frank Walker deduced that the father of her children, long believed to have been the impresario Merelli, was in fact the tenor, Napoleone Moriani. That he was indeed the father of the last-born, Adelina, who came into the world prematurely in November 1841, there can be no possible doubt. His paternity of the boy Camillo (b. 1838) and Giuseppa (b. 1839 and later adopted) is more difficult to establish. The theatrical agent Cirelli made himself out to be the father, possibly in order to protect the name of a star tenor with a family, but no less possibly because the children were in fact his. Hopes of regularising her position by marriage to an admirer – referred to by Moriani as 'that nasty lame devil who gives her such bad advice' – or of forming a liaison with an unnamed Count (probably Camerata) – came to nothing. At one point her doctors threatened her with consumption. Yet through all her misfortunes there shines a noble and courageous spirit.

Her attraction to Verdi seems to have begun with his music. It was she, together with Ronconi, who first pressed the cause of *Oberto*; it was to her that Verdi brought the score of *Nabucco* in December 1841 when Merelli had failed to include it among the operas announced for the Carnival season; and it was her agreement to sing in it that carried the day in the composer's favour. True, by the time of the première she was in wretched vocal condition, but her friendly relations with Verdi were unaffected. The next year they met in Parma, where she gave him sound financial advice; and there was another encounter in Bergamo in the spring of 1844 where she wrote a letter on his behalf to Giovannina Lucca about the 'sei romanze' for which Verdi had contracted with the firm. Letters to Giovannina from Paris give the clearest evidence of her continuing interest in Verdi and his career. She was especially concerned that his interests in France should not be compromised by Lucca's dealings over *I masnadieri*. ('The Escudier brothers are still gazing open mouthed and with eye-glasses to their eyes to make sure that they've read correctly for the amount you are demanding for *I Masnadieri* (10 thousand francs!)[17] There is even some evidence that she may have travelled to Florence for the première of *Macbeth*: a portrait said to be of Giuseppina Strepponi (though looking nothing like her) was painted in Florence in the spring of 1847. Certainly by the time Verdi arrived in Paris to work on *Jérusalem* she and the composer were seeing a good deal of one another. Barezzi, who had been persuaded to pay Verdi a visit in November writes warmly to Verdi about the kind reception given to him by Verdi himself and 'La Signora Peppina' from whom he is expecting a letter. But the clearest proof of the relationship between composer and prima donna is to be found in the autograph score of *Jérusalem*. The new text of the lovers' duet is written out partly in Verdi's, partly in Giuseppina's hand, the lines being so apportioned between them as to form a declaration of love in terms appropriate to the situation of each. It was a union that would endure to Giuseppina's death fifty years later. Their qualities complemented one another. Verdi was short on tact and humour;

[17] AGV, I, p. 709.

Giuseppina had an abundance of both. Where Verdi was tough and sometimes over-exigent, she was vulnerable and compassionate. For all his intelligence and culture Verdi was never much of a linguist; Giuseppina had an aptitude for languages which stood him in good stead in the operas which he took from foreign sources. It is even arguable whether *Il trovatore* or *Simon Boccanegra* would ever have come into being without her to translate the original plays. Above all, though she adored Verdi with all her heart and put up with his often tyrannical moods with the patience of a Griselda, she never ceased to be a 'person' in her own right with her own views on everything – views which were by no means always those of her husband.

Over the political events of 1848 they were of one mind. Ever since the accession of Pope Pius IX, Italian patriots had been foreseeing the imminent dawn of freedom. The Austrians could no longer count on La Scala as a weapon of government. In February Fanny Elssler was hissed during the course of a ballet, fainted on stage and abruptly returned to Vienna. There had been demonstrations when Cardinal Romilli succeeded Cardinal Gaisruck as Archbishop of Milan, and hymns were sung in praise of Pope Pio Nono. Satires circulated; riots broke out. 'All is quiet now', Muzio had written to Barezzi, 'but only a spark is needed to set everything in flames.'[18] On 18 March the powder keg exploded. The Austrians were driven out of Milan in the 'five days' (Cinque Giornate) of street-fighting. Then Venice declared itself a republic. Verdi and Giuseppina, both ardent Mazzinians wrote to their friends exultantly, Giuseppina from Paris to Pietro Romani, musical director at the Teatro della Pergola, Florence, Verdi from Milan (en route for Busseto) to Piave, now a soldier citizen in the Republic of Venice: 'Honour to all Italy which at this moment is truly great! The hour has sounded – make no mistake – of her liberation. It is the people that wills it, and when the people wills there is no absolute power that can resist.' (Needless to say he was using the word 'people' in the Mazzinian not the Marxist sense – a nation united by culture and language, not the toiling masses of the world.) 'You talk of music to me!! What are you thinking of? Do you think I want to concern myself now with notes and sounds? There is and should be only one

18 GMB, p. 355.

kind of music pleasing to the ears of the Italians of 1848 – the music of the guns!' But Verdi was not a fighting man. 'I too if I had enrolled would wish to be a common soldier, but now I can only be a tribune and a wretched tribune at that as I am only eloquent by fits and starts.'[19] That by 'tribune' he was intimating that Mazzini had devised for him a special position in the event of victory seems unlikely. To the classically educated Verdi the term probably meant no more than a popular orator. It might even be conjectured that his main motive for coming to Italy at the time was less the desire to be present at a historic occasion but rather to buy his property under cheap wartime conditions.

But he undoubtedly had the Italian cause at heart and did his best to serve it in the way his talents would allow. In October he composed a battle hymn, 'Suona la tromba', to words by Goffredo Mameli, hoping that it might be 'sung amid the firing of the guns upon the plains of Lombardy.'[20] But it was Mameli's 'Fratelli d'Italia' composed by the less gifted Novaro that was destined to become the Italian Marseillaise. In July, when the war had taken a bad turning for Italy and Milan was forced to capitulate, Verdi was one of the signatories to an appeal for French aid handed to General Cavaignac. But it was with an opera that he hoped to make his most valuable contribution to the Italian cause. At first it was to have been a setting of Guerrazzi's *L'assedio di Firenze*, a novel that tells of the downfall of the Florentine Republic under papal forces assisted by the Prince of Orange. He despatched a synopsis to Piave, whose military duties however prevented him from doing anything about it. Meanwhile a contract remained outstanding for an opera to be given in Naples. The upheavals of 1848 had temporarily unseated Flauto from the management of San Carlo; so Verdi suggested writing the commissioned work with Cammarano for Ricordi under the same kind of contract that he had had with Lucca. Ricordi would place it in a suitable theatre and arrange for a worthy cast. The opera was to be called *La battaglia di Legnano* and would deal with the defeat of the Emperor Frederick Barbarossa by the army of the Lombard League in 1184. For lack of an existing play on the subject Cammarano had recourse to Joseph Méry's *La bataille de Toulouse*. Into

[19] WMV, pp. 187–8.
[20] LCC, pp. 469–70.

this, at Verdi's suggestion, he wove suitably topical scenes, including a confrontation between the two heroes and Barbarossa. The opera was composed in Paris during the autumn and winter of 1848. The première took place on 27 January 1849 at the Teatro Argentina in Rome with Teresa De Giuli-Borsi (the second Abigaille) Fraschini and Filippo Colini, creator of Giacomo in *Giovanna d'Arco*. Verdi travelled to Rome for the production.

Time and place could not have been better chosen. Despite the setback in the North, the Italian cause was by no means lost. Venice still held out. There were uprisings in Tuscany and the Papal States; in Central Italy Garibaldi was recruiting an army. Meanwhile, by his Allocution of April 1848, in which he dissociated himself from the Risorgimento, Pope Pio Nono forfeited all the sympathy his previous amnesty had gained him. Indeed the end of the year found him a prisoner in the Vatican, from which he managed to escape to Gaita, just across the Neapolitan border, disguised as an ordinary priest. On 9 February, two weeks after the première of Verdi's opera, Rome was proclaimed a republic. That *La battaglia di Legnano* was a clamorous *succès d'occasion* could have been foreseen. The last act, in which the slayer of Barbarossa is borne in on a litter and dies amid the acclamations of his people was encored at each performance. But when the tide of war turned against the Italians the opera's fortunes waned accordingly. On 20 March Carlo Alberto of Piedmont denounced the armistice and once more invaded Lombardy, only to be defeated by General Radetzky. Venice was besieged and capitulated, leaving Radetzky to pick off the remaining cities of the north at his leisure. Austrian troops re-entered Florence in May and Rome in July. Garibaldi became a fugitive, eventually reaching safety in America after a series of dangers and misfortunes which included the death of his wife. The Pope was restored to Rome with the aid of French troops. From Paris Verdi could only wring his hands; 'Force still rules the world', he wrote to Luccardi, 'Justice? What use is it against bayonets? All we can do is to weep over our wrongs and curse the authors of so many misfortunes.'[21] A fortnight later he returned to Italy with Giuseppina.

Once he had taken the decision to write *La battaglia di Legnano* for his publisher, Verdi thought he had finished with the Neapolitan

[21] AGV, II, p. 23.

commitment. But Naples had not yet finished with him. By the autumn of 1848 Flauto was back in the saddle and demanding the opera stipulated in the original contract. Unable to put pressure on a Verdi resident in Paris, he and the management turned the heat on Cammarano. Either the said opera would be given in 1849 or the poet would be fined and, if unable to pay the fine, put in prison. With a wife and six children to support, Cammarano wrote to Verdi in a panic begging him to come to his rescue; and Verdi agreed grudgingly to do so ('I will write the opera for Naples next year *for your sake alone*; it will rob me of two hours peace every day and of my health').[22] However the project was as yet months away. First there was the subject to be chosen. Verdi wanted to return to *L'assedio di Firenze* but could hardly have been surprised when the censors of Royalist Naples turned it down. Cammarano then took up an earlier suggestion of the composer's for an opera based on Schiller's *Kabale und Liebe*, a product of the author's 'Sturm und Drang' period with a political element that Cammarano could be guaranteed to defuse. It is also a 'bourgeois tragedy' and as such offers the composer opportunities for a more intimate, poetic style of expression. Beginning with Abramo Basevi all commentators have recognised in *Luisa Miller*, as it came to be called, a 'second' manner, gentler and less grandiose than the first.[23]

Correspondence about the opera continued throughout the spring and summer of 1849. Much of it is of interest as showing the collaboration between two experienced men of the theatre. From Cammarano, unlike Piave, Verdi was prepared to learn. As usual he liked to keep as close as possible to the original source. But he allowed his desire to include Schiller's Lady Milford 'in the full extension of her character'[24] to be set aside on the grounds that no prima donna could be induced to play a character of such doubtful morals, especially if she had a rival in the title role. He also yielded to Cammarano's insistence that Luisa's false declaration of love should be written to the villainous Wurm rather than to the Court Chamberlain, as in Schiller. 'Did I not fear the imputation of being Utopian', Cammarano wrote, 'I would be tempted to say that to achieve the

[22] LCC, p. 55.
[23] BSV, pp. 156–9.
[24] LCC, pp. 470–2.

highest degree of perfection in an opera it would be necessary for words and music to be the product of one and the same mind, and from this ideal follows my firm opinion that when it has two authors they must at least be like brothers, and that if Poetry should not be the servant of Music still less should it tyrannise over her.'[25] Not altogether sound, perhaps, but indicative of a thoughtful and serious attitude toward his craft all too rare in theatrical poets of the time.

The scheme finally agreed, Verdi returned from Paris early in August to begin work on the score. His base was no longer Milan, but his home town of Busseto, where a new, more settled existence awaited him.

[25] Ibid., pp. 473–4.

5

Return to Busseto

If as a rule great artists are rarely good business men, Verdi must be accounted an exception. From the start he was determined that the money he earned should not lie idle. In 1844 following the success of *Ernani* he had bought some property near his native hamlet of Le Roncole. This he sold in 1848 putting the proceeds to the purchase of the farm house, S. Agata. In 1845 he had acquired the Palazzo Dordoni in the main street of Busseto. Clearly the Bussetani can have been in no doubt that their most distinguished citizen would sooner or later come to live amongst them. What they underestimated was his desire for independence. Already when arranging for the dedication of *I Lombardi* there are signs that he was finding the behaviour even of such a valued friend as Demaldé intolerably officious. About this time it was planned to build a municipal theatre in Busseto. Verdi had given the idea a cautious blessing, adding that he might be prepared to write an opera for it when his other engagements should permit; that even Frezzolini and Poggi might be persuaded to appear. Soon this began to be talked about as a certainty; and Verdi felt obliged to write to Barezzi pointing out that he had promised nothing. When the theatre project did eventually come to fruition in 1859 it was to prove one of the biggest bones of contention between Verdi and the Bussetani. In the meantime a greater cause for friction had arisen. Verdi took up residence in the Palazzo Dordoni in August. A month later he was joined by Giuseppina, on her return from Florence where she had visited her son Camillino now in the care of one Livia Zanobini with the sculptor Lorenzo Bartolini as his tutor. That Verdi should be living openly in their midst with a woman not his wife – and of a by no means unblemished reputation at that – was deeply shocking, not only to the clerical party that had opposed him years before. Little is known of his life in Busseto for the next two or three years; but more than one letter to Piave hints at an intolerable state of affairs. Meanwhile Giuseppina was ignored in the street and no one sat near her in church. For all her native charity she would not forget these insults in the years to come.

That Barezzi did not as yet join in the general disapproval, that relations between him and Verdi were unimpaired is clear from the fact that both men left for Naples on 3 October for the production of *Luisa Miller*. It was a slow journey: first by land to Genoa then by sea to Pisa and Rome where they were detained by a cholera epidemic; here Verdi received an ominous letter from Cammarano indicating that the financial affairs of the San Carlo Theatre were in disorder, that the management had not yet paid him his fee and that Verdi would do well to demand the advance due to him as soon as he set foot in Naples. Sure enough the advance was not forthcoming; whereupon Verdi declared that he would suspend rehearsals. The management countered by threatening to invoke a law whereby he could be detained indefinitely at His Majesty's pleasure. In that case Verdi would seek asylum aboard a French vessel anchored in the Bay. Fortunately it did not come to that. Verdi was paid and rehearsals proceeded normally. Barezzi, having visited the sights of Naples, was obliged to return home before the first performance. *Luisa Miller* was on the whole well liked; the highly original last act, coolly received at first, grew in popularity with each performance; and Verdi left Naples having again added to the list of lasting friendships – the composer Capocelatro, the clarinettist Sebastiani, the character bass Marco Arati, who had created Wurm in the opera, and most important of all, the merchant Cesare De Sanctis. For the next thirty odd years until his failure to repay a loan put an end to their friendship Cesare De Sanctis was to be Verdi's 'man in Naples'. If it was a matter of prodding the dilatory Cammarano into action or sounding out the affairs, financial or artistic, of the San Carlo or arranging accommodation, De Sanctis was the contact. Verdi and Giuseppina would stand as godparents to his son.

By 1850 Verdi had made enough money to retire on his earnings had he so wished. Rossini had done so at the same age; and Verdi made this ambition the burden of many a letter to his friends in Milan. Yet in fact the next three years were to be the most fertile of his life. He left Naples with grandiose plans for a *King Lear* in which all the traditional forms were to be abandoned and the 'convenienze' or class distinctions of singers left out of account. In fact this meant five principal roles and at least four heavy supporting ones. Cammarano dutifully promised to mull this over; but though Verdi continued to talk of this project as though it were a possibility for

Naples the following year, it proceeded no further than the drawing board. Presumably word of his intentions had spread abroad because that same year, 1850, he received two suggestions for Shakespearean operas: from Marie Escudier for a *Tempest* at Her Majesty's and from Giulio Carcano for a *Hamlet* to his own libretto. The second Verdi declined on the ground that 'if *King Lear* is difficult to set to music, *Hamlet* is still more so';[1] the first because the time proposed was too short and the fact that Lumley had commissioned an opera on the same subject from Halévy looked suspiciously like an impresario's stunt. Nevertheless 'I do plan to compose *The Tempest*, indeed I plan to do the same with all the major works of the great tragedian'.[2] But his next Shakespearean venture would be a long way in the future.

Because they could not agree on terms the Neapolitan contract came to nothing; and Verdi proposed to write *Re Lear* for Ricordi under the same conditions as *La battaglia di Legnano*. Then in the spring of 1850 he was approached by Marzari of the Teatro La Fenice, Venice, for an opera for the carnival season of 1850–1. Dumas' *Kean* and *Gusmano il Buono* were considered; also a *Stiffelius* by Souvestre and Bourgeois; 'but I would have another subject', he wrote to Piave, 'which, if the police were prepared to allow it would be one of the greatest creations of the modern theatre. Who knows? They permitted *Ernani* and might permit this too; and there would be no conspiracies in this one.'[3] Later 'Oh, *le roi s'amuse* is the greatest subject and perhaps the greatest drama of modern times. Triboulet is a creation worthy of Shakespeare!'[4] – than which he could bestow no higher praise. Piave was urged to get the subject approved as quickly as possible; this he did but only by word of mouth. The consequences would be felt later.

By June it was clear that Cammarano would not finish *Re Lear* in time for the autumn. Accordingly Verdi allowed *Stiffelio*, a synopsis of which he had read and liked, to be announced for production in the Teatro Grande, Trieste, with Maria Gazzaniga Malaspina (now a countess), Gaetano Fraschini and Filippo Colini. The choice of subject

[1] LCC, pp. 482–3.
[2] AGV, II, pp. 56–7.
[3] Ibid., pp. 59–60.
[4] Ibid., pp. 62–3.

bears witness to Verdi's growing spirit of enterprise: a Protestant minister who discovers his wife in an adulterous intrigue and is thus impelled by honour to a course of action which his cloth forbids; and who ends by forgiving her publicly from the pulpit. Nothing like that had ever been seen on the Italian stage. That summer Piave came to Busseto where, blessedly unaware of what lay ahead, both he and Verdi worked on *Stiffelio* and *Rigoletto*, as it would eventually be called. From this period we may presumably date that remarkable document, the so-called *Rigoletto* sketch: fifty-six pages of text, vocal line and bass with indications of connecting material, all relatively free from cancellations and differing so little from the finished opera as to suggest that never had Verdi's creative powers been more spontaneously ignited.

In September he went to Bologna to supervise a revival of *Macbeth*; thence he returned to Busseto where a feverish chill prevented him from setting out for Trieste at the appointed time. Luigi Ricci who had directed *Il corsaro* at the same theatre took charge of the early rehearsals. Verdi arrived with Piave at the end of October to find everything proceeding smoothly. But they had reckoned without the censor. Protestant ministers were not allowed to have spiritual authority, least of all if they were married. Certain lines, essential to the dramatic logic were therefore changed and rendered meaningless; worst of all in the final scene there was no church, no Bible and only a vague platitude for Christ's words of forgiveness for the woman taken in adultery. Verdi was used to having certain subjects rejected and to seeing his works bowdlerised when revived in Naples or the Papal States. This was the first time he had suffered the mutilation of a work at its première. It was received with respect and its composer with enthusiasm; but Verdi was determined for the future to find some way of rendering it censor-proof.

Piave had completed the libretto of *Rigoletto*, or *La maledizione* as it was called at the time, and sent it to Verdi in Busseto, Brenna having assured both parties that the authorities would not make any difficulties about the subject. Together they put the finishing touches to it during the rehearsals for *Stiffelio*; after which the submission of it to the censors could be regarded as a mere formality. Then on 1 December Marzari reported that 'despite all the effort of the Presidenza and the poet the subject has been absolutely forbidden; it is even prohibited to make any amendments whatsoever'. Enclosed with the letter was a copy of the censor's report, regretting that 'the poet Piave and the celebrated Maestro Verdi have not been able to choose some other theme on which to exhibit their talents than one of such repellent immorality and obscene triviality as the subject of the libretto entitled *La maledizione*'.[5]

Undoubtedly what alarmed the Venetian authorities was the spectacle of royal profligacy in action; and even while the letter was on its way to Busseto, Piave, with the unlikely help of the police official Martello who had signed the censor's report, was already trying to render the plot more palatable. Francis I was turned into a Duke of Ventignano, a nobleman having an affair like any other; there was no specific plot to have him murdered; and Gilda was spared the indignity of being thrust into a sack.

Verdi meanwhile had reacted violently against the censorial ban, as usual throwing the blame on Piave for having given false assurances and suggesting *Stiffelio* with a new ending by way of a substitute. Nor was he much impressed by the first redraft of the new libretto. 'The Duke is a nonentity', he wrote.

> The Duke absolutely must be a libertine; without that there can be no justification for Triboletto's fear that his daughter might come out of her hiding place . . . In the last act why ever should the Duke go to a remote tavern without an invitation and without an appointment?
>
> I don't understand why the sack should have been taken out. How does the sack concern the police? Are they afraid it won't be effective? But might I be permitted to ask why they suppose themselves to be better judges in the matter than I? . . .
>
> I observe finally that we are to avoid making Triboletto ugly and hunchbacked . . . Putting on the stage a character who is grossly deformed and absurd but inwardly passionate and full of love is precisely what I feel to be so fine. I chose this subject precisely for those qualities, those original traits, and if they are taken away I can no longer write music for it. If you tell me that my music can stay the same even with this drama I reply that I don't understand this kind of reasoning, and I must say frankly that whether my music is good or bad I don't write it at random, but I always try to give it a definite character.[6]

[5] LCC, p. 487.
[6] Ibid., pp. 109–11.

An irrefutable testimony, this, both to Verdi's humanity and to that feeling for dramatic logic which is sometimes denied to him.

The Presidenza saw the point, and a suitable compromise was worked out whereby locale and period were changed but the characters and situations remained as in Victor Hugo. (Curiously, although Francis I was turned without difficulty into Vincenzo Gonzaga, patron of Rubens and Monteverdi, he was not allowed to be mentioned by name, but only as The Duke of Mantua, even if, as Piave pointed out, everybody knew who was reigning in Mantua at that time.) The only casualty was the scene in which Blanche (Gilda), abducted into the palace, flees into a nearby room and locks the door; whereupon her seducer triumphantly produces the key – and enters. At about the new year Piave paid a visit to Busseto with his old friend Brenna to give moral support (they would have to share a room Verdi told them as he had his mother staying in the house). Piave and Giuseppina took to each other at once; and from now on Verdi's letters to his collaborator would often be accompanied by Giuseppina's postscripts. Verdi arrived in Venice early in February to begin rehearsals. The première took place on 11 March 1851 with Felice Varesi, the first Macbeth, in the title role, Raffaele Mirate as the Duke and Teresa Brambilla, one of the many singers of that name, as Gilda. Verdi's boldest and most revolutionary opera to date, it had a success which surpassed all expectations and of which the caution of *La Gazzetta di Venezia* and the grudging respect of Lucca's *L'Italia Musicale* can give very little idea. When it reached Paris even Victor Hugo was won round; having pronounced Verdi's *Ernani* a clumsy counterfeit of his own work, he now regretted that in a spoken drama there was no way of making four characters express different sentiments simultaneously, as in the *Rigoletto* quartet. Rossini declared that *Rigoletto* was the first opera which made him aware of the composer's greatness.

Verdi's elation, his renewed strength of artistic purpose can be glimpsed from his letters to De Sanctis and Cammarano during the following summer over his next operatic project. Cammarano was still dragging his feet over *Re Lear*; so Verdi had suggested another subject – *El trovador* by Garcia Guttiérez – 'very beautiful, imaginative and full of strong situations'.[7] And to De Sanctis 'the more

Cammarano provides me with originality and freedom of form the better I shall be able to do'.[8] But it was to be a long time before Cammarano was to be able to give Verdi what he wanted; and when at last after nearly two years *Il trovatore* reached the stage it did so in a form rather different from that which Verdi had originally envisaged.

Meanwhile life at Busseto was becoming increasingly irksome. In May Verdi moved with Giuseppina to the farmhouse S.Agata which would become his home for the rest of his life. His parents he settled at nearby Vidalenzo. Carlo had proved an inefficient 'fattore'. Verdi had not only to pay off his debts but found it necessary to correspond with him through a lawyer about their mutual rights in the property. In June in the midst of a painful family situation his mother died. In the months that followed he and Giuseppina withdrew further and further from Bussetan society into their rural solitude. Then in the winter they left for Paris where Verdi would arrange a contract with the Opéra, this time for a wholly original work (it would become *Les vêpres siciliennes*). While he was away Verdi received a letter from Barezzi which really upset him. ('If this letter were not signed 'Antonio Barezzi', that is by my benefactor, I should have replied very sharply or not at all.') Unfortunately the document has not survived; but Verdi's reply contains enough to suggest to the romantic biographer that he may have reproached his son-in-law for living with a loose woman – a Germont to Verdi's Alfredo.

> 'In my house', Verdi retorted, 'there lives a lady, free, independent, a lover like myself of solitude, like myself possessing a fortune that shelters her from all need. Neither I nor she owes anyone an account of our actions . . . Who knows whether she is or is not my wife? And if she is, who knows what the particular reasons are for not making the fact public? . . . In my house she is entitled to as much respect as myself – more even . . .

But this is mere self-defence against the routine gossip of the Bussetani. Barezzi himself had never shown the slightest disapproval of Giuseppina. The nub of the quarrel must be sought in an earlier passage.

[8] LCV, I, pp. 4–5.

> What harm is there if I live in isolation? If I choose not to pay calls
> on titled people? If I take no part in the festivities and rejoicings of
> others? If I administer my farmlands because I enjoy doing so . . . I
> come to the sentence in your letter: 'I know very well that I am not
> the man for serious charges because my time is over, but I should
> still be capable of doing small things.' . . .⁹

In other words Barezzi was blaming his son-in-law for cutting
himself off from his old friends; for no longer entrusting him with
little errands as he once did. But he was not asking him to give up
Giuseppina; and if a faintly caustic note occasionally creeps into her
own references to 'Father Antonio' and his reverence for the nobility,
he was a frequent and welcome visitor to S.Agata. His touching
devotion to Verdi almost amounting to worship is attested by Léon
Escudier who later that same year visited Verdi to bring him the cross
of the Légion d'Honneur.

While Verdi and Giuseppina were still in Paris a daring play by
Alexandre Dumas the younger was produced at the Vaudeville
Theatre, *La dame aux camélias*. At about the same time Verdi
received fresh overtures from the management of La Fenice, Venice,
anxious to follow up the success of *Rigoletto*. Whether or not the
two events were linked in Verdi's mind from the start we cannot be
sure. Certainly before accepting the contract for Venice he insisted
that there should be a good soprano available; only his term, 'donna
di prima forza' raises doubts as to whether he had in mind a
consumptive heroine. On the other hand the account given by
Brenna of his visit to S.Agata in late April contains a reference to one
Giani Vives who had played the comprimaria in *Il corsaro* (also on
the cartello of the forthcoming carnival season) whom it would be as
well to keep in reserve for the new opera. But the question was still
unsettled when Verdi finally signed the contract in May, and the
subject remained to be chosen. For the moment he had the more
pressing matter of *Il trovatore* to contend with. Cammarano had still
not completed the libretto. The faithful intermediary De Sanctis had
reported that the poet was ill but forebore to say how seriously. Not
till August did Verdi read in a theatrical journal that Cammarano
had died on 17 July, having completed the libretto a week earlier; the
composer's enthusiastic reply had arrived too late to cheer his bed of

⁹ LCC, pp. 128–31.

sickness. Verdi had lost a valued friend as well as a collaborator; and still much remained to be done to the libretto of *Il trovatore* before he was satisfied with it. It was again De Sanctis who found a suitable poet – the young Leone Emanuele Bardare ('he is in his seventh heaven at the prospect of writing for Maestro Verdi').[10] Under the composer's guidance the role of Leonora, originally a comprimaria, was brought into parity with that of Azucena, a fresh romanza written for the count and the opera shaped into the form that we know today. Out of respect for the dead man, Cammarano's was the only name to appear on the printed libretto and the published score.

It was about the time of Cammarano's death that the authorities of La Fenice became restive over the opera for the carnival season. The libretto should have been ready for the censor by early September and the subject had not even been chosen. Letters to Piave and the baritone Varesi, then in Spain, show that the search was still going on but without result. At length, as in the past, it was decided to send Piave to Busseto with a view to working out something on the spot. From the 'Thebaid' of S.Agata in the middle of a rainy November in which 'one must continually look at oneself in the mirror to be sure that . . . one hasn't been turned into a toad or a frog' Piave was able to announce to Brenna that when he had practically finished the libretto (unnamed) Verdi suddenly asked him to draw up a scenario for *La dame aux camélias*. 'I think that Verdi will write a fine opera, because I can see he is very worked up.'[11] Certainly if there was a theatre at which so bold and unconventional a subject would be likely to pass unscathed it was La Fenice; and apart from changing the proposed title from *Amore e morte* to *La traviata* the censorship raised no objections. On New Years Day Verdi announced triumphantly to De Sanctis, 'For Venice I'm doing *La dame aux camélias* . . . a subject for our time! Others wouldn't have attempted it for a thousand reasons – the costumes, the period and a thousand other silly scruples. But I'm doing it with the greatest of pleasure.'[12] By this time *Il trovatore* was ready to go into rehearsal. Verdi, it seems, was still putting the finishing touches to one opera while working on another (he had stipulated with the impresario, Jacovacci, that a

[10] LCV, I, pp. 11–14.
[11] CIV, pp. 85.
[12] LCV, I, pp. 16–17.

piano should be put at his disposal during his stay in Rome). Despite the presence of only two stars among the four principals – Carlo Baucardé and Rosina Penco ('take care, Maestro', De Sanctis had warned, 'she's a very devil and will certainly make mincemeat of the other prima donna')[13] – the première of *Il trovatore* was an outstanding success. One or two critics complained about the excessive number of deaths – 'but isn't life all death?',[14] Verdi wrote to Clarina Maffei.

He now hurried back to S. Agata to complete *La traviata*. He had heard disturbing reports of the cast, even of Varesi who was to sing the baritone lead. A clause in his contract had allowed him to engage a different prima donna if Fanny Salvini Donatelli, for whom he had agreed somewhat reluctantly to write, should prove unsuitable; in which case the management would need to be informed before the middle of January; but Verdi was too engrossed in the rehearsals for *Il trovatore* to observe the date of expiry. His subsequent protests were therefore ignored. However he once again obtained permission for Piave to come to S.Agata for the final modifications. Having done all in their power to meet his terms the management were dismayed to receive a letter written in Piave's hand but dictated by Verdi to the effect that the entire company of singers was unworthy of a theatre such as La Fenice; that Verdi himself was suffering from rheumatism in the arm and might not even be able to complete the opera: in which case he would suggest *Il trovatore* instead which would at least be new for Venice. This was too much; in firm but friendly terms the Presidenza recalled the composer to his obligations. In a thoroughly bad humour Verdi set out for Venice. 'I've just received a note', he told Piave, 'that unless the tenor and baritone are changed the opera will be a disaster. I know, I know and I'll prove it to you.'[15]

As to what happened during that notorious first night of 6 March 1853 writers are still disposed to argue. Some declare that the so-called fiasco was not a fiasco after all or that if it was, Verdi himself engineered it out of pique. A sober consideration of the documents shows that while not a fiasco on the scale of that of *Un giorno di regno*, it failed not only at its first performance but at all

[13] Ibid., pp. 11–14.
[14] LCC, p. 532.
[15] CBM, p. 324.

others given that season. Two of the old myths may be disposed of straight away. It did not fail because it was given in contemporary costumes. Indeed Verdi had intended that it be played in modern dress but he had been overruled. The time was put back to the beginning of the eighteenth century; and even when Gemma Bellincioni began the fashion of playing Violetta in a crinoline the men continued to wear full-bottomed wigs and breeches. Also it is not true that Fanny Salvini-Donatelli disappointed. An old-fashioned florid soprano, she distinguished herself nobly in the first act and won considerable applause; the rest of the opera however gave no scope for her particular skills; and the spectacle of so robust a soprano apparently dying of consumption carried little conviction. Varesi, on the other hand, was sufficiently stung by criticisms of his singing as to write to Lucca's *L'Italia Musicale* a letter of self-defence in which he declared roundly that if anyone was to blame for the failure of *La traviata* it was Verdi, who had simply not known how to make use of the qualities of his singers; he added with characteristic singer's egotism that the public were angry with Verdi for not having provided Varesi himself with a part such as Macbeth or Rigoletto.

His letter concludes with an account of the third performance. 'A wretched house. A little applause for the brindisi and a good deal for Salvini's cabaletta, with two curtain calls. In the grand duet between Salvini and myself there was some applause for the adagio and cabaletta. Applause for the finale to Act II and two curtain calls for the composer and the artists. Third act—no applause; one curtain call to say good-bye to the composer who was known to be leaving the next day.'[16] For a composer who used to declare that the thermometer of success was the box office takings at the sixth performance this was a poor omen. Clearly *La traviata* had not taken off. 'My fault', Verdi wrote to Muzio 'or that of the artists? Time will tell.'[17] In the meantime he refused to have the opera mounted anywhere else until he could be assured of a suitable cast, so depriving himself of a considerable source of revenue. Composers with Verdi's eye to profit do not act thus without good reason. A year passed before *La traviata* was revived at the Teatro Gallo (formerly San Benedetto)

[16] Letter from Varesi to Lucca, 10.3.1853. F. Schlitzer, *Mondo teatrale dell' ottocento*, (Naples, 1954) pp. 157–8.
[17] LCC, p. 533.

under the nose, so to speak of La Fenice. The proprietor, Antonio Gallo, had urged Verdi to tone down the third act; but Verdi refused. He did however make some significant changes in five of the numbers, improving the opera immeasurably in the process. This done he was content to let Piave take charge of the production in his absence. The result was all that he could have hoped for. The 'poor sinner',[18] as he put it, had been redeemed in the eyes of the world and soon joined the front rank of Verdian favourites.

Despite his defiant words to Barezzi, it was some time before Verdi was prepared to take Giuseppina with him to his Italian premières. Sometimes she would take the opportunity of his absence to visit her son, Camillo, in Florence; most of the time she remained at S.Agata, from which she regaled her lover with a series of letters, half plaintive, half humorous in tone. Through all of them her devotion runs like a refrain. Thus, after his departure for Venice for *La traviata*:

> Our youth is over; nevertheless we are still the whole world to each other and watch with high compassion all the human puppets running hither and thither, climbing, slipping, hiding, reappearing all trying to get to the top place or to the first row of the social masquerade . . . As long as God leaves us good health, our simple and modest pleasures and desires will cheer and comfort us even in old age; our affection and characters, so well matched, will leave no room for those frequent and bitter altercations which diminish love and end by destroying every illusion.[19]

In fact their fifty years of life together would have to weather more than one such altercation; but the bonds of mutual affection proved strong enough to hold.

Characteristically the first Italian city to which Verdi was prepared to travel with Giuseppina was Naples – then as now foreign territory to a North Italian. De Sanctis was asked discreetly if he could find an apartment where two people could pass the winter together incognito. De Sanctis hastened to make the necessary arrangements; but by October it became clear that Verdi's presence was required in Paris in connection with his contract with the Opéra. Accordingly he and Giuseppina left for France where they were to

[18] LCV, I, 23–4.
[19] WMV, pp. 213–14.

remain for more than two years. Neither was sorry to leave Busseto. Already in the summer Verdi had received what he considered another snub from his fellow citizens. The post of municipal musical director had again become vacant. Muzio's application was strongly supported by Verdi who recommended that he be spared the competitive examination and allowed the free time necessary to fulfil certain conducting engagements. The Council refused both conditions. Muzio withdrew and had the humiliation of seeing a rival applicant appointed without any examination whatever. 'In any other town', Verdi wrote to the Philharmonic Society, 'where music is concerned I should have succeeded in obtaining what you and I want; in any other town I should have had the support of the civil and ecclesiastical authorities . . . Elsewhere I should have succeeded; at Busseto – ludicrously – I have failed. It is an old saying: Nemo propheta in patria.'[20] it was not the last time he would invoke that adage.

[20] Ibid., p. 217.

6

Viva V.E.R.D.I.

By the third week in October 1853 Verdi and Giuseppina were installed in the Rue de Richter 4, Paris. The opera for which Verdi had been contracted in 1852 was not due for production for at least a year; but the schedule had fallen behind. Eugène Scribe – and Verdi would not settle for a less distinguished collaborator – had not supplied the libretto by the date stipulated (July 1853) for the good reason that the subject had not yet been agreed between them. From the start Verdi had demanded 'something grandiose, original and full of passion; an imposing and overwhelming mise-en-scene'.[1] Scribe proposed *Les Circassiens*; Verdi turned it down, as he did *Wlaska ou les Amazones de Bohème*, ('those female soldiers strike me as odd').[2] Then *Il trovatore* and *La traviata* claimed his attention and so time went by until it became clear that only a personal meeting would resolve the problem. At this point Scribe, according to his own account, proposed adapting *Le Duc d'Albe*, a libretto intended for Donizetti, only a part of which the composer had set. Verdi at first demurred at this offer of second-hand goods but finally agreed if the setting were changed from the Low Countries to Sicily, the scheme enlarged from four to five acts and certain of the situations and characters modified. Verdi's own recollection of the event is somewhat different. He was to insist that he had no idea that *Les vêpres siciliennes* had originated in *Le Duc d'Albe* until he saw Donizetti's opera mounted in 1882 with additions by Matteo Salvi. Be that as it may, he professed himself satisfied with the libretto when it arrived on the last day of 1853. To De Sanctis, to whom he had already applied for information about Sicilian history and local customs he wrote, 'I can't tell you the name of the opera because I don't know it . . . All I can tell you is that the scene of the action will be Naples or

[1] PVS, p. 96.
[2] Ibid., p. 98.

Sicily, probably, the latter',[3] and he continued with a request for examples of Sicilian folk-music.

Throughout 1854 Verdi remained in France, moving from Paris to the country town of Mandres for the summer months. He set to work on the new opera slowly, taking plenty of time to spy out the land. Since the events of 1848 Italians of the Mazzinian persuasion were not looked upon with much favour in a country whose government had seen fit to restore the Papal authority in Rome. True, by sending 15,000 men to fight alongside the British and French in the Crimea, King Victor Emmanuel had helped to win respect for the cause of Italian unity but the attitude of Paris to all things Italian remained patronising. In the Great Exhibition of 1855 Italy would earn prizes only for the wines of Baron Ricasoli in Tuscany and the manufacture of watches in Turin – by a French workman; while there was much talk of Italian decadence in the field of the visual arts. Accordingly Verdi remained aloof and mistrustful. He scornfully repudiated the suggestion that he might, like Rossini, put down roots in France. 'I'm too fond of my wilderness and my sky', he told Clarina Maffei. 'I certainly don't intend to spend the few thousand francs won by the sweat of my brow in advertisements, claques and all such filth', a reference, this, to the publicity that had preceded the appearance of Meyerbeer's *L'étoile du nord* at the Opéra Comique. 'I was at the first performance', he added 'and I understood little or nothing; but this good public understood it all and found it all sublime, beautiful, divine . . . And this same public after twenty-five or thirty years has not yet understood *Guillaume Tell* . . .'[4] Any line in *Les vêpres siciliennes* which cast the faintest aspersion on Italian courage or sense of honour he was careful to remove.

But the new opera was not the only project that he had on hand. There were the alterations – small but significant – to be made to *La traviata* before its triumph, in the composer's absence, at the Teatro Gallo in Venice in May. He was also concerned to restore *La battaglia di Legnano* to circulation by fitting it out with a plot more acceptable to the Italian censors and adding fresh music where required.

[3] LCV, I, pp. 22–3.
[4] LCC, pp. 539–40.

Meanwhile the groundwork was being laid of a far more ambitious undertaking – the *Re Lear* which was to remain Verdi's cherished but unattained goal for years to come. During his last visit to Venice he had made the acquaintance of Antonio Somma, a lawyer by profession and the author of several plays, two of them in the repertoire of the actress Adelaide Ristori. An ardent Italian patriot and republican, he had also served as secretary to the Assembly of the Venetian Republic of 1848. For today his plays have no more literary merit than a libretto by Piave or Solera; but Verdi had singled him out to inherit the mantle of Cammarano, as the only possible poet for what would be his own operatic masterpiece. From their correspondence, most of which runs from the summer of 1853 to 1854, it is clear that Somma had much more to learn about the librettist's craft than Piave; and it was a long time before the text had been pared and shaped to Verdi's satisfaction. Whether a note of the score was written at the time remains a mystery. Certain it is however, that during the 1850s *Re Lear* came nearer to being realised than at any other time.

By September Verdi could inform De Sanctis that the first four acts of his new opera were complete; all that remained were the fifth act, the ballet and the scoring. ('An opera for the Opéra is enough work to fell an ox. Five hours of music. Phew!')[5] Rehearsals began the following month only to be suspended by the sudden disappearance of the prima donna, Sophia Cruvelli. Known throughout Europe for her caprices *à la Malibran*, her latest exploit instantly became universal news. (London saw a new burlesque entitled 'Where's Cruvelli?'.) Verdi's reaction was to demand to be released from his contract, but without success. Soon Cruvelli re-appeared; she had been on a pre-marital honeymoon with her prospective husband, Baron Vigier. Someone had been instructed to inform the management, she said, but had evidently forgotten. The resultant scandal cost Roqueplan his post as intendant and he was replaced at the end of the year by Crosnier, to whom Verdi addressed a long letter of complaint, chiefly about Scribe. Not only had he failed to provide moving and dramatic situations; he could not be bothered to come to rehearsals to make adjustments where required. Above all he had not kept his promise to remove everything that reflected badly on the

Sicilians; that he had made of the patriot Procida 'a common conspirator with the inevitable dagger in his hand. Good Heavens!
There are virtues and crimes in the history of every people and we are
no worse than the others. At all events, I am Italian before all else and
come what may will never be party to an insult offered to my
country.'[6] He went on to complain of the criticisms of his music he
was continually overhearing in the foyer and ended by once more
asking to be released from his contract. Evidently he was pacified for
the moment but rumours of further disputes and difficulties continued
to circulate. 'Verdi is having to wrestle with all the Opéra people',
Berlioz wrote to a friend. 'Yesterday he made a terrible scene at the
dress rehearsal. I feel sorry for the poor man; I put myself in his
position. Verdi is a worthy and honourable artist.'[7] Nevertheless *Les
vêpres siciliennes* was on the whole well received at its première in
June and achieved a respectable number of performances, exceeding
those which the contract had stipulated. But it never entered that
charmed circle of grand operas that were repeated year after year,
such as Meyerbeer's *Robert le Diable, Les Huguenots* and *Le
Prophète*, Halévy's *La Juive*, Auber's *La muette de Portici* and even,
in its mutilated form, Rossini's *Guillaume Tell*. Nor was Verdi
justified in blaming Scribe for negligence, since the existing correspondence between them makes it quite clear that the final shaping of
the opera was Verdi's work. At all events they appear to have parted
with mutual good will.

Still Verdi did not return to Italy. After a brief visit to London to
arrange about the English rights of the new opera he passed the rest
of the summer at Enghien-les-bains, whence he dispatched the score
to Ricordi together with its Italian translation which the poet Eugenio
Caimi had made under his supervision. ('I feel for all translators,
because it's impossible to make a good one'.)[8] Just as *La battaglia di
Legnano* had had to be transformed into *L'assedio di Arlem* with a
total disregard for Dutch geography, so *Les vêpres siciliennes* was
transformed into *Giovanna de Gusman* and set in Portugal. Not
until the liberation of Italy were both operas permitted to resume
their original titles.

[6] LCC, pp. 157–9.
[7] AGV, II, p. 293.
[8] Ibid., p. 297.

But Verdi's chief reason for remaining in France was the necessity of defending his interests at the Théâtre des Italiens, where several of his operas had been given in pirated versions. After some acrimonious correspondence with the manager, Calzado, he agreed to supervise the first performance there of *Il trovatore*, given an adequate cast. He also discussed with Crosnier the possibility of a *Trovatore* in French at the Opéra; and a translation by Emilien Pacini was put in hand. However, nothing was concluded for that season, and Verdi returned to Italy in December for the first time without having a firm contract to meet. 'Sometimes I fear,' Giuseppina had written to him during the rehearsals of *Il trovatore*, 'that the love of money will reawaken in you and condemn you to many years of drudgery. My dear Mage, that would be very wrong of you.'[9] And Verdi, it seems, had taken her advice.

Not that he was indifferent to money, then or at any other time. From Paris he had written to Tito Ricordi, Giovanni's son and successor, complaining of the conditions under which his foreign rights were being sold, and especially of the firm's habit of making available the plates rather than the scores, so depriving him of his own percentage. He was much concerned over his rights in England, where the House of Lords had recently passed a bill refusing copyright in a stage work unless the author were the subject of a country with which England had a special treaty. He therefore urged the lawyer Ercolano Balestra to promote such a treaty between Parma and Britain; he even considered changing his citizenship. In 1848 Verdi had been a republican. Now he had a more practical reason for favouring a united Italy under the Kingdom of Sardinia which had just such a treaty with England. In February 1856 through the agency of Cavour, soon to be his political hero, he was awarded the order of S.Maurizio and S. Lazzari.

Meantime he had purchased another property and would soon, he told Crosnier, need to take up his pen once more to clear his debts, But he was in no hurry. There were three projects on the horizon: the revision of *Stiffelio* with Piave, of *La battaglia di Legnano* with Bardare and, more important, a possible *Re Lear* for Naples. Hence a long drawn out exchange of letters with Somma, the impresario Torelli and a certain Paolo Mitrovich who seems to have acted as

[9] WMV, p. 209. 'Mage' or 'Wizard' was one of her pet names for Verdi.

agent for the soprano Marietta Piccolomini, London's favourite Violetta and Verdi's ideal choice for Cordelia. For the Fool he wanted the contralto Giuseppina Brambilla; in the title role he would prefer Coletti to Colini. There was no need to engage Fraschini because the tenor, Edmund, was a comprimario; and so on. Whether because the right combination of singers could not be found or whether in the event Verdi felt unequal to the subject (later he told the young Mascagni that he had always baulked at the scene on the heath), nothing was settled. Meanwhile Bardare dutifully sent, via De Sanctis, drafts for a revised *Battaglia di Legnano* but none of them satisfied Verdi; so this plan was also shelved. There remained the re-fashioning of *Stiffelio*, for which Piave, now resident stage director at La Fenice, had hoped for a visit from Verdi early in 1856. But Verdi, remembering what he had suffered during rehearsals for *Attila*, had no intention of spending the winter months in Venice. However, against the possibility of a '*Giovanna de Gusman*' at La Fenice, he sent Piave the so-called 'mise-en-scène' of *Les vêpres* – that is the booklet containing a detailed description of the stage action with the help of diagrams, that was regularly compiled for most if not all productions at the Paris Opéra. 'It's very fine', Verdi wrote, 'and if he read it with care, a child would be able to mount the opera.'[10] Under the title of 'disposizioni sceniche' these booklets were from then on printed by Ricordi for all Verdi's operas, though only a handful have survived. They provide an invaluable insight into nineteenth century notions of staging and should be consulted by all who aspire to produce Verdi's operas today (see p. 387).

In mid-March Verdi allowed himself to be lured to Venice to witness the triumph of *La traviata* on the very stage on which it had failed so disastrously three years before. There followed a return visit of Piave to S.Agata which lasted most of April. It was decided, much against Verdi's inclination, to turn the Protestant minister into an English crusader and add an entirely new last act setting the scene of reconciliation in the Scottish Highlands. The first performance, envisaged for Bologna in that autumn, would not take place till nearly a year later, by which time much had happened. For during that spring Verdi had been persuaded to compose a new opera to be given at La Fenice during the carnival season of 1857 to a libretto by

[10] AGV, II, pp. 315–16.

Piave. There is no mention of the subject on the contract which Verdi signed during May; nor do we know for certain how he came to settle for *Simon Boccanegra*; but as the playwright was Garcia Gutiérrez and no Italian version of it exists we may guess that, like *El trovador*, it was brought to his attention by Giuseppina. Both spent a brief holiday in Venice in June (the first time that Giuseppina had ever accompanied him there) during which he can only have discussed the subject with Piave very briefly if at all. But he promised to send him a synopsis from Paris, where events had once again called him.

Calzado had wanted to follow up the success of *Il trovatore* with productions of *La traviata* and *Rigoletto*. Verdi, convinced that if he were not there to assist, the operas would fail, instructed Escudier to withhold the scores. Accordingly Calzado availed himself of pirated editions, and Verdi decided to take him to court. The case was heard during the autumn of 1856 and Verdi lost it. But he was amply compensated with the production of *Le trouvère* at the Opéra on 7 January 1857, for which he added the statutory ballet music and made a number of modifications to suit the exigencies of the Opéra and of Parisian taste. But all this had taken up valuable time which should have been spent on polishing the score of *Simon Boccanegra* with the help of his librettist. There are letters to Piave with copious suggestions for the casting and staging and always promising his imminent return to Italy so that they could arrange details by word of mouth. But as delay followed delay Verdi felt the necessity of having a collaborator on the spot. He therefore turned to Giuseppe Montanelli, an exiled Tuscan patriot. How much of the final text is his and how much Piave's remains uncertain. Verdi merely despatched it to Piave with the words, 'Here is the libretto of *Boccanegra* shortened and altered more or less as it had to be. You can put your name to it or not as you like. If you're sorry about this I am sorry too, perhaps even more so than you; but I can only repeat, "It had to be".'[11] Piave made no demur at the time but in a subsequent letter to a friend he came nearer than at any other time to complaining of his lot as a librettist ('. . . a donkey tied up in his master's stall; Verdi is my tyrant and you cannot believe how many and how various are the demands he makes on me and my poor verses'.)[12]

Produced on 12 March 1857 with the French baritone Leone

[11] CBM, p. 401.

Giraldoni in the title role, the Spanish basso profondo Giuseppe Etcheverria as his antagonist and a soprano and tenor both 'di forza' (Luigia Bendazzi and Carlo Negrini), *Simon Boccanegra* was not a success. Some blamed the plot and the libretto; others the experimental nature of the music. Dr Cesare Vigna, a psychiatrist by profession and Venetian correspondent of the *Gazzetta Musicale di Milano* and a friend of Verdi's since the time of *La traviata*, had a more sinister explanation. The opposition was organised by one Levi 'of the ancient tribe' whose opera *Giuditta* had suffered the fate of Holophernes in Venice. 'Some', Vigna continued, 'see in all this the hidden hand of Meyerbeer.'[13] It was to Verdi's credit that he paid no attention to this kind of gossip; but he was furious when he heard also from Vigna that he himself was rumoured to be the author of the much-abused libretto; and he concluded that the canard must have been started by Piave, to whom he had said nothing about Montanelli's contribution. The letter that he wrote to Piave has not survived, but from the poet's deeply wounded but dignified reply its contents can all too easily be guessed. The storm died down at once, however; and one can even sense a somewhat uneasy conscience in Verdi's reply to Vigna: 'that story about the libretto being my composition was just about the last straw! A libretto with Piave's name on it is always judged thoroughly bad poetry in advance; and frankly I should be quite happy if I were good enough to write lines like "Vieni a mirar le cerule . . . Delle faci festanti al barlume" and various others . . .'[14] The contretemps was all the more unfortunate since Verdi had tried without success to include in his contract a clause that entitled Piave to a small percentage of the hire fees, since he considered the librettist's position 'neither just nor honourable'.[15]

Unlike *La traviata*, *Simon Boccanegra* in its original form never won acceptance except when directed by Verdi himself. At Florence that same year it was laughed off the stage. A disastrous performance in Milan in 1859 prompted Verdi to some bitter reflections on the public that had once 'maltreated the opera of a poor sick young man pressed by time and with his heart torn by a horrible bereavement . . .

---

[12] AGV, II, p. 429.
[13] Ibid., p. 395.
[14] LCC, p. 553.
[15] CBM, p. 400.

I don't intend to condemn the public; I allow its right to be severe; I accept its hisses on condition that I'm not asked to be grateful for its applause.'[16] By the late 1860s the fortunes of *Simon Boccanegra* had reached so low an ebb that Giulio Ricordi, Giovanni's grandson, and already the most powerful voice in the family's firm, suggested that Verdi might care to revise it; and so he did, but many years later.

By contrast the première of *Aroldo* (the revised *Stiffelio*) at the Teatro Nuovo, Rimini, in August was all that Verdi could have wished for. Press and public were alike enthusiastic; no one could foresee that the opera would end in an even more profound obscurity than *Simon Boccanegra*. Today it is among the most rarely revived. But it had brought Verdi one lasting benefit; the experience of working with Italy's leading conductor, Angelo Mariani, with whom he would form a close friendship, artistic and personal, that would last for the next twelve years.

The conductor's art is of fairly recent provenance. It came into being with the growth of the Romantic orchestra; and it is fitting that the first composer-conductors of distinction should have been Weber and Berlioz, the first using a role of manuscript paper grasped in the middle, the second the new-fangled baton, said to have been introduced by Spohr. Without a central control of this kind the grandiose orchestral effects of a Wagner or a Meyerbeer could not have been conceived. By the mid-century the conductor was established throughout most of Europe even if at the Paris Opéra, for instance, he might still conduct from a first violin part with the more important cues marked in. But in Italy his function remained divided between the maestro concertatore, who rehearsed the singers at the piano, and the primo violino, who gave the beat with his violin bow at points where it was particularly needed. Italian conductors such as Spontini, Costa and Arditi who had learned the new system remained working abroad. There was no place for them in the tightly-knit organisations of La Scala or La Fenice.

To Angelo Mariani must go the credit for bringing about a change – a gradual one, admittedly, and by no means painless; as late as the mid-1860s the singer Charles Santley recalls the altercations at La Şcala between the conductor Alberto Mazzucato and Ernesto Cavallini, the first violin, who considered that his position was being

[16] LCC, pp. 556–7.

usurped. Mariani himself, born in Rimini in 1821, had begun his career as a primo violino in various small theatres in the peninsula. By the age of twenty-one he had already begun to make a name for himself, as well as (by his own account) numerous enemies – presumably the maestri concertatori whose authority he had successfully challenged. A letter of Verdi's to Lanari, the impresario at Florence, suggests that he would have liked Mariani to conduct the première of *Macbeth* if his demands had not been beyond the management's purse. By 1852 Mariani had been appointed resident conductor at the Teatro Carlo Felice, Genoa, a comfortable post which allowed him opportunity to travel and which he retained to the end of his life. It was from Genoa that he wrote to Verdi in 1853 offering to secure a worthy performance of *La traviata* that would redeem the opera's failure in Venice. Verdi declined, but in terms that suggested that he had a warm regard for the conductor. The last act of *Aroldo* with its orchestral storm, its elaborately written 'Angelus' prayer sung by the chorus behind the scenes, bear witness to the stimulating effect on a composer's imagination of properly co-ordinated forces. From this time on new possibilities of sound and technique were brought within Verdi's reach.

As a person Mariani seems to have been amiable but with little strength of character. He was vain, indecisive, loquacious ('If only', Giuseppina said, 'he would manage to chatter for 23 instead of 25 hours a day'),[17] a snob who loved to move in titled society, a boaster, and, so it is said, a womaniser (his only marriage had broken up when as a biographer puts it, he surrendered to the flattering smile of a local countess). But to Verdi his devotion was simple and profound. He soon became a frequent visitor at S.Agata; together he and Verdi would spend hours at the piano or shooting in the woods by the banks of the Po. From Genoa and elsewhere Mariani would give detailed accounts of the operas of Verdi's that he was conducting, interspersed with many a flattering comment on the music. No commission was too great or too trivial for him to execute on Verdi's behalf. It was through Mariani that in 1866 the Verdis acquired their winter quarters in the Palazzo Sauli in Genoa, where they would spend the first three or four months of each year. The cooling of that friendship and its change into open enmity is one of the saddest

[17] LCV, I, pp. 77–8.

episodes in Verdi's life; nor can we do more than guess as to the cause. But this is to anticipate.

During this time Verdi's interest was ever more engrossed in his estates. In July 1857 he wrote to his friend the sculptor Luccardi in Rome for his advice in buying two large Friulian horses (Friuli was Luccardi's native province). But he had kept the Neapolitan management dangling too long over a possible *King Lear* for him to let them down. In a letter of September to the impresario Torelli he recounted his search for a suitable subject for their Carnival season of 1857–8; that he was working on a scenario of *Gustavus III* on a subject by Scribe of which he was only half convinced; and he ended by suggesting that for that year he could direct revivals of *Simon Boccanegra, Aroldo* and a *Battaglia di Legnano* with altered venue and some extra pieces added. This would not do for Torelli, who wanted an entirely new work, preferably *Lear*. 'I hear that *La traviata*, a real musical and social revolution' he wrote, 'was written in a very short time. Let this be another *Traviata* for us.'[18] But Verdi, with many misgivings settled for *Gustavus III*, eventually and after many a difficulty, to be called *Un ballo in maschera*. As for *Re Lear* the librettist was to be Antonio Somma, who for this occasion chose the pseudonym Tommaso Annoni possibly because he knew the subject to be a dangerous one and feared that his lines would be maltreated by the censorship. In 1789 Gustavus Adolphus, King of Sweden, had been assassinated during a court ball by an officer, Anckarstroem, whose motives were unknown and who even under torture refused to name any accomplices. In 1833 this event had been made the subject of a grand opera by Scribe and Auber who turned the murder into a crime of passion – the revenge of a private secretary, with whose wife Gustavus had been having a love affair – and spiced the action with a mischievous page and a witch who prophesies the disaster. The fictional nature of this version of events was doubtless apparent to all, especially to those who were aware of Gustavus' real proclivities. But in the Austrian dominated Italy of the 1850s regicide of any kind was, theatrically speaking, tabu. Verdi was well aware that Scribe's plot would need to be disguised; none the less he preferred to set Somma to work on the libretto even before sending the synopsis to the Neapolitan management. As Somma declined an

[18] AGV, II, pp. 447–8.

invitation to S.Agata, Verdi was compelled to instruct him at a distance. Like the letters about *Re Lear*, those on the genesis of *Un ballo in maschera* tell us much about what Verdi, and doubtless many of his fellow opera composers, expected from a libretto. Thus:

> The only thing that needs to be retouched is from 'Strega mia' down to 'ti tradi'. All this passage is insufficiently theatrical. True, you say what has to be said but the words don't sculpt properly, they don't stand out and therefore Gustavus' indifference, the witch's astonishment or the terror of the conspirators do not emerge clearly enough. Perhaps the metre and the rhyme prevent this. In that case make this passage into a recitative, I prefer a good recitative to mediocre lyrical verses, I would ask you to change me 'e desso – a desso'. These rhymes being so close, sound badly in music. Remove too 'Dio non paga il sabato' [God does not pay on the Sabbath]; believe me, all proverbs . . . are dangerous in the theatre . . .[19]

This concern with the 'parola evidente e scenica' recurs more and more frequently in Verdi's correspondence. Important words had to leap to the ear; they must express the situation as immediately and graphically as possible. The result might look odd on paper, but, as Verdi would often put it, 'there are times when both poets and musicians should renounce their calling in the interest of theatre'.[20]

In due course the memorandum from Naples arrived insisting on a change of locale. 'We can have all the North', Somma noted, 'except for Norway and Sweden. But what century should we choose for the action?'[21] His own suggestion was for twelfth-century Pomerania at the time of the Teutonic Knights, the opera to be called *Il Duca Ermanno*. Verdi approved the place but not the time. 'It's such a rough, brutal period,' he wrote, 'especially in those parts that it seems to me utter nonsense to set in it characters who are tailored to the French style like Gustavus and Oscar and a drama that has such sparkle and is so much modelled according to our modern ways. We must find a princeling, a duke, or some devil or other, so long as he's from the North, who has seen something of the world and had a whiff of the court of Louis XIV. Once you've finished the

[19] PRB, pp. 79–80.
[20] See for instance LCC, p. 641.
[21] LCV, I, p. 227.

drama you can think about it at leisure.'[22] They solved the problem (or so they thought) by moving the action forward five centuries. Its new title was to be *Una vendetta in domino*.

Verdi arrived in Naples on 14 January 1858 in time to attend a performance of *Batilde di Turenne* (his own *Vêpres siciliennes* again rechristened) with Fraschini and Coletti as Arrigo and Monforte. He was recognised, cheered, dragged to the footlights. The orchestra repeated the overture in his honour. But the cordial atmosphere did not last long. Early in February Verdi was writing to Somma 'I'm in a sea of troubles! It's almost certain that the Censorship will forbid our libretto. Why, I don't know. . . . They've begun by taking exception to certain expressions, certain words, and from words they've gone on to scenes. They've suggested the following modifications (and that by way of kindness):

(1) Change the protagonist into a gentleman, completely removing the idea of a sovereign
(2) Change the wife into a sister
(3) Change the scene with the witch, putting it back into an age in which such things were believed in
(4) No ball
(5) The murder must take place behind the scenes and so on and so forth.[23]

Somma replied somewhat drily authorising Verdi and the Neapolitan censorship to make what use they wished of his verses provided that the title was changed and no librettist's name mentioned. The management duly refashioned the libretto along the lines suggested above, setting it in thirteenth-century Florence, with the title *Adelia degl' Adimari*. (It was probably the work of Domenico Bolognese, resident librettist and stage director at the San Carlo after Cammarano's death.) Verdi annotated the text of *Adelia degli Animali*, as he called it, with satirical comments.

The management removes and adds lines at its own good pleasure, as who should say 'You're a composer, cobble your notes around this . . . what, you've already written the piece? What does that matter? Lengthen it, shorten it, twist it around, it

22 PRB, pp. 85–8.
23 Ibid., pp. 90–1.

will be all right . . . We want music, we want your name and you as
our accomplice in gulling that poor public that pays! . . . Drama,
good sense? . . . Bah! Rubbish!' That's how it is; and that's the
respect they have for their public, for art and for artists . . .[24]

Verdi offered the management two alternatives: to release him from
his contract or to take him to law. The management chose the
second; Verdi's defence was that the opera which he was being asked
to set was not the one for which he had been contracted. With the
help of an able lawyer, Arpino, he won his case. The Tribunale di
Commercio ruled that 'the difference between the two libretti was
sufficient to do harm to the music'. Verdi was free to take his score
elsewhere; while on its part the San Carlo management would commission the composer to mount a revival of *Simon Boccanegra* in the
autumn. In general Neapolitan feeling was running strongly on
Verdi's side. Prominent among his supporters was the King's brother,
the Count of Syracuse, who led more than one demonstration in his
favour. Even Mercadante, once an embittered rival, had been won
over; new friends would include the distinguished sculptor Domenico
Morelli and the archivist of the Conservatory, Francesco Florimo,
known as Lord Palmerston for his aristocratic presence. (It was in
Naples that the slogan 'Viva Verdi' first acquired the hidden significance: 'Viva Vittorio Emanuele Re d'Italia'.) The autumn visit was a
particularly happy one, commemorated by the cartoonist Melchiorre
Delfico in a series of lively cartoons: Verdi at the piano rehearsing
Coletti and Fraschini and singing more vigorously than either; Verdi
on stage stamping and flinging his arms around to get some life into
the performance; Verdi scowlong over a sixteenth-century motet
presented to him by a graciously smiling Florimo; Verdi and
Giuseppina, voluminous in black crinoline, finding the errant
Maltese spaniel Lulu ('Ah there you are, you son of a bitch!').
Cesarino De Sanctis, married for over a year, had now become the
father of a son. Correspondence between the two families continued
with unremitting cordiality for nearly twenty years, until De Sanctis,
a victim of the economic recession of the 1870s, was unable to repay
a substantial loan with which Verdi had helped to set him up in
business. He agreed to have the debt liquidated by a regular supply of

[24] LCV, I, p. 251.

good Neapolitan pasta; but from then on it was Giuseppina who wrote the letters.

Even while the case against him was pending Verdi had written to his friend Luccardi in Rome for information about a play on the subject of *Gustav III* which he had heard was being performed there. If it resembled *Una vendetta in domino* might not the same censorship permit the opera? And if so, what a triumph to be able to produce it on Naples' doorstep, so to speak, if Jacovacci, impresario of the Apollo Theatre, could be persuaded to spend enough to assemble a suitable cast. The reply was sufficiently encouraging for Verdi to send the libretto to Jacovacci, who, as one who prided himself on having influence in priestly circles, promised to get it approved. He was over-optimistic: whether because lyric as distinct from prose drama was supposed to have greater power to corrupt, or whether because the political clouds were gathering ever more densely, the Roman censorship threatened to be as obstructive as that of Naples. But here Verdi had a valuable ally in the lawyer Antonio (Toto) Vasselli, Donizetti's brother-in-law; and throughout the summer of 1858 he was ready to bargain and haggle over the various modifications suggested by the censors, despite the growing exasperation of Somma who could not understand why Verdi refused to have the opera produced in Turin or Venice where the subject might have passed unharmed. Forbidden the whole of Northern Europe as a venue for the plot, it was Verdi himself who suggested North America 'at the time of the English domination'; later he would even declare that the opera had gained thereby. During a brief visit to Venice in July he persuaded Somma to modify certain expressions which the censors had found unacceptable, but not to acknowledge paternity of the libretto; and so the last obstacles to a performance were removed.

In the middle of January 1859 Verdi and Giuseppina travelled to Rome via Genoa and then by boat in rough weather to Civitavecchia ('almost nineteen hours at sea' Verdi wrote to De Sanctis; 'Peppina was very ill; the great Lulu wasn't well either'; I gave nothing to the sea but that *malaise* and then having to lie in bed sixteen hours without moving!').[25] Arrived in Rome, his ill-humour persisted. Their lodgings (arranged by Luccardi) were ugly. The cast

[25] Ibid., p. 51.

for *Un ballo in maschera*, as the opera was finally called, was inadequate, the heroine, Madame Julien Dejean being particularly ill-prepared. 'But Maestro,' she remonstrated, 'I expected you to teach me the part yourself.' 'I am not a professional repetiteur', Verdi snapped;[26] and it needed all Giuseppina's tact to restore peace. Leone Giraldoni, the baritone, creator of Boccanegra, was continually indisposed and at one point had to be taken to the theatre under police escort. And yet the première on 17 February was a huge success and all subsequent performances played to an increasingly packed house. All the same, Verdi wrote to Torelli at Naples, 'after the third performance I couldn't help saying to Jacovacci, "Look, you hound of an impresario, if I had a good ensemble, what a success that would have been!" Do you know what he replied? "Heh, heh! What more do you want? The theatre is full every night. Next year I'll find some good women and the opera will be new again for the public. Half this year . . . half later on!" '[27]

It was the last time that Giuseppina Strepponi would ever have to accompany the composer in an equivocal capacity. For on 29 August 1859 at Collonges-sur-Salève, in the diocese of Annecy, Haute Savoie, in a ceremony conducted by one Mermillod, rector of the Church of Notre Dame in Geneva, and with the same secrecy that had characterised all his actions with regard to her in the eyes of the world, Verdi at last made Giuseppina his wife. They would have no children – 'since God is perhaps punishing me for my sins in ordaining that I shall have no legitimate joys before I die,'[28] as Peppina put it six years before – but they would adopt the orphaned child of one of Verdi's cousins, Maria Filomena, who would in due course marry the lawyer Alberto Carrara, from whom the composer's heirs are descended.

[26] MVA, pp. 75–6.
[27] AGV, II, p. 529.
[28] WMV, p. 209.

7

The new order

For all that Verdi considered *Un ballo in maschera* the most harmless drama in the world, the scruples of the Roman and Neapolitan censorship were not hard to understand. True, order had been restored often brutally throughout the peninsula since 1849 but during the decade that followed the symptoms of unrest grew ever more alarming. In 1857 there had been an attempt on the life of Ferdinand I of Naples. In Verdi's own province of Parma Carlo III, the restored Bourbon monarch, as profligate and irresponsible as an Emperor from the pages of Gibbon, was assassinated in the theatre. His successor, another Maria Luigia, far less politic than the first, attempted to rule with the aid of an Austrian garrison, which, after much hostile demonstration she was persuaded to withdraw. Cracks in the Holy Alliance were deepening, to the advantage of Italy as well as France. In England, popular sympathy was on the Italian side, Gladstone having described the rule of King Ferdinand II as 'the negation of God erected into a system'. If the republican ideal of Mazzini seemed a lost cause, a united realm under Victor Emmanuel of Piedmont offered a distinct prospect of success. Not only did Piedmont have a constitution; under the leadership of statesman such as Gioberti and Cavour its subjects prospered; it could put an army in the field; and, to the approval of liberal opinion throughout Italy, the laws exempting the priesthood from civil jurisdiction had been abolished. Eventually Napoleon III entered into an agreement, the Treaty of Piombières, with the tacit blessing of Palmerston's England to end Austrian influence in Italy. In the spring of 1859 hostilities began. The combined troops of Piedmont and France fought successful if indecisive battles at Magenta and Solferino; but that was as far as Napoleon III was prepared to go. By the Treaty of Villafranca Austria was made to cede Lombardy but retained Venetia; elsewhere the status quo was to remain.

At the start of the war Verdi had been all enthusiasm. He would have liked to follow the example of the patriot Montanelli, his part-collaborator on *Simon Boccanegra*, and take up arms himself even at forty-five – 'but what could I do', he wrote to Clarina Maffei, 'who couldn't even undertake a march of three miles? My head won't stand five minutes of sun, and a breath of wind or a touch of damp sends me to bed for weeks on end.'[1] But in June 1859 he led his fellow citizens in a subscription for the families of those fallen in battle. Napoleon III he was ready to adore 'as I adore Washington and even more; and I would bless that great nation and even put up with their insolent *politesse* and contempt for everything that isn't French'.[2] But he resisted Carcano's invitation to collaborate on a Hymn for the Emperor's nameday, ostensibly because time was short but more probably because this kind of occasional ode had never appealed to him. He would decline a similar invitation to write a hymn in honour of Victor Emmanuel, while prepared to subscribe handsomely to the gift of a cannon from the citizens of Busseto.

The terms of Villafranca depressed him utterly. To Clarina Maffei: 'Where is the longed-for independence of Italy that we've been promised? What an outcome after so many victories! How much blood spilt to no purpose! And Garibaldi who even gave up his long-held convictions to the cause of a king without achieving his purpose! It's enough to drive one mad . . . It's perfectly clear that we have nothing to hope for from foreigners, no matter of what nation.'[3] Much would be gained nevertheless. The smaller states of Northern and Central Italy, papal territory excepted, were now relieved of the Austrian presence and were thus free to decide their own destiny. Temporary 'dictators' were established in Modena, Parma, the Romagna and Tuscany to preside over a plebiscite. All voted for annexation with Piedmont. Next year, with Cavour once more at the helm after a brief retirement Victor Emmanuel's troops invaded Umbria and the Marches while Garibaldi landed with an army in Sicily and speedily toppled the Bourbon Kingdom. The Italian nation was now set to become the Italian state.

As one who had long been identified in the popular mind with the cause of Italian freedom, it fell to Verdi to carry the votes of his fellow citizens to Turin; a mandate which he acknowledged to the

[1] LPB, II, pp. 517–19.
[2] LCC, pp. 577–8.
[3] Ibid., pp. 579–80.

mayor in a rare moment of rapport with the Bussetani; 'In the annexation to Piedmont resides the future greatness and the regeneration of our common fatherland. Anyone who feels Italian blood flowing in his veins must wish for it deeply and steadily so the day will dawn for us in which we can say that we belong to a great and noble nation.'⁴ Perhaps the lid had been taken too suddenly off the cauldron. On the steps of Parma station the hated chief of police Colonel Anviti was recognised and murdered by an enraged mob. With Mariani's help Verdi was instrumental in procuring rifles with which to arm the national guard of Busseto against similar outbreaks.

That he should stand as parliamentary candidate for the local borough of Borgo San Donnino was never in Verdi's mind; nor would anything short of a personal appeal from Cavour, seconded by the British ambassador, Sir James Hudson, have induced him to do so. But Cavour had spoken of the need for every patriotic citizen to make sacrifices for his country, and Verdi reluctantly yielded, adding that he would resign as soon as decently possible. The story of his political career he summed up in a letter to Piave six years later:

> I was elected and during the early days I frequented the Chamber up till the great day in which Rome was declared Capital of Italy. Having recorded my vote I then approached the Count (Cavour) and said to him,
> 'Now I think it's time for me to go about my business.'
> 'No', he answered, 'let's first go to Rome.'
> 'Will we go?'
> 'Yes'.
> 'When?'
> 'Oh, when, when? Soon'
> Those were the last words I heard him speak. A few weeks later he was dead.
> . . . For two long years I was absent from the Chamber and afterwards I attended only rarely. Several times I was about to hand in my resignation but some obstacle always came up at the last moment and I'm still a deputy against every wish, every desire, without having the slightest inclination nor aptitude nor talent. There you have it. Anyone who wishes or who has to write my biography as member of Parliament has only to print

⁴ Ibid., p. 580.

in large letters in the middle of a blank sheet of paper 'The 450 are really only 449 because Verdi as a deputy doesn't exist.'[5]

The main benefit to Verdi of those parliamentary days was his growing intimacy with two public figures: Giuseppe Piroli, deputy for Parma and his old ally Count Opprandino Arrivabene, now editor of the *Gazzetta di Torino*, his future confidants on matters of politics and art respectively.

Composition seems to have played little part in Verdi's life during those momentous years. His hobbies were now shooting, collecting autographs, planting his garden with various blooms and shrubs acquired with Mariani's help and developing his estates. To Léon Escudier, who had recently announced Verdi's nomination as a member of the Académie Française, he wrote asking him to procure a rifle of the latest type 'now that I no longer manufacture notes but only plant beans and cabbages'.[6] Even when Piave, now married and a father, reported the success of *Un ballo in maschera* in Bologna he professed himself indifferent, adding

> If people knew this they would howl me down and accuse me of ingratitude and of not liking my art.
>
> Oh no! I've always loved it and do so still. And when I'm alone and at grips with my notes my heart throbs, the tears pour from my eyes and my joy and emotion are indescribable, but when I think that these notes of mine have to be thrown to beings of no intelligence and to a publisher who then sells them for the amusement and mockery of the masses, then I don't like anything any more.'[7]

He had already been disturbed by an unwelcome voice from the past: 'Fate that decrees that I shall ever be a wanderer has brought me here to Bologna . . . Could you dispense a little charity to an old friend before he loses all hope?'[8] It was Solera, destitute after, it is said, a series of adventures worthy of Casanova. Verdi complied with his request only to receive another, this time from Leghorn, asking him to put Solera's name forward for the editorship of the *Gazzetta Ufficiale* of Piedmont which 'I would promise to raise to the level of

---

[5] Ibid., pp. 601–2.
[6] AGV, II, p. 568.
[7] Ibid., p. 591.
[8] Ibid., p. 668 ff.

France's *Le Moniteur*'. Understandably Verdi took no action. To Clarina Maffei who suggested raising a subscription for Solera's benefit he wrote, 'If you intend doing something for Solera I commend your goodness of heart but it would be to no purpose; after a week you would be back where you started.'[9] None the less he would be prepared to contribute, but anonymously. In the end Clarina took his advice and did nothing. Happily Solera's luck took a turn for the better: and for some years he ran an antiquarian bookshop in Florence, where he had the pleasure of a visit from Verdi in 1870. To the end of his life (he died in Milan in 1878) he would regret that Verdi had come to prefer Piave's libretti to his own, 'but then', he would conclude, 'he is as weak as a woman'.[10]

That Verdi's farewell to the muses was not as absolute as might appear had already been hinted by Giuseppina ('he doesn't feel like swearing never to write again; for in that case he would become a slave of his own vow, and he likes his independence so much'[11]). Indeed no one did more than she to start the wheels of creation turning once more. The occasion presented itself in the form of a letter from the tenor Enrico Tamberlick, engaged at the Imperial Theatre St. Petersburg for the winter season of 1860–1. Would Verdi accept a commission to compose an opera for the following winter? 'I have heard from Corticelli who has arrived here with Signora Ristori that it might not be impossible to induce you to add another gem to the splendid crown of your operas, the series of which you are threatening to close.'[12] Mauro Corticelli, secretary to the actress Adelaide Ristori, and soon to be 'fattore' at S.Agata, was an old friend of Giuseppina's from her theatrical days. The invitation had in fact been his idea, as he explained in a letter to her; and she in turn promised to do all she could to persuade her husband, then about his Parliamentary duties in Turin, to accept, 'using the methods which are said to be successful with the most illustrious St. Peter . . . that is, to worry and make a nuisance of oneself until you get what you want. It is true that Verdi is less patient than St. Peter; but after all if he packs me off to bed it won't be the first time . . .'[13]

[9] LCC, pp. 520–1.
[10] WMV, p. 146.
[11] VBISV, IV, p. 287.
[12] AGV, II, pp. 625–6.
[13] Ibid., p. 627.

In the event Verdi needed little persuading. The only problem was the subject. *Ruy Blas*, his first choice, was unacceptable to the Imperial censors; whereupon Verdi declared himself in a quandary and unable to proceed. At once the objection to Hugo's drama was removed and Verdi was allowed any conditions he cared to impose 'short of proclaiming a republic in Russia,'[14] as Giuseppina put it. But the interest in *Ruy Blas* had now retired in favour of a 'huge, powerful and very singular drama' which I like very much and I don't know if the public will find it as I do but certainly it's something out of the ordinary'.[15] This was *Don Alvaro o La fuerza del sin* by Angel de Saavedra, Duque de Rivas, which he had considered setting as long ago as 1856. Accordingly a search was instituted for a copy of Sanseverino's Italian translation which would serve as basis for the libretto. Having found one, Verdi drew up a synopsis and sent it to Piave; at the same time he made contact with Maffei, whose translation of Schiller's *Wallensteins Lager* he intended to draw upon for the encampment scene of the third act. Even Arrivabene, apprised of developments, submitted a gipsy-girl's song for the same context, which however Verdi never saw fit to use. A series of letters, brisk, often peremptory, written to Piave between August and November 1861 bear witness to the care which Verdi brought to every detail, and show us how much of the eventual wording was his. By 22 November *La forza del destino* was finished, all but the scoring. Five days later, armed with a good supply of Neapolitan pasta and French wines the Verdis set off for St. Petersburg by way of Paris. A few weeks later their friends were surprised to hear that the opera would not be given that season after all. 'The singers' voices', wrote Giuseppina to Arrivabene, 'are as fragile as —— I leave you to finish the sentence.'[16] La Grua had fallen ill; so the opera would be deferred to the following winter. Not greatly distressed, the Verdis returned for a few weeks to Paris, where the composer accepted a commission to contribute a piece for the Great London Exhibition of 1862. At a grand concert on 1 May at Kensington Palace four of the great nations of Europe were to be represented each by a new composition from their senior composer: Auber for France, Meyerbeer for Prussia; Sterndale Bennett for England and if possible Rossini for Italy. But the

[14] Ibid., pp. 629–30.
[15] Ibid., p. 634.
[16] AVI, pp. 13–15.

'swan of Pesaro' had protested age and infirmity; and so the choice fell on Verdi who, for the last time and most reluctantly, agreed to compose a ceremonial piece, introducing the anthems of England, France and Italy. Partly on the advice of Auber, who had written an overture for the occasion, Verdi had decided on a cantata with a prominent solo part for Tamberlick. The text was by a young man of twenty, fresh from his studies at the Milan conservatory and fortunately resident in Paris at the time, having been awarded a travelling scholarship; his name was Arrigo Boito. Already a protegé of Clarina Maffei, he was received affably by Verdi, who approved the text and rewarded the poet with a gold watch. But the performance did not go according to plan. The concert was given but without Verdi's contribution on the grounds that he had not sent it in on time and that in any case he had been commissioned for an instrumental piece. In a letter to *The Times*, translated into suitable English by his old friend Maggioni, Verdi defended himself against both charges. The resultant publicity did far more good than the scheduled performance would have done; and at last through the good offices of James Henry Mapleson on 24 May in Verdi's presence the *Inno delle nazioni* was performed at Her Majesty's Theatre, conducted by Luigi Arditi and with the soprano Therèse Tietjens as soloist. Honour satisfied, Verdi returned to Paris, and thence to S.Agata. 'Artistically speaking', he wrote to Tito Ricordi, 'it's a stroke of good fortune not to have "occasional" pieces performed. Nothing in them is or can be effective.'[17] However he gave instructions for his *Inno delle nazioni* to be printed.

In September, deeply saddened by the recent death of their dog Lulu, Verdi and his wife again set out for St. Petersburg. The opera took place as planned with Tamberlick outstanding as the hero and De Bassini once a 'noble baritone' amusing in the part of Melitone (this was Verdi's own casting). If the criticisms were more mixed than might have been expected, the reason lies rather in Verdi's position as a foreigner in a land where musical nationalism was burgeoning. To his insignia was now added the Order of the Royal and Imperial Order of St. Stanislas.

The Verdis were back in Paris by the end of the year, whence they proceeded to Madrid for another production of *La forza del*

[17] AGV, II, p. 698.

destino scarcely less prestigious than the first, inasmuch as it was given in the country of the play's origin and in the presence of the author. 'Admirably performed by chorus and orchestra; well done by Fraschini (Alvaro) and Legrange (Leonora); the rest . . . null or bad. Despite that, a success.'[18] Nevertheless he was already aware that something would have to be done about the dénouement with its excess of corpses; but it was not till six years later that the solution occurred to him. After a tour of Andalusia and of the major Spanish cities he returned yet again to Paris where for the first time for some years a revival of *Les vêpres siciliennes* was in view at the Opéra with a new tenor, Villaret, in the part of Henri. For his sake Verdi was prepared to break a rule of nearly eighteen years standing – never to compose an alternative aria for an old score; hence the romance 'O toi que j'ai chérie' in place of the aria 'O jour de peine'. It was not a happy occasion. Discipline in the orchestra was at a low ebb. Dietsch was no more able to secure an efficient performance of Verdi's opera that he had been of *Tannhäuser* in 1861. Verdi, exigent as ever, had insisted on his repeating a passage which he had taken too slowly. The orchestra responded by playing it slower still and Verdi left in a fury. Dietsch was dismissed forthwith and replaced by Hainl; and Verdi reluctantly consented to stay for the first three performances. But the revival had hardly been worth the trouble. Villaret proved a mediocre interpreter; the star of the show was the ballerina Mlle Vernon, in whose honour Auber's *La muette de Portici* was given for the 450th time, while Verdi's opera relapsed once more into obscurity.

The Italy to which the Verdis returned after two years of travel had changed from the time they had left. New cultural forces were coming into play; and a climate was being created to which Verdi felt himself increasingly alien. These were the days of the 'scapigliatura milanese' a radical artistic movement dedicated to the overthrow of traditional values, not least the liberal Christianity of Verdi's idol, Manzoni. Like the 'Sturm und Drang' of the previous century it was essentially a reaction against decades of emotional conformity. Its adherents lived disordered lives, argued and declaimed in cafés, drank absinthe and fought duels. Its chief musical representative was Boito, already acquiring the reputation of a young firebrand with his

[18] AVI, p. 23.

critical writings. Many of his notions are pretentious and vapid. ('To the Sublime only the grand form, the divine eternal universal form will match: the spherical form. The horizon is sublime, the sea is sublime, the sun is sublime. Shakespeare is spherical, Dante is spherical, Beethoven is spherical; the sun is simpler than the carnation, the sea simpler than the brook, the adagio of Mendelssohn is spherical and simpler than the andante of Mozart.')[19] Yet much of what he said was valuable. He preached boldness and variety of invention, the dissemination of German music, the exploration of new paths and, not least, the revival of Italy's instrumental tradition. When the Quartet Society of Milan was formed in 1864 Boito was one of its members and chief critic of its 'giornale'. Even the professors of the Milan Conservatoire such as Mazzucato and Ronchetti-Monteviti did their best to keep up with the new trends. Much publicity attended the première in November 1863 of *I profughi fiamminghi*, words by the 'scapigliato' poet Emilio Praga, music by Boito's fellow-student Franco Faccio. It is not a specially novel type of opera; nor did it have more than a modest success. But at a dinner given in Faccio's honour Boito toasted his friend in a Sapphic Ode in which he is described as the man who is perhaps born to raise up Italian art upon an altar which is now 'befouled like the walls of a brothel'.[20]

If Verdi had any sympathy with the ideals of the new movement that would have been enough to kill it. For against whom could Boito's gibe have been directed except himself? To Clarina Maffei who wanted a word of encouragement for her latest protegé he wrote in guarded, somewhat ironical vein. He had heard and read great things about this opera amid a profusion of words like 'Art, Aesthetics, Revelations, the Future' etc. – words which meant nothing to him – 'great ignoramus that I am'. But he had no intention of getting to know the work for fear of having to pass judgment on it. 'If Faccio is really destined to raise up the art on an altar foul with the stink of a brothel [Verdi never failed to misquote the phrase], so much the better for him and for us all. If he is on the wrong path, let us hope that he soon finds the right one.'[21] He refused to associate

[19] See WMV, p. 455.
[20] Ibid., p. 449.
[21] LCC, pp. 506–7.

himself with the Quartet Society. ('You known that I'm an ass in music and I can't understand what the learned ones mean by their talk of "classical".')[22] Boito's jargon caused him much amusement (*'Spherical, focal point, carnation* are all very fine but what you need to make music is something very different – *music*').[23] His resentment was fed by Piave whose application for the newly instituted professorship of dramatic poetry at the Milan conservatory had recently been turned down in favour of Emilio Praga. But for all his protestations of cultural ignorance, of never judging music from the printed page, he ordered all Ricordi's latest publications of old and new music. He showed especial interest in Clementi's Sonata in F sharp minor ('I don't know whether it belongs to the Classical or the Romantic school; whether to the past or to the future, but it's very fine'). A pity that the same collection did not include Scarlatti's 'Cat' Fugue ('with such an odd subject a German would have made something chaotic: an Italian has made it as clear as sunlight').[24]

For some years the Théâtre Lyrique, Paris, had been in the hands of the enterprising Carvalho. Among his successes had been Gounod's *Faust* of 1859 and the French *Traviata* of 1864, rechristened *Violetta*; his noble failures had included the second part of Berlioz's *Les Troyens*. For the spring season of 1865 he counted on a French *Macbeth* with an added ballet of witches. Verdi who had cherished the idea of a revised Parisian version of his favourite opera as long ago as 1852 readily assented, provided that he was not expected to take charge of the production. As usual the revision took longer than anticipated and required new verses from Piave. Verdi himself was as meticulous in his instructions over the second version as he had been over the first. He plotted the scenario of the ballet almost phrase by phrase; he countered (though in vain) Carvalho's proposal that Macduff should sing the second verse of Lady Macbeth's drinking song, and sketched an ingenious mechanism for the 'shew of kings'. Only on one aspect of the interpretation did he appear to have changed. For the *bel canto* singers of the 1840s he had insisted on the greatest possible realism of delivery even to the extent of uglifying the voice. Having heard the curious 'death-rattle' which

[22] AGV, II, p. 744.
[23] Ibid., pp. 777–8.
[24] Ibid., p. 779.

Adelaide Ristori brought to the sleepwalking scene in Shakespeare, he now warned against all naturalistic touches of this kind – whether a cough for Violetta in *La traviata* or a laugh for Riccardo in the first finale of *Un ballo in maschera*. He had little to say about the French translation beyond insisting that Lady Macbeth's 'Follie!' should be rendered by 'Folie'.

The première on 7 June 1865 was not a notable success. Most of the critics found it an unsatisfactory mixture of the old and the new. ('I thought I had done something passable', Verdi wrote, 'but evidently I was mistaken.')[25] He was particularly annoyed with the critic who accused him of not understanding Shakespeare. ('It may be that I have not done justice to *Macbeth* but that I don't know or understand or feel Shakespeare – no, by God, no. He is one of my favourite poets; I've had him in my hands since my earliest youth and I read him over and over again.')[26] Though never popular in his lifetime, the new *Macbeth* would find a place of high honour in the Verdi renaissance of the present century.

Meanwhile Verdi continued to work at his garden and his estates. A small chapel was built for household use on Sundays. Additions to his library included Darwin's *Origin of Species* and the *Canzoniere* of Heine. From outside echoes reached him of the *succès d'estime* of Faccio's *Amleto* on a libretto by Boito, of the fulsome praise of the 'scapigliato' critic Filippi and the enthusiastic support of Giulio Ricordi, Tito's son, from whom Giuseppina thought it prudent to intercept a defensive letter to her husband. Nearer home an old subject of discord had reared its head – the Busseto theatre.

When building operations began in 1859 Verdi considered that public money was being wasted at a time of national crisis. By 1865 the theatre was finished; it was to be named the Teatro Giuseppe Verdi and the dedicatee was expected to subscribe handsomely to its upkeep and activities. This was too much. Unfortunately Giovanni Barezzi, always ready in the past to put himself out for his famous brother-in-law, though clearly much disliked by Giuseppina, became caught in the cross-fire and a long friendship came to a disagreeable close. Finally in August an agreement was reached whereby Verdi accepted the dedication and presented a cheque for 10,000 lire (a

[25] PLVE, p. 189.
[26] Ibid., p. 187.

considerable sum in those days) against the opening, which took place three years later. Although a box was reserved for his use, Verdi never set foot inside it. Giuseppina's comment: 'To the minor and modest composer Coppola the citizens of Catania are coining a gold medal worth 1227 francs as a token of their joy at his return home after fifteen years absence. Giuseppe Verdi who has filled the world with the glory of his music the citizens of Busseto have rewarded by poisoning his life with every sort of vileness . . .'[27] From then on the trees grew ever thicker round the walls of S.Agata.

If Verdi was, as he so often protested, without honour in his own country all the more reason why he should accept another commission from abroad. 'It seems that the main difficulty', wrote Giuseppina to Leon Escudier, 'as regards writing for the Opéra is the libretto. I put my hope in the imagination of the poets . . .

'I know him. Once he's caught up the scene will change. He will leave his trees, his building, his hydraulic machines, his guns etc. He will abandon himself to his poem and I hope that the whole world will gain by it.'[28] This after an apparently fruitless visit to S.Agata in which the publisher had submitted various ideas. Nor was she mistaken. A letter from Lulu's successor, Blach, to Ron-Ron, master of the Arrivabene household, announced that 'my secretary' is disposed to make a few 'hooks'[29] (i.e. notes). The subject would be Schiller's *Don Carlos*, possibly associated with a French *Forza del destino* if a suitable denouement to the latter could be found. With this in view the Verdis left in November for Paris, where they had their first sight of Baron Haussman's city. ('Really very fine', was Verdi's comment, 'a pity the sun doesn't shine more often.') They heard *L'Africaine* ('Certainly not Meyerbeer's best opera') and the overture to *Tannhäuser* ('he's mad!').[30] They visited Rossini – 'Ex Compositeur de Musique et Pianiste du 4ième classe', as he liked to style himself. New acquaintances included the Polish poet Mickiewicz, friend of Mazzini, who presented Verdi with two volumes of

[27] WMV, p. 259.
[28] Ibid., p. 251.
[29] 'rampini' – a standing joke. One of Verdi's farm labourers had been overheard to express his wonder that the master could make so much money by drawing little hooks on straight lines.
[30] AVI, p. 61.

his poetry, and the sculptor Dantan, whose bust representing the composer with the claws and mane of a lion date from this time. Of the two poets who were to prepare the libretto of the new opera Joseph Méry, an old Bonapartist whose *Battaille de Toulouse* had served as a basis for *La battaglia di Legnano*, was already confined to his room with the illness of which he would die; and it fell to Camille du Locle, son-in-law of Perrin, director of the Opéra, to complete the work and make the changes that Verdi required. For of all his operas based on Schiller *Don Carlos* is the one in which Verdi was determined to squeeze as much as possible from the original drama, while being content (for the time being) to retain such extraneous elements as the Fontainebleau act (derived from a play on the same subject by Eugène Cormon), the ballet, the voice from heaven and the equivocal figure of the Monk/Emperor. From the start he had insisted on including two scenes which the librettists had omitted – for Philip and the Inquisitor ('whom I should like to be blind and very old')[31] and for Philip and Posa, in which the Marquis startles the King with his liberal ideas.

Verdi remained in Paris until the middle of March, by which time he had completed the first act. Then he returned to S.Agata to complete the rest undisturbed. But it was not to be. In April Italy signed a treaty with Prussia; and both prepared to go to war with Austria. 'I expect any moment now', Verdi wrote to Escudier, 'to hear the roar of cannon and I'm so near the field of battle that I wouldn't be surprised to find a cannon ball rolling into my room one fine morning'.[32] It was even rumoured that the Prince Umberto intended to take up his quarters at S.Agata. As Italian troops gathered massively along the Po Verdi's first thoughts were to pack his bags for Paris; his second were to remain in Italy as long as the war lasted as a patriotic gesture even if this meant arriving in Paris later than stipulated; his third were to ask for the dissolution of his contract.

For the war had gone badly for Italy. The Prussians had won a decisive victory at Königgratz; but from the North Italian forts, which the peace of Villafranca had allowed them to keep, the Austrians routed the Italian forces at Custozza, while the Italian fleet

[31] GGDC, p. 30.
[32] AGV, III, pp. 79–80.

was no less soundly defeated at the Battle of Lissa. Garibaldi's march into the Trentino, in which Boito, Faccio and Giulio Ricordi took part, was a brave but futile venture since the war was over before a shot was fired. By the terms of the treaty Austria handed over the Veneto to France who in turn handed it to Italy. This was not the way in which Venice had hoped to become Italian. Verdi was in Genoa, arranging for the lease of the appartment in the Palazzo Sauli which was to be his regular winter quarters, when the news broke; and it needed all Piroli's and Perrin's firmness to persuade him to honour his contract with the Opéra. Finally on 22 July he and Giuseppina left reluctantly for France leaving Mariani to busy himself with the furnishings.

The Verdis took an appartment in the Champs Elysées, having first insisted that it be properly dusted beforehand to prevent any throat infection. In mid-August they left for Cauterets in the Pyrenees. The voice parts meanwhile had been sent to the singers and the répétiteurs. Immediately the bass engaged for the Monk/Emperor declared that his part was not a principal; the management replied that it was of equal importance with those of Philip and the Inquisitor. As the singer remained unconvinced it was decided that the score should be examined by a composer of authority – Thomas or Reyer – to see if Verdi had written three principal bass parts or not. Verdi refused absolutely to let anyone see a score which was not yet complete; and in the end it was found easier to engage another singer. By the middle of September Verdi was back in Paris where the rehearsals ran their long and laborious course and the 'tortoises of the Opéra', in Giuseppina's phrase, 'take twenty-four hours to decide whether Mme Sasse or M. Faure should raise one finger or the whole hand'.[33] Rivalry between the prima donnas was also a problem; and Verdi preferred to miss a day's rehearsal rather than watch the grimaces of La Sasse whenever Pauline Gueymard-Lauters was singing. But he found time to keep up a busy correspondence with Ricordi about the contract for the Italian *Don Carlos* and with his bailiff Marenghi regarding the administration of the farm. ('. . . I gather from your letters that you are making "Milord" do little work and that you haven't harnessed the hack [puledra]. I don't like this because the horses won't stay healthy or at least they'll become big

33 WMV, p. 267.

and heavy like Rosso's.')[34] He had instructions for his father who had been left in charge of little Filomena. By December it became clear that the opera was assuming vast proportions; two substantial duets had been dropped and the ballet not even begun. At the final rehearsal it was decided to omit a twelve-minute choral introduction to the first act so that the performance should finish before midnight and the patrons of the Opéra be able to catch their last trains home. The performance on 11 March 1867 was at least a *succès d'estime*. Both Reyer and Theophile Gauthier praised the opera highly, as marking a new stage in the composer's development. Bizet on the other hand found it full of good intentions and nothing else. ('Verdi is no longer Italian. He is following Wagner. He no longer shows his well-known faults, but neither does he show a single one of his virtues.')[35] Another writer compared *Don Carlos* to St. George's Chapel, Windsor, full of the coats-of-arms of various knights of the Garter: Wagner, Gounod, Donizetti . . . Back at his new flat in Genoa Verdi read the notices with irritation. 'In fact I'm an almost perfect Wagnerian! But if the critics had paid a bit more attention they would have seen that there are the same ideas in the trio from *Ernani*, the sleepwalking scene from *Macbeth* and in so many other pieces . . .'[36] In Paris *Don Carlos* barely lasted out the year. But two highly successful performances were given in the Italian version of Achille De Lauzières at Covent Garden under Costa and later at Bologna under Mariani, both in Verdi's absence. But even in Italy its length told against it; and it rarely escaped without the cutting of the ballet (which Verdi allowed) and the first act (which he was powerless to prevent).

On 15 January, barely two months before the première of *Don Carlos*, Carlo Verdi died, aged 82. 'Verdi is deeply grieved', Giuseppina wrote, 'and so am I despite the fact that we had lived with him hardly at all and were at opposite poles in our way of thinking.'[37] A far greater blow was the death in July of Antonio Barezzi, though for some months it had been foreseen. 'You know that I owe him absolutely everything,' (to Clarina) '. . . I've known

[34] AGV, III, p. 107.
[35] H. Imbert, *Portraits et Etudes: Lettres à un ami* (Paris, 1894), p. 168.
[36] PLVE, pp. 524–5.
[37] AGV, III, p. 115.

many people in my life but never a better man than he.'[38] His depression and bouts of ill-humour are all too evident from Giuseppina's diaries.

> Yesterday he came [to my room] and in his usual way, especially nowadays, he no sooner sat down than he got up again. I said to him, 'Where are you going?'
> 'Upstairs.'
> . . . And as he doesn't usually go up there I said, 'What for?'
> 'To look for Plato'
> '. . . But don't you remember, it's in the cupboard in the dining room? . . .'
> I should never have said it! It was a serious matter, premeditated on my part and almost an abuse of power . . .
>
> This evening there was a row about an open window and because I tried to calm him down. He went into a fury saying that he would dismiss all the servants and that I take their part when they don't do their duty rather than his when he makes perfectly justified complaints. But, good Heavens, he sees these lapses on the part of the servants through a magnifying glass when he's in a bad mood and these poor devils need someone to look after their interests . . . God grant that he calm down because I suffer very much and I lose my bearings.[39]

Rumours of Verdi the severe landlord and the domestic tyrant were not without foundation.

Earlier that year, however, Giuseppina had sown a seed that would bear important fruit. Soon after their return from Genoa she had visited one of her husband's oldest friends, Clarina Maffei, who in turn had taken her to see Alessandro Manzoni, now in his eighties. All this was kept from Verdi until after the event; and his surprise and delight both women found deeply touching. He sent the poet a photograph of himself accompanied by a humble dedication to 'one who did true honour to this strife-torn country of ours. You are a saint, Don Alessandro.'[40] Not till July of the following year did he meet the poet personally and was charmed by the old man's

[38] LCC, pp. 521–2.
[39] WMV, pp. 400–1.
[40] AGV, III, p. 142.

simplicity. ('I would have knelt before him if it were possible to adore mortal men.')[41]

In the autumn of 1867 the Verdis went with Mariani to Paris for the Great Exhibition and were present at the première of Gounod's *Roméo et Juliette* ('it has neither the variety nor the originality of *Faust*,'[42] Mariani wrote) then returned to S.Agata. After a brief visit to Bologna during the rehearsals of the first *Don Carlos* in Italy, where, it is said, Verdi was moved to tears by the Posa of Antonio Cotogni, Verdi was back in Genoa where he heard of the opera's and of Mariani's triumph.

The early months of 1868 saw the moderate success of *Don Carlos* at La Scala under Mazzucato and the total failure of Boito's *Mefistofele* conducted by the composer. The Minister of Education, Emilio Broglio felt it was time to apply drastic measures to remedy the state of music in Italy. He set forth his views in an open letter to Rossini. The maintenance of the Conservatories was an unnecessary burden on the state. What had happened to the glorious Italian tradition of opera since Rossini had retired? It had become a matter of musical mastodons and Mephistofelean pretensions. Far better the formation of a voluntary society of music lovers to take care of the musical education of the young – a society of which Rossini himself was invited to be president. Rossini declared his acceptance and sent a copy of his latest 'péché de vieillesse', the *Chant des Titans*, as an inaugural piece – surely in a spirit of mockery, though not everyone saw it in that way. Verdi read Broglio's letter on the same day that he received the Order of Commendatore of the Crown of Italy. He immediately sent it back on the grounds that it must have been sent to the wrong address, 'not on my own account,' he told Arrivabene, 'but in memory of those two (i.e. Bellini and Donizetti) who have filled the world with their melodies:[43] Boito replied to Broglio with an ironic 'Letter in Four Paragraphs' in the course of which he touched on the achievements of the Italian romantics – *Norma*, *I Puritani*, *La favorita* and in 1851 *Rigoletto* and in 1853 *Il trovatore* and all the glorious, spell-binding ever fertile theatre of Verdi.[44] It

---

[41] Ibid., p. 215.
[42] AGV, III, p. 153.
[43] AVI, pp. 96–7.
[44] P. Nardi, *Vita di Arrigo Boito* (Milan, 1942), p. 319.

was a short but significant step towards a rapprochement between the young iconoclast and the middle-aged idol.

In December 1867 Piave succumbed to a stroke that left him paralysed and speechless till his death. Verdi at once offered financial assistance to his wife and daughter on condition however that they refused a similar offer from Giovanni Barezzi. For the Album Piave he suggested approaching Auber, Thomas, Federico Ricci, Mercadante and Wagner (needless to say this last suggestion was not followed up though it is fascinating to speculate on Wagner's reaction if it had been acted upon). Verdi's own contribution was the delicate and witty *Stornello*. About this time he entered Filomena in a boarding school in Turin. But his main achievement of 1868 was to have found a solution for the denouement of *La forza del destino*. Over the past six years Piave, Perrin, De Lauzières and even the Duke of Rivas himself had been canvassed for ideas. Now it was the turn of Antonio Ghislanzoni, ex-baritone, poet, pamphleteer and destined to become one of the leading librettists of the 1870s and 80s. A renegade 'scapigliato', he had already endeared himself to Verdi by his satirical attack on the publicity attending Faccio's *Amleto*; and he would soon be a frequent visitor to S. Agata of which he has left a charming description in his so-called *Libro Serio*. Yet from the tantalisingly incomplete letter that survives it is clear that Verdi himself, not Ghislanzoni, hit upon the idea of a final terzetto during which Leonora dies and Don Alvaro reconciles himself to the necessity of living on. 'I have great doubts about this', he wrote to Giulio Ricordi, 'which will either grow or diminish when I've slept on it. Meanwhile let Ghislanzoni be the judge and if he doesn't like it we'll look for something else.'[45] But the poet approved; and the opera, revised and mostly strengthened, was scheduled for performance at La Scala on 27 February 1869, the first Verdi première to have been given at Italy's leading opera house since *Giovanna d'Arco*. More sadly it was the last occasion on which Verdi and Mariani worked together in perfect amity. The break-up of their friendship is puzzling since the initiative was all on Verdi's side. The conductor had not ceased to be his devoted slave in matters artistic and material. Yet all of a sudden Verdi began seeing hidden motives in Mariani's every word and action. Foibles which he had once affectionately tolerated now

[45] AGV, III, p. 234.

began to get on his nerves. Undoubtedly there were contributory factors. Mauro Corticelli, now installed as 'fattore' at S.Agata, clearly disliked the conductor and did much to influence his employers against him. Later, by insisting on conducting the Italian première of *Lohengrin*, the first of Wagner's operas to be given in that country, Mariani involved himself in the war of the publishers and thus had the Ricordis to contend with. More significantly, perhaps, there was a woman in the case. Her name was Teresa Stolz. Born in Kostelec nad Leben, near Prague, in 1834 of a family of musicians, she trained as a singer in Prague and began her career in 1857 at the Italian opera at Tbilisi; from there she passed via some of the remoter theatres of Europe to Rio de Janeiro and London and in 1864 established herself in the Italian circuit. She scored a notable success in a revival of *Giovanna d'Arco* at La Scala the following year. But it was not until the Italian première of *Don Carlos* in 1867 that she entered Verdi's orbit. Mariani, at first unenthusiastic, waxed lyrical over her Elisabetta and still more over her Amelia in *Un ballo in maschera* in Genoa early in 1868. ('The range and beauty of her voice, the artistry with which she inflects it, sentiment, mastery of line – all perfect, sublime.')[46] Later that year she and Mariani became engaged.

Exactly when she began to interest Verdi is not clear. It may be significant that he was unwilling to invite Giuseppina to the rehearsals of the revised *Forza del destino* in which Teresa Stolz was singing Leonora: hence her desolating letter a fortnight before the première ('. . . when last Spring my heart counselled me boldly to introduce myself to Clarina Maffei and to Manzoni so as to come home bearing all sorts of things you would like – when we took that trip together to Milan and visited Manzoni and sailed along the lake and the consequence of it was to bring you back to the land of your early triumphs, little did I foresee the strange and cruel outcome, that I should be disowned thus . . . May God forgive you the sharp and humiliating wound you have dealt me.')[47] In his mid-fifties Verdi doubtless resented the encroachments of middle age after a youth which had been far from care-free. Giuseppina had aged before her time. Teresa Stolz, plump and equable, was neither very beautiful

[46] Ibid., p. 174.
[47] WMV, pp. 404–5.

nor clever but she had two assets: vitality and an instinctive feeling for the interpretation of Verdi's music, allied to an impeccable vocal technique to which others bore witness besides the infatuated Mariani. How natural to regret that she should have been thrown away on anyone as trivial as the conductor, who had the unfair advantage of being eight years younger than himself! Only by some such reasoning can one explain Verdi's extraordinary behaviour to a close friend of twelve years standing.

The first occasion of discord originated in the death of Italy's senior composer, Rossini, in November 1868. Preparations for commemorating the anniversary were planned for both Pesaro, where he was born, and Bologna where he was brought up. The programme for Pesaro was put in the charge of Mariani, its centrepiece being Cherubini's Requiem in D minor. For Bologna Verdi conceived from the start a much more imposing plan – to commission from the senior composers of the day a composite Requiem, to which each would contribute a piece; the composers to be chosen and the pieces allocated by a committee of which Giulio Ricordi would act as secretary. Verdi himself expressed a preference for the 'Libera me'. The plan was approved and the composers duly selected, more, it would seem, for their learning and familiarity with the sacred style than for their distinction; but Verdi professed himself satisfied. By the end of the summer the various pieces, including Verdi's, had been composed; only Mercadante and Petrella had declined, the first because of age and blindness, the second in order to supply an opera on Manzoni's *I promessi sposi*. The chief problem would be the choir since the chorus of the Teatro Comunale was clearly inadequate. It was at this point that Mariani offered to put the Pesaro choir at the disposal of the Commissioners; and when Verdi declared his intention of coming to Pesaro to hear it, 'you can imagine how happy that would make me', he wrote; 'come, come and come!'.[48] Little did he expect the withering letter that was already on its way to him. 'You can slumber in peace as I've already decided that I can't come to Pesaro.'

The rest of the letter is startling in its savagery:

Do you mean to say that we have to beg you to be allowed the

[48] Ibid., pp. 353–4.

chorus that you have at Pesaro? . . . I have never known whether the project of a Mass in honour of Rossini has had the good fortune to meet with your approval. When it's a matter not of personal interest but of art and of the lustre and glory of one's own country then a good deed needs nobody's approval . . . It becomes a fact of history not of musical charlatanism . . . What does it matter if it doesn't satisfy such and such a composer's vanity or such and such an artist's arrogance? . . .[49]

and more to the same effect. To Giulio Ricordi; 'He (Mariani) is the usual donkey . . . but it's as well that the Commission should know that he will never be more than lukewarm about our Mass because he wasn't the promotor of it and still more because the Commission didn't give him a piece to compose . . .'[50]

Whether or not Verdi had intended to provoke Mariani into resigning as conductor-designate of the Mass was rendered of academic interest by a scathing letter from the impresario Scalaberni which appeared in the *Monitore di Bologna*. He had never undertaken, he said, to lend his forces for the performance of the Rossini Mass; he was not rich and he had a family of six to feed from the proceeds of the operatic season; nor did he see why he would put himself out for an event from which the best of the younger composers had been excluded.

That was the end of the Rossini Mass – at any rate for the time being. Giulio Ricordi proposed mounting a performance in Milan instead; but Verdi, understandably, objected. To have presented the Mass in any other place than Rossini's home town, as a spontaneous, and disinterested act of homage, would have lowered the value of the gesture. The various pieces were returned to the firm of Ricordi, in whose archives they would remain until resurrected at the Stuttgart Bach Festival of 1988, since when they have been commercially recorded.

'The Bologna affair was an ugly business for many people and also for my distinguished friend Mariani', Verdi wrote to Clarina Maffei, 'who never moved a finger in a matter which I so strongly recommended to him.'[51] Later, to Giulio Ricordi again, 'I've learned

[49] LCC, pp. 210–3.
[50] AGV, III, p. 298.
[51] LPB, II, pp. 527–8.

my lesson over the Rossini-Mass and I will never get mixed up in musical affairs where Mariani is involved.'[52] To Arrivabene: 'He has failed to do what he ought to have done both as a friend and an artist.'[53] Bewildered by the thunderous silence from S.Agata, Mariani turned first to Corticelli then to Carlo Del Signore, a mutual friend and neighbour at Genoa. Reluctantly Verdi agreed to a meetin Del Signore's presence; and the correspondence was resumed, cool on Verdi's part, cringing and fearful on Mariani's. In the summer of 1870 Mariani tormented by symptoms of the illness that would kill him three years later wrote of a visit to Loreto where 'who knows whether Madonna will manage to cure me'.[54] The reply, brutal and would-be satirical, came not from Verdi but from Corticelli; incredibly, a draft of it can be found in Giuseppina's hand. Whether she was revenging herself for those months when the intimacy of Verdi and Mariani seemed to exclude herself; whether she blamed him for bringing Teresa Stolz into their lives; or whether her misplaced confidence in Corticelli allowed him to poison her against him, Giuseppina had developed a dislike of Mariani of which he himself was quite unaware. Indeed it would be a long time before he could bring himself to believe that Verdi had finished with him altogether.

[52] AGV, III, p. 311.
[53] AVI, pp. 114–15.
[54] WMV, p. 364.

8

The dark decade

No sooner was the première of the revised *Forza del destino* over than Verdi was beset with suggestions for new operas by Perrin, Du Locle, Giulio Ricordi and others. He was loth to try his luck in Paris again for reasons which he explained to Du Locle:

> In your theatres there are too many savants. Everyone wants to judge by the yardstick of his own insights, his own tastes and, what is worse, according to a system, without taking into account the character and the individuality of the author. Everyone wants to give an opinion, express a doubt and if the author lives for a long time in that atmosphere of doubts, he can't help in the long run being rather shaken in his convictions and he will end by correcting and adjusting and, to put it better, spoiling his work. At any rate he will have on his hands not an opera which is all of a piece but a mosaic, however fine. . . . Certainly no one would deny Rossini's genius! And yet despite that genius in *Guillaume Tell* you can sense that fatal atmosphere of the Opéra and sometimes, though more rarely than in other composers, you can feel a little too much here, not enough there and that the course of the music isn't as sure and free as in *Il barbiere*.[1]

However, he did not rule out the possibility of writing for the Opéra Comique of which Du Locle was now manager, if he could find a subject to his liking. Sardou's *Patrie* had some fine situations but the character of the prima donna was unsympathetic. *Froufrou* by Meilhac and Halévy was gripping for the first three acts but fell off badly in the last two. Dumas' *Acte et Néron* was sent for, together with a French translation of Wagner's prose works ('since I want to get to know that side of him too')[2] but was in the end rejected; on hearing which Giulio Ricordi tried to tempt Verdi with the libretto

[1] LCC, pp. 219–22.
[2] PUVD, p. 86.

on the subject of *Nero* that Boito was preparing for his own use; but though Boito had no objection, again Verdi drew back. Meantime he asked Ricordi to obtain from Madrid Gutierrez's *Catalan vengeance* and Zorilla's *El zapatero ed el rey*.

Yet the stimulus to compose again came from an unexpected source. In November 1869 the Khedive of Egypt planned to open a new theatre in Cairo as part of the celebrations attending the opening of the Suez Canal. A keen admirer of Verdi, he invited him to compose an inaugural hymn; and Verdi, following his usual rule, declined. But having successfully launched an operatic season with *Rigoletto* conducted by Muzio, the Khedive hoped for a new work from Verdi's pen on an Ancient Egyptian subject for the following year. He was encouraged in this by August Mariette, a French Egyptologist in the Vice-regal service, who saw in the project a long-desired trip to Paris at his employer's expense in order to give expert advice on the costumes. He had an ally in his old friend Camille Du Locle to whom he outlined the plot he had in mind. During the winter of 1869–70 Du Locle made an attempt to engage Verdi's interest; but it was not until April that Verdi took the bait, having read a synopsis to which was attached a letter to the effect that Gounod or Wagner might be interested if he himself was not. Who, he wanted to know, was the author? Clearly someone with theatrical experience. Du Locle refused to say but hinted that might be a person of high rank (i.e. the Khedive himself), so creating a false mystery which has lasted almost to this day. For the plot was Mariette's and nobody else's. Verdi signed a contract to write the new opera for performance at Cairo early in 1871; Giulio Ricordi signalled his joy in an extravagantly hilarious cartoon; and so *Aida* was born.

From the start Du Locle had offered himself as a disinterested intermediary, preparing a 'treatment' for which he could expect no advantage since the opera would be given in Italian. This was in turn broken down into recitative, scena and formal number by Verdi himself with Giuseppina's help. The resultant text was handed to Ghislanzoni for versification. The correspondence that survives between composer and librettist is mostly on Verdi's side but it paints a remarkably vivid picture of the opera's genesis and in particular the blend of traditionalism and innovation which gives *Aida* its special character. Thus of the terzettino in Act I:

It will be better to do without the first lines so as not to give Aida too much to say, and I don't care for Amneris' threats.

Of the hymn:

I would like Radames and Amneris to have a real part in the scene, avoiding those two asides which are always ineffective . . . Amneris could grab a sword, a flag, or some other piece of devilry and address her verses to Radames, warm, loving, war-like.

Of the consecration scene:

The characters don't always say what they ought to say and the priests aren't sufficiently priestly. It seems to me too that the 'parola scenica' is lacking, or if it's there it's buried beneath the rhyme of the line and therefore doesn't emerge cleanly and clearly as it should.

Of the duets in Act III:

I see that you are afraid of two things: of certain, I would say, theatrical audacities and of *not writing cabalettas*! I always believe in writing cabalettas when the situation demands it. Those of the two duets are not required by the situation, and in particular that of the duet between father and daughter seems to me out of place. In her state of terror and moral prostration Aida cannot and must not sing a cabaletta.

He was particularly detailed in his metrical requirements – a far cry from the days when he professed himself agreeable to whatever metre the poet chose.[3]

Preparations for the casting began in the autumn, not only for the première in Cairo but for the first performance in Italy three months later. For Cairo Verdi wanted Muzio as conductor, and shrugged off Mariani's final, pathetic attempt to put himself at the composer's service. ('Once before you wrote to me that you would like to go with me to Egypt; I told you I wasn't going. If I had thought fit you should go in my place I would have asked you. The fact that I didn't is proof that I didn't find it convenient and therefore I've given the job to someone else.')[4]

[3] For Verdi's letters to A.Ghislanzoni see LCC, pp. 638–75, chronology revised in P. Gossett, 'Verdi, Ghislanzoni and *Aida*: the Uses of Convention', *Critical Inquiry* i/2 December 1974), pp. 291–334. For some of Ghislanzoni's replies see BVA.

[4] LCV, II, p. 34.

But all such plans were for the present to be frustrated by political events. In July 1870 the French declared war on Prussia, only to be defeated with a swiftness which surprised the whole of Europe. Verdi's attitude to the French had been ambivalent; but the present crisis found him a staunch Francophile. 'In the last resort', he wrote to Clarina Maffei, 'France gave freedom and civilisation to the modern world. And if she falls, don't let us delude ourselves, all our liberties and civilisation will fall with her. By all means let our statesmen and men of letters sing praises to the knowledge, science, and, God forgive them, the art of these conquerors, but if they looked a little more closely, they would see that the blood of the ancient Goths flows in their veins . . . Men of head but no heart.'[5] And to Arrivabene 'Ah, the North! It's a country, a people that terrify me.'[6] He and Giuseppina wrote letters of commiseration to the Du Locles, now their close friends. From his commissioning fee for *Aida* Verdi set aside 2,000 francs for the benefit of the wounded at Sedan. With the rest he authorised Du Locle to buy Italian government stock on his behalf, the certificates of which he was free to use as surety for his own management of the Opéra Comique (a thoroughly unwise decision as it turned out). By November the French capital was under siege and with it the scenery and costumes for *Aida*; and it soon became clear that the opera's première would have to be deferred to the following winter. Verdi took advantage of the extra time allowed to make one or two modifications and additions which included the romanza in Act III, 'O patria mia'.

In the meantime he was free to turn his attention to two major events in Italy's music life. In the winter of 1870 Mercadante died, leaving vacant the directorship of the Conservatory of Naples. Florimo at once wrote to Verdi inviting him on behalf of the teaching staff to take up the post. For various reasons Verdi refused; he had a home in the North which he had no intention of leaving; he needed his independence in order to compose; whereas to carry out his theories of musical education would require constant surveillance on his part. He was all for basic grounding, constant exercise in fugue and counterpoint accompanied by a wide study of literature. He concluded with an epigram that was to become all too famous for

[5] LPB, II, pp. 528–9.
[6] AVI, p. 121.

Verdi's own liking 'Torniamo all' antico e sarà un progresso' (Let us return to the past; it will be a step forward).[7]

He did however reluctantly consent to form part of a committee on the reform of the conservatories which sat during the early months of 1871 in Florence, capital of the new Italy since 1864 and soon to give way to Rome. As one who had little use for official seats of learning his views can hardly have carried much weight. Indeed he wrote via Piroli to the then Minister of Education that he was for leaving the conservatories as they were on the somewhat illogical ground that they never taught a composer what mattered and such of their alumni – Bellini or Rossini – as achieved greatness did so in spite of the training they had received. He urged the minister rather to subsidise the theatres – without result. In the next decade the theatres would languish, while the conservatories prospered and the study of modern, ultramontane music which Verdi so much deplored would flourish.

The performance of *Lohengrin* in November 1871 struck a decisive blow for the modernists as well as marking a new stage in the war of the publishers. For years the advantage had lain with Ricordi, who had secured the rights of all the leading Italian composers of the day. Lucca had nothing more impressive to show than three operas by Verdi of which only *Attila* made him any money. But the growing popularity of foreign opera combined with Tito Ricordi's indolence to turn the tide in Lucca's favour. The acquisition of Wagner's rights was his last and greatest coup. He died shortly afterwards; but his business was carried on by the unremitting energy of his widow – uneducated but shrewd and with a heart as large as her large frame (she would be a mother to the disreputable Petrella no less than to the delicate ailing Catalani). More than a match for Tito Ricordi, she found an adversary worthy of her steel in his son Giulio, to whom more and more of the firm's business was being entrusted. The trim, spare, little man with spade-shaped beard surmounting a wing collar who figures in so much of the late Verdian iconography was already a dynamic force in Italy's musical life.

> A writer of graceful, measured prose, a sharp mordent satirist, a fluent, elegant composer, any one who had dealings with him realised at once that they had to do with a superior intellect. . . . In

[7] LCC, pp. 232–3.

his study there was a constant procession of composers, librettists, singers, conductors agents and impresarios. His manner was rather reserved with something in it of the aristocrat and the soldier.[8]

Such is the description given by a contemporary of 'Sör Giüli' as he was known to his Milanese intimates. Not all his prognoses were proved correct; his early backing of Massenet rather than Bizet was clearly a mistake. But posterity has confirmed his estimate of Puccini whom he 'discovered' and to whom he held fast at a time when his compatriots were convinced that Italy's future lay with Mascagni and his followers. Despite his years he obtained a far greater measure of Verdi's confidence than either his father or his grandfather before him.

An assiduous reader of Ricordi's *Gazzetta Musicale di Milano* Verdi went to a performance of *Lohengrin* in a mood of mistrust, having been further irritated by the publicity that had attended the première ('Lohengrenades',[9] as he would call it). Characteristically, Ricordi's agent made Verdi's presence known in the theatre – a fact which can hardly have had a beneficial effect on the performance. Verdi meanwhile jotted down his impressions on a copy of the libretto. Much he liked, including such details as the combination of cor anglais and bass clarinet that accompanies Lohengrin's warning. But his summing up was lukewarm: 'Fine music where it's clear and there are ideas. The action moves slowly as do the words. Hence boredom. Fine instrumental effects. Too many sustained notes so that it becomes heavy.'[10] Yet in time he was to warm towards *Lohengrin*; for Verdi's horizons never ceased expanding with age. The year before he died he told an interviewer of his admiration for *Tristan und Isolde*.

Aida was now scheduled for December in Cairo and for February in Milan. Casting for the first was in the hands of Draneht Bey (in fact a Greek Cypriot who had changed his family name of Pavlidis); for the second in the care of Giulio Ricordi. Never was Verdi so difficult to please. As Muzio was no longer available

---

[8] G. Depanis, *I Concerti Popolari ed il Teatro Regio di Torino* (Turin, 1914), I, p. 175.
[9] AGV, III, p. 518.
[10] Ibid., p. 511.

Draneht attempted to engage Mariani together with his fiancée on highly lucrative terms. This arrangement was blocked by Verdi who was determined to secure Teresa Stolz for the Milan revival but without Mariani. He agreed however to the engagement of Antonietta Anastasi-Pozzoni, whom he heard on his visit to Florence; after which he reverted to the idea of Mariani for Cario, especially since he did not intend to go there himself. But Mariani, irresolute as always and by now terrified of 'his Maestro', prevaricated and finally declined. 'Ah c'est vraiment trop fort! trop fort! trop fort!' Verdi fumed. Their last meeting was at Bologna station at the time of *Lohengrin*, when Mariani offered to carry Verdi's bag and was curtly refused.

In the end Verdi reluctantly agreed to Giovanni Bottesini as conductor at Cairo. But he raised interminable objections to the proposed mezzo-soprano for the role of Amneris, Eleonora Grossi, only giving way when his intransigence threatened to cost Draneht his job. For her counterpart at Milan he was reluctantly persuaded to have the young Austrian Maria Waldmann, whose talent made up for her inexperience. The Milan conductor would be Franco Faccio, Mariani's assistant at the revivals of *La forza del destino*, who had already decided to abandon composition in favour of what was clearly his true vocation.

On 23 September 1871 Teresa Stolz paid her first visit to S.Agata to study her part under the composer's guidance. Assuming that Giuseppina was aware of the danger, it seems from her first letter to the departed visitor that she had decided to take the course recommended by the average women's magazine: '. . . what I want above all is to embrace you again and stay as long as possible in your company, because I love you, admire you and am attracted by your frank, sincere and elevated character in no way tainted by the air of the *coulisses* . . .'[11] How successful her tactics were over the next few years can only be guessed. In her letters to Giuseppina Teresa Stolz is all sisterly affection. To Verdi she was kittenish ('Couldn't you spare a moment of your precious sleep to come and say hello to us in the theatre . . . Maestro you are *naughty*! very naughty'.)[12] Whatever the truth, her husband's attentions to the prima donna caused

[11] WMV, p. 406.
[12] AGV, III, p. 576.

Giuseppina much distress for some time to come. It may be significant too that it was after her visit to S.Agata that Teresa Stolz broke
off her engagement to Mariani.

The success of *Aida* in Cairo was all that could have been wished
and earned Verdi the title of Commendatore of the Ottoman Order.
None the less for Milan Verdi made an important alteration in the
cabaletta that concludes the first scene of Act II. He also wrote an
overture to replace the original prelude, as he had done with the
revised *Forza del destino* but, having heard it rehearsed, decided that
it sounded pretentious and tasteless. But he never destroyed the
score; so performances have been possible, beginning with Toscanini's in America in 1940. Not since *Macbeth* in 1847 had Verdi
taken so much trouble over every aspect of the opera's presentation –
the performance, the staging, the scenery and costumes, even the
lay-out of the orchestra; and all his instructions had been faithfully
carried out by Giulio Ricordi. The first night was predictably a
brilliant occasion. Seats were shared, boxes crammed. At the end of
the second act Verdi was presented with a gem-studded sceptre and a
parchment scroll.

But he was not entirely happy. Though the public had been
enthusiastic the critics were captious. In the contentious climate of
the new Italy where modernism and the music of the future, however
little understood, had become a central issue the conventional
aspects of *Aida* were not entirely welcome. Indeed Filippi considered
that its mixture of old and new did not fuse as well as in *Don Carlos*
(it should perhaps be remembered that Verdi had snubbed his offer
to go to Cairo and report in rehearsals). He added that to deny that
Verdi had been influenced by Gounod, Meyerbeer and Wagner was
like denying light to the sun. 'Stupid criticisms and even stupider
praise; not one noble idea; no one who wanted to point out what I
was aiming at.'[13] A young man called Prospero Bertani who lived at
Reggio Emilia went to one of the later performances and was highly
dissatisfied with what he saw and heard. As he was a 'figlio di
famiglia' with no independent income, the outing had made considerable inroads on his purse, which in all justice the composer
ought to make good. He accordingly wrote to Verdi asking him to
refund the price of his ticket, the return fare to Milan and the cost of

---

[13] Ibid., p. 553.

his evening meal. Verdi wrote to Ricordi authorising him to pay the necessary sum, excepting the price of the meal since Bertani could have eaten before he set out. Ricordi did so and published the whole story in the *Gazzetta Musicale di Milano*. Bertani at once found himself the object not only of ridicule but of opprobrium. He wrote again to Verdi complaining that he had been threatened with the fate of Colonel Anviti; and would Verdi please exonerate him. But the joke had gone far enough and Verdi this time ignored him. It was not the only instance of fatuous presumption. A minor composer, Vincenzo Sassaroli, challenged him to a trial of skill; they would both compose an opera within a fixed number of days; both works would then be performed and compared. Verdi and Ricordi chose to ignore him − a sure acknowledgment, Sassaroli thought, of his rival's inferiority.

The influx of new, mostly German ideas, due partly to the moral effect of the Prussian victory and the presence in Italy of distinguished foreigners such as Liszt and Bülow, the continuing artistic campaign of the 'scapigliati' and the war of the publishers combined to create an atmosphere of faction from which Verdi himself had not reached that position of unassailable eminence to be immune. Younger composers such as Catalani made it clear that they regarded the Bear of Busseto as something of a sacred monster. It was a time when sound reputations were attacked and false ones created. *Lohengrin*, applauded at Bologna in 1871, was hissed off the stage in Milan in 1873. That same year *I Goti* by Stefano Gobatti was hailed at Bologna, now a Lucca stronghold, as a noble specimen of the music of the future. Posterity however upheld Verdi's view that 'Gobatti is writing a language of which he simply has no knowledge'[14] and that *I Goti* was 'a musical abortion'. At a time when at every première the agents of Ricordi and Lucca could be seen, as Depanis puts it, 'looking daggers at each other' and controversy raged in the press, personal scandal was always a useful weapon. In March 1872 Mariani wrote to a friend from Genoa 'As for my *fellow tenant* I can tell you nothing. He is here, but I have never seen him, nor do I seek him out . . . All I will say is that if the gossip one hears about him and another person, who has also behaved very badly

[14] AVI, pp. 166–76.

towards me, were true, they would both deserve contempt.'[15] If such gossip reached Giuseppina's ears, she none the less continued to write cordially to Teresa Stolz and invite her to S.Agata. From November to March the Verdis and Teresa Stolz were together at Naples for revivals of *Don Carlos* and *Aida*. To De Sanctis's plea that he should help to mount his latest works at the San Carlo he had always replied that Naples did not have the elements necessary for the performance of what he called 'opere d'intenzioni' (operas of ideas); that the theatre was still living in the world of cavatinas and cabalettas. He had refused point blank even to allow his *La forza del destino* to be performed there. But now, having ensured the participation of Teresa Stolz and Maria Waldmann, he yielded. At the same time he came to De Sanctis's assistance with a loan of 25,000 lire free of interest, of which he was only to see 5,000 returned to him; for like many businessmen De Sanctis had fallen victim to the recession of the 1870s and would remain a poor man for the rest of his life.

For the performance of *Don Carlos* Verdi took the opportunity of making two notable changes, one to the duet between Philip and Posa in Act II, the other in that between Elisabeth and Carlos in Act V, from which he removed two movements. The changes were incorporated in all subsequent editions of the vocal score until the revised edition of 1884, so proving a rich source of confusion to scholars. But the principal fruit of that winter in Naples was something wholly unexpected. On the evening of 1 April friends of the composer were bidden to the Hotel delle Crocelle. There, in the foyer, they found four chairs and four music-stands of an eighteenth century design with candle attached. Four players entered and without a word of explanation began to play – Verdi's String Quartet in E minor. To begin with Verdi seems to have regarded it as a private diversion, like Wagner's *Siegfried Idyll*; later, like Wagner, he agreed to its publication.

On 22 May, in his eighty-eighth year, his mind already clouded by the tragic death of his son, Alessandro Manzoni died as the result of a fall on the steps of the Church of San Fedele. Less than a fortnight later Verdi announced to Giulio Ricordi his intention of composing a Requiem Mass in his honour to be performed on the anniversary of his death. Clearly this decision was not as sudden as it

[15] WMV, pp. 384–5.

might appear. Shortly before the Italian première of *Aida*, Alberto Mazzucato, the conductor and professor had happened to glance at Verdi's contribution to the Rossini Mass where it lay gathering dust in Ricordi's archives. Astonished and deeply moved he wrote spontaneously to the composer, complimenting him on having written 'the finest the greatest and the most vastly poetic piece of music that could be imagined.'[16] 'Your remarks', Verdi replied, 'would almost have planted in me the desire to set the Mass in its entirety at some later date; especially since with a little more development (of the material) I would find that I'd already written the *Requiem* and the *Dies Irae* to which there's a back reference in the *Libera*. . . . But don't worry. Its a temptation that will pass like so many others. There are so many Requiem Masses; there's no point in adding one more.'[17] An indication, surely, that the idea of writing a large-scale liturgical composition had been germinating in his mind for some time and needed only a solemn occasion to bring it to fruition.

That it sprang from some deeply religious impulse is unlikely, even if it has the spiritual quality of one who has reflected profoundly on first and last things. The face that Verdi showed to his intimates was that of an agnostic. In the year preceding Manzoni's death his Venetian friend the doctor and 'alienist' Cesare Vigna sent Giuseppina a copy of a treatise in which he had, as he thought, successfully reconciled religious faith with scientific thought. In her reply she could not resist remarking that in all such matters her husband presented the strangest phenomenon in the world. 'He isn't a doctor, he's an artist; everyone agrees in granting him the divine gift of genius: he's the soul of honesty, he understands and feels every lofty and delicate sentiment, yet with all that this *brigand* allows himself to be, I won't say an atheist, but certainly not much of a believer – and all with a calm obstinacy that makes one want to hit him.'[18] Later that year to Clarina Maffei: 'there are some highly virtuous natures that need to believe in God; there are others no less perfect who are quite happy to believe in nothing at all, while rigorously observing every precept of strict morality. Manzoni and Verdi . . . These two men are for me a real subject for meditation.'[19] For Verdi,

[16] LCC, pp. 242–3.
[17] Ibid., pp. 243–4.
[18] WMV, p. 280.
[19] Ibid., p. 282.

then, as for Brahms or Vaughan Williams, agnosticism was no bar to the composition of a religious work.

On 25 June Verdi left with his wife for Paris to begin work on the Requiem. Meanwhile another death seems to have left him quite unmoved; that of Mariani, alone in his attic flat in the Palazzo Sauli, after weeks of excruciating pain. Only once, two years later, in a letter to the impresario Antonio Gallo do we find an oblique reference: 'Charlatan! How often have I used that word to a poor fellow who is no longer with us but was worth all the rest put together?'[20] Mariani is not mentioned by name, but who else could he have meant? In September the Verdis were back at S.Agata and arrangements for the performance of the Mass were going ahead. The team of four soloists included the by now traditionally associated pair, Teresa Stolz and Maria Waldmann; and at Verdi's insistence the venue was to be the Church of S. Marco, Milan, Verdi himself conducting. The work was completed by 10 April 1874; rehearsals began at the beginning of May. Predictably there was some opposition. Certain members of the Milan City Council objected to defraying the very considerable costs of the undertaking on the grounds that, however prestigious, the occasion would be of no benefit to the local poor; and it needed all Boito's eloquence as a fellow-member to persuade them to change their minds. On the eve of the performance Hans von Bülow published in the *Allgemeine Zeitung* an attack on Verdi's 'latest opera, though in ecclesiastical robes', at which he admitted to having sneaked a 'furtive glance',[21] no more; but it had taken away all desire on his part to attend the performance. Predictably this set the Italian press in an uproar; but the most crushing rejoinder came from Brahms: 'Bülow has made an almighty fool of himself. Only a genius could have written such a work.'[22]

Certainly that was the prevailing opinion at the time of its performance; after which the Verdis set out for Paris followed by their team of soloists for seven performances at the Opéra Comique: 'apparently genuine success' Verdi reported both to his publisher and Clarina Maffei; and indeed the series could have been prolonged were it not for the refusal of the tenor and bass, Capponi and Maini,

[20] AGV, III, pp. 764–5.
[21] Ibid., p. 690.
[22] J.V. Widmann, *Johannes Brahms in Erinnerungen* (Berlin, 1898), p. 132.

to exceed the terms of their contracts. Escudier's brother-in-law, Maurice Strakosch, had explored the possibility of a London performance that year but found that the Handel Festival had made it impossible to secure a good choir. Not convinced, Verdi himself paid a four-day visit to London at the end of June ('nobody must know of this' he told Ricordi *'no one, no one, no one, no one'*[23]). He was unimpressed by a Handel Festival concert at the Crystal Palace ('. . . these three or four thousand performers are just an immense humbug . . .');[24] yet, as before, he liked the capital ('. . . very curious, this city . . . none the less very exciting . . .'). His immediate concern was to arrange for the Mass to be given the following year not at the acoustically unsatisfactory Crystal Palace nor yet at one of the opera theatres, which would have involved him with the impresarios Gye and Mapleson and their 'old crocks'[25] of singers, but in that latest wonder of public engineering, the Royal Albert Hall. Having arranged this he returned to Paris and then to S.Agata, once more to enjoy the peace of country life while from time to time issuing complaints or orders to the House of Ricordi regarding past and future performances of the *Requiem* and *Aida*. To Giuseppina fell the task of organising their move from the Palazzo Sauli in Genoa to the Palazzo Doria, which was to remain their winter home from now on. In November Verdi had the satisfaction of being nominated Senator, an honour which no more required his attendance in the Italian Parliament than does a peerage in the British House of Lords.

During the preparations of an extended European tour of the Requiem to take place in the spring of 1875 Verdi decided to make an important change in the score; he would turn the choral fugue of the Liber scriptus into a solo for Maria Waldmann. On reflection he decided not to include it in the Paris performances at the Opéra Comique, partly because, as he told the singer, she would not have had sufficient time to study it but chiefly since 'the public's first impressions are always terrible, and even should this piece make its effect, people would say, "It was better as it was before" '.[26] So it was

[23] AGV, III, p. 700.
[24] Ibid., p. 703.
[25] Ibid., p. 733.
[26] Ibid., p. 740.

1 Rocca di Busseto

2 Antonio Barezzi

3 Verdi in 1843

4 *Rigoletto:* original set design for Act I, scene 2 by Giuseppe and Pietro Bertoja

5 *Il trovatore:* original set design for Act II, scene 1 by Giuseppe and Pietro Bertoja

5 Temistocle Solera

7 Francesco Maria Piave

8 Verdi rehearsing *Un ballo in maschera*

9 Antonio Ghislanzoni

10 Teresa Stolz

11 Teresa Stolz as Aida

12 Verdi and Boito at Sant' Agata

13 Giulio Ricordi

14 Giuseppina Strepponi Verdi in old age

15 Verdi, with La Scala in the background

in London where he arrived in mid-May 1875, after having been awarded the Cross of the Légion d'Honneur, that the new setting was first heard. Critical reception of the Requiem, conducted by the composer in the Albert Hall on 15 May, was on the whole favourable; but the performance was poorly attended and the box-office receipts correspondingly low. Clearly Verdi had reckoned without the Puritanism of the Victorians, who liked their liturgical music solemn and sedate. Mawkishness they could tolerate; theatricality never. So Verdi left London in a black mood before the performances had run their course, handing over the baton to Joseph Barnby. In Vienna, by contrast, success was complete and 'into the torrid zone',[27] as Giuseppina put it. Having conducted a performance in the Hoftheater, Verdi for the first time since *I masnadieri* mounted the operatic podium for his *Aida*. Later that year in a season which included the Viennese première of *Carmen*, the revised *Tannhäuser* and the first night of Goldmark's *The Queen of Sheba*, the Requiem was revived in the composer's absence. Among the audience was Richard Wagner; but only Cosima provides the evidence of his reaction to it – a work of which 'it would certainly be best to say nothing'.[28] In the eyes of the Wagners Verdi ranked below Donizetti.

A performance in Berlin was to have followed; but Tito Ricordi had taken fright at the financial disaster of the London venture and had accordingly cancelled it. On his return to Italy Verdi duly vented his wrath on the unfortunate publisher, all the more forcibly for having discovered some irregularities in past accounts. Tito Ricordi retreated into illness and the mountains, leaving his son to settle matters as best he could; and it was due both to his ability and tact that a settlement was reached and that Verdi's fears expressed to Piroli that 'our relations can never be the same again'[29] were proved groundless. As usual Giuseppina had proved an invaluable go-between. Tirelessly active on her husband's behalf she was also directing the restoration of their first Busseto home, the Palazzo Dordoni, which she had bought from Verdi with her own money, so that it could serve as a memorial to him. It is all the sadder, therefore,

---

[27] Ibid., p. 753.
[28] Cosima Wagner, *Diaries*, trans. G. Skelton, 2 vols (London, 1978–80), I, p. 873.
[29] LCV, III, pp. 115–16.

that her peace of mind should have been continually troubled by public gossip of a particularly unpleasant kind.

The previous year Pietro Scalaberni, now manager of the Pergola and Pagliano theatres in Florence, applied for permission to perform the Requiem. Remembering his behaviour over the Rossini Mass in Bologna, Verdi refused. Now in 1875 one Ducci persuaded the impresario to lease him the Teatro Pagliano for 'four concerts'; and it was only after Scalaberni had signed the agreement that he learnt that the four concerts were four performances of the Requiem. Although the 'poisonous insect' (Teresa Stolz's description) pretended not to mind, he seems to have taken his revenge by inspiring a series of scurrilous attacks on the prima donna in successive issues of the *Rivista Independente*. Totally without natural gifts, the writer declared, she had bluffed her way into the Italian operatic world. Her career had been saved from shipwreck by the conductor Mariani who fell in love with her. Under his guidance she had distinguished herself mightily in *Don Carlos*, previously thought to have been one of Verdi's weaker operas; but instead of being grateful to her mentor she transferred her affections to Verdi; hence a rift between composer and conductor, who thereafter pined and died. Then the writer raked up an incident which had occurred during rehearsals for the Requiem in 1874. Verdi had gone to visit the 'rotund and appetizing soprano' in her hotel. After his return he discovered the loss of a wallet containing 50,000 lire. His first reaction was to blame the servants; but the missing wallet was found on Teresa Stolz' sofa, having slipped out during – well, the intelligent reader would be able to hazard his own guess. Other revelations were promised but none were forthcoming. Teresa Stolz was sufficiently upset to write to Giuseppina suggesting that from now on she might be *de trop* at S.Agata. Giuseppina replied cordially assuring her that she would never be *de trop* 'as long as you and we remain the honourable and loyal people that we are'. But the proviso was not a mere form of words. Giuseppina was indeed worried; and the following year in Paris her fears seem to have precipitated some sort of a crisis. In the draft of a letter to her husband she complains that since 1872 there have been 'febrile periods of assiduity and attention' in his relations with La Stolz. 'If there's nothing in it . . . be calmer in your attentions . . . Remember that I, your wife while despising past rumours am living at this very moment à trois and that I have the right to ask if not for your caresses at least for your consideration.'[30] How and in what manner the crisis was surmounted with Teresa Stolz remaining a friend of the family – this like so many of the more intimate details of Verdi's life has remained sedulously shrouded from posterity.

Indeed, 1876, the year which saw the realisation of Wagner's wildest dreams in the opening of the Bayreuth Festspielhaus, was an especially black one for Verdi. In March he travelled once again to Paris to rehearse the first production of *Aida* at the Théâtre des Italiens now managed by Escudier with Muzio as conductor. Now for the first time a rift opened between Verdi and his French publisher. The immediate cause was the poor spectacle. ('What I said yesterday in a moment of rage I now repeat in utterly cold blood: *I shall not come to the theatre unless I can be materially certain that the scenic indecencies of the fourth act are put right.*')[31] Then came the matter of the translation. Escudier, as his contract with Ricordi allowed him to do, had commissioned a French version from Nuitter which Verdi found metrically correct but thoroughly bad as regards the relation between music and action. He himself meanwhile was preparing with Nuitter's help a new one which might not be very beautiful stylistically but would at least bring out the musical and dramatic sense. A somewhat acrimonious correspondence followed between Verdi and his two publishers which ended with a new agreement being struck with Escudier in the presence of two witnesses, according Verdi full translation rights and a more favourable share of Escudier's hire fees. Fortunately *Aida* at the Théâtre des Italiens was a success, so too another Requiem at the same venue; so, still more gratifyingly, was another performance of the quartet before a large invited audience at the Hotel de Bade; and Verdi at last made up his mind to have it published. One matter however had remained unsettled when Verdi left Paris in early June. Before his arrival there he had informed Du Locle by letter that he wished to recover the 48,000 lire which he had deposited with him in 1870, together with the accumulated interest. Du Locle had promised faithfully to make restitution, then had pleaded ill-health to excuse the delay. The truth was that under his management the Opéra Comique had fared poorly and the fiasco of *Carmen* the previous year had ensured bankruptcy. Verdi arrived in Paris to find the theatre closed, Du

[30] WMV, pp. 427–32.
[31] BVA, p. 397.

Locle himself on the high seas recovering from a breakdown, and only a tearful Marie Du Locle about to separate from her husband on the grounds of being a burden to him. But he did not despair of getting his money back. He applied first of all to Emile Perrin, Du Locle's father-in-law, now in charge at the Comédie Française; but it was not a debt for which Perrin was prepared to assume responsibility. Verdi's next move was to write to a wealthy aunt of Du Locle's, the Comtesse Mollien from whom the poet might one day expect to inherit. Marie Du Locle, however, had Verdi's letters intercepted on the grounds that the payment of so large a sum would deprive her children of the means of subsistence. Eventually Verdi took legal proceedings against Du Locle. The case was announced for August; but there is no record of its having come to court. Presumably some kind of settlement was reached beforehand.

No one had been more zealous in Verdi's cause than Escudier; but soon he too fell once more into disgrace. News reached Verdi of slipshod revivals of *Aida* at the Théâtre des Italiens, not to mention the failure in October of the first performance in France of *La forza del destino*; worst of all Escudier was unable to pay Verdi according to the terms of their new agreement. 'Among your many and complicated affairs', Verdi wrote with ominous sarcasm, 'you will certainly have forgotten one which is tiny, indeed a mere bagatelle . . .'[32] Like Du Locle before him Escudier could only promise; for the following year the Théâtre des Italiens also went bankrupt; and a stinging letter from Verdi put an end to their friendship, though not to their business dealings; for he remained the publisher for the French *Aida* of 1880. When he died in 1881 Verdi characteristically sent money to his widow.

Finally it was the turn of De Sanctis to default on the interest-free loan that Verdi had made him; and from then on only Giuseppina was prepared to maintain the contact that the Verdis' position as godparents to his son demanded. Meanwhile death, as well as debt, was starting to take its toll of Verdi's friends. That of Piave in March had been a happy release from eight years of a vegetable existence. More unexpected was the death of the sculptor, Vincenzo Luccardi, the oldest of Verdi's Roman friends. 'He was so nimble, so active and cheerful when I saw him last year', Verdi wrote to Piroli. 'What is

[32] AGV, IV, p. 29.

life? All those efforts, desires, aspirations, then suddenly . . . death.'[33]
He was also saddened by the political scene in Italy, which saw the
fall of the governments of the Right and with it the exclusion of
friends such as Piroli from Parliament. In foreign affairs it was to see
a progressive moving away from France towards Germany which
would culminate in the Triple Alliance of 1882. The one gleam of
light that remained to console the composer from an otherwise
sombre year was the graduation with honour from her college of his
adopted daughter Fifao and her engagement to Dr Alberto Carrara
of Busseto – 'just the kind of husband we could have wished for
her',[34] Verdi told his friends. 'I could never have wanted her to
marry above her station.' The following year they were married.
Fifao would be a mother before she was twenty.

In January 1877 Verdi received an invitation from Ferdinand
Hiller, Director of the Lower Rhine Festival, to conduct his Requiem
at the Festival of Cologne in May. A friend of Rossini and Mendelssohn, Hiller had at one time been viewed with mistrust by Verdi who
suspected him of contempt for the contemporary Italian tradition.
In the event he was to find him remarkably sympathetic. He too
deplored the Germanising tendency of the younger Italians as well as
the more bizarre flights of fancy of his own countrymen. True, the
Verdis were not strong on German; and Verdi himself complained of
the appearance of German grammars on the table at mealtimes
weeks before their departure. The occasion itself was outstandingly
successful. The large but very efficient amateur chorus presented him
with an ivory baton with a golden handle; the ladies of the city gave
him a crown of silver and gold, and the organisers of the festival a
huge album containing views of the Rhine by one of their leading
painters. George Henschel, who sang the bass solo, had very pleasant
recollections of the composer whom he remembered as 'very taciturn
for an Italian.'[35] The local quartet performed his one composition in
that medium; and he heard a quantity of choral and chamber music
which impressed him greatly. His friendship with Hiller which lasted
until Hiller's death in 1885 was to prove the revitalising spark in a
creative career which seemed to have run its course. Topics of

[33] LCV, III, pp. 121–2.
[34] Ibid., p. 120.
[35] G. Henschel, *Musings and Memories of a Musician* (London, 1918), p.
166.

discussion included the political events of both countries, such questions as who were the best singing teachers, the unexpected emergence of two English composers, Frederick Cowen and Arthur Goring Thomas ('How nice it would be if that nation that never has been musical should now join hands with us . . .'[36], Verdi wrote.) Hiller sent to Verdi his own *Rebecca at the Well* which Verdi found admirable. The surprise occurred when Hiller told him of his intention of setting a *de profundis* in Dante's translation. 'The beauty of it is', Verdi replied, 'that I too had the idea last winter of setting that very psalm, but happily I changed my mind and decided to set the *Paternoster* for five voices in Dante's own translation:'[37] the first indication that Verdi was beginning, however modestly, to compose again.

None of this was apparent to his friends. The Verdi of the late 1870s remained the same incorrigible grumbler. Asked by Faccio for his advice on compiling a programme for the orchestra of La Scala to perform at the Paris Exhibition of 1878, he refused to offer suggestions since he thought that the entire venture was ill-conceived; though he was agreeably surprised by subsequent reports from the French press. Though unable to comprehend the recession that pervaded the European economy at the time, he was distressed by its effects – the poverty of the peasants, the signs of unrest that the government was attempting to quell by a show of force; the closing of the theatres for lack of a subsidy; the invasion of foreign works such as Goldmark's *Queen of Sheba*. ('We're nearly there; another step and we shall all be completely Germanized.');[38] the bizarrerie of Boito's *Mefistofele* which was being praised to the skies in the *Gazzetta Musicale di Milano*. ('I had always read and understood that the Prologue in Heaven was a thing of spontaneity, of genius . . . yet hearing how the harmonies of that piece are almost all based on dissonances I seemed to be . . . not in heaven, certainly!!')[39] As for the various Orchestral and Quartet Societies that seemed to be springing up everywhere, 'Sometimes I have a thoroughly paltry idea and I whisper to myself, "But suppose we in Italy were to form a vocal

---

[36] LCV, II, p. 342.
[37] Ibid., pp. 330–1.
[38] AVI, pp. 226–33.
[39] Ibid.

quartet to perform Palestrina and his contemporaries, Marcello etc., wouldn't that be Great Art?" '[40] He continued to travel abroad. On his return from Cologne he had passed through Holland, which he found totally depressing apart from its museums. Early in 1878 he and Giuseppina paid a two-day visit to Monte Carlo and were half fascinated, half appalled by its Casino. Twice that year they went to Paris, the second time to view the International Exhibition. In December he was elected honorary member of Modena's Accademia di Scienze, Lettere e Arti. None of this seemed to lighten his mood. When at the turn of the year Faccio reported to him a highly successful performance of *Don Carlos* which he had conducted at La Scala a deep bitterness shows in his reply. He pointed out that you cannot measure the success of a production merely by the applause on the first night especially when, as seems to have been the case here, the wrong pieces were applauded.

> But all this doesn't matter. What matters is that attention should be paid to the present condition of our theatres. They are sick unto death and they must be kept alive at all costs. And you and Giulio who are omnipotent must take care not to fall into a trap with failures. Find operas good or bad (for the moment, I mean) just so long as they draw an audience. You will say that that is inartistic, that it befouls the altar; no matter, you can clean it afterwards.
>
> Meanwhile keeping alive is what matters. If the theatres close they won't open again. And if *Don Carlos* doesn't make money, put it aside and ask for *Le Roi de Lehore*, an opera of many virtues, an opera of the present without human interest, most suitable to this age of *verismo* in which there is no verity, an almost surefire opera especially if you have the composer who is a gentle creature, and not too difficult and will gain the sympathy of the chorus and orchestra and so of the public. Then he is a foreigner! . . . Hospitality! . . . the usual artistic banquet![41]

But already the tide of depression was on the turn.

[40] Ibid.
[41] DFV, pp. 182–5.

9

Indian summer

The Spring of 1879 saw the devastation by flood of many Italian provinces. Active as always in charitable causes, Verdi agreed to direct a performance in Milan of his *Requiem* for the benefit of the victims. Teresa Stolz and Maria Waldmann came out of retirement to give their services. The proceeds were gratifyingly large; and the composer himself was feted by the Milanese quite beyond his expectations. The following evening he and his wife dined privately with the Ricordis and Faccio. 'Quite by chance', the publisher recalled, 'I steered the conversation on to Shakespeare and Boito. At the mention of *Othello* I saw Verdi look at me with suspicion but with interest. He had certainly understood and had certainly reacted . . .'[1] Next day Faccio brought Boito to see Verdi with a libretto of *Otello* already sketched. Verdi was impressed but would not commit himself. 'Now write the poetry', he said; 'it will always do for me or for you or for someone else.' Indeed there were many difficulties to be surmounted before the 'chocolate project', as it came to be called, could be realised. To begin with Verdi took offence at an extract from the sculptor Dupré's memoirs which had appeared in Ricordi's house magazine quoting Rossini's remark that Verdi would be incapable of writing a comic opera. He instantly wrote to the publisher declaring that he had at last found the perfect subject for a comedy, but that, naturally, if he managed to set it, he would offer it to another firm. Ricordi replied diplomatically that he had not been responsible for that issue of the *Gazzetta Musicale di Milano* but that if he were he would certainly have added a footnote to the effect that Verdi had already shown himself a master of comedy in parts of *Un ballo in maschera* and *La forza del destino*; and the composer was mollified. But when at the end of August Ricordi offered to bring Boito to S.Agata to show him the completed libretto, Verdi drew

[1] G.Adami, *Giulio Ricordi, amico di musicisti* (Milan, 1933), pp. 92–3.

back. He could not offer an opinion good or bad in Boito's presence without in some way committing himself. The best course, he maintained, would be for Boito to send him the libretto by post so that he could peruse it at his leisure and then make up his mind whether or not to set it. For the next two months Boito worked at the libretto amid bouts of toothache and facial neuralgia spurred on by the relentless Ricordi. By November it was complete and in Verdi's hands. 'He must have liked it', Giuseppina wrote, 'for after reading it he bought it; but whether or not he would set it . . . there was no knowing'[2]. She was especially anxious that no one should bring the slightest pressure to bear. ('Let the river find its own way to sea', she wrote to Giulio Ricordi; 'it's in the open spaces that certain men are destined to meet and understand one another.')[3]

Meanwhile in September Verdi had received a visit from Vaucorbeil, the new director of the Paris Opéra, hoping to succeed where his predecessor, Halanzier, had failed in persuading the composer to direct a production of *Aida* in the city's only theatre which could do justice to its spectacle. Nor was he disappointed. The first performance took place on 22 March 1880, Verdi having extended the ballet music to its present definitive length; Gabrielle Krauss and a certain Victor Maurel were 'stupendous' (Verdi's words) in the roles of Aida and Amonasro respectively. The composer's triumph was acknowledged by his nomination as Grand Officer of the Foreign Legion. Two months earlier Vienna had made him an honorary member of the Gesellschaft der Musikfreunde; while on his return to Italy in April the King of Italy conferred on him the title of Cavaliere of the Great Cross. That same month his settings of the Pater Noster and Ave Maria in a translation attributed to Dante were given their première at a benefit concert at La Scala. He had certainly no reason to think himself forgotten.

That summer Boito returned from directing the English première of his *Mefistofele* at Covent Garden and together with Verdi set about revising details of the libretto. Their first concern was with the finale of Act III where Verdi had wanted a traditional concertato followed by a *coup de théâtre* with which to bring down the curtain. Not finding any help in Shakespeare, he suggested, rather naively,

[2] WMV, p. 476.
[3] Ibid.

that the ensemble of horror occasioned by Othello's striking of his wife should be interrupted by the news of a Turkish attack; Othello would 'shake himself like a lion' and lead his troops to victory while Desdemona and the women would pray for his safe return. He was not altogether convinced of this solution himself and wrote to Boito asking his advice. Boito first supplied the kind of text he had been asked for before proceeding with infinite tact to point out the flaws resulting from this break with Shakespeare's dramatic scheme. It would be like letting in fresh air to a room in which two people were slowly suffocating to death. The fatal atmosphere would have to be recreated from the start; but, he added, 'in opera eight bars can restore a sentiment to life; a rhythm can re-establish a character.'[4] If Verdi liked the verses he had sent, that meant that the musical setting was already present in his mind, and that his own criticisms would be silenced. But Verdi was persuaded of his error and no more was heard of the Turkish invasion.

However all this was the merest groundwork. Before setting to work on the composition of *Otello* Verdi evidently felt the need for a trial run with something much less ambitious – namely the revision and reclamation of *Simon Boccanegra*, which had never satisfied the high hopes he had had for its success. Boito was unenthusiastic. He had not read the play, but only Piave's libretto, which he found lame, like a table with uneven legs. But Verdi was firm; the characters were admittedly not altogether 'drawn to the life';[5] but there was still something to be made out of men such as Boccanegra and Jacopo Fiesco. He wanted an entirely new scene in the Council Chamber at which the Doge would read aloud a letter from Petrarch calling for unity amongst the Italian cities; Boito amplified it with the splendid address to the people of Genoa ('Plebe! Patrizi! Popolo') to which Verdi would respond with some of the finest music he had written to date. The revisions, not all of which involved Boito, were finished by February 1881; and the opera was first given in its new form on 24 March with Victor Maurel in the title role, Edouard De Reszke as Fiesco (despite Verdi's fears that his voice might be too bland for the implacable patrician) and Francesco Tamagno as Gabriele. Much acclaimed on its opening night, *Simon Boccanegra* proved scarcely

4 MCVB, pp. 1–2.
5 Ibid., pp. 12–13.

more popular in its revised than in its original form; only in recent years has it acquired the status of a connoisseur's piece.

Work was then resumed on *Otello*, but they had still not progressed beyond the finale of Act III, the coping stone of the opera's musical architecture. However, that Verdi had never ceased thinking about the subject is attested by his exchange of letters with the Neapolitan artist Domenico Morelli, whose notion of representing Iago with the face of an honest man greatly appealed to Verdi (*Iago* was at that stage to be the title of the opera). There were further meetings between librettist and composer during the autumn but no documents to tell us what was said. Then came another interruption. Late in 1881 Léon Escudier died in poverty, his firm bankrupt. Though there had been no reconciliation between them he had remained Verdi's publisher; and Verdi was characteristically generous to his family for old times' sake. Also there were his copyright interests to be looked after; therefore in May he set out for Paris to enter into negotiations with the firm of Choudens. While he was there, so Muzio tells us, he worked out a third version of *La forza del destino* to a French text by Nuitter and Du Locle, presumably the one prepared in 1865 with a performance at the Opéra in view. The new *Force du destin*, first given in Antwerp the following year, was a much more modest affair: a utility version designed for the lesser French-speaking theatres, with the number of scene-changes reduced, the situations simplified and the role of Fra Melitone eliminated. Although it was revived as recently as 1931 in Brussels, no trace of it remains except for rare copies of the vocal score published by Choudens.

It had been Verdi's intention for some years to reduce *Don Carlos* to more manageable proportions. This however could be done only with the help of Du Locle, who would otherwise have been in a position to prevent its performance in France, and the breach between him and Verdi had not yet been repaired. Nuitter now volunteered to approach him on Verdi's behalf; and so began a laborious three-way exchange of correspondence, from Rome or Capri, where Du Locle had now retired, through Paris to Busseto or Genoa and back again by the same route. Inevitably the revision took far longer than that of *Simon Boccanegra* and was not completed until March of the following year. Even then Verdi was in no great hurry to return to the 'chocolate project'; he wrote irritably to Boito regarding the offer of the French critic Blaze de Bury to make a

French translation of the new opera on the grounds that 'Un jour ou l'autre *Iago* existera.'[6] This he maintained was a surprising assumption; not even he himself knew whether it would ever exist. Meanwhile Verdi continued his by now habitual yearly round; Montecatini Spa at the height of the summer, S. Agata for late summer and autumn, Genoa for the winter months. Early in the year Wagner had died in Venice. 'Sad, sad, sad', Verdi wrote to Giulio Ricordi, '. . . A great personality has vanished! A name that has left a most powerful mark in the History of Art.'[7] But he continued to fulminate against the pernicious influence of all German art on native Italians. Meanwhile the New Year passed without any evidence of composition on Verdi's part, though Ricordi sent his usual reminder in the form of a Christmas cake surmounted by a chocolate figurine.

In January 1884 Faccio conducted the new *Don Carlos* at La Scala in an appropriately revised Italian translation by Angelo Zanardini. To his old friend Arrivabene, who asked him whether he had not had qualms about sacrificing the Fontainebleau act, Verdi retorted that there would always be people who, now that it had been cut, would want it restored even if they had disliked it previously; for himself he considered that the four-act version was an improvement upon the old: it had more concision, more 'sinew'.[8] None the less the *Don Carlos* in five acts without ballet, first performed in Modena in 1886 could hardly have come into being without his sanction. With the Fontainebleau act re-instated and most of the 1884 revisions retained, this is the form in which the opera is mostly given to-day. An unequivocally happy outcome of the revision was Verdi's reconciliation with Du Locle. Though they would never meet again, they now corresponded amicably; and Du Locle would collaborate with Boito on the French translation of *Otello*.

At last in mid-March the composition of *Otello* began, only to run into an obstacle of a different and more serious kind. Boito had gone to Naples for a revival of *Mefistofele* at the San Carlo theatre. At a dinner given in his honour he mentioned in the course of his

---

[6] Ibid., p. 65.
[7] LCC, p. 323.
[8] AVI, pp. 305–6.

speech the new Shakespearean libretto as a project on which he had embarked reluctantly, but which now he would have been only too glad to be able to set to music himself. This was reported in the local press as implying that Boito regretted having sold it to Verdi. It never occurred to Boito that Verdi would have read the report; nor did he himself attach the slightest significance to it. He said nothing about it therefore when he visited S.Agata shortly afterwards. But Verdi had indeed read it and could not understand Boito's failure to provide an explanation. Accordingly he wrote not to Boito himself but to Faccio as Boito's oldest friend, offering to return the libretto without payment 'without a shadow of resentment or rancour of any kind'.[9] Boito was not to receive the message until three weeks later when he and Faccio met in Turin, where Faccio was rehearsing his cantata for the International Exhibition. He at once wrote to Verdi a long letter of apology and explanation. 'You alone can set *Otello* to music', he insisted. 'If I have been able to divine the inherent, powerful musicality of the Shakespearean tragedy, which at first I did not feel and if I have been able to demonstrate it in fact with my libretto, that is because I put myself at the view point of Verdian art . . .'[10] In any case he could not have considered setting any subject other than *Nerone* with which he had been engrossed for the last eight years and which he might or might not finish. Verdi replied civilly enough that he might or might not finish *Otello*; but for the moment he felt unable to continue. Boito reacted by sending a new and definitive version of Iago's Credo, written 'for my own comfort and personal satisfaction, because I felt the need to do so. You can interpret this as you like – childishness, sentimentality or superstition – it doesn't matter. All I ask is that you do not reply, even to say "thank you".'[11] But reply Verdi did, not with a 'thank you' (as Boito did not wish it) but a 'well-done'. 'Most beautiful this Credo; very powerful and wholly Shakespearean.' But he suggested that *Otello* be left in peace for a while 'for he too is on edge as we are – you perhaps more than I'.[12] So the spring and summer passed away in inactivity apart from a visit to the Turin Exhibition. In May there occurred a small portent – the

[9] WMV, p. 489.
[10] MCVB, pp. 69–73.
[11] Ibid., pp. 74–6.
[12] Ibid., p. 76.

première at the Teatro dal Verme Milan of a one-act opera *Le Villi* (*Le willis* at it was then called) by a twenty-six-year-old composer, Giacomo Puccini. It had been submitted for a competition for one-act operas organised by the publisher Edoardo Sonzogno, but the judges had found the score illegible and the prize was awarded elsewhere. Boito was among those who had heard Puccini play it on the piano and were sufficiently impressed to promote a performance. 'I have heard the composer Puccini highly spoken of', Verdi wrote to Arrivabene. 'He follows the modern trends, which is natural, but he keeps to melody which is neither ancient nor modern. However the symphonic vein appears to predominate in him. No harm in that, but one needs to tread carefully here. Opera is opera and symphony symphony and I don't think it's a good thing to put a symphonic piece into an opera merely to put the orchestra through its paces.'[13] Such is the only reference in Verdi's entire correspondence to his destined 'successor'. What he thought of Puccini's music once he had heard it we may never know.

In September Boito stayed three days at S.Agata with his friend the poet and playwright Giuseppe Giacosa; then on 9 December came the news from Genoa: 'It seems impossible, and yet it's true!! I am busy. I'm writing!!'[14] After a hiatus of eight months *Otello* was at last going forward, to be interrupted only by the customary summer visits to the spas. By October Verdi could announce that Act IV was complete except for the scoring, but as usual the end was still a good way off. Not until March 1886 did the Act I love duet reach its final shape; while May brought the inspiration for Otello's famous entrance 'Esultate!' There remained the problem of casting. In March Verdi left for Paris to engage Maurel as Iago, in accordance with an understanding that had existed between them since Maurel's triumph as the Doge in the revised *Simon Boccanegra*. Tamagno was clearly indicated for Otello; Desdemona was less easily decided upon. Giulio Ricordi was all for Gemma Bellincioni, a noted Violetta of the time and the first to portray the consumptive heroine in a crinoline. Verdi retorted that even a nobody could succeed in *La traviata*, whereas Desdemona must have the capacity to represent ideal womanhood (he had already received reports from Boito on

[13] AVI, pp. 311–15.
[14] MCVB, pp. 78–9.

Bellincioni's vocal shortcomings). He finally agreed with some misgiving to the choice of Romilda Pantaleone. True, she was better suited to 'nervy' parts but Faccio, who would conduct, was in love with her and doubtless she would respond to coaching. The final touches to the score were administered in mid-December 1886, after which, 'Poor *Otello*!', Verdi wrote. 'He won't come back here anymore.'[15] 'The moor will come no more to knock on the door of the Palazzo Doria', Boito replied, 'but you will go to meet the Moor at La Scala. *Otello* exists. The great dream has come true.'[16]

The première on 5 February 1887 was an international occasion, attended by correspondents from all over the world. Joseph Bennett of the *Daily Telegraph* tells how the first night was constantly being postponed because of some detail with which Verdi was not satisfied (of all composers that he had known, none, he maintained, was so exigent regarding the performance of his own works). Fresh honours were showered on him – the Great Cross of the Order of SS Maurizio and Lazzaro, the Freedom of the City of Milan – and a sum of money sufficient to enable him to proceed with certain charitable projects: the building of a hospital at Villanova, begun in 1882, which would spare the sick of his neighbourhood a long journey to Piacenza, and the purchase of a site in Milan for a musicians' rest-home, of which Camillo Boito, Arrigo's brother, would be the architect.

In September 1888 Tito Ricordi died; the widow Lucca, after prolonged negotiation, sold out to Giulio Ricordi, so ending a war which had lasted more than half a century. Ricordi now found himself the proprietor of Wagner's Italian rights. That same year saw the first performance of *Tristan und Isolde* in Italian at Bologna conducted by Giuseppe Martucci. *Die Meistersinger* would come to La Scala the following year. The musical climate in Italy was changing ever more in the direction which Verdi had always deplored. But if his friends were dying around him – Andrea Maffei in 1885, Clarina and Arrivabene in 1886 to be followed by Muzio and Piroli in 1890 – he himself was being rejuvenated by the influence of Boito and Giulio Ricordi. He was also becoming infected with Boito's love of conundrums. So when in August 1888 a certain professor Crecentini published in the *Gazzetta Musicale di Milano* an 'enigmatic

---

[15] Ibid., p. 118.
[16] Ibid., p. 119.

scale' inviting readers to try their hand at a harmonisation, Verdi decided to enter the lists – with a full-scale polyphonic composition to the text of the Ave Maria ('. . . when we're old we become boys again').[17] 'An Ave Maria!', he added, 'It will be my fourth! Perhaps I shall be beatified by the Holy Father.' Boito retorted that he would need to write a good many more Ave Marias to be excused Iago's Credo. To which Verdi, 'It's you! You're the main culprit who needs to be pardoned for that Credo. Now you can do no less than set to music a Catholic Credo in four parts à la Palestrina – that is after finishing him whom I dare not name . . .'[18] So the first of the Four Sacred Pieces came into being, though Verdi never intended it to be given along with the other three. He regarded it as a 'sciarada', a 'rebus' and with difficulty was persuaded to allow it to be performed privately by the students of Parma Conservatoire. That it exists in two versions (one in manuscript in Parma, the other published by Ricordi) was due to the fact that Verdi had temporarily mislaid his original solution.

He was unable to prevent a revival of *Oberto* at La Scala fifty years after its première (how could a modern audience put up with its two long acts? he wondered) and he declined to attend it himself. Meanwhile a far more important idea was starting to burgeon in his brain, as we first hear from a letter to Boito from Montecatini in July. 'Excellent! Excellent! Before reading your sketch I wanted to re-read the *Merry Wives*, the two parts of *Henry IV* and *Henry V*, and I can only repeat excellent, for one could not do it better than you have done.'[19] He had slight reservations about the last act; no matter; a dream was once more taking on flesh and blood. But the next day qualms arose.

> In outlining *Falstaff* did you never consider the extreme number of my years? I know you will reply exaggerating the state of my health, which is good, excellent, robust . . . So be it but in spite of that you must agree that I could be accused of being very rash in taking on his work! Suppose I couldn't stand the strain and was unable to finish it? You would then have wasted your time . . . Have you a sound argument to oppose to mine? . . . if you can find

[17] Ibid., p. 138.
[18] Ibid., pp. 139–40.
[19] Ibid., p. 142.

one for me and I some way of throwing off ten years or so, then . . . what fun to be able to say to the public: Here we are again!! Roll up![20]

And of course Boito was not short of arguments. He was never aware of Verdi's age when working with him; and comedy would not exhaust the composer as a tragedy might, since (and he quoted from Ugo Foscolo's translation of Lawrence Sterne's *A Sentimental Journey*) 'a smile adds a thread to life's tapestry'.[21] 'We'll write this *Falstaff* then', Verdi replied '. . . I too', he added, 'wish to preserve the deepest secrecy . . . But wait . . . Peppina knew it, I believe before we did! Be sure, however, she will keep the secret: when women have this quality they have it in greater measure than we.'[22] Boito then enlarged upon his ideas for the dramatic treatment. There were to be no love duets. The love between Nannetta and Fenton 'must appear suddenly at very frequent intervals . . . I should like, as one sprinkles sugar on a cake, to sprinkle the whole comedy with that merry love, without concentrating it at any one point.[23] Verdi meanwhile, doubt- less with the final scene of *Don Giovanni* in mind, was sketching fugues. ('Yes sir; a fugue . . . and a *comic fugue* which would fit in with *Falstaff*.) But this was mere preliminary skirmishing, a flexing of musical muscles. Boito completed the first two acts in November and brought them to S.Agata. The third was ready by March 1890.

Meanwhile the Carnival season at La Scala had opened on 26 December with the first Italian performance of *Die Meistersinger*. Earlier Puccini had accompanied the conductor Faccio to Bayreuth to decide on the necessary cuts – much to the indignation of the Wagnerian Catalani whom the absorption of Lucca by Ricordi had left out in the cold. ('Not all of us have the good fortune to be able to travel there at a publisher's expense, like Puccini, armed with a pair of scissors and entrusted with cutting the score so that it fits the good Milanese like a suit . . .')[24] The conductor's health was clearly break- ing down and his behaviour becoming increasingly erratic. Having

[20] Ibid., p. 143.
[21] Ibid., pp. 145–7.
[22] Ibid., p. 147.
[23] Ibid., pp. 152–3.
[24] Letter to G. Depanis, 20.8.1889, *Catalani: Lettere*, ed. C. Gatti (Milan, 1946), pp. 100–1.

conducted the first act of *Die Meistersinger* he imagined that the opera was over and had to be brought back to the theatre to complete the performance. Suspecting over-work, Verdi and Boito had tried to persuade him to undertake the directorship of the Conservatory of Parma left vacant by the death of Bottesini. But by the time he yielded, it was too late. His brain was now seriously affected. 'One of the causes', wrote Boito ominously, 'is a disease of the blood which is cured with injections of mercury.'[25] In March he went to Krafft-Ebbing's clinic in Graz which specialised in maladies of the brain; but Krafft Ebbing refused to accept the case. Faccio returned to Italy to die a year later at an asylum in Monza. Boito agreed to fill the post at Parma in order to draw the salary necessary for Faccio's support. Such hours as he could spare he spent at the invalid's bedside; but he continued with *Falstaff* and urged Verdi to do the same. ('This world is full of sorrows; our friend's condition grows steadily worse . . . Let us try to keep our health, dear Maestro, and forget life in working.')[26]

It is not easy to chart the progress of *Falstaff*, partly because Verdi gave different accounts of it to different people. To Boito he claimed to have written the entire first act without altering a line of the poetry by 17 March 1890 and to have sketched the third act and part of the second by October. To the journalist Eugenio Checchi two months later he declared that he had written hardly a note of the music; to Ricordi in the New Year he said that he had sketched about half the opera and would probably not finish it within the following year. There was a burst of activity in June 1891. 'Big Belly is going crazy', he wrote to Boito, 'There are days when he doesn't move but sleeps and is in a bad humour. At other times he shouts, runs, jumps and causes a devil of a rumpus . . .'[27] 'Three cheers!' Boito replied, 'Let him go, let him run; if he breaks all the windows in your house it doesn't matter; you can always replace them.'[28] In September Verdi broke off the third act to begin scoring the first 'because I'm afraid of foregetting some passages and instrumental combinations.'[29] The first act was in score by April 1892 and the whole opera complete by September. Only then was he prepared to discuss the staging. Deter-

[25] MCVB, pp. 161–2.
[26] Ibid., pp. 175–6.
[27] Ibid., pp. 190.
[28] Ibid., p. 191.
[29] Ibid., p. 196.

mined not to be hurried, and possibly fearful of not being able to finish the work to his own satisfaction, he had been at pains to insist that he was writing *Falstaff* merely as a pastime.

Nor had he allowed it to restrict his other activities. At some point during those years he managed to complete a setting of lines from the last Canto of Dante's Paradiso, the *Laudi alla Vergine Maria*, which forms the third of the *Quattro pezzi sacri*. He continued to take an interest in the latest musical events and developments. That he attended *Die Meistersinger* at La Scala in 1890 can hardly be doubted; the evidence lies in the end of the first act of *Falstaff*. This was the year of *Cavalleria Rusticana* and the explosion of *verismo*. Verdi received Mascagni cordially, though as usual refused to discuss his music. However Giulio Ricordi reported that after playing through the score of the opera the old man had remarked 'evidently the tradition of Italian melody is not yet exhausted' – a remark which reached the newspapers as 'Now that I have heard *Cavalleria Rusticana* I can die happy.'[30] Verdi was much less impressed by *L'amico Fritz*. ('I started reading it but soon got tired of all those dissonances, false relations, interrupted cadences and so on, and all those changes of tempo at almost every bar.')[31] In general he seems to have found the harmonic pallette of the 'giovane scuola' far too rich in relation to the drama. In Bruneau's *La rêve* he longed for the vent-hole of a consonance – like Falstaff in the buck-basket.[32]

Towards Catalani he was more tolerant: 'At least he knows how to write even if he has an exaggerated idea of the orchestra's importance.'[33] Thus to Giulio Ricordi after the success of *La Wally* at La Scala early in 1892, so giving the lie to those three letters to Perosio hostile to Catalani which Frank Walker demonstrated con-clusively to be forgeries yet which continue to appear in modern Italian biographies. After two years of total neglect Ricordi had suddenly taken an interest in *Loreley*, the revised version of *Elda* and had seen his faith in it justified. It was conducted with brilliant success by Toscanini in Genoa in 1892; and Catalani took the opportunity of paying a call on Verdi who 'received me with the utmost cordiality . . . He mentioned your article in the *Gazzetta*

[30] CIIV, pp. 303–4.
[31] AGV, IV, pp. 426–7.
[32] MCVB, pp. 191–2.
[33] AGV, IV, p. 428.

Musicale, saying that "Nothing is truer than what Depanis writes: that in art Wagner's name is synonymous with artistic tyranny." '[34]

In April Verdi was in Milan to conduct the prayer from *Mosè in Egitto* at La Scala at centenary celebrations of Rossini's birth. On his return to Genoa he found Bülow's celebrated letter of recantation. The man who had publicly sneered at the *Requiem* without even taking the trouble to listen to it now declared himself an enthusiast for all things Verdian.

> I have begun by studying your latest works: *Aida, Otello* and the *Requiem* of which a recent rather poor performance moved me to tears; I have studied them not only according to the letter which kills, but also the spirit which gives life. And so, illustrious Maestro, I now admire you and love you. Will you forgive me, will you avail yourself of the sovereign's privilege of granting a pardon? However that may be . . . I feel the necessity of confessing my sin if only to set an example to our lesser, erring brothers; and faithful to the Prussian motto Suum cuique I cry with all my heart Long live Verdi, the Wagner of our dear allies![35]

Verdi replied with a touch of irony that there was no shadow of sin in Bülow – indeed that he might have been right the first time. Nevertheless he was grateful for such a tribute, which showed that the really great artists could judge without prejudice as regards school or country. He then returned to his favourite theme: that composers should be true to their nationality. 'How lucky you are still the sons of Bach! And we? We too as sons of Palestrina will one day have a school which will be great – and our own? At present it is a mongrel affair . . .'[36]

The end of the year was taken up with anxious preparation for the première of the new opera. Maurel was clearly destined for the title role though his exorbitant claims nearly caused Verdi to cancel the opera altogether. (Nothing less than a visit from Mme Maurel was deemed sufficient to avert this calamity.) An excellent Mistress Quickly in Giuseppina Pasqua led Verdi to expand the role for her benefit. It is interesting to note that most of the original cast were to make their names chiefly as exponents of *verismo*. Antonio Pini

[34] Letter to G. Depanis, 17.2.1892, *Lettere* p. 129.
[35] LCC, pp. 375–6.
[36] Ibid., p. 375.

Corsi (Ford) created Schaunard in *La Bohème*. The Nannetta and Fenton, Adelina Stehle and Edoardo Garbin were to be a favourite Rodolfo and Mimì. Maurel himself was fresh from his triumph as Tonio in *Pagliacci*. Verdi attached especial importance to the casting of Alice. 'She must have a touch of the devil in her. . . . It is she who stirs the polenta';[37] eventually he settled for Emma Zilli whose shattering tremolo (as recorded by Stanford and others) was less apparent to one in his eightieth year. The première took place on 9 February 1893. Verdi conducted the first performance then handed over the baton to Edoardo Mascheroni. The King and Queen of Italy, unable to be present, sent telegrams; the prime minister, Francesco Crispi, sent a signed portrait of himself. Later that night Verdi's hotel was besieged by wellwishers. 'The public has been kind to *Falstaff*', Verdi remarked, 'as it was towards *Otello*.'[38] He had no illusions that either would prove popular in the manner of *Il trovatore*.

A still greater triumph awaited him in Rome three months later, where at the Teatro Costanzi *Falstaff* was given with notable modifications in what is, essentially, its definitive form. On his arrival at the railway station the crowd of well-wishers was so importunate that he was obliged to take refuge in a tool-shed (a plaque commemorating the event is to be found in the Rome Museum). It was from the royal box, in the presence of King Umberto and Queen Margherita, that Verdi, now a freeman of the City of Rome, acknowledged the tumultuous applause. The summit of his public career had finally been attained.

[37] AGV, IV, pp. 442–3.
[38] Ibid., p. 476.

10

The last years

So fresh, so apparently effortless had been the miracle of *Falstaff* that Boito had little doubt that it could be repeated. His biographer, Nardi, relates an anecdote to the effect that one day in the company of some friends Boito approached Verdi and said, 'Now dear Maestro, we must set to work on *King Lear*', only to see a look of desperate alarm on Giuseppina's face. Later she drew him aside: 'For Heaven's sake, Boito! Verdi is too old, too tired.'[1] That was the end of that.

Not, however, of their collaboration. There were the French premières of *Otello* and *Falstaff* to look forward to, both planned for the following year. Meantime an incident occurred which might well have ended Boito's days prematurely. When Ricordi took over the firm of Lucca in 1888 he was conscious of having to face a far more dangerous rival in Edoardo Sonzogno. Like Lucca, Sonzogno had specialised in foreign works, his greatest asset to-date being *Carmen*, which he rightly regarded as a pointer to an operatic style destined to reflect the contemporary literary fashion for Zola-esque naturalism. After *Cavalleria Rusticana* had won the award instituted by Sonzogno himself a host of 'veristic' composers flocked to his banner – Leoncavallo, Giordano, Cilea – who together with Mascagni would almost monopolise the scene throughout the 1890s. Indeed Sonzogno succeeded in capturing Ricordi's stronghold, La Scala, and holding it for two years, during which not a single Ricordi opera was produced there. In 1893 he had bought the rights of Frederick Cowen's *Signa*. Having stipulated three performances, Sonzogno decided to cancel the second two; when Cowen held him to the terms of their contract, he doubled the prices of admission for the second performances and adduced the meagre takings as his reason for cancelling the third. Informed of this Boito wrote to Cowen expressing the hope that he

---

[1] P. Nardi, *Vita di Arrigo Boito* (Milan, 1942), p. 594.

would not judge Italians by the standards of Sonzogno. This letter Cowen had published in the *Daily Telegraph*; Sonzogno retorted by calling Boito a coward in print. The duel was not yet obsolete in Europe; accordingly Boito sent a pair of seconds to call on the offending editor. Sonzogno took up the challenge; and a time and place was fixed. All this was recounted by Giacosa to Verdi, who sent an urgent telegram to Boito begging him not to keep the appointment. Eventually through the good offices of friends of both parties the duel was averted.

It had been proposed that *Otello* and *Falstaff* should run concurrently during the Spring, one at the Opéra, the other at the Opéra Comique; but Verdi objected and succeeded in getting *Otello* postponed to the autumn. Rehearsals for *Falstaff* began in April. Paul Solanges, Boito's collaborator on the French translation, reported that musically all was going well but that the academic traditions of the Opéra Comique were stifling the comedy; the only remedy for this would be Verdi's presence. Reluctantly Verdi agreed to go. ('I just wonder what am I supposed to do in Paris; exhibit myself like the "ours Martin" . . . And is that worthy of a man of 80?'.)[2] But he had to admit that the performance of 18 April was a great success. It had included the last addition of any importance to the score – a snatch of dialogue preceding Nannetta's solo in Act III. Boito duly translated the words into Italian and they appear in every subsequent edition in the opera.

During the composition of *Otello* Verdi had refused to countenance the idea of a ballet for the French version. Now he was disposed to fall in with the age-old traditions of the Opéra; but where would he place it? Who would it be danced by? Originally, it seems, Boito had suggested that it should occur during the islanders' homage to Desdemona in Act II. Finally Verdi opted for the arrival of the Venetian ambassador, in whose honour the dances would naturally be given. By 1890 the cosmopolitan idiom of *Les vêpres siciliennes* would no longer do; genuine local colour was required. Accordingly from the spa at Montecatini Verdi wrote to Ricordi for specimens of Greek, Turkish and Venetian folk music to serve as models. As usual, however, he never made use of them but invented his own folk music. ('I've found a Greek song written 5,000 years B.C. if the world didn't

[2] AGV, IV, p. 540.

yet exist, so much the worse for the world . . .'.)[3] He did however make use of a 'cry of the Muezzin' taken from Félicien David's *Le Désert*, presumably convinced of its ethnic authenticity. He also re-wrote in shorter form the concertato which follows, partly to keep up the dramatic situation and partly to throw Iago's lines into stronger relief.

In September Verdi travelled to Paris for the last time, where on his eighty-first birthday he witnessed the French première of *Otello*. During one of the intervals the French President came to his box to tell him that he had been awarded the Grand Cross of the Légion d'Honneur. Ten days later he returned to Genoa having attended a memorial service for Gounod and been the guest of honour at a State Banquet in the Elysée Palace. His last composition of that year was a short setting of *Pietà Signor*, the words adapted by Boito from the *De profundis* published in the magazine *Fata Morgana* for the benefit of victims from the recent Sicilian earthquakes.

The early months of 1895 saw the composer in Milan discussing with Camillo Boito the plans for the musicians rest home. It was to be a two-story building designed to accommodate a hundred musicians – sixty men and forty women – who had reached the age of sixty-five and found themselves in a state of poverty. Camillo Boito's ideas that they should be housed in dormitories was rejected by Verdi in favour of double rooms so that couples could help each other during the night. Anything that smacked of institutionalism was scouted; therefore no uniforms. But by an uncharacteristic stroke of vanity Verdi suggested that the men be encouraged to dress like himself – large, wide-brimmed hat and flowing necktie. Construction began the following year on what Verdi would later describe as the favourite of all his works, musical or otherwise.[4]

But he continued to take an interest in the progress of *Falstaff* around the world. If mildly piqued at the refusal of the Berliners to encore 'Quando ero paggio', as had become the tradition in Italy, he can only have been gratified to receive a score of a first opera by an unknown young German by way of homage '. . . unable to find words to describe the extraordinary beauty of *Falstaff* or to express my gratitude for this re-birth of the intellect, I beg Your Honour to

[3] Ibid., pp. 551–2.
[4] TGV, p. 213.

receive this score.'[5] His humble suggestion that they might meet was not followed up by Verdi who, however, replied civilly enough to the composer and went so far as to write to Ricordi asking whether one Richard Strauss of Munich, composer of *Guntram*, was the same as the Waltz-King. His opinion of *Guntram* we may never know; but for Richard Strauss *Falstaff* remained an undying masterpiece, his own favourite Italian opera.

Verdi's operatic career was now over; but he could never keep from composing. Every man has his destiny, he once wrote to the conductor Mascheroni. 'As for me, with my tongue hanging out like a mad dog, I'm fated to work till my last gasp.'[6] This time the project under consideration was a setting of the *Te Deum* 'a thanksgiving not on my part but on the part of the public who is now set free after so many years from having to hear new operas of mine'.[7] But though he pored over fragments of plainchant he seems to have done little work on it that year. In the autumn he was concerning himself with the affairs of the Parma Conservatory, now running smoothly under the excellent directorship of Gallignani, like Verdi, a fervent admirer of Palestrina, but constantly threatened with bureaucratic interference. In December Giulio Ricordi, ousted from La Scala, mounted a first-class revival of *Falstaff* at the Dal Verme under Leopoldo Mugnone. Among the audience was the young Ermanno Wolf-Ferrari recently returned from his studies in Germany. The performance inspired him to write a set of variations for piano on the Minuet from Act III, which, with Boito's encouragement he sent to Verdi. Indeed, to find the inspiration behind ninety per cent of Wolf-Ferrari's output one need look no farther than Verdi's comic masterpiece.

But not even the success of *Falstaff* could compensate Ricordi for the total exclusion of his operas from La Scala. He even begged Verdi to write to the prime minister, Crispi, on his behalf. But this Verdi refused to do. Not only would it have no effect; he himself was totally out of sympathy with Crispi's conduct of Italy's affairs. A Mazzinian liberal at heart, he disapproved of Crispi's colonial adventures in Eritrea. ('Unfortunately we too are playing the tyrant

[5] AGV, IV, p. 567.
[6] LCC, pp. 717–18.
[7] AGV, IV, p. 572–3.

in Africa; we are wrong and we shall pay for it.')[8] The crushing defeat at Adua seemed to him a just recompense. He hoped something of the sort would befall the English in India.

In February 1896 he decided to consult Boito as to the form and character of his new *Te Deum*. They agreed it should not try to ape an archaic style; but where was the model for a modern *Te Deum*? Boito mentioned a certain Abbé Perosi; but it was Verdi whose subsequent researches led him to the archives of S.Antonio at Padua, where he found listed a Te Deum by the eighteenth century composer Padre Vallotti. His letter to the director of music and archivist, Giovanni Tebaldini, asking for his assistance includes an interesting observation:

> I know several of the old Te Deums and I've heard a few modern ones and I've never been convinced by the way this canticle has been interpreted – quite apart from the value of the music. It is usually sung during grand, solemn and noisy ceremonies for a victory or a coronation etc. The opening lends itself to that since Heaven and Earth are rejoicing, Sanctus Sanctus Deus Sabaoth. But towards the middle the tone and colour change: 'Te ad liberandum . . .' This is Christ is born of the Virgin and opens to humanity the 'Regna coelorum'. Humanity believes in the Judex Venturus, invokes Him in the Salvum fac and ends with a prayer, 'Dignare Domine die isto', which is moving, melancholy and sad even to the point of terror.[9]

In the event the Vallotti setting proved too difficult to trace; Tebaldini offered others by Victoria and Purcell; but once more Verdi decided to proceed without a model. His setting was completed that summer, to be followed by the *Stabat Mater*. All four sacred pieces were consigned to the publisher in June 1897.

In January came a warning. One day Giuseppina found him lying in bed seemingly paralysed and unable to speak. While she and Maria Carrara were anxiously debating whether or not to call a doctor, Verdi managed to indicate that he wanted pen and paper. In a shaky scrawl he wrote 'Coffee' which was straightaway brought to him; within a few days he had completely recovered. The death which occurred later that year was not his but Giuseppina's. For

[8] CIIV, p. 341.
[9] AGV, IV, pp. 588–9.

some time she had been crippled with arthritis; and her appearance at Montecatini that year had made a strong contrast with that of her husband – he alert and erect, she unable to walk without help. In November a severe bronchitis set in; a few days later she was dead. The family lawyer Amilcare Martinelli recalled seeing Verdi standing at the piano, his head bowed, his cheeks flushed, the picture of silent grief. The funeral service was held in Busseto Cathedral and the body was then transported to a cemetery in Milan. Verdi spent lonely weeks at S.Agata. 'Great sorrow', he wrote to a friend, 'does not demand great expression; it asks for silence, isolation, I would even say the torture of reflection.'[10]

However, he had a welcome Christmas visitor in Boito. The poet had already persuaded Verdi to allow three of the *Four sacred pieces* to be performed in Paris in Holy Week 1898; and the New Year found Verdi in Milan supervising their publication. He fully intended to travel to Paris for the event, but the doctors advised him against it. Accordingly he sent Boito in his place, writing him copious letters with the most detailed instructions as to the musical interpretation. A telegram from Boito assured him of the concert's complete success. 'To show you my gratitude', he replied, 'I could offer you some trifle or other, but what would be the point? It would be embarrassing for me and useless to you. Permit me therefore when you are back from Paris to clasp your hand here. And for this handclasp you will say not a word, not even "thank you".' [11]

Only a month later the same three pieces were due to be performed at the International Exhibition at Turin under the baton of Toscanini whose career had been linked with Verdi almost from the start. In 1887 he had played the second solo cello in the opening of the *Otello* love duet; and it was with *Aida*, deputising at short notice, that he achieved his first triumph as a conductor at the Teatro Colòn, Rio de Janeiro, the year before. While studying the score of the *Te Deum* he began to feel strongly that at a certain point a slowing down of the tempo was required; but how could he be justified in applying it if Verdi himself, known for insistence on a strict adherence to the markings of the score, had not given his sanction? Eventually he asked the Festival director to write to Verdi on his

[10] MVLT, p. 470.
[11] MCVB, pp. 264–5.

behalf requesting permission to come and discuss the matter. The reply was encouraging: 'Maestro Toscanini and Maestro Venturi (the chorus master) may come when they wish. I am always at home after mid-day.'[12] When they arrived Toscanini had hoped that Verdi would play the *Te Deum* at the piano; but the old man insisted that Toscanini play it himself. 'Well done', he said when Toscanini had finished, having dared to make the rallentando, 'a bad musician would have exaggerated it; but if one is a good musician, one feels it and plays it just as you have done without the necessity of having it written down.'[13] It is a good story and a salutary reminder that all agogic instructions are only relative. Only the fact that Depanis, who was present, makes no mention of it raises the faintest doubts of its authenticity, since this is just the kind of anecdote of which his book is full. Moreover, Toscanini, who gained an unjustified reputation for strict fidelity to every composer's intention, would have every reason to invent such a tale and eventually come to believe it himself.

Native resilience seems to have restored Verdi to something like his old self. 'He plays the piano, eats as he pleases, walks, argues with youthful vivacity. He is as merry as a lark.'[14] Thus Boito of the 85-year-old composer. But his creative days were over. When in 1900 King Umberto was assassinated by an anarchist, he wished to set the poem written by Queen Margherita in her husband's memory. A few sketches for it exist but nothing more.

He spent more and more time in Milan at the Albergo Milano within easy reach of his friends – Boito, Giulio Ricordi, Teresa Stolz. A photograph preserved in the Milan Conservatory and clearly taken without his knowledge shows an erect figure presbyopically perusing a newspaper as he walks along the street in front of La Scala. That the administration of his estates at S.Agata had deteriorated need not surprise. The evidence was discovered recently among the municipal archives of Parma by the journalist Maurizio Chierici, author of the semi-fictional novel *Un delitto a Casa Verdi*, built round an incident which actually occurred: the accidental shooting of a maidservant by Fifao's son, Angelo. A lawyer sent from Rome to investigate the unrest among the peasantry in 1898 heard tales of

[12] H. Sachs, *Toscanini* (London, 1978), p. 58 ff.
[13] Ibid.
[14] WMV, p. 508.

Verdi, the harsh landlord, whose 'fattori' gave flour and meal to his tenants that made even the pigs vomit. But it is unthinkable that if Verdi was aware of this he would not have put a stop to it – witness his letter of ten years earlier regarding the hospital at Villanova:

> I think it right to warn you that I have had bad reports about the hospital . . . and I hope and pray they are not true. Here is what they are saying:
>   1. That the food is meagre.
>   2. The wine even more so (though the cellar is well stocked).
>   3. That the milk costs more than it is worth and that it is not whole milk.
>   4. That the oil is of the commonest kind, with a bad effect on both food and lighting.
>   5. That they wanted to buy half-spoiled rice and coarse, dark, native spaghetti.
>   6. That funeral expenses are charged even to persons of absolutely no means.
>   7. Many more things which for the sake of brevity I omit.
> I am far away and can say nothing to this . . . but in any case these reports distress me extremely and make me wonder if I can achieve the purpose for which I devoted part of my fortune in endowing this charitable foundation.[15]

Certainly Verdi was authoritarian, sometimes unreasonably so, as Giuseppina's diary makes clear; but the patriarch of S.Agata and the benefactor of his region would not knowingly stint his dependants. On the other hand it was probably not difficult to cheat an 85-year-old landlord who spent a large part of the year away from home.

Various people came to visit him in Milan during those last years – journalists, writers, musicians. All found him keenly interested in the musical life around him though he could rarely be prevailed upon to pronounce on a particular work. He approved of the fact that operas were much shorter than they used to be and that there was no longer any need to think up some chorus or other to fill out the scene (indeed liberation from 'grandeur' had been one of the positive achievements of the 'veristi').

When Toscanini visited him on 20 January 1901 he was eager for news of Mascagni's *Le maschere*, of which his guest had given the

---

[15] LCC, p. 350.

Milan première – one, incidentally, of seven which had been planned to be given simultaneously in different cities throughout the peninsula. Did Tartaglia sing with a stutter he wanted to know. 'Yes', Toscanini replied. 'In fact', Verdi replied, 'stutterers rarely stutter when they sing.' The piece that had been most successful had been the pavane. 'A pavane? What is that?' Verdi asked, 'then added hurriedly, 'Yes of course, I know, I know.'[16] But Toscanini noticed with sadness that the old man was somewhat confused. The next day, while dressing, he had a stroke. Six days later, at 3 a.m. on 27 January, he died.

'He died magnificently', Boito wrote to Bellaigue,

> like a fighter, redoubtable and mute . . . With his head bent, his eyebrows set, he seemed to measure with half-shut eyes an unknown and formidable adversary . . . Thus he put up a heroic resistance. The breathing of his great chest sustained him for four days and three nights; on the fourth night the sound of his breathing still filled the room; but what a struggle, poor maestro! How magnificently he fought up to the last moment! In the course of my life I have lost persons whom I idolized, when grief was stronger than resignation. But I have never experienced such a feeling of hate against death, such loathing for its mysterious, blind, stupid, triumphant infamous power![17]

Giuseppina's coffin was removed from the cemetery in Milan and placed beside that of her husband in a memorial ground in the Casa di Riposo. Her will had concluded with these words: 'Now, addio, my Verdi. As we were united in life, may God rejoin our spirits in Heaven.' Whether in their last years together she had converted Verdi to the faith in which she was to die we may never know. Boito left the matter open.

> He gave the example of Christian faith by the moving beauty of his religious works, by the observance of rites (you must recall his fine head bowed in the chapel of S.Agata), by his homage to Manzoni, by the ordering of his funeral, found in his will; *one priest, one candle, one cross*. He knew that faith is the sustenance of the heart. To the workers in the fields, to the unhappy, to the afflicted around him, he offered himself as example, without ostentation, humbly, severely to be useful to their consciences.

[16] Sachs, p. 76.
[17] WMV, p. 509.

And here one must halt the enquiry; to proceed further would take me far into the windings of psychological research where his great genius would have nothing to lose but where I myself would be afraid of missing my way. In the ideal, moral and social sense he was a great Christian. But one must be very careful not to present him as a Catholic in the political and strictly theological sense of the word: nothing could be further than the truth.[18]

At his funeral the 28,000 people who lined the streets broke softly but spontaneously into the chorus, 'Va, pensiero'. But the man who had given the new Italy her artistic voice remained to the end a very private person.

[18] Ibid., p. 506.

11
Verdi as man and artist

Great artists rarely live up to their best work. The more they put into their art, the more they are likely to be found wanting in the prosaic dealings of everyday life. The ruthless egotism of a Wagner or a Bellini can be seen as a necessary protection of their genius. While Beethoven the composer rose to ever greater heights, the man, beset by growing deafness, became ever more difficult and disagreeable. Mozart was feckless and often undignified. Schubert was an impractical Bohemian, Bruckner pathetically naïve, Mahler a neurotic, and so on.

With Verdi, however, the man and the artist in many ways developed side by side. The composer of *Oberto* was not especially prepossessing. The small mouth mentioned in the passport of 1832 and confirmed by the earliest portraits, gives him a peevish, faintly distrustful air. But from the start there was something in his character that won him many friends and admirers whom he did not cast off with the years: a certain loyalty, integrity and liveliness in the pursuit of his ideals. Yet together with the warmth that transpires from Muzio's letters to their joint benefactor, Barezzi, there is also evident a strong objection to being taken for granted. When Barezzi suggests that Verdi could well afford to advance his pupil a small sum of money, it is clear from Muzio's reply that his teacher considered this an unwarrantable assumption. Yet the money would be forthcoming none the less; for it was Verdi's habit to treat his friends generously.

Throughout those early Milan years a certain awkwardness is apparent. His letters to the countesses to whose salons his celebrity had gained him admittance breathe a rather embarrassing elephantine gallantry. Clearly by the time of *Macbeth* in 1847 he had not learned how to convey his intentions clearly to his performers, as Marianna Barbieri-Nini makes clear in her memoirs. The conductor Pietro Romani was driven nearly to despair, as were the soprano herself and her baritone partner. But Verdi persisted with them until he was satisfied. A softer side of his nature is recorded from the same period by the sculptor Giovanni Dupré who was cordially received and entertained in the composer's lodgings. In general Verdi liked the company of his fellows in the other arts, whether of poetry, painting or sculpture. But just as the musician had earned the nickname 'the composer with the helmet', so the man was known as 'the bear of Busseto'. As he became a man of property and underwent the civilising influence of Giuseppina, so Verdi acquired assurance and authority. In the photographs of the 1850s and 60s it is now the straight blunt nose that dominates together with the steady gaze. He could still be formidable, and even brusque, as the baritone Charles Santley was to find out when he visited the composer during the rehearsals for *Don Carlos* in 1867. Antonio Ghislanzoni, however, who remembered Verdi in 1846 as a taciturn young man glowering amidst a happy throng of artists and musicians, was astonished at the change he found when first invited to S.Agata in 1868. 'I have known artists', he wrote, 'who in their youth were carefree and overflowing with merriment and affability but later, under their glossy coating of honours and fame became reserved and almost unapproachable. One would say that Verdi, as he pursued his triumphant career, at every stage shed a part of that hard, prickly carapace that enclosed him in the years of his youth.'[1] Giuseppe Depanis, son of the manager of the Turin opera house, who knew Verdi in his last years never failed to be struck by the old man's affability and a 'courtesy all the more exquisite for being unaffected and spontaneous'.[2] No mean tribute, this, from an ardent Wagnerian and friend of Catalani, who in his youth had ascribed Verdi's fame to nothing more than astute publicity. In a word it would seem that collaboration with Boito had rejuvenated the man as well as his music.

Independence, the desire to be beholden to nobody, was among the mainsprings of Verdi's life. Hence his carefulness with money. From the start he drove hard, though not unreasonable bargains with publishers and managements and was always ready to 'cavil on the ninth part of a hair'. He never forgot a debt; and though he could be generous to a defaulting debtor, it was often the end of a friendship. For Verdi was curiously Victorian in his attitude to bankruptcy. Those who could not manage their financial affairs as well as he managed his had no right to his respect. He knew nothing of the

[1] CIIV, pp. 72–3.
[2] Ibid., p. 295.

Marxian trade cycle.

However, he was in no sense a miser. All the proceeds from the composition and hire of his operas (and he was probably the highest paid opera composer in Europe) were – literally – ploughed back into the land. In his works of public beneficence – the Casa di Riposo in Milan and the Hospital at Villanova – he was the typical Lombard-style patriarch, supervising every detail from the human as well as the practical angle.

'You pose as an advanced man', Shaw's Roebuck Ramsden exclaims with a snort. 'Let me tell you that I was an advanced man before you were born!' To which John Tanner, drily, 'I knew it was a long time ago.' Verdi, also a Liberal in his youth and often claimed by the left as one of themselves, would be seen in his maturity to stand rather towards the right of the political spectrum. In the Risorgimento years he had followed the republican ideals of Mazzini and consorted with patriots such as Luciano Manara and others who frequented the salon of Clara Maffei. Later he became an enthusiastic follower of Cavour. But with the radical governments that predominated in Italy after 1876 he had no sympathy, partly because of their tendency to side with Germany against France, partly because of their colonial policy in Africa. By the 1890s England was already urging Italy to take up the white man's burden in Eritrea. The result was the devastating defeat at Adua in 1896. This Verdi regarded as a salutary lesson; however much he had modified the political views of his early days, he retained the Mazzinian belief that no nation had a right to rule another. He hoped that the English would likewise be expelled from India as the Austrians had been from Italy. It is sad that his last-known reference to Shakespeare's countrymen, to whom he had generally shown himself benevolent, should be as 'sons of bitches'. And the South African War had not yet broken out!

In music, literature, the visual arts, as in politics, he always kept abreast of events. In matters visual his taste was that of his age, no more. The French journalist Etienne Rouillet-Destranges waxed ironical over the furnishings of Verdi's apartment in Genoa, in particular a tapestry depicting a pheasant – 'the pride and joy of a country parson'.[3] Many of the scenic ideas – undoubtedly Verdi's

[3] Ibid., pp. 205–6.

own – indicated in the production book of *Aida* would raise a smile if realised to-day. The garden of the Villa Verdi is a typical piece of Victorian fantasy with its grotto, lake and rowing boat. His reading was wide, especially in the classics, and his taste very personal. He preferred imaginative variety to formal perfection; hence Ariosto to Tasso, and Shakespeare to everyone, including the Greek dramatists. He disliked 'naturalism' or 'verismo' which he regarded as mere photography as opposed to painting. His favourite Italian novel remained Manzoni's *I promessi sposi*.

His musical views were to some extent coloured by his concern to protect his country's national heritage. But they were less rigid than he made them appear. Like most of his coevals he undervalued Monteverdi and the early masters of Venetian baroque. For him great music ceased for a while with Palestrina (whom he revered as the father of Italian music) and began again with (surprisingly) Benedetto Marcello and Corelli. Otherwise the contents of his private library are astonishingly varied. All the leading German composers are represented from Bach to Brahms; from France Gounod, Bizet, Saint-Saens; Smetana and Dvořák are also there. He might protest that vocal not instrumental music was what suited the Italian genius; but on the shelf above his bed are all the quartets of Haydn, Mozart and Beethoven alongside the works of Shakespeare, Schiller, Dante and Byron. He also possessed Bach's Partitas, chorale preludes and the Well-tempered Klavier and the symphonic poems of Liszt. Choral masterpieces include the B minor Mass, Beethoven's Missa Solemnis, several of Handel's oratorios and the Requiems of Mozart, Cherubini and Brahms. His comments on individual composers are worth noting. On Berlioz, whose 'Traité d'instrumentation' he possessed as well as the scores of *La Damnation de Faust*, *Benvenuto Cellini* and the Carneval Romain overture: 'a brilliant power of invention, though lacking that calmness and poise that produces the greatest works of art'. However he had a real feeling for the orchestra and anticipated Wagner in some of his most original effects. 'The Wagnerians won't have it so, but it's the truth.'[4] Of Gounod: 'a great musician, a great talent who writes chamber and instrumental music of high quality and in a manner quite his own. But he is not an artist of dramatic fibre. Even *Faust*, though

4 AVI, p. 295.

successful, has become diminished in his hands . . . He is good at the intimate piece but his dramatic situations are weak and his characterisation poor.'[5] Of Gluck's *Orfeo ed Euridice*, seen in 1890: '. . . the second act is really fine. Hearing it I couldn't help being confirmed in my view that the Germans should stay German and the Italians Italian. Even in those days in which one only wrote melody or rather melodic phrases in opera, the German was far more successful with the instrumental part, despite the meagre orchestra of the time. In this same second act the choruses and dances of the Furies are most powerful. But the music which Orfeo sings accompanying himself on the lyre is not good enough. He couldn't manage to find a calm, broad, deeply felt melody that was needed . . .'[6] As a musician he considered Gluck inferior to Handel. Of Rossini and Bellini, in a letter to Camille Bellaigue, author of 'Les musiciens': '. . . I confess I can't help believing that for wealth of real musical ideas, comic verve and truth of declamation *Il barbiere di Siviglia* is the best comic opera ever written. Like you I admire *Guillaume Tell* but how many sublimities do you find in many of his other operas? It's true that Bellini is poor in harmony and orchestration! . . . but rich in feeling and in a melancholy entirely his own. Even in his less-known operas, in *Straniera* and *Pirata* there are long, long melodies such as no one wrote before him. And how much truth and power of declamation there is especially in the duet between Pollione and Norma! And how much loftiness of thought in the first phrase of the Introduzione of *Norma*, followed after a few bars by another phrase . . . which is badly scored but which no one has surpassed for heavenly beauty.'[7] All these quotations have something to tell us about Verdi the composer; and several of the phrases that he singles out find an echo in his operas.

After a certain age the mind tends to become closed to new impressions, but not Verdi's. True, there is no evidence that he ever came fully to terms with the music of the 'veristi'; but his appreciation of Wagner undoubtedly developed over the years. His earliest reactions to *Lohengrin*, which he saw in Bologna in 1871, were not especially enthusiastic. He liked certain orchestral effects but found

[5] Ibid., pp. 221–2.
[6] MCVB, pp. 172–3.
[7] LCC, pp. 415–16.

the opera as a whole slow and boring. By 1886 he had come round to it. 'I have a great admiration for Wagner', he told a French journalist . . . 'Whatever one may say, there is melody in Wagner; but you have to know where to find it. But in general I have to admit that I prefer his earlier works to his later style and I wouldn't put any of them above *Lohengrin*.'[8] Thirteen years later he pronounced the second act of *Tristan und Isolde* 'one of the sublimest creations of the human spirit'.[9] No further evidence is needed of Verdi's ever-widening creative horizons.

Over his private life Verdi was careful to draw a veil from the start, more from a natural 'pudeur' than from having anything to hide. Those who wanted information he would often deliberately mislead, just as he misled the critic Filippo Filippi when he told him that 'in my house there is hardly a note of music'.[10] In the same way he liked to pose to his Milan countesses as a cynical money-grubber who would retire as soon as he had made his pile. Later he would pose as a farmer who had forgotten all he knew about music and just wanted to plant cabbages. Would-be biographers were shown the door. Only the wily Giulio Ricordi succeeded in 1879 in obtaining an account of Verdi's early triumphs and failures in Milan and one which consciously or not was already encrusted with legend. But it is unlikely that there were any skeletons to be found, apart from those bouts of nervous irascibility recorded by Giuseppina in her diaries. From certain references in the letters we might gather that he was not above the occasional flirtation, if not more than that, when in Piave's company, even after he had begun to live with Giuseppina; but the disordered sexual life of a Donizetti, Pacini or Petrella was certainly not for him. We shall probably never know why he did not marry Giuseppina until 1859, nor why he – and his wife – should have turned so violently against Mariani, nor yet the precise nature of his relations with Teresa Stolz, nor what, if any, were his religious beliefs. In a word the secrets of his own life were guarded as closely as those of his musical workshop.

For the fundamental consistency of Verdi's output across a style that develops from crude simplicity to the utmost refinement and

---

[8] CIIV, p. 165.
[9] Ibid., p. 317.
[10] LCC, pp. 616–17.

sophistication is one of the most baffling phenomena in music. Time and again serious music lovers reared on the German classics and prepared to recognise only *Otello* and *Falstaff* as worthy of the European tradition have found themselves carried further and further back in the canon, discovering greatness where they had expected only triviality. Where lies the explanation? Partly in the fact that alone among his Italian contemporaries Verdi invariably treated each opera as an entirely separate artistic proposition, each with its own terms of reference and its special musical 'tinta' or 'colorito', to use Verdi's own term. It is not easy to define, though Verdi's earliest commentator, Abramo Basevi, understood it well enough: a predominance of certain melodic contours, rhythmic patterns, harmonic progressions, phrase-lengths and so on, so blended as to give the opera concerned a recognisable physiognomy.[11] The abundance of minor tonality, dark and strange scoring and melodic intervals of a minor second and third all make up the 'tinta' of *Macbeth*, just as the leaping sixths (soh to mi) and vigorous upward scales precipitate that of *Ernani*, and the pentatonics, the parallel sixths and the barcarole rhythms that of *Simon Boccanegra*. *Il trovatore* could be said to have a double tinta, derived from Azucena and Leonora respectively. One reason why Verdi's revisions even at twenty-five-years' distance from the original succeed as well as they do is that in every case he takes care to preserve the original colouring.

All this implies a very precise calculation of means to ends and a complete absence of that facile hedonism that marks the operas of Verdi's older contemporaries such as Pacini and Mercadante. Verdi's music is always dramatically functional. 'I don't like pointless things',[12] was a favourite saying of his; also 'I do not write my notes at random but try to give them a definite character.'[13] In other words he aimed to realise the dramatic essence of a given subject as far as his currently available means would allow; and if the means developed with the years, the end never changed. It used often to be said that until his meeting with Boito Verdi, partly from a defective education, too readily accepted bad libretti which inhibited his

[11] BSV, pp. 114–16.
[12] LCC, pp. 243–4.
[13] Ibid., pp. 109–11.

genius. The truth is that with few exceptions, and those very early, he drew up the schemes of the libretti himself with a view to getting the subject on his own terms and those of contemporary Italian opera, whose conventions are for some reason considered so much less respectable than those of eighteenth century opera seria. At the time of *Ernani* Verdi was able to encompass the high heroism of Hugo's drama but not its moments of irony and humour; seven years later, in *Rigoletto*, he was able to encompass both. 'In der Beschränkung zeigt sich erst der Meister', Goethe remarked; and it is that keen sense of its own limitations, its total consistency within precise boundaries that makes the earlier work as satisfying on a modest level as the later on a far more exalted one. In neither does Verdi lapse into that unconscious absurdity that makes most of Hugo's plays unperformable today. When Donizetti's Lucrezia Borgia (another Hugo subject) pointedly reminds Don Alfonso that he is her fourth husband it is difficult to suppress a snigger at this vignette of Borgia home life. But we do not smile at Ernani's fatal bargain over the horn any more than at the absent-mindedness of Azucena. Verdi has an astonishing faculty of making us take the most extravagant situations seriously.

New subjects, new forms – this was Verdi's constant cry. If the more adventurous subjects (*Rigoletto, La traviata, Macbeth, Simon Boccanegra*) were the most obvious sources of self-renewal, it is the works of consolidation (*Il trovatore, Un ballo in maschera, Aida*) that show most clearly the steadily developing resources. In his early operas Verdi scored for emphasis, doubling the voice-parts here and there with the brighter instruments and supporting them with elaborate fidgety accompaniments. Woodwind, strings and brass are combined in set patterns; the colouring is hard and heraldic with no half tones. But gradually the combinations become more varied and imaginative; the colours soften into more delicate shades. Rhetoric turns into poetry; the sharp shocks which drive the earlier operas forward become smooth transitions, aided by an ever-widening melodic and harmonic vocabulary. All these processes keep pace with one another, so preserving the integrity of each opera. But Verdi never scruples to draw on earlier procedures where they serve his purpose. At the same time, though his language becomes increasingly acceptable to academic ears, his later style remains far from orthodox. Harmonic ellipses, a personal use of seventh inversions and of the 6/4 chord and a discreet inclination for non-functional harmony in the manner of Richard Strauss, all contribute to an entirely personal idiom. Some of the progressions to be found in *Otello* are much harder to 'parse' than anything in Wagner.

Just as the man rose from a humble provincial environment to become one of the most revered patriarchs of the new Italy, so the artist born into a decaying and devitalised operatic tradition succeeded in creating a musical world of infinite depth and variety. Both are a source of continual wonder.

THE MUSIC

12

The background

Before considering Verdi's own contribution it may be useful to take a brief look at the operatic world into which he was born and the kind of opera to which he was heir. It was not the cosmopolitan Italian opera of the eighteenth century; for by Verdi's time Italy's musical hegemony was in the past. She had long been a stranger to the German symphonic tradition which was to nourish German opera. The Napoleonic Wars had disrupted communications between peoples; and Napoleon himself, if only for tactical reasons, had fostered nationalism in his subject states and nowhere more successfully than in the Peninsula. Italian patriots looked on him as their friend and deliverer just as they viewed Nelson as their enemy. The collapse of the empire was followed by an explosion of opera in which the sense of national identity awakened in the previous decade was powerfully affirmed. In 1823 that staunch Italophile Stendhal wrote: 'Napoleon is dead; but a new conqueror has already shown himself to the world; and from Moscow to Naples, from London to Vienna, from Paris to Calcutta, his name is constantly on every tongue. The fame of this hero knows no bounds save those of civilisation itself; and he is not yet thirty-two!'[1]

The new conqueror was Gioachino Rossini, architect and foremost exponent of a style of opera which, with modifications, would survive into the mid-century. He was Napoleon's successor only by analogy, being himself the most unpolitical of men; indeed he had no scruples about setting loyalist verses at the time of the Congress of Verona in 1821 – a fact which would be remembered against him twenty-seven years later. Nor would Rossinian opera have flourished as sturdily as it did had it not been wholly acceptable to the powers of the Holy Alliance. Ornate, artificial, essentially hedonistic,

[1] Stendhal, *Vie de Rossini*, trans. R. Coe (London, 1956), p. 1.

it was well calculated to divert attention from the prowess of Italian soldiers to that of Italian singers. For this was the age of vocal virtuosity, when the French husband of an Italian prima donna could declare that to fill a theatre he needed only 'ma femme et quatre ou cinq poupées'. The castrato had nearly vanished from the scene, but the vocal values he represented continued to prevail. All voice types from bass to soprano aspired to total flexibility and show. Virtuoso tenors floated up to c' and d' in head voice. Whether the juvenile lead was a tenor or a contralto *en travesti* made little difference since both shared the same cool agility.

Rossinian opera was a highly successful concordat between singer and composer. Its structural features – the aria in two movements, one slow and expressive, the other fast and brilliant; the multi-movement duets that allow the singers to vie with each other, now with the same material, now with different; the choral interventions that set the soloist on a pedestal, the noisy orchestral conclusions designed to whip up applause – all these represent a concession to the star performers of a golden age of song. Yet at the same time Rossini was able to contain singers' licence with a wealth of vocal floridity which accorded perfectly with his own flamboyant personality. The articulation of the drama in situations rather than a steady developing action suited his essentially classical instinct for balance and contrast. His skill in large scale construction and part-writing is given scope in the grand 'concertato' which invariably ends the first of the opera's two acts. This too will be in two contrasted, essentially static, movements with intervening transitions during which the action moves forward. The concertato is the opera's centre of gravity, usually occurring at some fatal discovery or revelation which will determine the destiny of the hero or heroine.

On the negative side is the lack of expressive harmony which a florid style necessarily entails, and for which Rossini was much blamed by his German contemporaries (Wagner compared his clusters of fioritura to artificial flowers). But Rossini's strengths lie in other directions; in his readiness with the apt, if totally unexpected, modulation, in a sureness of rhythmic grasp and in his aristocratic sense of style. Nor, except at the moments where the sheer joy in pattern-making led him to 'instrumentalise' the voices, is his vocal writing lacking in expression. Within its essentially classical idiom the music is by turns noble, tender and rhetorically powerful. But one consequence of his restricted harmonic vocabulary is that the expression is somewhat generic, so that the same music may serve for quite different situations – a fact which did not go unnoticed by the hostile Berlioz, who wrote of the composer's 'melodic cynicism' and 'disregard of the dramatic proprieties'.[2] Weber also railed against the Italian habit of clothing tragic sentiments in sweet harmonies. None the less Rossini had bequeathed to his successors an operatic groundplan which they had only to fill out in a personal variant of his own manner to be sure of success; and this they were only too ready to do. As Pacini put it, 'Everyone followed the same school, the same fashions and as a result were all followers of the Great Luminary. But, good heavens, what was one to do if there was no other way of making a living? If I was a follower of the great man of Pesaro, so was everyone else.'[3]

Verdi was born in the year of Rossini's first international triumphs – *Tancredi* and *L'italiana in Algeri* – and his early youth was passed under the Rossinian ascendancy. But by the time he arrived in Milan in 1832 the climate had changed. The tide of Romanticism had washed against Rossinian opera, leaving its structure intact but altering its facade. Chief agent here was Bellini whose *Il pirata* of 1827 had proclaimed a new, more emotional style, marked by a sparing use of floridity, a longer melodic articulation, a more expressive use of harmony, including an abundance of discords and appoggiaturas on strong beats – the whole suffused with that indefinable melancholy characteristic of Romantic lyricism. Bellini died in 1835; but his influence was wide and lasting – at its best in Chopin, at its worst in 'The Maiden's Prayer'.

The vogue for Bellini also brought with it a fundamental change of vocal style, most evident in the case of the tenor. No longer was he required to show the light flexibility demanded by Rossini, but rather a sustained intensity of expression suitable to a romantic lover. The pioneer was Rubini for whom Bellini wrote most of his tenor roles and whom he personally instructed in their interpretation. Like his successor, Mario, Rubini retained his head-notes, but most tenors of the time followed the example of Gilbert Duprez who,

[2] H. Berlioz, *Mémoires* (Paris, 1870), p. 102.
[3] G. Pacini, *Le mie memorie artistiche*, 2nd ed. (Florence, 1873), p. 54.

brought up in the high Franco-Italian tradition, proceeded after 1830 to cultivate the 'voix assombrée', singing everything up to high C with full chest resonance. He it was who created that archetypal romantic tenor role, Edgardo in Donizetti's *Lucia di Lammermoor* which never exceeds B flat. At the same time floridity vanished from the lower male voices, remaining only to the soprano, whom it surrounded with an aura of angelic purity of the unattainable. To conservatives like the Belgian encyclopædist Fétis all this spelt the death of good singing. If Verdi was blamed for destroying the singer's art with his emotional demands, so to a lesser degree were Bellini and Donizetti.

Meanwhile the forms of Italian opera had changed hardly at all, despite the increasing incidence of romantic subjects. By now the commonest plot was that of star-crossed lovers and a tragic ending. The central concertato would occur at the point where hero and villain confront one another in the presence of the heroine and a host of bystanders. The emotional situation would be gathered up into a climax of sad sweet song, to be followed by a burst of noisy energy with which to bring down the curtain.

The most resourceful practitioner of romantic opera was Donizetti. Less original than Bellini, he had a far keener feeling for dramatic pace. No one was more skilful at combining and varying the various operatic forms to achieve swiftness of action without compromising the structural balance. Gifted with a remarkable power of self-renewal, he maintained a gradual ascent over the course of some seventy operas, the last of which sometimes antici- pate the dramatic conquests of Verdi. Only his tendency to remain within the bounds of bland Rossinian harmony combine with a certain over-facility to arouse expectations which are not always fulfilled. The most learned among his contemporaries was Saverio Mercadante, who was much admired by Liszt. Not the most spon- taneous of composers, he nevertheless achieved both distinction and dramatic force with a group of operas written round about 1840, before relapsing into mannerism and self-repetition. Lesser lights of the period were Pacini, whose *Saffo* remained in the repertory for some fifty years, and the brothers Luigi and Federico Ricci, remem- bered today for their fairy-tale comedy *Crispino e la comare*. Ultramontane influence impinged, mainly through the French operas of Rossini which began to find their way to Italy in the 1830s and were to result in an increased participation of the chorus. But in the main Italian opera of the period remained almost provincially Italian.

What, then, was the secret of its phenomenal international success which made French and German composers grind their teeth in envy and Berlioz want to blow up the Théâtre des Italiens and all its aficionados? Partly Italian singers, still the best in Europe in pure vocal accomplishment; partly the Northerners' traditional *Sehnsucht* for the land where the lemon trees bloom. But more than that Italian opera possessed a purely musical fluency which French and German were much slower to attain. The reason lies in the wealth of ancillary elements of which the Italians had disposed for two centuries. First was a uniquely flexible system of verse metres which had obtained since the time of Monteverdi and Busenello and would last throughout most of the nineteenth century; next a tradition of conversational recitative in 'versi sciolti' which stood composers in good stead when through-composed opera became the rule. It was a long time before German composers found such suitable connecting tissue for their formal numbers. After the noble experiment of *Euryanthe* Weber returned to spoken dialogue for *Oberon*. Lortzing, Marschner and Nicolai had never departed from it. Finally Italy never lacked a recognised style of dramatic poetry. True, by the nineteenth century the pure, chiselled language of Metastasio had given way to a more high-flown jargon. Yet the profession of operatic poet was well regarded; and there was no dearth of skilled fabricators of 'musicable' verse – Felice Romani, Jacopo Ferretti, Gaetano Rossi, Domenico Gilardoni all knew how to extrapolate from dramas old and new just those situations that would lend themselves most readily to operatic treatment; how to trim the casts so as to arrive at no more than four full principals; and above all how to render every plot harmless in the eyes of the censor. Such is the advantage of a centuries old tradition. In the nineteenth century France, Germany and Russia had 'operas'; Italy had an 'opera'.

13

From Oberto to Ernani

For his first opera Verdi characteristically chose a subject out of the common run. The provenance of *Oberto, Conte di San Bonifacio* has never been established; nor can we be sure how much of it was carried over from *Rocester*. The hero is an outraged father who returns to the land of which he has been dispossessed to find his daughter, Leonora, seduced and abandoned by the usurper, Riccardo. Together they present themselves to Cuniza, the bride-to-be; then having enlisted her sympathy they confront Riccardo in the presence of his followers (the usual concertato-finale). The wedding is broken off; but this does not prevent Oberto from challenging Riccardo to a duel and being killed by him. Riccardo, remorseful, goes into exile bequeathing his possessions to Leonora, who concludes the opera with the prima donna's traditional 'rondò-finale' of grief and delirium.

At the centre of the action, therefore, a prototype of Rigoletto: a brooding father, torn between tenderness for his daughter and an implacable desire to be avenged on her seducer; a character who expresses himself most vividly in recitative and arioso. Yet throughout the opera Verdi's individual voice is heard only by fits and starts. Bellini's influence is evident in the andante of the overture with its two cantabili trumpets (the melody is heard again as a bridal chorus); in a somewhat languid duet between Cuniza and Riccardo; in two male choruses of Act II; in the andante of the rondò-finale 'Sciagurata! a questo lido', reminiscent of Amina's 'Ah non credea mirarti' but with a powerful dramatic thrust; and in a duet-movement for the two women 'Al cangiar di sorte infida', cut from the first performance and therefore the vocal score, in which the two voices move in thirds over a typically Bellinian accompaniment of cello arpeggios, sustaining violas and pizzicato violins.

The hand of Mercadante can be sensed in the grand gestures of the Act I concertato and in the terzetto in the form of a false canon for Leonora, Cuniza and Oberto. Cuniza has a highly Rossinian cabaletta at the start of Act II; and even Mozart's Commendatore seems to stand behind two of Oberto's more melodramatic appearances. In every case Verdi is simpler and blunter than his models. The result can be naif to the point of embarrassment, as in parts of the Leonora/Oberto duet and Oberto's one aria; but it can also be dignified and touching, as in Riccardo's somewhat Donizettian romanza in Act II. Verdi prefers to end an idea abruptly rather then extend it by means of 'sweet nothings'. Hence the unusually concise and condensed nature both of Riccardo's cavatina in Act I and Leonora's rondò-finale.

The most prophetic moment, however occurs just before the duel, where, at Merelli's suggestion, Verdi had inserted a quartet for the four main principals. Here for the first time we encounter that huge rhythmic span, based on a simple pattern of slow accompanying triplets, that wealth of ideas within a small compass that marks so many ensembles of the young Verdi. Indeed the following phrase turns up again almost unaltered in *Il corsaro* of 1848.

Ex. 1

The second act succeeds better than the first, not because the music is superior, but rather because the drama is better paced; as so often with Verdi, the opera gathers momentum as it proceeds. A contemporary reviewer noted at the first performance that the applause for Act I was meagre, that for Act II enthusiastic. This is equally true of modern revivals. The first act drags; the second holds the attention from start to finish; nobody leaves the theatre with a sense of anti-climax.

Still less characteristic as a whole is *Un giorno di regno*. In none of his compositions published to date had Verdi shown any propensity for comedy. Opera buffa was still a genre apart demanding four stereotyped ingredients – the witty sprightly soprano or mezzo, the romantic tenor, much sentimentalised since 1830, the chattering basso buffo and the basso cantante who sings lyrically, if ironically, with the upper part of his voice but who can turn himself into a basso buffo for purposes of a comic duet. If *Il barbiere di Siviglia* remains the classic of the pre-Romantic age, Donizetti's *L'elisir d'amore* is that of the Romantic, its humour infused by a not too serious pathos. The libretto which Verdi chose, not willingly but as the least uncongenial of those available, dated from 1818; despite a sentimental tenor, it is much nearer to the Rossini than the Donizetti model. A young French officer is required to impersonate Stanislas Lescinsky, King of Poland, so that the real monarch can return home incognito, thus giving his enemies the slip. As honoured guest of the Baron Kelbar in Brittany the false Stanislas makes use of his position to effect the wedding of his host's daughter with the man she loves in the teeth of parental opposition and at the same time is reconciled to his former sweetheart who is on the point of marrying someone else. The plot requires as well as the standard four roles an extra female principal for the daughter and an extra basso buffo for her unwelcome suitor. But clearly everything depends on the delineation of the Chevalier Belfiore; he must combine the resource and cunning of a Figaro with the manner of a Dandini – one moment all regal authority, the next chuckling with delight at his own cleverness. The contrast was not one that came easily to Verdi, whose penchant, evident from his earliest years, was for making the audience take the most unlikely events seriously. His Belfiore errs throughout on the side of solemnity. Typical in this respect is the Act I duet where the young lover Edoardo begs the 'sovereign' to take him into his service as a soldier. Belfiore goes one better; he appoints Edoardo his personal equerry much to the young man's delight. The model for the duet is clearly 'Venti scudi' from *L'elisir d'amore*. It is laid out in the same three movements: an allegro opening in dialogue, a central section of asides and a final cabaletta. Neither of the first two movements has any distinction, the second being downright clumsy; but the cabaletta strikes a new note that is clearly reflected in the tenor's text;

> Infiammato da spirto guerriero
> Scorrerò della gloria il sentiero

Not Romani, but the swaggering decasyllabics of the Risorgimento; of the young Manzoni and Temistocle Solera, who as resident poet of La Scala was doubtless responsible for any alterations in Romani's libretto. Verdi responded like a war-horse to the trumpet with a martial variant of Ex. 1 in *Oberto*:

Ex. 2

Most of the opera relies on cheerful buffo commonplace, coarser and heavier than that in Rossini or Donizetti and with much banda-like scoring; nearer in fact to the style of Luigi Ricci whose opera semiseria, *Chiara di Rosemberg*, had been one of the successes of La Scala during Verdi's student days. The best of the opera is to be found in the ensembles: there are two vigorous quarrel duets between the buffi, one of which ('Diletto genero') hints at the *Aida* trumpet march.

Especial care went to the concertato of Act I where Belfiore surprises the Baron and Treasurer and temporarily shames them into making peace. The movement builds up impressively voice by voice after the Baron's opening stanza ('In qual punto il re ci ha colto!') – an irregular declamatory melody which Verdi would perfect three operas later in *Ernani* at a similar dramatic moment. There is an ingenious sestetto ('Cara Giulia, alfin ti vedo!') in which the various threads are effectively picked out – the 'billings and cooings' of the lovers, the military talk of Belfiore and the Baron, the Treasurer's grumbling – all cut short by the appearance of the Marchesa, which sets off a general 6/8 scramble ('Madamine, il mio scudiere'). A haunting terzetto for Giulietta, Edoardo and a distracted Marchesa carries memories of the minuet from *Don Giovanni*. Feeblest among the ensembles is the settimino 'A tal colpo preparata', a plodding imitation of Rossini's 'Quest'è un nodo avviluppato' from *La cenerentola*.

Although at the time Verdi considered *Un giorno di regno* sunk beyond recall and took no further interest in it, the opera enjoyed two fairly successful revivals in Venice in 1845 and in Naples in 1859. Ricordi paid it the compliment of publishing it under the original title of *Il finto Stanislao* thereby indicating that it had completely eclipsed Gyrowetz' opera. Indeed to insist as we do nowadays on the meaningless *Un giorno di regno* is rather like calling Rossini's comic masterpiece *Almaviva o l'inutil precauzione.*

None the less the Verdi boom of the last twenty-five years has not succeeded in bringing his second opera back into the repertory. In his early years Verdi's most conspicuous talent was for the cumulative effect, here precluded by bouts of recitativo secco. The moments which remain most in the mind are those of chuckling drollery that Verdi will recall in the music of Fra Melitone:

Ex. 3

In *Nabucco* the influence of Verdi's predecessors still operates. The model for this work is Rossini's *Moïse*, the French version of his *Mosè in Egitto* and familiar to Italian audiences as '*Il Mosè nuovo*' to distinguish it from its predecessor. Like *Moïse*, *Nabucco* is concerned with the persecution of the Jews by a foreign power, their captivity in exile and their eventual triumph. The equivalent of Moses is Zaccaria the prophet, likewise a bass with all the bass voice's aptitude for calm authority. The persecutor is in both cases a dynamic baritone. As in Rossini's opera there is a love interest that spans the opposing sides; but it no longer occupies a prominent place. Both Ismaele the Israelite and Nebuchadnezzar's daughter Fenena are comprimario roles. Even a love duet for which Solera had written the verses was rejected by Verdi who wanted a prophecy by Zaccaria instead. The soprano lead is also the villainess of the piece, Abigaille, supposedly a daughter of Nabucco but in fact the child of a

167

harem slave by one of the King's wives. She it is who admits the Assyrian troops into Jerusalem by a ruse and assumes the crown when the king is struck down by madness. But in the depths of his abasement Nabucco prays to the God of Israel; his faculties are restored to him, and he leads out his troops in time to save Fenena and the Jews from execution. In a fit of remorse Abigaille commits suicide.

Whatever the order in which the score was composed, its stylistic heart is to be found in the great chorus of Hebrew slaves ('Va, pensiero') which remains its chief adornment to this day, a transfigured national anthem, embodying the longings and aspirations of a whole people. Its principal features will appear in many a Verdi opera from here on – a slow, simple line articulated in long strains and underpinned by triplet pulsations. Though it seemed entirely new to the Milanese of its time, its prototype can be found, unexpectedly, in the choral pendant to Raimondo's narrative aria in *Lucia di Lammermoor* ('Dalle stanze ove Lucia').

Ex. 4

Thicken the orchestral texture, simplify the rhythm and extend the scale of Donizetti's melody and you arrive somewhere near the manner of early Verdi. But while Donizetti slips unobtrusively into harmony at the final cadence, Verdi explodes into it at the start of the third stanza ('arpa d'or') with electrifying effect. Characteristic too is the pattern of woodwind semi-quavers that decorate the reprise of Ex. 4, a rather naive device for increasing the rhythmic momentum.

The 'Va, pensiero' style is the opera's main artery. It is pre-figured directly in Zaccaria's cavatina 'D'Egitto là sui lidi' in which he rallies the terror-stricken Israelites (significantly the unison chorus breaks in on both movements); in the concertato finales of both the first two acts, but particularly the second – a false canon of remark-able rhythmic weight and tension in which once more the unison chorus plays a prominent role. The same manner, lightened by hope, pervades the 'prophecy' that concludes Act III. Above all it determines the scale and character of the ensembles. The opening scenes of both *Nabucco* and *Moïse* run parallel; but whereas Rossini is happy to make do with two contrasted ideas, one minor and one major, Verdi lays out the scene in three massive paragraphs, each with its own scoring and rhythmic cut: the first a hurricane of scales and dimin-ished sevenths in E minor ('Gli arredi festivi') using full orchestra; the second for unison basses and a chorale of lower brass and bassoons; the third for women only with harp and woodwind in E major ('Gran Nume che voli') in which full voices and orchestra eventually join. Here is primitive grandeur on a huge scale and a driving force which makes Rossini's score seem almost sedate.

The three principals are correspondingly larger than life. Zaccaria is the spearhead of the Israelites, an Oroveso more closely identified with his people than Bellini's Archdruid. Nabucco and Abigaille are both monsters with the occasional redeeming moments of pathos. For the first Verdi had the benefit of the finest baritone of his day, Giorgio Ronconi; for the second Giuseppina Strepponi proved so manifestly inadequate that it is more likely that Verdi conceived this very demanding role more in terms of Sofia Loewe, a well-known 'donna di forza' who had appeared at La Scala earlier in the season. From her first appearance, when she interrupts the tender colloquy of Ismaele and Fenena, now a hostage to the Israelites, Abigaille shows her claws, first in phrases of snarling sarcasm ('Prode guerrier!'); then her fury erupts in full force (Ex. 5).

In this as in most of Verdi's early operas the characters define themselves more sharply in ensembles than in solo arias. Thus in the concertato finale of Act I ('Tremin gl'insani') Verdi breaks with tradition in keeping the participants musically separate without disturbing the sense of a melodic unit. Nabucco blusters; Abigaille vents her anger in soaring leaps and plunges; Zaccaria remains

Ex. 5

steadfast; the lovers plead lyrically. Only with the release of Fenena by Ismaele just as she is about to be stabbed by Zaccaria does the music plunge into a noisy, indiscriminate stretta.

Act III offers an early example of the Verdian 'dynamic duet'. Outwardly it follows the traditional three-movement plan – a dialogue, a joint soliloquy and a cabaletta sparked off by an off-stage signal. But instead of being set out in parallel verses the first movement is designed as a series of short exchanges over an orchestral theme in what Basevi called a 'parlante misto'[1] (compare 'Or siam soli' from Donizetti's *Lucrezia Borgia*). It is a particularly apt solution since the characters are not merely expressing their points of view. Nabucco must sign the Jews' death warrant, then realise that Fenena is amongst them; while Abigaille must tear up the evidence of her humble birth before Nabucco's eyes. Her mockery is summed up in an impudent orchestral phrase with woodwind prominent (Ex. 6).

The central section is, as usual, a joint aside but one in which the voices remain as far apart as possible. Nabucco expresses himself in simple phrases in an unstable F minor suitable to his wandering state of mind; Abigaille remains firmly in D flat major glorying in her new authority with many an imperious vocal gesture. When the voices eventually join, it is in her key, though each singer retains his own identity throughout. In the last movement Nabucco makes one last appeal to Abigaille in a slow melody quite unlike that of a normal cabaletta. She replies with Ex. 6, now a vocal, not an orchestral theme. Both musical ideas are repeated before a final coda winds up the duet. It would be easy to point to more graceful, better balanced

[1] BSV, p. 32.

Ex. 6

and more delicately scored duets by Verdi's predecessors; but there is none in which the dramatic current moves so swiftly.

The remaining solos are more variable in quality. Abigaille's double aria ('Anch'io dischiuso un giorno') is assured in style if not especially characteristic; but we may note in the first movement Verdi's penchant for throwing the main weight of a cantabile on its final phrase; also a Bellini-like use of expressive fioritura without Bellini's fondness for appoggiature. More remarkable is Zaccaria's prayer, 'Tu che sul labbro', following the offstage conversion of Fenena. Here to a rich tapestry of six solo cellos he speaks not as the leader of his people but rather as a man of God with a noble simplicity of utterance and a richness of harmonic inflexion that almost carries us outside the world of Italian opera. There follows a stormy scene between Ismaele and the Levites which could be described as 'exasperated' Donizetti. Nabucco's 'Dio di Giuda!' preceded by a 'nightmare' prelude – a montage of previously heard themes – and a powerful recitative shows Verdi's ability to create something moving out of Italian opera commonplace when aptly sited; so too does Fenena's small *preghiera* 'Oh, dischiuso è il firmamento!'. Two solos stand out as entirely sui generis: Nabucco's ('Chi mi toglie il regio scettro?') with its manic alternations of major and minor, andante and allegro, and Abigaille's death scene ('Su me morente esanime') a free arioso scored only for cor anglais, harp, cello and bass with touches of clarinet, bassoon and finally – signifying death in a state of grace – arpeggiating flute. It is the first of those miniatures scored for a mere handful of contrasted instruments to be found in all the operas up to *Macbeth*.

If Verdi had written nothing else, *Nabucco* would have ensured him a place in musical history. Everything about it breathes a new air of confidence even down to the recitatives. Very little of it is poor – the banda march in Act IV, reputedly based on one which he wrote for Busseto; the hastily written overture based on themes from the opera including 'Va, pensiero' twisted, Rossini-fashion, into a different time: a jolly, Sunday bandstand piece containing an anomaly of tempo which few conductors manage to resolve satisfactorily.

Of all Verdi's operas *Nabucco* depends for its effect on the excellence of its chorus. It is not well-served by recordings whose chief attraction lies in star principals and a refinement of orchestral sound. At this stage of his career Verdi scored for emphasis, sonorous or rhythmic. To turn the full searchlight of stereophonic technique on the reach-me-down devices whereby he maintains the scale and momentum of numbers such a 'Gli arredi festivi' is to do them no service whatever. *Nabucco* will always be heard to best advantage in live performance by a repertory company with adequate choral resources.

I Lombardi alla prima crociata (1843) was clearly designed to follow up the success of *Nabucco* with as little self-repetition as possible. Accordingly Verdi and Solera chose a plot which was not only far removed from that of *Nabucco* but a very unlikely choice for an opera at all: an epic poem of the crusades by Tommaso Grossi, a friend of Manzoni. Partly a family saga, partly the story of a campaign, its events span more than twenty years; yet they must be compressed into as few as will make the young heroine remain plausibly young throughout. It begins with the public reconciliation of two feuding brothers, Arvino and Pagano. Both had been rivals for the hand of Viclinda, who had eventually chosen Arvino. But Pagano has never become resigned to her loss even after she has borne Arvino a daughter who is now grown up. Later that night he sets fire to the family home, only to find that his victim is not Arvino but their father, Folco. He is banished, turns hermit and spends the next few years living in a cave near Antioch; here he is able to render valuable assistance to the Crusaders including his own brother, who fails to recognise him. The rest of the opera is the story of Arvino's daughter, Giselda. Captured by the Sultan of Antioch she falls in love with the Sultan's son Oronte and he with her. Even after her rescue by the Lombards she joins him in the desert where he dies in her arms, a converted Christian. During the great drought which causes the Crusaders to drop like flies Oronte appears to Giselda in a dream, directing her to 'cool Siloim's shady rill'. Refreshed, the Christian army joins battle with the Muslims and defeats them. Pagano, fatally wounded, dies in the odour of sanctity, having revealed all to his brother and niece.

Solera's adaptation is skilful and reasonably true to the original, even if the *convenienze* require Giselda to appear in a scene which in the poem takes place before she was born and prolonging her life beyond the end of the opera (in the poem she dies a victim of thirst); but there was no making a dramatic unity out of such a sprawling narrative. Indeed, variety rather than unity seems to have been the aim here; and for this Verdi was as yet inadequately equipped. The musical quality of *I Lombardi* fluctuates disconcertingly. A chattering narrative chorus, words syllabicated over a march-like tune of incredible banality, is followed by a sextet with a chorus ('T'assale un tremito') that has the dramatic force of some of his later ensembles, each singer's mood defined by his or her vocal line. Then there is a chorus of crusading fervour ('All'empio che infrange'), which is little more than a series of emphatic gestures; this in turn gives way to a naive, not unattractive march ('Or basta!... nè l'odio'); a scene of almost comic villainy for Pagano and his henchmen rubs shoulders with one of the gems of the score, Giselda's 'Salve Maria'. Erminia Frezzolini who created the role was noted for her smooth, expressive legato singing; accordingly her melody is remarkably plain and unadorned even for a 'preghiera'. As in Abigaille's death-arioso, the scoring is selective – 8 violins, 2 violas, one bass, flute and clarinet. The melody evolves in two periods; only with the second does the tonality unequivocally declare itself with a melody that Verdi will recall in his *Pater noster* of 1880 (Ex. 7).

A similar heartfelt simplicity pervades the love duet from Act III ('O belle, a questa misera') whose long melodic lines are not spoilt by over-emphasis either in the voice-parts or the accompaniment. Even where extreme bravura would have been in order, as in the cabaletta ('Non fu sogno!') following her vision of Oronte, Giselda's joy is expressed rather by syncopations, variegated wind doublings of the vocal line and the occasional bold progression, all of which combine to make it one of the most effective numbers of the opera. The rondò-finale, 'Se vano è il pregare', which ends Act II is, despite

Ex. 7

the fiery outburst of its cabaletta, disappointingly commonplace, using material that Donizetti would have developed to much better purpose.

Once he has turned hermit, Pagano acquires the somewhat generic nobility of his calling, which does much to redeem the crudely scored 'Ma quando un suon terribile', his cantabile of Act II, cast in the usual minor/major form of a romanza. Oronte presents himself with a cavatina in which, for once, the cantabile with its massively swinging three-pulse rhythm and second beat ('La mia letizia infondere') cadence is more energetic than the cabaletta which follows it ('Come poteva un angelo'), which is possibly why Verdi provided an alternative cabaletta to the same words but in a lighter, fleeter rhythm. Both are printed in the score. Oronte's solo, delivered from Heaven to an accompaniment of harps and stage band, may be passed over in silence.

It was with his choruses that Verdi had created the greatest impression in *Nabucco*. Accordingly in *I Lombardi* there are choruses galore; choruses of nuns, of 'sbirri', of Musulmen ambassadors, of mocking odalisques and of course crusading armies. For these last Verdi devised a particularly brash theme to serve as the Crusaders' motif:

Ex. 8

The Act IV chorus 'O Signore, dal tetto natio' deliberately exploits the vein of 'Va, pensiero'; and indeed for many Italians of the time it seemed even more poignant. For listeners of to-day its dignity may be somewhat compromised by the woodwind trillings and gurglings that represent the streams of Lombardy, of which the thirst-stricken Crusaders are dreaming. Far more striking is the pilgrims' chorus at the start of Act III ('Gerusalem!') another one of those pieces in which Verdi seems to anticipate the noble austerity of his final religious works.

As if all this were not enough, the opera includes an orchestral interlude descriptive of the battle between Christians and Muslims, the first represented by full orchestra and Ex. 8, the second by the military band; while the third scene of Act III is preceded by a prelude with concertante violin written in the style of a Paganini concerto. The violin supplies an obbligato for the entire scene, which, fortunately, Verdi brought to a truly fine conclusion with a terzetto for Giselda, Pagano and the dying Oronte ('Qual voluttà trascorrere'). This is the high point of the score: a majestically unfolding andante, Bellini-like in length but more varied in its texture and with a wider tonal range and, above all, with a harmonic climax beautifully calculated on its final phrase.

I Lombardi, then, is a patchwork; an opera of indiscriminate vitality in which there are several inspired moments; these include not only whole numbers but also snatches of lyrical arioso that anticipate those phrases which in the mature Verdi will do duty for whole arias. But it is impossible for us to recapture the enthusiasm of its first audiences for whom it had the charm of being based on an Italian subject by a popular Italian poet. Besides, it is a difficult opera to stage, having no less than eleven changes of scene. It is rarely to be seen today.

Ernani on the other hand has never left the Italian repertoire since it was first staged in 1844. This is a unique distinction for an early opera of Verdi's, but it can easily be understood. Here the composer has returned to dramatic concentration. The logic that underlies Victor Hugo's most extravagant conceits provided him with the premise that he needed. As Bernard Shaw aptly remarked, 'It was Victor Hugo's chief merit as a dramatist to furnish Verdi with librettos.'[2] No longer harnessed to Solera, this time it was Verdi who planned the shape of *Ernani*, having perceived the operatic skeleton beneath the trappings of the play. Three men are in love with the

---

[2] Bernard Shaw, *Shaw's Music*, ed. Dan H. Lawrence, 3 vols. (London, 1981), II, p. 724.

same woman, Dona Sol (Elvira in the opera): her elderly uncle, Silva, who is also her guardian; Don Carlo, King of Spain; and Ernani, a young nobleman with a price on his head, who has turned bandit. Knowing that she returns his love, Ernani decides to carry her off. But Don Carlo has had the same idea; and Ernani arrives to find Elvira repulsing his advances. All three are surprised by the appearance of Silva; only Don Carlo's presence of mind saves the situation. He had merely come, he said, to canvas Silva's support for his candidature as Holy Roman Emperor. Ernani he passes off as one of his followers. From then on alliances dissolve and re-form. Ernani, pursued by Carlo, seeks shelter in Silva's castle disguised as a palmer. Despite evidence that Ernani has abused his hospitality, Silva hides him from the King who then takes Elvira as hostage. Ernani and Silva now unite in a conspiracy against Carlo. In earnest of his good faith Ernani gives Silva the horn that he carries at his side. Silva has only to sound it, and Ernani will yield up his life. In the third act the conspirators gather but are foiled by Don Carlo, who, as Emperor Charles V, finally decides to pardon them; he also agrees to the restoration of Ernani's titles and estates and his marriage to Elvira. But on the wedding night the implacable Silva sounds the horn and Ernani obediently kills himself; Elvira faints over his body.

In the average Italian opera of the time one expects no more than a single scene of confrontation – namely the central finale, to which the plot has been working. In *Ernani* there are confrontations at every turn. In Act I Elvira versus Don Carlo; Ernani and Elvira versus the same; Silva versus Ernani and Don Carlo; In Act II Silva versus Ernani and Elvira; Don Carlo versus Silva. In Act III Don Carlo versus the conspirators; and in the last Act Silva versus Ernani and Elvira. It is by the elementary clash of personalities that early Verdian opera takes fire.

There is of course a difference between a clash and an argument. The former hardly applies where the singers, however antagonistic, share the same material, as do Enrico and Edgardo in the Wolf's Crag scene in *Lucia di Lammermoor*. In *Ernani* Verdi develops still further the procedure first adopted in *Nabucco* whereby the two contendants are kept musically as far apart as possible. In Act I Don Carlo woos Elvira with a rising arpeggio phrase in the major. She retorts with an indignant downward arpeggio in the minor. When Ernani appears the lines of battle are again drawn up. Don Carlo leads with a declamatory melody in dialogue with the orchestra ('Tu se' Ernani! Mel dice lo sdegno'); Elvira and Ernani reply with a convulsive cantilena in unison, much as Leonora and Manrico will reply to the Count in Act I of *Il trovatore*. In Act II where Silva rages at the two lovers there is another opposition of minor and major. The hostile exchange between Don Carlo and Silva 'Lo vedremo, veglio audace') is in fact an aria for the king with 'pertichini' from his subject; but so contrasted are the latter's interventions that the effect is that of a duet — the irresistible force against the immovable object:

Ex. 9

Throughout the opera Verdi shows a rare gift for honing the commonplaces of Italian opera to his own dramatic purposes. One of the hardest worked openings of any ottocento aria is the rising sixths from soh to mi falling back towards doh. In slow time it usually connotes love and tenderness. Here Verdi uses variants of it as a means of differentiating his characters. Both Ernani and Elvira take it in a single leap or, where they do not, continue the movement upwards. Don Carlo, more mature, approaches the higher note more cautiously; even in anger he includes the intervening doh. Silva drags himself almost painfully to the apex, as befits a character who regularly moves by small intervals. In this way Verdi establishes certain vocal archetypes: the heroic, pure-hearted tenor, now ardent now despairing; the implacable, granite like bass; and the baritone who partakes of both natures and commands a far wider range of expression than either. This, too, serves the drama; for while Ernani and Silva remain fettered by their own strange codes of honour, he alone can be moved by wider considerations. Hence his magnanimity towards his enemies.

The momentum is even better sustained in *Ernani* than in *Nabucco*; and once again it is the ensembles that stand out: the afore-mentioned duets and trios; finale to Act I; the conspiracy of Act III which culminates an another famous unison chorus ('Si ridesti il Leon di Castiglia') of more energetic stamp than those of *Nabucco* and *I Lombardi*; the finale of Act III, effortlessly dominated by Carlo; and the final trio of Act IV, a linear descendant of the quartet in *Oberto*, in whose relentlessly rolling phrases we sense the noose being slowly tightened round the hero and heroine. But the arias are far from negligible. Nothing could be more hackneyed than the situation of the opening scene with its chorus of bandits and cavatina for Ernani, but it is redeemed by its sheer wealth of melodic ideas. Elvira's cavatina, written for the wide range and technical bravura of Sofia Loewe, is the first of Verdi's solos to bear transplantation to the concert hall.

To Bernard Shaw *Ernani* typified 'that ultra-classical product of Romanticism, the grandiose Italian opera in which the executive art consists in a splendid display of personal heroics, and the drama arises out of the simplest and most universal stimulants to them.'[3] This is an acute judgment and one which makes due allowances for the fact that Verdi's technique is still relatively crude. His accompaniments consist mainly of waltz-like pulsations, guitar-like thrummings, elaborate, fidgety patterns (see Ex. 9) which lends emphasis if not substance to the utterance of the singer. He still uses wind instruments to pick out certain contours of the singer's line. Except for a little duettino for the lovers in Act II, scored for a handful of solo instruments like Abigaille's death scene, the instrumentation is still heavy and undistinguished. No matter; the opera has a freshness and vitality that should ensure its continuance in the Italian repertory.

[3] Ibid., p. 725.

14

The prison years

In 1858 Verdi wrote to Countess Maffei, 'Ever since *Nabucco* I haven't known an hour's peace and quiet, sixteen years of hard labour.'[1] The expression 'anni di galera' has been picked up by his biographers and used to designate that period between the triumph of *Ernani* and the moment when Verdi settled in his own property in Busseto and could accept or reject commissions as he felt inclined. During this time his power of self-renewal could not always keep pace with the demands made upon him; and though he never repeated himself, one sometimes senses the language of *Nabucco* and *Ernani* applied almost automatically without any of the composer's former zest.

He began, however, by striking out in a different direction. Byron's *Two Foscari* he described to Piave as 'a fine subject, delicate and full of pathos'.[2] Certainly the plot is of the simplest, concerning as it does the attempts of Jacopo Foscari to defend himself against a false charge of murder and the powerlessness of his father, the Doge to help him.

A closet drama is not the best subject for an Italian opera. Byron's play consists of five acts of argument, recrimination and rhetoric, all couched in high-flown verse and with a minimum of action. There are none of those surprise incidents and confrontations that drive *Ernani* forward so effectively. 'I notice that the play doesn't quite have the theatrical grandeur needed for an opera',[3] Verdi noted, 'so rack your brains and try to find something to make a bang, especially in the first act.' Piave's solution was to introduce a few contrived shocks which in no way alter the course of the plot but merely serve to precipitate a change of mood. Thus Loredano, who is

[1] LCC, p. 572.
[2] AGV, I, p. 516.
[3] Ibid.

not even a comprimario, twice makes a melodramatic appearance, causing the Foscari family to switch from lamentation to anger. Even the sudden appearance of Lucrezia, Jacopo's wife, together with their two children in the Hall of the Council of Ten has the sole function of detonating a concertato finale to Act II. In later years Verdi complained of the gloomy monotony of his first Byronic opera.

The positive achievement of *I due Foscari* is a new sense of intimacy which will not be found again until *Luisa Miller*. By that time, of course, he had acquired a richness and suppleness of harmonic vocabulary which in 1844 was as yet beyond his reach. The melodies of *I due Foscari* are as straightforward as those of *Ernani*, but they are mostly much shorter. The rhythms of 3/4 and 4/4 are plain, without triplet subdivision. 3/8 and 6/8 andantinos abound with the kind of barcarolle-like accompaniment much favoured by Donizetti. The scoring is lighter than in previous works; and none of the three act-finales finishes with a stretta. There is considerable formal compression, even innovation. The duet between Lucrezia and her father-in-law that ends the first act forestalls that of Violetta and Germont in *La traviata* in its multi-movement design where the music seems to be shaped entirely by the dialogue. It is just unfortunate that dramatically it leads nowhere since the position of the two singers remains exactly what it had been at the beginning.

Within this new, reduced scale the music often shows a remarkably long reach. Thus Act II begins with a prelude for viola and cello depicting the 'pozzo' in which Jacopo is imprisoned; from this Verdi generates a dramatic scena for the hallucinating Jacopo, ending with a brief cantabile, after which he falls in a faint. Lucrezia arrives and rouses him with one of those long magical phrases which in the later operas will function as surrogate-arias (Ex. 10).

Their brief scena leads to a two-movement duet broken off an off-stage chorus with band. Thence by way of an excited transition, marking the entrance of the Doge to a terzetto which ends in a quartet with the arrival of Loredano. In this way solo, duet, trio and quartet are comprehended in a simple sweep. Jacopo's farewell in the following act ('All'infelice veglio') is a blend of romanza, duet and concertato.

But the main innovation of *I due Foscari* is the use of recurring instrumental motifs to characterise the three principals and the Council of Ten. Of these only the last is ever sung. Yet it would be

Ex. 10

wrong to call them leitmotives, since they are never developed in Wagner's manner. Rather they serve to limit the horizons of the drama, reminding us how little the situation has changed with the progress of the action, such as it is. The Council remains secretive and inflexible (Ex. 11d); Lucrezia harassed and angry (11a); Jacopo pathetic (11b); the Doge an impotent shadow, his theme scored with a diaphanous sonority (11c).

Only in the finale ultimo does the wounded lion turn upon his tormentors with a revival of Verdi's massive risorgimentale manner ('Questa dunque è l'iniqua mercede'). Here is the true climax of an opera in which up to this moment the chief vehicle of power has been the soprano.

Thematic reminiscence will form an important part of Verdi's dramatic technique; but only in *Aida* will he again use labelling themes, and then far more sparingly than in the present opera. But despite its restricted horizons, its static plot and its lack of romance, *I due Foscari* is quite often revived, its charm lying not only in its simplicity and lack of routine emphasis but also in a certain 'marine' atmosphere, to be recaptured in *Simon Boccanegra*.

With *Giovanna d'Arco* (1845) we are back with the grand gesture. Solera's libretto, which he claimed as 'an entirely original drama'[4] – is in fact an operatic distillation of Schiller's *Jungfrau von Orleans*. Its heroine dies not at the stake but on the field of battle, having earlier been denounced not by the Church but by her own father. Solera pointed out that he had not followed Schiller and

[4] Ibid., p. 534.

Ex. 11

Shakespeare in making Joan 'fall basely in love with the foreigner, Lionel'. No indeed; since that would have added an extra principal to the cast and therefore have restricted the opera's circulation. So Joan's lover is Carlo, the Dauphin, if only for reasons of economy. The rest is according to Schiller.

That Verdi's love-affair with the German poet who furnished the basis of four of his operas had yet begun seems unlikely. There is nothing in his letters to suggest that he was any more committed to this subject than Donizetti to *Maria Stuart*. Rather he seems to have been content to fill out Solera's canvas in the manner that was expected of him. His prima donna was once more Erminia Frezzolini, heroine of *I Lombardi*; and for her he undoubtedly wrote the best music of the score: the prayer beneath the oak tree ('Sempre all'alba ed alla sera') with its fitful undercurrent of martial spirit in the accompaniment; the pastoral romanza ('O fatidica foresta') with its delicate *ranz des vaches* scoring; her duet from Act III with her forgiving father, Giacomo ('Amai, ma un solo istante'), whose long simple lines recall Giselda's duet with Oronte; her death scene; and greatest of all, her love duet with Carlo in Act I, a worthy forebear of that in *Un ballo in maschera*. In both it is the tenor who makes the running, while the soprano is oppressed by a sense of guilt. Angel voices in the form of an unseen contralto choir accompanied by harp and small harmonium have warned her against succumbing to earthly passion. Demon voices (an unseen male chorus with harmonium and triangle) have urged her to gather her rosebuds while she may. Hitherto she has held out against their blandishments; but now she falls from grace. The trivial interventions from Heaven and Hell cannot spoil the beauty of the duet whose central movement contains this transfiguring phrase:

Ex. 12

The great scenic tableaux are designed on an especially massive scale and show a growing pictorial sense of a somewhat poster-ish variety. A backcloth of orchestral sighs and groans sets in vivid relief the hopelessness of the soldiers and villagers of Dom-Rémy, in a scene which Solera designed as an *introduzione e cavatina* with Carlo as soloist. In between his spacious dream narrative ('Sotto una quercia parvemi') and its complementary cabaletta ('Pondo è letal martiro') there is a swift chorus warning him against the unholy spot he proposes to visit that points forward to the sensational manner of *Il trovatore*. Carlo, like Jacopo Foscari, is a sensitive tenor; and his music throughout tends to a similar refinement, especially in his last act arioso ('Quale più fido amico') with its selective scoring. In the finale to Act II, set in Rheims Cathedral, Giacomo's denunciation of Giovanna, commonplace in itself, generates a richly woven concertato, moving from abrupt shortwinded gestures to a long cantilena for soprano and tenor underpinned by a design of continuous semi-quavers and pizzicato strings; even the stretta has a certain Bellini-like intensity. The last scene of all evolves from a funeral march through a parade of interlocking themes to the moment of triumph where Giovanna is called aloft by the angels while the demons gnash their teeth below, fortunately without doing more than heighten the general sonority.

The weakest music is that written for Giacomo, partly, no doubt, because the creator of the role, Filippo Colini, no Ronconi, was a light, flexible baritone more suited to the style of an earlier period. Not so much weak as thoroughly banal are the chorus of demons ('Tu sei bella') and the interminable 'processional' for banda and orchestra that opens Act II.

There are one or two further attractive touches: a trio for flute, clarinet and oboe, sounding like a Flotenühr in the overture; a chorus of English soldiery with a distinct and possibly deliberate reference to 'Heart of Oak'; a trim little march to represent the battle in Act III. But in general *Giovanna d'Arco* falls below its two immediate predecessors. It is an opera of brilliant, not to say garish patches; but the sustained drive is wanting and much of the invention lacks freshness.

The same passiveness that marked Verdi's attitude to Solera's libretto is shown in his unquestioning acceptance of Cammarano's scheme for an opera on Voltaire's *Alzire* – with perhaps more reason. Cammarano was the foremost librettist in Italy, now that Romani was no longer in the field; and Verdi doubtless considered that he had much to learn from him. An inhabitant of the most repressively governed state in Italy, he could be guaranteed to remove any inconvenient rationalist sting from Voltaire's drama.

The plot is laid in Peru at the time of the Conquistadores. Gusman, the Spanish governor is to wed the Inca princess Alzira. But she is still in love with the Inca warrior Zamoro, thought to have died under torture by the Spaniards. Zamoro has in fact escaped and returns to claim her. Gusman would have him arrested and tortured but his father, whose life Zamoro had saved on an earlier occasion, begs him to show mercy. An Inca uprising is announced; Gusman allows Zamoro to go free, predicting that they will meet on the field of battle. Once again the Incas are defeated. Alzira agrees to marry Gusman to save her lover from death. But at the height of the celebrations Zamoro, who has entered the governor's palace in disguise, stabs his rival to the heart; whereupon Gusman gives his murderer a lesson in practical Christianity by ordering that he be set free. *Alzira* is the only one of Verdi's serious operas, apart from *Jérusalem*, with an unequivocally happy ending.

Cammarano constructed the libretto with his usual expertise, making the rescue of Gusman's father, narrated in the play, into a self-contained prologue – an 'introduzione e cavatina' for Zamoro. So where did it go wrong? Partly in the lack of ensembles. Apart from two finales and two duets all the principal numbers are solos. Deprived of the opportunity of pitting themselves against one another, Verdi's characters are apt to become purely generic and over-forcible. This is especially true of Zamoro, the noble savage. All the Verdian tenors we have so far considered have their tender side and most make their entrance with a gentle andantino. Not so Zamoro; from his cavatina ('Un Inca – eccesso orribile') onwards he is unremittingly emphatic. The cabaletta ('Dio della guerra') in which characteristic use is made of the male unison chorus has strength without beauty; yet we can only admire the propulsive effect of shifting the triplet from the end to the beginning of the phrase:

Ex. 13

The duet with Alzira, introduced by an excited pounding over a dominant pedal, consists of two allegro movements only – surely the most perfunctory love duet in opera. In the course of the finale to Act I Zamoro taunts Gusman with a stanza ('Teco sperai combattere') which irresistibly brings to mind Edgardo's curse from *Lucia di Lammermoor* and with good reason, since it was in this role that Zamoro's creator, Gaetano Fraschini, had earned for himself the soubriquet 'il tenore della maledizione'. In general it would seem that Verdi's melodic inventiveness was sorely tested by Cammarano's spaciously conceived arias; and he compensated for lyrical breadth with swiftness of action. The result is an opera with the brevity of *I due Foscari* but without its charm.

Yet *Alzira* is not without its memorable moments. There are two essays in imaginative scoring: a section of the overture for high woodwind and percussion of a distinctly exotic colour, and a prelude in Act II descriptive of the lonely cavern in which the Incas have taken refuge. Both finales are impressive; the first with its gradual build-up of voices, first singly then in pairs; the second with the baritone line of Gusman running like a golden thread through the choral and orchestral tapestry. But they are not enough to restore the opera to the repertory – if indeed it can ever have been said to have entered it.

Attila (1846) is the last in the line of homespun 'grand' operas which began with *Nabucco*. So long as it had been intended for Piave Verdi had been disposed to take charge of the dramatic scheme; but once Solera had taken over he was only too ready to rely on the judgment of a librettist whose formulae had never yet failed with the public. Solera freely manipulated the events of Zacharias Werner's turgid drama, turning it into a vehicle for Italian – and more specifically Venetian – patriotism. To the opening scene, set during the sack of Aquileia, he added another showing the founding of Venice on the mudflats of the Adriatic lagoon. The two principal scenes – Attila turned back from the gates of Rome by Pope Leo, and the banquet at which the heroine thwarts a plot to poison Attila since she wants to stab him herself on their wedding night – are placed in that order, contrary to Werner's scheme. The heroine herself, the Burgundian Hildegonde, becomes the Italian warrior-maid Odabella; the tenor hero is the historical Aquileian knight Foresto; Attila's chief adversary and baritone lead remains the treacherous if patriotic Roman general Ezio. Attila himself is a bass role written for Ignazio Marini, creator of Oberto.

Here at least was a subject far better suited to Verdi's early manner than *Alzira*; and indeed within the blunt, not to say bludgeoning style there is considerable progress in melodic craftsmanship even where inspiration is lacking. Odabella's cantabile of defiance ('Allor che i forti corrono') and Foresto's 'Ella in poter del barbaro!' are conceived on an unusually large scale, the opening phrase of each yielding three variants so graded as to produce a particularly strong climax towards the final cadence. In Ezio's 'Dagli immortali vertici' we have the archetypal baritone cantabile of this period – plain, massive, articulated in long phrases. The last two lines proclaim their author instantly:

Ex. 14

Indeed Verdi's melodic style is as well integrated in *Attila* as it is in *Ernani*. Its salient feature is a simple arch-like contour which marks sometimes the opening, sometimes the most emphatic moment in the principal numbers. Examples other than Ex. 14 include the main motif of the highly concentrated prelude which appears again as the Druids' warning in Act II; in Foresto's cavatina and in his romanza from Act III ('Che non avrebbe il misero'); in Ezio's famous proposal to Attila, 'Avrai tu l'universo, resti l'Italia a me', which found so ready a response in the hearts of Italian patriots, and in the solemn concerted finale to Act I.

There is a similar advance in pictorialism, admittedly of the formal heraldic sort – no question as yet of 'Mehr Ausdruck der Empfindung als Malerei'. The storm in the prologue is followed by the breaking of dawn, an essay in orchestral colour clearly inspired by Félicien David's *Le Désert* which had enjoyed a huge success in Milan the previous year. Odabella's romanza in Act I ('Oh! nel fuggente nuvolo') evokes a moonlit scene with its bright tapestry of harp, cor anglais, flute and cello. The sense of unease that invades the priestesses' choral dance at the banquet in Act II – the chill wind from the tomb – is symbolised by a figure of demisemiquavers on the strings played at three bar intervals. Unfortunately the big ensemble that follows the extinguishing of the candles, with its unaccompanied voices and instrumental punctuations, remains on the level of commonplace theatricality. Very different is the concertato-finale of Act I. Nothing shows more clearly Verdi's ability to rise to the great moment using the simplest of means than the scene where Attila awakes from a dream to confront the dream's reality – a saintly old man who forbids him to enter the Holy City; behind him a procession of Christian maidens and children robed in white and carrying palms; and in the sky the figures of St. Peter and St. Paul seeming to bar his way with flaming swords. Pope Leo's command 'Di flagellar l'incarco' is declaimed over a sequentially developed figure as pregnant with meaning as that of Ernani's fatal vow or Monterone's curse in *Rigoletto*.

Ex. 15

In the hymn that follows, the 'Risorgimentale' choral style is transfigured in music of the utmost simplicity. The rosalia in the third phrase would make us smile in any other context. Here it seems the perfect way of arriving at the climax of the melodic period.

It will be noticed that the young Verdi gets more out of his comprimario than his principal basses. The reason is simple; a comprimario bass can be required to sing in every register of his voice; the principal likes to be kept in that area where he can sing lyrically and make most noise. Which is why Leo is so effective in his confrontation with Attila, while the duet between Attila and Ezio in the prologue, apart from the Roman's patriotic line, is not especially memorable. The clash is not between baritone and bass but rather between high and low baritone. The duet between Foresto and Odabella ('Si, quell'io son, ravvisami!') has tension and excitement from its long allegro preparation over a dominant pedal (a favourite device of Verdi's to signify a lovers' reunion) through the andante of opposition to the cabaletta of reconciliation. However, as in *Alzira* there is no time for tenderness. Once Foresto has accepted Odabella's argument about Judith and Holofernes the two are off in a scampering unison.

The third act stands a little apart from the rest. It had been no part of Solera's scheme that Odabella should flee before her wedding with Attila, or that her bridegroom should come after her unescorted and fall straight into an ambush. But he had failed to supply the last act; and Piave had to do the best he could under Verdi's guidance. The succession of numbers from solo to quartet finale, certainly makes possible a long formal reach; while the reduced scenic scale allowed Verdi to infuse a little humanity into his rather odious characters. But despite a beautiful terzetto with harp for Odabella, Foresto and Ezio ('Te sol, te sol, quest' anima') the final honours lie with the victim. Scourge of God he may be; but he is far more sympathetic than his enemies.

For all its beauties *Attila* has more than its fair share of noisy strettas and cabalettas – all indiscriminate energy and pounding accompaniments. Even the unison chorus, once the great strength of Verdi's scores, begins here to lose its freshness. Clearly the way forward lay in a different direction; and happily in his next opera Verdi found it.

In describing his *Macbeth* to the impresario Lanari as belonging to the 'genere fantastico',[5] Verdi seems to imply that some kind of precedent for it existed. But the student of Italian opera will seek it in vain. *Macbeth* breaks fresh ground in a number of ways. It is the first Italian opera which attempts to reflect the spirit of Shakespeare; and for that purpose it makes free with the conventional forms in a way that had never been done before. In no previous opera is there such a wealth of minor tonality; nowhere has the gloom of the north been so powerfully evoked by instrumental means. True it was not the first opera to dispense with a conventional love interest. Yet even today it is sometimes known in Italy as 'l'opera senza amore' just as Mozart's 'Prague' symphony is called in Germany the 'symphony without minuet' – surely a measure of its stature.

Verdi's enthusiasm for Shakespeare was by no means general in Italy at the time. The version of *Macbeth* with which he was familiar was not, as is sometimes said, that of Andrea Maffei, which was a long way in the future, but of Carlo Rusconi, published in 1838. For the prose synopsis which he sent to Piave Verdi extracted the witches' prophecy on the blasted heath and its partial fulfilment; Lady Macbeth's soliloquy on receiving her husband's letter; the 'dagger speech'; the murder of Duncan and its discovery; Banquo's murder and his apparition at the feast; Macbeth's second visit to the witches and the shew of Kings; the meeting of Malcolm and Macduff on the English border; Lady Macbeth's sleepwalking scene and, finally, Macbeth's demise at the hands of Malcolm. Appropriate

[5] Ibid., p. 656.

choruses fill out the design, including those of the witches, increased from three to eighteen so as to accommodate all the female choristers. Only Macbeth and his wife are principals.

In 1865 Verdi re-wrote almost a third of the opera for Paris, enriching it with the fruits of eighteen years' experience. But it is the original version that demonstrates how far Verdi was departing from the standard patterns of the 1840s. After the unremitting F minor of the prelude, based on thematic fragments from the sleepwalking scene and the shew of kings, the dizzy plunge into the A minor of the blasted heath in which noises of storm blend with eldritch cacklings on woodwind must have come as a shock to conservative-minded Italian audiences; so too the witches with their shrill staccato mode of utterance. What would normally have been a cavatina for Macbeth ('Due vaticini compiuti or sono') turns out to be a duettino for him and Banquo. Instead of a cabaletta with chorus to round off the introduzione there is merely an allegro of triumph for the witches ('S'allontanarono!') making play with a fidgeting orchestral figure which will later function as reminiscence motif for the witches themselves. Neither of the first two act finales has a stretta. As for the hallucinations at the banquet, the shew of kings and the sleep-walking scene, there had never been anything like them in Italian opera.

But Verdi could not afford to break with convention entirely. Lady Macbeth makes her first appearance with the regulation two-movement cavatina ('Vieni t'affretta!') which by a happy chance corresponds neatly with Shakespeare's two speeches ('Hie thee hither' and 'Come you spirits that tend on mortal thoughts'). The restless patterned accompaniments proclaim the music early Verdi; but the vocal line of both movements has a rare strength and energy (it had been written with Sofia Loewe in mind); which may explain why the composer did not see fit to replace it in 1865. Likewise in Act II Banquo is given a standard minor-to-major romanza ('Come dal ciel precipita'), rich and powerful in its sonority, preceded by a chorus of murderers, pianissimo in bland C major but with those sudden explosions which were Verdi's usual way of conveying villainy. Macbeth, too, has a formal romanza in the last act ('Pietà, rispetto, amore') corresponding to 'I have lived long enough', broadly articulated and heavily scored, the Risorgimentale style infused with a new pathos. Macduff also has a romanza in minor/major form ('Ah, la paterna mano'); but being a mere comprimario he has to share the consequent cabaletta with Malcolm.

The original score contained two isolated cabalettas: one for Lady Macbeth in Act II of somewhat routine brilliance ('Trionfai, sicuri alfine') and Macbeth's 'Vada in fiamme' at the end of Act III, equivalent to 'The castle of Macduff I will surprise'. The first was replaced by the wonderfully sinister 'La luce langue', the second by a duettino for Macbeth and his Lady ('Ora di morte e di vendetta'), although Verdi had been pleased with it at the time and had instructed the singer Varesi to study it well as it was not in the usual form, the baritone singing continuously, without the respite of a ritornello. In both cases the musical gains were huge. 'La luce langue' with its wide range of modulation and richness of harmony reminds us that in the 1860s sopranos were no longer expected to use mere coloratura as a means of forceful dramatic expression. The duettino has all the pith and concentration of Verdi's later manner. The most drastic revisions occur in the fourth act. This Verdi had originally opened with a chorus of exiles after the fashion of 'Va, pensiero' and 'O Signore, dal tetto natio', no longer however in the decasyllabic rhythm and strictly related to the melodic style of the opera as a whole. In 1865 Verdi re-wrote it to the same text employing a wealth of harmonic dissonance that points forward to the Requiem.

The end of the act was entirely altered. Originally there had been a perfunctory battle interlude, a brief exchange between Macbeth and Macduff, and a dying solo for Macbeth ('Mal per me chi m'affidai') in dialogue with bassoons and lower brass. 'You should be able to make the death very effective', Verdi wrote to Varesi, 'if you can combine singing with intelligent acting . . . You must treat it in an entirely new manner. Let it be pathetic: but more than pathetic – terrible!'[6] Indeed so effective is this death scene that many modern performances splice it into the revised ending where it has no place. For in 1865 Verdi depicted the battle in an orchestral fugato during which he had Macbeth die offstage. The opera now concludes with a stirring triumphal chorus of a nation set free from tyranny. Presumably the composer had discovered that Macbeth's dying speech, to be found in early Italian translations of Shakespeare derived from Garrick's performing edition, was not written by Shakespeare at all. Verdi allowed no trifling with the Bard!

Both the banquet and the apparition scenes are enhanced in the

---

[6] GVIM, pp. 438–9.

revision, especially the latter where Macbeth's interventions have all the essence of condensed arias; but even in their original form they must have seemed startlingly novel. The two visions of Banquo take the form of free arioso, predominantly lyrical in 1847, more declamatory in 1865 with richer harmonies and sharpened orchestration. The scene is held together by recurrences of the conventional party music and Lady Macbeth's drinking song 'Si colmi il calice' – also conventional but with something peremptory about it as befits the character of the singer. Only with the beginning of the finale concertato ('Sangue a me') does the music return to something like a normal design. Likewise in the scene of the apparitions formality is delayed until Macbeth's final cantabile ('O mio terror! dell'ultimo').

Not all the modifications of 1865 are important. Beside those passages where Verdi contrived miraculously to re-enter his original vision and expand it are others where he merely elaborates for the benefit of the sophisticated Parisians. The chorus of aerial spirits ('Ondine e Silfidi'), much in the vein of the Druidesses in *Attila*, is merely prettified in the revision. A parlante during the grand duet in Act I is embellished by 'interesting' inner parts which in no way affect the musical substance. The ballet is usually omitted save in festival performances though it is one of Verdi's most impressive, by turns majestic and demonic. Only the first and last movements are danced. The rest is a mime built round the appearance of Hecate and her instructions to the witches – a more fruitful scheme, musically, than the usual succession of dances.

But some of the finest music in *Macbeth* passed from the first to the second version with little or no modification: the dagger speech ('Mi si affaccia un pugnal?') which in depth and richness of suggestion anticipates the arioso-recitatives of Rigoletto; the grand duet following Duncan's murder – yet another instance of the dynamic duet in which the lineaments of the Rossinian tripartite scheme are barely discernible and the listener is only aware of a continuous dialogue. In the opening verse ('Fatal mia donna! un murmure') the accompanimental pattern is for the first time organically related to what has gone before (Ex. 16).

The central cantabile ('Allor questa voce m'intesi nel petto') is lit up by one of those transcendent phrases similar to Carlo's in *Giovanna d'Arco* ('E puro l'aere'), the words evidently taken from Macbeth's speech of vacillation from one of the scenes which the

Ex. 16

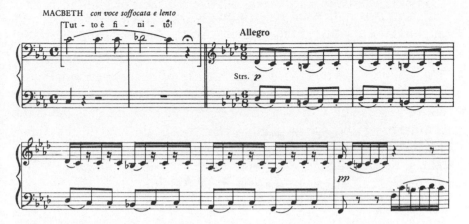

libretto omits. The only difference between the two versions occurs in the fourth bar where the chromatic E natural was originally a plain E flat.

Ex. 17

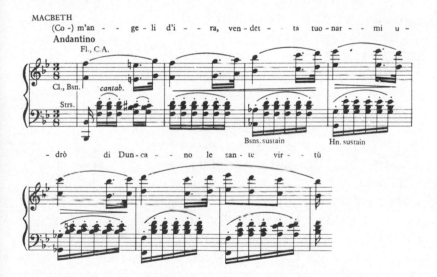

The tension is sustained in the 1847 version till half way through the cabaletta where tradition ordained that sooner or later a minor movement must end in the major. In 1865 the rule no longer applied and Verdi was able to conclude his grand duet in the tonality in which it had begun. Most famous of all the original numbers is the

193

sleepwalking scene. Once again Lady Macbeth's solo ('Una macchia è qui tuttora') is launched by a fidgety patterned accompaniment; but here it is harnessed to a dramatic purpose. The recurrent cor anglais lament conveys the eerie sorrow: the restless string figuration the continual washing of the hands.

Ex. 18

Observe too that the same pattern does not persist throughout. At bar 19 it is succeeded by another, returning only in fits and starts as the sense of the verse requires. The huge design of 63 slow bars pivots on a typical Verdian axis of D flat and E, including at the words 'co' suoi balsami' what will become one of the composer's hallmarks – a plunge onto a 6/4 chord in a remote key. A unique conception for 1847, it is no less striking in its later context. Significantly, soon after the first performance the great actress Adelaide Ristori took the corresponding scene in Shakespeare into her repertory.

In no previous opera had Verdi given such careful thought to the orchestra. The witches utter their first prophecies to a combination of oboe, trumpet, clarinet, bassoon and brass bass. The 'shew of kings' is accompanied by a subterranean band of two oboes, six clarinets, two bassoons and a contra-bassoon. The dagger speech, the grand duet and the sleepwalking scene all employ selective scoring: a basic palette of clarinet, cor anglais, horns, bassoons, muted strings and timpani in shifting combinations, to which the first two add a flute, while the second is reinforced by trombones and bass drum at the sequence beginning 'Methought I heard a voice cry "Sleep no more!" '. The difference between such numbers and the brightly scored panels in *Attila* and the preceding operas is that they are no longer merely decorative. All contribute to the prevailing 'tinta'. To Varesi Verdi wrote regarding the 'scena e gran duetto', 'Remember that it's night; everyone's asleep; so this duet should be sung sotto voce but in a hollow voice such as will inspire terror. Macbeth himself will sing one or two phrases in full voice as though carried away for the moment. . . . The orchestra will be very quiet and therefore you two on stage will have to sing with your mutes on.'[7] Hearing that *Macbeth* was to be revived in Naples with Eugenia Tadolini as prima donna, Verdi wrote to Cammarano pointing out that she would sing the music too beautifully: 'Tadolini has a marvellous voice, clear limpid and strong; and I would rather that Lady's voice were rough, hollow and stifled.'[8] He concluded that 'both duet and sleepwalking scene should not be sung but rather acted and declaimed in a voice that is hollow and veiled'. By the time of the Paris revision, when Adelaide Ristori was performing Shakespeare's scene with a snore or a death rattle between each line Verdi had realised the dangers of unbridled realism; and in a letter to Escudier he recommended simplicity and restraint. But his concern for dramatic truth and fidelity to Shakespeare never wavered.

Francis Toye described the opera as 'an uncommonly interesting failure.'[9] Nowadays it is the fashion, especially in Italy, to consider it the best of Verdi's three Shakespearean operas on the grounds that in it the composer experiences Shakespeare at first hand, not diluted through the preciosity of Boito. It is also possible to admire the work and wonder at its boldness while having reservations about certain passages which Verdi did not think it necessary to replace in 1865. Not the music of the witches, whose 'trivial and gossipy' tone when not engaged in prophecy Verdi himself intended. Not the concerted finale of Act I which, although old-fashioned for the 1860s, is too closely welded into its context, rhythmically and thematically, to be changed. But the finale of Act II with its jaunty lilt makes an incongruous effect after the terrors of Banquo's ghost. As for the 6/8 banda march which introduces the silent figure of Duncan, upholders of the '*Macbeth* at all costs' school perform wonderful mental acrobatics to justify its existence – 'a suitably trivial expression of a trivial event' – and so on. Most of us will be content to call it trivial and leave it at that. But with all its shortcomings *Macbeth* is nowadays a repertory work and rightly so. 'If we

[7] Ibid., p. 437.
[8] LCC, pp. 60–2.
[9] TGV, p. 277.

cannot make something great, let us at least make something out of the ordinary.'[10] And this they did.

If by comparison the cut of *I masnadieri* seems old-fashioned, it should be remembered that by his own account Verdi had begun it before *Macbeth*. Not only that. The libretto was by that noted man of letters and Germanist Andrea Maffei, whom Verdi held in high esteem. It was his first and only essay in libretto-writing and he brought to it considerable skill and intelligence, turning, as he put it 'a huge conception into a miniature without altering its physiognomy, like a concave lens which diminishes objects while preserving their shape'.[11] But he solved the problem along strictly conventional lines. Poet and composer must have agreed the scheme between them during their stay at Recoaro together in 1846. Only one letter of Verdi's, written in September of that year, can be found asking for certain details of Act II to be adjusted. Verdi was usually much more successful when he assumed command of operations from the start.

Schiller's first play is a typical product of the German *Sturm und Drang*, a movement of blind revolt against a rationalist society in the name of emotion. It concerns a young man who, disinherited through the machinations of a younger brother, turns Robin Hood, rescues his old father from starving to death in a dungeon and drives the brother to a remorseful suicide. But this is no simple tale of a wrong righted. The hero is given to Hamlet-like self communings and feelings of guilt and shame. He cannot bring himself to reveal his identity to his father; and sooner than allow his beloved to join the robber band to whom he has bound himself by an oath he prefers to stab her in their presence. The dramatic exposition is laid out in what was for Verdi that most uninspiring of routines – a chain of cavatinas. As in *Alzira* the characters have no opportunity to define themselves by contrast. However one may notice in each a new tendency to articulate the melodies from short rhythmic figures capable of variation and development rather than the long, inflexible lines of *Attila* and *Nabucco*. But Verdi was not yet ready to follow up the implications of this new trend, so that *I masnadieri* remains essentially a 'grandiose' work in the composer's early manner. The cavatina of Francesco ('La sua lampada vitale') poses the problem of villainy in

[10] AGV, I, p. 643.
[11] Ibid., pp. 718–19.

music and in Italian opera in particular. A principal baritone expected to make a sympathetic impression on his audience so long as the plot allowed him to do so. Even his anger, like Enrico Ashton's, must be expressed in bland lyrical phrases however tensely uttered. But Enrico's feelings are not wholly unjustified according to his own code of honour. Francesco Moor on the other hand is a self-confessed monster. Not yet having acquired the technique that would enable him to depict Iago with the lightest of brush-strokes Verdi can only think of making Francesco bluster and shout. A very different problem arose with Amalia's cavatina. For though Verdi had been very keen to write for Jenny Lind, he discovered in the event that hers was not the kind of voice that interested him. For her cavatina ('Lo sguardo avea degli angeli') he employs the same rather tinselly style that had served for Alzira's cabaletta ('Nell' astro che più fulgido') with prancing bass and little spurts of bravura. Far more affecting is her andante at the start of Act II ('Tu del mio Carlo al seno') with its delicate accompaniment of harp, cello and bass touched in here and there by sustaining woodwind – a Victorian ballad sublimated. But the news that her beloved Carlo is still alive plunges Amalia into a shallow cabaletta ('Carlo vive!') which is all trills and fioritura. Indeed it is to the Swedish Nightingale's limitations that we must ascribe the failure of her subsequent duet with Francesco in Act II. The situation is precisely that of Elvira and Don Carlo in Act I of *Ernani* – he pleading, she angrily repelling. But somehow no contact is made; the spark fails to ignite; and what should be an exciting duet of confrontation remains rather flat.

Not until the duet between Francesco and Pastor Moser in Act IV do we find the clash of vocal archetypes that make early Verdian opera so exciting. Significantly Moser is a comprimario bass, disposed to parade the full extension of his voice and so providing the granite rock against which Francesco's force dashes itself in vain (Ex. 19).

Carlo's music is engagingly fresh, from the heroics of his cabaletta 'Nell' argilla maledetta' (in which he may seem to take the task of forming a robber band rather lightly) and the 'giuramento' following the discovery of his father starving to death in a dungeon to the pathos of his Donizettian romanza ('Di ladroni attorniato') from Act II, one of those haunting minor-key melodies which achieve resolution without repose in the relative major. There is novelty in the love duet in Act III ('Qual mare, qual terra') with its dialogue of repeated

197

Ex. 19

phrases; also in Carlo's duet with Massimiliano ('Come il bacio d'un padre amoroso') where each seems to be continuing the other's thought. There is an abundance of choruses, chiefly male voice, some highly inventive and exciting, like that of Rolla's rescue in Act II, some unbelievably banal ('Gli estremi aneliti'), also two important narrative arias for Massimiliano and Francesco respectively. The first ('Un ignoto, tre lune or saranno') is the less effective of the two, being designed as a minor/major romanza hardly suitable to the horrible events it describes. But Francesco's vision of the Day of Judgment ('Pareami che sorto de lauto convito') has a much more original form which anticipates the long narrative reach of Azucena's 'Condotta ell'era in ceppi', and is marred only by a schematic use of a three-fold pattern of sequences, as though Verdi were playing unduly safe in his organisation of the large space the text allowed him. All the act-finales are strong, but especially the quartet of Act I following the false news of Carlo's death. This is in the best tradition of Verdian ensembles with partwriting which allows the character of the participants to stand out and a climax enhanced by that idiosyncratic use of the remote 6/4 already noted in Lady Macbeth's sleepwalking scene. Nor should we forget the grave Prelude with its concertante cello, written for Verdi's old friend Alfredo Piatti. Yet *I masnadieri* remains unsatisfying as a whole. All of it is recognisably Verdi; but the central dramatic conception is lacking and with it the unifying 'tinta'.

Jérusalem is essentially a work of reclamation; but it also represents Verdi's first attempt to come to grips with the Paris Opéra, that cynosure of the ambitious Italian composer ever since the time of Piccinni. Like Rossini with *Le siège de Corinth* and Donizetti with *Les martyrs*, Verdi made his debut with an adaptation of a previously written work, *I Lombardi*. In his case the plot was completely re-fashioned, only the Crusading ambience being retained. But the Crusaders are now French marching under the banner of the Count of Toulouse. Hélène, the new Giselda, is his daughter; and she, not her mother, is the object of her uncle's crime. But Roger (formerly Pagano) succeeds in throwing suspicion on her lover, Gaston, her father's hereditary enemy. Thereafter all four characters make their separate ways to the Holy Land. Roger becomes a hermit, Gaston is captured by the Sultan of Ramla, Hélène goes in search of him, only to suffer the same fate. Both are freed by the Count at the head of his Crusaders. But Gaston is stripped of his armour and condemned to death, to be saved at the last moment by Roger's confession. Like his counterpart in *I Lombardi* Roger dies fatally wounded after having beheld the sun rising over the gates of the Holy City.

All this necessitated a re-shuffling of many of the old numbers; but this matters little since *I Lombardi* is essentially episodic. The 'cabaletta della visione' is now prompted by Hélène's discovery that Gaston is alive, though in captivity; 'O Signore, dal tetto natio' ('O mon Dieu, ta parole est donc vaine') is assigned not to the crusaders but to a company of weary and thirst-stricken pilgrims, for whom the arrival of the Count and his troops bring salvation. The terzetto takes place in the equivalent of a condemned cell, where Gaston is granted absolution and a promise that he will in the end be vindicated.

Just as the librettists, Royer and Vaez, had removed the implausibilities of the original plot, so Verdi set himself to eliminate all that was embarrassingly *naïf* in the music. The battle interlude was cut, likewise certain march themes, to be replaced by better ones. Even the pieces which pass to the new version are improved. The terzetto is shorn of its concertante violin. Gaston's 'Je veux encore entendre' (originally Oronte's cavatina) is more lightly scored and extended up to a high C, doubtless so as to exploit Gilbert Duprez' famous 'ut de poitrine'. Many of the transitions are strengthened by the introduction of new motifs; and in general the new version gives the impression of being more through-composed than the old. There is some vivid mime-music (a French speciality) at the point where Hélène first presents herself at the hermit's cave. Newly composed numbers include a Meyerbeer-like jewelled miniature in the form of a duettino for Hélène and Gaston accompanied by solo horn only and followed by a 'sunrise' interlude as in *Attila* but more subtly scored; a rather commonplace cabaletta of rage for Roger which is not perhaps an improvement on what it replaces; and a no less commonplace ballet, after the style of Pugni, whose only point of interest is the adagio of the *pas seul* (no 3A) in which flute, oboe clarinet and harp weave a complex tapestry of bright threads such as we shall meet again in the ballet music to *Le trouvère (Il trovatore)*. But by far the most significant of the additions is the new finale to Act III, set in the public square of Ramla, where Gaston is publicly disgraced and sentenced to execution by the Papal Legate. Here is a canvas of contrasting musical and scenic elements typical of Parisian grand opera, which Verdi exploits to greater effect in the operas to come. The herald's proclamation, Gaston's protests, the knights' brutal response, the chanting of the monks, the women's plea for mercy to be shown – all these form a triple pattern of rising sequences, linking Gaston's moving andante ('O mes amis, mes frères d'armes') with his final, desperate stretta ('Frappez, bourroux, frappez').

That *Jérusalem* improves musically upon *I Lombardi* is beyond question. How, then, can we explain the fact that it remains the least often revived of all Verdi's operas? Partly because it is something of a hybrid. In the reckless primitive vitality of *I Lombardi* there is a certain charm, which is stifled by the refinement of the later work; nor is there sufficient new music in *Jérusalem* to compensate for its loss. Then, too, it requires all the resources of a French grand opera without offering the rewards of *Les vêpres siciliennes* and *Don Carlos* which are entirely fresh creations. But as a step on the road to those masterworks it will always be of interest to the Verdi student.

Il corsaro (1848) is traditionally rated along with *Alzira* at the lowest end of the Verdian canon, a judgment which might seem reasonable to those who have never heard it. For while for a time he cherished high hopes for *Alzira*, he seems to have written off *Il corsaro* even before he began writing it. His Byronic phase had by then passed. At first, it is true, he had waxed enthusiastic over the subject, but it seems that *Macbeth* wiped it from his mind. Originally intended as the opera for London, it was replaced by *I masnadieri*. When he eventually came to compose *Il corsaro* it was merely by way of discharging his obligations to Lucca. He did not bother to go to Trieste to mount its première, though he sent a letter to the prima donna Marianna Barbieri-Nini with instructions for its interpretation – a sign that he was not wholly indifferent to it. However, it failed and Verdi showed no further concern for its fate.

Certainly it is minor Verdi and highly conventional in form: a string of arias and duets with the central finale-concertato located at the point where Corrado falls into the hands of the Turks. The solo cabalettas are without exception generic, not to say perfunctory; indeed Corrado's 'Sì: de' Corsari il fulmine' plunders from Carlo's 'Nell' argilla maledetta', doubtless because the situations are similar (both cabalettas are sparked off by the singer's receipt of a letter). There are also a few of those 'Risorgimentale' gestures which have become tarnished with age – such as Pasha Seid's hymn 'Salve Allah! tutta quanta la terra' with its unison chorus; while the action music during the attack on Coron is on the lowest level of invention. But there are some striking novelties as well: the prelude to Act III for violin, cello and strings where Corrado lies in prison, not unlike the corresponding piece in *I due Foscari* but with richer, more poignant harmonies; the duet between Corrado and the Pasha's favourite, Gulnara, no longer cast in a succession of contrasted movements but unfolding on a continuous thread with an accompaniment that reflects the shifting mood of the speakers. (These two pieces, it should be remembered, are the first music composed by Verdi during his convalescence after the première of *Attila*.) There is genuine drama in Gulnara's duet with the Pasha ('Vieni, Gulnara') whose false suavity erupts into fury as he senses her sympathy for his deadliest enemy; and in the cabaletta that follows Verdi breaks with tradition in keeping the voices apart throughout as though indicating the gulf that separates slave from master – Seid blustering, Gulnara muttering furiously ('You know better than I', Verdi wrote to Marianna Barbieri-Nini 'that anger need not be expressed by shouting.')[12]

[12] CIIV, pp. 308–9.

There is an unexpectedly humorous vignette where Corrado, disguised as a palmer, first confronts the Pasha, lifting up his voice in a priestly whine while his enemy huffs and puffs. A duet of a very different sort is that between Corrado and his frail, flower-like Medora ('No, tu non sai comprendere') which in its delicacy and pathos recalls that archetypal duet of parting lovers, 'Dalla tomba' from *Lucia di Lammermoor*, and especially in the cabaletta ('Tornerai, ma forse spenta'), which has all the inspired simplicity of 'Verranno a te sull'aure'.

In other words, beneath the often conventional surface of *Il corsaro* the process of refinement is ceaselessly at work. The cantabile of Gulnara's cavatina ('Vola talor dal carcere') proceeds tunefully but unremarkably until its final phrase, which breaks into a cluster of Chopinesque harmonies (x). This stepping up of the harmonic rhythm is a device which Verdi will often employ to heighten a lyrical climax.

Ex. 20

Two principles may be observed at work throughout the opera: thematic economy and variation. Examples of the first are the concertato and stretta of the finale to Act II both for the first time in Verdi evolved from a short rhythmic cell which paradoxically yields more variety than many a chain of separate ideas; others are Medora's romanza ('Non so le tetre immagini') and the first two movements of her duet with Corrado; and Corrado's narrative in Act III ('Per me infelice'). Variation is to be found in the second strophes of Medora's romanza and Seid's 'Salve Allah', the one encrusted with fioritura, the other set in the minor key; and in Corrado's cantabile 'Tutto parea sorridere'. All this gives to *Il corsaro* a trim compactness which marks it out from the other operas written about that time, and does much to compensate for the variable quality of the music.

The rule 'no-repeat-without-variation' is still more evident in *La battaglia di Legnano* (1849), Verdi's belated tribute to the political events of the time. Here, deprived by the duality of the plot of a long dramatic reach, Verdi made up the loss by a meticulous attention to detail. The truth is that Méry's *La bataille de Toulouse* needed fairly drastic treatment before it could become suitable for an Italian opera. Cammarano showed all his old skill in the adaptation from nineteenth-century Spain to twelfth-century Italy. The hero, Arrigo, is accommodated with that favourite prop of Italian juvenile leads – a saintly, but invisible mother. His beloved Lida, believing him dead, has married his best friend in obedience to a dying father's wishes. But the outstanding trait of Méry's two comrades-in-arms is their reticence – hardly a valuable quality in an Italian opera. Cammarano's solution was to make his hero rage at Lida while remaining strictly correct in his behaviour towards her husband. The triangle drama is interwoven with patriotic scenes which proceed on a different level altogether. As a result, that delicate balance between public and private sentiment, between love and patriotism, so perfectly struck in Rossini's *Guillaume Tell* and later in Verdi's own *Les vêpres siciliennes*, is here lacking. Arrigo is one of the most unsympathetic of Verdian heroes.

None the less the special données of the plot produce unusual and interesting solutions. The opening scene, which sees the gathering of the Italian contingents outside the gates of Milan and the reunion of Arrigo with his friend Rolando, is laid out with classical symmetry, choruses alternating with solos and culminating in a grand 'giuramento' led alternately by the two principals. The whole is framed by an instrumental march. The Hymn of the Lombard

League ('Viva Italia! sacro un patto'), a trenchant martial theme first heard in the overture, forms the central refrain:

Ex. 21

Cammarano's verses are as vivid and inspiring as one could wish; yet somehow that theme, like so much of the score, has more of France than of Italy. It is as though Verdi were deliberately offering his country all the fruits of his Parisian experience. Rolando's cavatina ('Ah! m'abbraccia, d'esultanza') is even cast in the French ternary mould with a modulating middle section; while the preceding dialogue is set not as recitative but as a free arioso with an accompaniment of studied elaboration.

Lida's cavatina ('Quante volte come un dono') has one of those self-perpetuating accompanimental patterns typical of Italian opera, but so permeated with morbid chromatic inflexions as to mirror to perfection the singer's mood of accidie. The melody, already halfway to a Chopin nocturne, avoids literal repetition throughout. Verdi's uncanny ability to find a form appropriate to every confrontation is shown in the duet finale between Lida and Arrigo. Here for once he reverts to a near-sonata form such as one finds in French opera at the turn of the century. Arrigo launches his accusation in the tonic; she replies at length with a new theme in the dominant. During the development he seems to pursue her from key to key. Finally both take up their positions in a new movement in the same tempo ('T'amai, t'amai qual angelo') with what is essentially the same theme; but where the melody is the same the harmonies are slightly different and vice versa. Unifying both movements is a persistent semiquaver figure symbolising the stage direction: 'shaking her roughly by the arm'. Lida, it appears, can never do anything right.

Of the grand scenes the most original is that in which Arrigo and Rolando rouse the city fathers of Como against the Germans only to be cut short by the sudden appearance of Frederick Barbarossa at the head of an army. The German Emperor, being a comprimario, can lead the concertato with a phrase which takes him down to A flat —

quiet but mocking; the two heroes keep up a muted defiance, while Federico's power is asserted with increasing vehemence. At a sign from him the doors of the council chamber are flung open to reveal the surrounding hills thronged with German soldiers. In the final allegro Federico proclaims himself as Italy's destiny; his two opponents rally; the Comaschi weigh in on the Emperor's side and the act ends in a huge trial of strength. It is one of the most effective uses ever made of the concertato-stretta formula, the two movements no longer polarised but moulded into a steady crescendo of feeling, to which the highly wrought accompaniment makes a significant contribution.

Arrigo's enrolment among the knights of Death (a select band of warriors who have pledged themselves to die rather than be taken prisoner) provides the excuse for a particularly sensational piece of writing. The ceremony takes place in a subterranean vault, whose atmosphere is evoked by a succession of funereal figures on trumpets, trombones cimbasso and bassoons with intervening gestures for lower strings and a timpani roll at the cadence. Verdi, who had once scored mainly for emphasis, is beginning more and more to score for colour. Once, we may be sure, he would have added horns and clarinets to the chords; but these would have blunted the feeling of menace and diminished the starkness. The harmonies, too, are correspondingly more sophisticated – a chain of dominant sevenths carrying the music far from its tonal roots before coming home to a strong A minor cadence. The chorus that follows ('Giuriam d'Italia por fine ai danni') with its massive two-part writing has all the sombre grandeur the situation requires. Verdi never wrote blacker music than this.

The final act forms a typical 'grand opera' tableau of musical and scenic contrasts: the praying congregation inside the church; Lida on her knees in the vestibule; the far off sounds of victory; the return of the Lombard army to the strains of Ex. 21; the joyous chorus of thanksgiving, interrupted by a funeral march as Arrigo is born in fatally wounded (having, however, dispatched Frederick Barbarossa), his death and reconciliation with Rolando; and the whole beautifully crowned by a lyrical phrase, announced by Arrigo, taken up by Lida and finally by the whole emsemble, 'Chi muore per la patria alma sì rea non ha!' – a well-worn musical coin that in Verdi's hands becomes new minted (Ex. 22).

Yet at the end of it all it is the solo scenes that remain most firmly

Ex. 22

etched in the mind: Lida's hysterical scena at the start of Act III with its turmoil of inchoate themes, as saturated in melody as any scena of Bellini; her subsequent duettino with Rolando as he gives their son his blessing on the eve of battle; the cantabile ('Se al nuovo dì pugnando') where he recommends his family to Arrigo's care should he himself be killed. Except in his one cabaletta Rolando is consistently characterised as a 'baritono nobile' with a smooth line capable of deep melancholy and tenderness. Even in the great terzetto where he confronts Lida and Arrigo, as he mistakenly thinks, in flagrante, his anger is conveyed more by harmony and rhythm than by vocal vehemence. In this opera at least Verdi had found how to make use of the limited means of Filippo Colini, the baritone of *Giovanna d'Arco*.

La Battaglia di Legnano undeniably represents an advance in musical craft upon anything that Verdi had yet written. This is evident in the overture alone with its variegated scoring, its clever superimposition of themes in the main allegro, its delicately patterned andante which re-appears as the Prelude to the second scene of Act III. All this tells in its favour in the eyes of foreigners who are often embarrassed by certain crudities in the early works. Italians, to whom the spirit is more important that the manner, find that the sophistication of *La battaglia di Legnano* militates against its impact as a tract for the time, or indeed for posterity. Compared to *Attila* or *Ernani* it seems 'sicklied o'er with the pale cast of thought'. Certainly the opera does to some extent suffer from its dual origins; but the consistently high level of invention should ensure it a worthy place in the canon.

All writers, beginning with Abramo Basevi, have hailed *Luisa Miller* (1849) as the opera that inaugurates Verdi's 'second manner' – that in which he abandons the grandiose gestures of his youth for a simpler and quieter style, more suited to the portrayal of ordinary human beings and human emotions. As we have seen, this process of refinement had already begun with Verdi's sojourn in Paris, if not earlier. It was like an organic process at work at the roots of his musical thought; but it was natural that it should first become generally apparent in an opera in which these qualities were especially called for. For Schiller's *Kabale und Liebe*, another product of his youthful *Sturm und Drang*, is a bourgeois tragedy of young lovers sacrificed to the intrigues of a cruel and corrupt regime. Needless to say, Cammarano removed from it all political overtones, making it a drama of individuals only and the first scene an operatic *Giselle* – artless village maiden wooed by the Count's son in disguise. (Curiously Verdi would often show a desire to venture into the world of *La sonnambula* or *Linda di Chamounix*, but Act I of *Luisa Miller* was the nearest he came to it.) The Tyrolean village ambience, the chorus of peasants bringing flowers to the heroine, Luisa's cavatina that turns to a duet when her lover appears and then to a terzetto as Luisa's father voices his unease – all these require an idyllic pastoral atmosphere such as Bellini and Donizetti knew so well how to evoke. And Verdi rises to the occasion with music of a matutinal freshness, delicately scored. Grandiosity however is not banished. It returns in both movements of Miller's aria ('Sacra la scelta') together with some old habits of instrumental doubling; and even more in Luisa's aria ('Tu, puniscimi, o Signore') where she prepares to sign the letter she has been blackmailed into writing. In the long emphatic lines supported by one of those fidgeting, inexpressive accompaniments that seem to date from five years earlier, the village maiden becomes engulfed in the prima donna. If there are inconsistencies in the portrayal of Luisa, Rodolfo remains one of the best integrated, most rewarding tenor roles in all Verdi. Here for the first time the composer exploits the essentially vulnerable quality of the tenor voice when pitted against baritone or bass. His is the tragedy of youth in chains like that other hero of Schiller's, Don Carlos. Only once does he break free from parental authority. At the end of Act I, after a finely differentiated and flexible concertato of confrontation, just where we should expect the conventional stretta, Rodolfo thrice threatens his father, his voice rising higher each time. Twice Count Walter shrugs him off with contempt; the third time he gives in and orders Luisa's release. This is the first time that an operatic 'curtain' has taken its form from that of the play from which it derives.

But Rodolfo is no mere ranting tenor. In his duet with Federica, the cousin whom his father wants him to marry, both recall their childhood days in music that savours of a dreamy Schubert Ländler ('Dall'aule raggianti di vano splendore'). The most famous number in the score is Rodolfo's 'Quando le sere al placido', a tenor melody as beautifully fashioned as any of Donizetti's and far more imaginatively scored. Chromatically shifting string chords and a cello gesture in the introduction, rippling clarinet in the accompaniment, all enhance the lyrical poetry. Wholly Verdian is the *slancio*, emphasized by a preceding modulation, of the refrain ('Ah, mi tradia!') that concludes both verses as in French couplets.

Ex. 23

By this time Verdi is ready to spare a thought for the opposing side as well. Count Walter is not the ogre of Schiller's play but a man of power who genuinely has his son's welfare at heart. So much is clear from his first cantabile ('Il mio sangue, la vita darei') in which sadness and regret alternate with authoritarian menace. Like many a Verdian bass, Walter is a smouldering volcano, quiescent but not extinct. The true villain is Wurm, to whom Verdi wished to give a touch of the comic; but Cammarano dissuaded him on the grounds that this would give him parity with Walter and therefore strain the resources of the average company. Apart from his duet of complicity with Count Walter ('L'alto retaggio non ho bramato') Wurm is confined mainly to transitional passages where he expresses himself with a sinister suavity. Federica on the other hand is a nullity. Announced with all the pomp of a female chorus she has only a recitative, a duet in which the interest is centred on Rodolfo and the final quartet – a string of *parlanti* finishing in an unaccompanied ensemble, which is a pretty piece of workmanship but quite undramatic. No wonder that when the great Alboni undertook the part at the opera's first London performance in 1858 she filled it out with Leonora's cavatina from *Oberto*!

Whatever the shortcomings of the first two acts, there are none in the third. From her scene with Laura and the village maidens, through the two duets, the *preghiera* and the trio finale Luisa's music is no longer that of a type but of an individual. The duet with Miller in which he dissuades her from suicide ('La tomba è un letto') is on the highest level of those in *Rigoletto* – and none the less so for carrying in its cabaletta distant echoes of a similar one in Donizetti's *Belisario*, where father and daughter set off to wander through the world as vagrants. In the duet with Rodolfo thematic transformation plays a notable part in the lyrical structure: the buds of *Il corsaro* bursting into full flower.

If in *La battaglia di Legnano* Verdi lavished unusual care on the orchestra, in *Luisa Miller* he brings it into the forefront of the action. Several times it will voice sentiments which the singers are too moved to utter, as when Rodolfo swears to Miller that his intentions are honourable, or when Luisa realises that she must write her self-incriminating letter if she is to save her father's life. (In both Verdi bore in mind the prowess of Sebastiani, first clarinet of the San Carlo Theatre.) It is the orchestra too that expresses the evil nature of Wurm with many a brutal gesture. It provides the thematic background to the sombre chorus that opens Act III. Finally it gives us what many people to this day consider Verdi's finest overture. Certainly it is his most classically designed, with first and second subjects and a closely worked development all carved out of a single theme. The spirit of Weber with the technique of Haydn.

Luisa Miller is said to be the first opera for which Verdi made extensive sketches, his invariable habit from now on. For though his rate of composition over the next few years slackened only gradually, he was no longer under the same pressure from managements as before. He was free to accept or to reject offers of commissions as he felt inclined. The prison years were over.

15

The high noon

From the third act of *Luisa Miller* to *Rigoletto*, the first full flowering of Verdi's genius, seems but a short step. Both proceed by a swift, succession of short, simple ideas spontaneously generated one from another. In between, however, Verdi found time to write a work of an entirely different character. *Stiffelio* concerns the minister of a Protestant sect who returns from his travels to find that his wife has committed adultery and whose feelings therefore impel him to a course of action which his cloth forbids. He is thwarted by his father-in-law, Stankar, not from any motives of Christian forbearance but because Stankar himself wishes to take vengeance in secret on his daughter's seducer and eventually succeeds in so doing. Stiffelio's conscience is embodied in the old minister Jorg, who, after the rather undistinguished overture, sets the tone of the opera with a magnificent recitative, pregnant with the suggestion of liturgical chant:

Ex. 24

The overlapping fourths are a well-known *topos* in the nineteenth century, standing for religious aspiration (compare the fourth movement of Schumann's Rhenish Symphony, Liszt's *Les Préludes* and Cesar Franck's D minor Symphony). They reappear in ascending form in the settimino of Act I ('Colla cenere dispersa') and in the concertato of the Act I finale, an elaborately worked piece in which the chorus are once again 'instrumentalised' into a pattern of staccato semiquavers. Generally speaking the melodies are articulated in long, wide-spanning phrases that suggest a determination to keep the strongest feelings under dignified control. Typical here is the opening of the duet in which Stankar comes upon his daughter in the act of writing a confession to her husband. Is she not content with having dishonoured her marriage? Is she determined to bring public disgrace upon their house and break Stiffelio's heart as well?

Ex. 25

Stankar only once loses control of himself. Tempted to take his own life after Stiffelio has learnt the truth, he is told that the adulterer, Raffaele, is still within his walls. Straightaway he breaks into a cabaletta of savage glee ('O gioia inesprimibile'). But for once it is sung pianissimo until the final phrase, whose impact is all the greater for the previous restraint.

The part of Stiffelio is unlike any tenor role that Verdi had yet written; a man no longer young, who, like Othello, is 'not easily jealous, but being wrought, perplex'd in the extreme'. To begin with he is all charm and kindness as he tells his family and guests in a graceful baracarolle ('Di qua varcando') how he recently destroyed the evidence of a guilty liaison offered to him by a boatman. (Little did he guess that his own wife was involved.) His first scene alone with Lina has something of the dialectical quality to be found in that between Lucrezia and Doge Foscari. But the two sides are unequal, since Lina is tongue-tied with guilt. Everything she manages to say produces the reaction she least hopes for and thus twists the knife in her wounds. Verdi therefore casts the scene not as a duet but as an aria *con pertichini*, but one of unusual flexibility since each stage in the argument is marked by a new movement. Gradually Stiffelio's suspicions are awakened; and his rage erupts in a final cabaletta ('Ah v'appare in fronte scritto').

But Stiffelio's outbursts are weighty and considered, with nothing of the volatility of an Arrigo or Rodolfo. By the start of Act III he is addressing his wife with the bland bitterness in the manner of Ex. 25 as he tells her that he is determined upon a divorce. Lina has so far come very badly out of the drama. Her excuses have been confused and inconsistent. But at her moment of total abjection she takes on an unexpected nobility. No longer distraught and barely coherent, she appeals to Stiffelio not as a husband but as a man of God. The harmonies are bare and hollow; but warmth is unmistakably breaking in.

Ex. 26

Appropriately, this piece is a genuine duet from which Lina emerges with honour.

Dramatically the best act is the second. The opening prelude depicting the cypress-girt cemetery by night is as fine a piece of tone-painting as any that Verdi has yet achieved; more, it is an 'expression of feeling', in Beethoven's phrase, reflecting Lina's mood of desolation shot through with moments of panic. Then the moon comes out and reveals her mother's grave. Her andante ('Ah dagli scanni eterei') is an extraordinarily subtle essay in divisi string writing, surrounding the cantilena with a soft, shimmering radiance. Raffaele arrives for his assignation with Stankar; Lina threatens to tell her husband everything; but once again Stankar enters in time to forbid her. The action moves swiftly and inevitably towards the duel, which is interrupted by the sudden appearance of Stiffelio. He bids the opponents put up their swords in the name of Christian duty, only to be told by Stankar that Raffaele is his wife's lover. The quartet that follows ('Ah era vero . . . ma no, è impossibile') is Verdi's most flexible to date and encompasses an especially wide range of emotion and of key. The act ends with the two motifs of the drama – earthly passion and religious duty – polarised. Stiffelio's savage denunciations are cut short by the sound of a congregational psalm and the reproving tones of Jorg.

The finale ultimo has a very different character, Stankar's murder of Raffaele has drained Stiffelio of all feeling; it has put the final touch to his nightmare. But the faithful await him. He allows himself to be led to the pulpit by Jorg; he opens the Bible at the story of the woman taken in adultery. So far the music has been almost athematic in its austerity. The continuity is afforded by sparse orchestral gestures such as Bellini will use in transitional passages. All the more heartwarming, therefore, is the richly harmonised cadence at the word 'Perdonata'. Economy can surely go no further.

Stiffelio demonstrates yet again how an unusual plot will elicit from Verdi an unusual solution. Its weak spots are few – an undistinguished overture, some trivial party music, a flashy cabaletta for Lina in Act II. If the censorship had not led Verdi to re-write the opera in a far less satisfactory form, it might have remained in the repertory to this day.

Rigoletto is a very different proposition: a drama of fierce passions, of black humour and mockery, of grotesque juxtapositions and bizarre logic. Verdi described it as a revolutionary opera. This is an exaggeration; for in it he never overturned the old forms as Wagner would do in *Das Rheingold*. Rather he adapted them to the particular demands of the drama; only where this was not possible did he strike out in a new direction. The cabaletta that ends

Rigoletto's first duet with Gilda ('Veglia, o donna') is entirely orthodox, Gilda echoing her father's music as she will soon echo her lover's, until Rigoletto suddenly breaks off on hearing a noise outside. He rushes to investigate, finds nothing, re-iterates his instructions to the duenna not to admit anyone and finally resumes the reprise. Likewise the earlier movements of the duet are packed with musical incident while keeping to the basic post-Rossinian pattern of 'tempo d'attacco ('Figlia . . . Mio padre'), cantabile ('Deh, non parlare al misero'), tempo di mezzo ('Già da tre lune'); only, as in the best of the earlier duets, the boundaries are submerged beneath the dramatic current. On the other hand the opening scene and the entire third act from the beginning of the storm onward are entirely without precedent. The result is that even the traditional elements appear dissolved within a wider perspective.

Like the *King Lear* that Verdi had always longed to write, *Le roi s'amuse* is a drama of paternity. Triboulet leads a double life: as jester to a licentious monarch and as protective father to a young daughter. The first he spurs on to vice and debauchery; the second he keeps in cloistered seclusion. One day he mocks another father whose daughter the king has seduced. The old man curses him; and from that moment Triboulet is haunted by the fear that the curse will strike him at his most vulnerable point – his own daughter. The fact that such a misfortune would have happened to him anyway, since the king is already wooing his daughter in disguise and the courtiers are only too ready to revenge themselves on the hated jester, is beside the point. The curse symbolises the retribution that will fall on Triboulet for his vicious behaviour. Verdi sums it up in a pregnant motif that dominates the prelude. It is not strictly speaking the curse but rather Rigoletto's recollection of it ('Quel vecchio maledivami'), and it falls over much of the first act like a shadow.

Ex. 27

In a letter to Cammarano of 1848 Verdi had expressed a wish to be able to blend the comic and the terrible 'in Shakespeare's manner'. This is precisely what happens in the opera's opening scene. There are no conventional choruses and cavatinas. Instead a string of banda melodies sets the atmosphere of the Mantuan court, while in the skipping elegance of his ballata ('Questa o quella') the Duke proclaims his Macheath-like philosophy. There are two further dances played by a string band on stage during the first of which, a *Don Giovanni*-like minuet, the Duke flirts with the Countess of Ceprano. Rigoletto makes fun of her husband, unaware that the courtiers have already discovered the house where he keeps his daughter (his mistress as they think) under lock and key. The music coalesces naturally into a kind of concertato with no preliminary surprise to set it off and no attempt at skilled part-writing. The voices hurtle against one another over the pounding of the banda. The shock comes with the appearance of Monterone. He is received by Rigoletto with a grotesque parody of regal ceremony. The vocal line, beginning in long notes topples over itself in a flurry of semiquavers. The orchestra seconds him with abrupt unison gestures, trills and gruppetti. Monterone responds with a violent denunciation backed by full orchestra and culminating in the famous curse. The Duke orders his arrest; and the scene is wound up with a conventional stretta in which the action freezes, even Monterone remaining on stage; but it begins hushed and in the minor key. Monterone has spoiled all the fun.

So far Rigoletto has figured as little more than a master of ceremonies. From the second scene onwards he fills out to become the most fully rounded character that Verdi has yet given us. The recitative 'Pari siamo' has no precedent save in Macbeth's dagger speech ('Mi si affaccia un pugnal?'). Framed by two statements of Ex. 27, it fetches a wide tonal sweep as it moves from fear to anger, to pathos, to tenderness and with the return of the curse motif, back to fear. A similarly powerful recitative occurs in Act III ('Egli è là . . . morto!'), but the mood is one of eagerness and triumph, as he contemplates the sack that he believes to contain the Duke's body. The sequence of arioso phrases beginning 'Ora mi guarda, o mondo' moving from G flat to B flat major has something of the exultant finality of Otello's first entry, though his triumph will be shattered far sooner than the Moor's by a mere voice singing offstage. The great centrepiece of the part is the scene with the courtiers in Act II.

The opening parlante ('La-ra, La-ra') is a masterpiece of dissimulation; but events soon cause the mask to slip until, with a violent wrench from F major to E flat, Rigoletto cries out that Gilda is his daughter. His aria ('Cortigiani, vil razza dannata') is in one movement articulated in three sections, each corresponding to his changing mood. In the first he inveighs indiscriminately and with utmost savagery against the venal courtiers; in the second ('Ebben . . . io piango . . .') he pleads with one of them to take pity on him; and in the third ('Miei Signori, perdono, pietate') he begs them all to forgive him; and just at the point where he has thrown away the last remnants of his pride he rises to a new nobility of utterance. The music moves from F minor into a warm D flat major: the singer's line is doubled at the sixth by the plangent cor anglais and accompanied by a pattern of cello semiquavers not unlike that which accompanies the heart-rending plea of another father, William Tell's 'Sois immobile'. The courtiers are not appeased, but they are effectively annihilated. When the distraught Gilda rushes to her father's arms they can only shuffle away muttering shamefaced excuses to themselves and each other. During the scene of Gilda's capture they had taken on a corporate entity, like the witches in *Macbeth*. Their chorus 'Zitti, zitti muoviamo a vendetta' and associated *parlante* have the explosiveness that we associate with Verdi's earlier collective villains; the unison 'Scorrendo uniti' has a certain swaggering humour as it recounts how Gilda was carried off with the jester's unwitting connivance. But after Rigoletto's outburst the courtiers have no further existence. In the next act Verdi will have a different use for his exclusively male chorus.

It is in the duets with Gilda that Rigoletto's tenderness bursts into full flower. These rather than the solos tax the baritone hardest since they call for sustained legato singing just below the highest part of his register. All three bend the traditional forms to meet the dramatic situation. In 'Tutte le feste al tempio' Gilda has two lengthy parallel strophes moving from E minor to C major in which to tell the story of her deception; as against this Rigoletto has only one in A flat ('Solo per me l'infamia') as he laments the overturning of his own private altar, before they find relief in the cantabile ('Piangi, fanciulla'). But it is the orchestra that weeps for them, while the voices unite in flights of the purest lyrical beauty – a superb example of musical catharsis (Ex. 28).

To this the final cabaletta ('Sì vendetta'), prompted by the reap-

Ex. 28

pearance of Monterone again in stentorian voice, provides a brilliant contrast, the tonic-dominant opposition between Gilda and her father increasing the forward thrust. The duetto finale to Act III ('V'ho ingannato') is essentially a minor-major romanza for two voices which never sing together. Its high point is an ethereal harmonic side-slip where Gilda, now an almost disembodied spirit, again promises to pray for her father in Heaven (Ex. 29).

The portrayal of Gilda has been a matter of debate. Ever since Toscanini cast Zinka Milanov in the part for his recording of the third act, the lirico spinto has tried to claim it from the 'piping coloratura'. The fact that Gilda never descends below the treble stave

Ex. 29

and that she sings in tenths with the tenor rather than the traditional sixths indicates a lighter soprano than Verdi usually demands; but her character does develop during the opera. Her first entrance to an impulsive orchestral melody, her artless pleas to Rigoletto, the delicate wisps of melody that colour her brief dialogue with Giovanna and her aria 'Caro nome' designed like the Liszt-Paganini study 'La Campanella' as continuous variations – the perfect illustration of a young girl weaving fantasy about the name of her beloved – all suggest youth and innocence. But the music of 'Tutte le feste al tempio' is unmistakably that of one who has woken from dreams to reality; while the Gilda who sacrifices herself for her lover and who dominates the symmetrical terzettino that crowns the height of the storm is no mere girl. During the course of the opera Rigoletto's daughter has come of age.

The Duke on the other hand is drawn entirely from the outside. In the duet ('È il sol dell'anima') we see him through Gilda's eyes – a Prince Charming, all passion and poetry. His grand aria in Act II ('Parmi veder le lagrime') is sometimes criticised as being out of character and a mere concession to the demands of a star singer. Yet it has a subtle aptness, since the Duke, like many who are used to deceiving others, may well be expected to deceive himself. The fact that Gilda, whom he has taken endless trouble to land, has suddenly, as he thinks, been removed from his reach lends her a very special quality for one who is accustomed to getting his own way. So there is nothing improbable in his singing a poetic and musically concentrated cantabile (note the telescoping of the third and fourth phrases) at a point where a certain stasis in the action comes as a needed respite.

But the moment he knows that Gilda is safely his he reverts to type with a noisy cabaletta ('Possente amor mi chiama').

Also in character is the canzone ('La donna è mobile'), carried over from the play ('Souvent femme varie'). Like all such 'stage items' (i.e. songs that would figure as such even if the opera were a spoken play), it is on a different more perfunctory level of expression than the rest of the opera. There is no need therefore to take offence at its catchiness, like Honegger, who declared that its banality is enough to stifle a barrel-organ in the Rue de Lappe.[1] Indeed it is precisely because it stands outside the language of its context that it serves as a vital prop later on. No such objections can be made to the quartet 'Bella figlia dell'amore', the musical gem of Act III. It was not the first time that Verdi had encompassed four different moods and characters within a single movement; but in no previous instance is the integration so faultless. The duke's ardour, Maddalena's flirtatious chuckling, Gilda's grief, Rigoletto's grim menace all merge in what seems a single, many-faceted melody. Hugo regretted that it was an effect beyond the power of mere poetry to achieve. He could have added that it was beyond the power of most composers as well.

What most impressed contemporary reviewers of *Rigoletto* was the use Verdi made of the orchestra. Certainly it is the scoring – a strange, phosphorescent blend of clarinets, bassoons, lower strings and bass drum – that lends so sinister an atmosphere to Rigoletto's first dialogue with Sparafucile; and it is the orchestra that speaks most eloquently of the grief of Gilda and Rigoletto in Act II. The 'tempesta' however is something new in musical dramaturgy. Storms in Italian opera are plentiful; mostly, however, they function as preludes and interludes, ceasing before the drama resumes its course. In *Rigoletto* the storm keeps step with the action, reaching its climax with the murder of Gilda. Again unlike most musical storms it does not preserve a continuous texture. Verdi takes a handful of short motifs, descriptive or merely atmospheric, alternates them with snatches of melody, including reminiscences of 'La donna è mobile' and 'Bella figlia dell'amore' and develops the drama across them with a sense of growing tension. Two features stand out: the use of wordless chorus to suggest the moaning of the wind and a figure

[1] A. Honegger, Presentation to the *Almanach de la Musique 1950* (Paris, 1949), pp. 3–7.

Ex. 30

whose precise significance is elusive but which powerfully contributes to the general eeriness (Ex 30).

As the drama proceeds the motifs follow ever harder on each other's heels to culminate in a formal trio melody ('Se pria ch'abbia il mezzo') – a regular Verdian device for giving cohesion to a scene that threatens to become amorphous. Even after the climax has passed and major harmonies have indicated the clearing of the skies the occasional flash of lightning and growl of thunder recur intermittently. Indeed it is one such flash that reveals to Rigoletto the body of his daughter.

Opera has always recognised two species of time: the ever rolling stream and the expanded moment. In the early eighteenth century it was the second that provided the musical interest with mere recitative to carry the action forward. In the nineteenth century time became ever more continuous; and the expanded moment tended to survive only in the concertati and cabalettas of Italian opera. What makes *Rigoletto* seem uniquely modern amongst Verdi's operas of the period is that it is the only one in which, but for a brief moment in the stretta of the first scene and in the Duke's often omitted cabaletta, time never stands still.

This is certainly not true of *Il trovatore* (1853), often regarded outside Italy as an amiable backsliding on the composer's part and the epitome of all that is most absurd in opera. Paradoxically, in choosing the subject Verdi seems to have wished to continue along the path of *Rigoletto* with the gipsy woman Azucena as protagonist – a figure in whom maternal and filial love fight for mastery. Yet despite Verdi's demands for novelty of form, Cammarano persisted along the well-trodden path of cavatinas, cabalettas and pezzi concertati, and Verdi ended by accepting his scheme with only minor modifications. At least Cammarano's command of traditional operatic language enabled him to encompass the complex events of Gutiérrez's plot, setting out in compendious narrative what could not be shown dramatically. The happenings of *Il trovatore* may be bizarre, but they are never unintelligible; and the situations themselves are always crystal clear. If the musical forms are old-fashioned, they are none the less suitable to an opera which, like *Lohengrin* and *Euryanthe* inhabits the world of medieval chivalry and romance. Though set in the sixteenth century, *Rigoletto* is essentially a modern drama. As recent productions have shown, it will bear transplanting to a nineteenth or even twentieth-century setting. *Il trovatore* will not.

But if the bottles are old the wine is excitingly new. *Il trovatore* is a late flowering of Italian Romantic opera possible only to one who has seen beyond it. If it is a drama of the expanded moment rather than a continuously developing action, the theatrical interest never slackens. The symmetry of the dramatic scheme – eight contrasted scenes each built round one or more finite numbers – results from the tension of opposing forces held in equilibrium; and for once the two forces are symbolised by the two prima donnas. In Azucena Verdi first exploits the potentialities of the mezzo-soprano voice as a female equivalent of the baritone. His model is sometimes said to be Fidès in Meyerbeer's *Le Prophète*, the first of the great mother-figures in opera. But Fidès is a 'noble mother' throughout; Azucena is far more varied and interesting. While the heroine, Leonora, is the epitome of everything lyrical, an aristocrat who expresses herself in long flowing melodies, Azucena is a woman of the people, speaking a demotic language, mostly in 3/8 or 6/8, mostly of short-breathed rhythmic patterns. Lyrical by fits and starts, she is otherwise the essence of everything dramatic. When Leonora tells the story of how she first met the hero, Manrico, the music makes no attempt to underline the events of her narration; nor do we expect this. Our interest is concentrated in the windings of her melody. But when Azucena relates how she saw her mother burned at the stake and heard her calling for vengeance; how she stole the count's son intending to throw him onto the still smouldering pyre, but the poor mite wailed so piteously that her resolve failed her; how a vision of her mother caused her to lose consciousness; and when she came to her senses, there was the Count's son beside her; it was her own baby that she had burned – the music outlines every detail with such vividness that what might sound like a subject for one of Harry Graham's Ruthless Rhymes becomes a horribly convincing tragedy. Each singer has her own tonal area: A flat major, D flat and related keys for Leonora, E minor and G major, C major and A minor for Azucena. Typically, where Leonora opens with a full 'scena e cavatina', Azucena's first solo is a short strophic canzona ('Stride la vampa!'), the central episode of a gipsy chorus.

Ex. 31

A stage item, like 'La donna è mobile', it none the less sums up during its course the two forces which motivate the singer – thirst for revenge (E minor) and maternal tenderness for the son that is not hers (G major). Bridging the two keys is the note B which recurs throughout the melody with the force of an obsession.

Azucena does not appear till the second act; but her presence has already been felt in the first scene of all. The formal part of Ferrando's narration ('Abbietta zingara') has the same triple rhythm, the same key with a similar tendency to oscillate between it and its relative major, even though the subject is not Azucena but her mother. Her narrative aria ('Condotta ell'era in ceppi') is open in form with Ex. 31 high up in the strings serving as its lynch-pin; it is a tour de force of graphic musical expression. From then on it is the pathetic side of Azucena that predominates. Her appearance at the Count of Luna's camp in fetters and her subsequent interrogation have all the drama of a recognition scene in a Greek play. Both are cast in the short-winded demotic idiom we have come to associate with her; but twice the force of her emotion prompts her to long lyrical phrases that approach the idiom of Leonora: both times the subject is her 'son', the comfort of her declining years, whom she calls upon to come to her rescue. The last scene of all shows us an Azucena transfigured, after a tumultuous, hysterical scena, in the haunting 'Ai nostri monti', in whose folk-like simplicity there is something of Brahms. Woven into the subsequent terzetto ('Parlar non vuoi?'), its nobility seems to rebuke the wranglings of Leonora and Manrico. Only at the curtain does Azucena's *Blutrache* re-awake as she tells the Count exultantly that he has killed his own brother.

By contrast Leonora has all the effulgence of Romantic womanhood – a less passive, more robust Lucia Ashton. Her opening scena passes from recitative through a delicious moment of arioso ('Come d'aurato sogno') to her cavatina ('Tacea la notte') which shows Verdi's melodic craftsmanship at its finest. Even his earliest arias show a tendency to throw their main musical weight towards the end. Here the melodic centre of gravity seems to rise with each successive strain, ending in a soaring flight up to a high B flat enhanced by chromatic inner parts, a roll on the drums and a steady reinforcement from the orchestra.

Ex. 32

The fioritura of the cabaletta ('Di tale amor') is of the 'angelic' variety. Again Lucia comes to mind (compare 'Quando rapita nell'estasi').

Balancing this 'scena e cavatina' is Leonora's grand aria in Act IV ('D'amor sull'ali rosee') constructed on an even larger scale since it encloses the famous 'Miserere' scene in which she remains the dominating figure. Again in the cantabile the music is minted from the purest gold of the Italian lyric tradition; but whereas in 'Tacea la notte' the phrases had mounted ever higher, here they tend towards a dying fall accompanied by poignant harmonies. The chanting of the monks prompts her solemn, declaimed melody 'Quel suon, quelle preci' which is answered by Manrico's voice floating down from the tower ('Ah, che la morte ognora') to be followed by her passionate rejoinder ('Di te, di te scordarmi!'). In a reprise the diverse elements coalesce in one of the most memorable of all Verdi's tableaux, suffused with a romantic beauty that is all the greater for being simple and unselfconscious. With the concluding cabaletta ('Tu vedrai che amore in terra') Leonora seems to regain a certain hope and will to action. Throughout the opera she irradiates every scene in which she takes part. Hers is the glorious melodic flight which frames the concertato finale of Act II ('Sei tu dal ciel disceso, o in ciel son io con te?'); hers too is the soaring refrain of her duet with the Count ('Calpesta il mio cadavere, ma salva il trovator').

The Count, as an aristocrat, belongs essentially to Leonora's world. A somewhat generic, unsympathetic role, it is redeemed by the poetic 'Il balen' with its velvety sonority and the martial vigour of 'Per me, ora fatale'. Manrico on the other hand is poised between the idioms of Azucena and Leonora. His opening harp-accompanied serenade ('Deserto sulla terra') imbues Azucena's style with a touch of mystery. Later Manrico will be found to take on the musical colouring of the prima donna in whose scene he takes part. The turning point of the action occurs where events cause him to cross from Leonora's sphere into Azucena's in his grand aria in Act III. The andante 'Ah! si, ben mio' is a masculine conterpart to 'Tacea la notte', making use of those reiterated notes with which Verdi likes to lead up to a tenor cadence (see Ex. 33a). But these same reiterations take on a very different significance in the cabaletta 'Di quella pira'. Here they become part of the short, obsessive phrase out of which the entire movement is generated (Ex. 33b). It is the language of Azucena elevated into high heroism.

Ex. 33

A quality identified by Basevi as characteristic of the opera as a whole is 'insistenza', an urgent driving home of the musical argument. Essentially a consequent of the Azucena style, it is noticeable in the demonic stretta ('Su l'orlo dei tetti') that ends the first scene of Act I, in the racing cabaletta ('Perigliarti ancor') with which Manrico takes leave of his protesting 'mother' in Act II and the stretta to Act III, scene 3 ('Deh, rallentate, o barbari') where Azucena is condemned to the stake. But it informs some of the Leonora scenes as well: the terzetto finale to Act I with its alignment of voices à la *Ernani*; in the concertato finale to Act II amid Leonora's tremulous happiness and the taut ferocity of her rival suitors; and in the Act IV duet between her and the Count, where she bargains for Manrico's life ('Mira, di acerbe lagrime'). It remains to be added that in no other opera is Verdi so prodigal of memorable 'tunes' – and not just in the solos and duets. The old unison choruses of the Risorgimento find an exhilarating echo in the colourful 'Vedi! le fosche', with its 'anvil' refrain, and the swaggering 'Squilli, echeggi la tromba guerriera', with its wholly novel treatment of decasyllabic metre.

For the French version of 1857 Verdi made certain modifications, mostly for the benefit of the new Azucena, Adelaide Borghi-Mamo; but they also included elaborations of the texture, doubtless designed to impress the Parisian cognoscenti. None of them are improvements. The headlong spontaneity of *Il trovatore* is not enhanced by such tinkerings. The ballet music, however, considered on its own is competent in a predominantly Spanish-gipsy fancy dress. For once in a ballet Verdi quotes from the opera itself; the *Pas des Bohémiennes* contains themes from 'Vedi! le fosche' cunningly woven into the material. The *Sevillana* features a whirling violin melody like a rustic perpetuum mobile. *La bohémienne*, a fortune-teller's pas d'action, is notable for some ingenious wind-patterning. In the final galop the rising star of Offenbach can be glimpsed.

'In the heart of Africa or the Indies you will always hear *Il trovatore*.' Thus Verdi to his friend Count Arrivabene in 1862. He was not exaggerating. From its première in 1853 until it was overtaken by Gounod's *Faust* it was the most popular opera in the entire repertoire. Parodies of it sprang up everwhere. 'Ah, che la morte ognora' and 'Il balen' were to be heard on every barrel organ and street piano in the world. To German Italophobes of the late nineteenth century it epitomised everything that was most vulgar in the Italian tradition. It is of course understandable that those to whom expressive harmony is everything should feel uneasy at the moments where negative emotions are conveyed in bright, major key melodies (Azucena's 'Rallentate, o barbari' is one case amongst many). This in German eyes is a common Italian failing. (Weber, in one of his literary sallies, describes the muse of Italian opera as wearing 'a saccharine look' and singing 'sorte amara' 'to the prettiest passages in thirds'.)[2] The truth is that when emotional utterance is immediate

---

[2] C.M. von Weber, *Writings on Music*, ed. J. Warrack, trans. M. Cooper (Cambridge, 1981), p. 343.

it is often undifferentiated; what counts is its force. The characters of *Il trovatore* are supremely unreflective. Manrico flies to Leonora the moment he hears that she is about to take the veil, just as he flies to Azucena's rescue the moment he hears of her capture. *Il trovatore* has all the confidence of the age in which it was written, hence its popularity at the time. Our own more self-doubting century tends to prefer its successor.

Within Verdi's idiom of the 1850s *La traviata* is as different from *Rigoletto* and *Il trovatore* as they are from each other. An Italian critic of the time described it as 'chamber music', rather misleadingly for it is in no sense a 'chamber opera'. But to a nineteenth-century Italian 'musica da camera' meant the kind of romanza or arietta which Donizetti and Mercadante turned out in great quantities to be sung in the salons of Naples and Milan. And here the comparison is apt; for the melodic style of *La traviata* with its simple, waltz-like rhythms and its themes that move by small intervals, does indeed approach that of Verdi's own romanze. *La traviata* is a very private opera in which the choral numbers often seem like an intrusion.

It is no less misleading to regard the opera as an early example of *verismo*. Even if Verdi had had his way and the work had been mounted in contemporary costumes, the language of the libretto would have kept realism at a distance. Besides, the demi-mondaine who abandons a life of promiscuity for the love of one man, then returns to it under pressure from the man's father undergoes a progressive idealisation from real life to novel, from novel to play and from play to opera. Dumas' Marguerite remains purely theatrical; Violetta is a creature of poetry.

The prelude is a portrait of the opera's heroine. It begins with the diaphanous blend of divisi violins, which will characterise the invalid of Act III; then comes the theme of her declaration of love for Alfredo, not as in the course of the opera, a sudden passionate outburst but as a steadily burning flame. If the opening phrase can be found note for note in Donizetti's *Pia de'Tolomei* the long, climactic conclusion with its sense of two phrases rolled into one stamps it with Verdi's patent (Ex. 34). In the tripping violin descant that decorates the repeat there is a suggestion of the veneer of frivolity that marks the hostess of Act I.

Violetta dominates the opera as no previous hero or heroine has done. Her presence gives life and individuality to the other two principals. Without it they tend to lapse into the generic. 'Far from

Ex. 34

her, life holds no joy' are Alfredo's first words at the start of Act II. None the less his cantabile 'De' miei bollenti spiriti' is a neat and pithy statement of a frame of mind, the lyrical line subduing the simmer of pizzicato strings. Likewise Germont's 'Di Provenza il mar, il suol' with its woodwinds in thirds, its see-sawing strings, its simple Donizettian conjugation of the opening phrase is a suitable expression of nostalgia, as befits one who is trying to persuade his son to return to simple ways and values. But Alfredo's 'Oh mio rimorso! O infamia!' is a touch heroic for one who has merely discovered that his mistress has been selling her possessions to keep them both in funds; while Germont's 'No, non udrai rimproveri' is utterly otiose. Both cabalettas are often omitted in performance. Yet a kind word from Violetta suffices to launch Alfredo on the brindisi ('Libiam ne'lieti calici'), a melody whose charm lies in the 5-bar structure of its phrases, so skilfully balanced that the listener is not aware of the irregularity but only of the forward thrust. Alfredo's too is the other main theme of the opera, a simple declaration of love clearly related to Ex. 34. (Strange that the generally perceptive Basevi should see in the downward curve an illustration of base love, so at variance with the idealistic feelings expressed in Bellini's 'A te, o cara'.)

Ex. 35

It occurs first as the crowning moment of Alfredo's first strophe in the cantabile of the 'Valzer-Duet' ('Un dì, felice, etereo'); it persists beneath the skittish frivolity of Violetta's reply ('Ah, se ciò è ver, fuggitemi'). It forms the major-key release of Violetta's 'Ah, fors' è lui' and at the same time a refrain to what is written as a French style 'couplets', though most Violettas always omit the second strophe. Alfredo recalls it in the distance during her cabaletta ('Sempre libera'). It is heard again on attenuated strings (two first violins on the melody, the rest tremolando) as for the hundredth time Violetta takes Germont's letter from her bosom and speaks it aloud – a device not yet vulgarised by Hollywood; and in a still more ethereal voicing of strings it accompanies her false recovery at the end of the opera. Each placing is exactly calculated to make a dramatic point.

Like Luisa Miller, Violetta is a developing heroine; but her progress is musically smoother and surer. In Act I she is the lively hostess, ready with repartee and concerned to make the party go. Even her duet with Alfredo is no more than a gentle dalliance as far as she is concerned. The first note of seriousness comes with her scena and aria ('Ah, fors' è lui'), only to be immediately contradicted by the waltz-like 'Sempre libera', whose immediate purpose was doubtless to allow full scope for the bravura of Fanny Salvini-Donatelli; yet it works perfectly well on the plane of dramatic irony. Violetta imagines herself to be heart-whole; but the distant intrusion of Ex. 35 tells us otherwise.

During the weeks that separate Acts I and II nothing bears witness more powerfully to Violetta's growing stature than the warmth and dignity of the seven-bar phrase with which she turns aside Germont's rudeness (Ex. 36a). Their grand duet ('Pura siccome un angelo') forms the centre-piece of the act and the turning point of the drama. It is dialectical in the manner of the duetto-finale of Act I between Lucrezia and the Doge in *I due Foscari* which it excells not only musically but dramatically as well. For in the earlier work although the moods change the situation does not. Father and daughter-in-law are no further forward at the end than at the beginning. But by the end of the present duet Violetta will have taken a decision and Germont scored a victory, though one which gives him less pleasure than he had hoped. Through a chain of short contrasted movements, as Germont's logic tightens its grip, Violetta passes from tremulous hope to panic fear, to despair and finally to resignation, at first infinitely sad, then transfigured in the andante 'Dite alla giovine'. This is the still heart of the duet, the moment at which the intimate *Traviata* style reaches spiritual heights (Ex. 36b).

The cabaletta ('Morrò, la mia memoria') is fragmented at its final reprise as though Violetta were on the point of breaking down. Her letter to Alfredo, like Luisa's to Wurm, is accompanied by a sighing

Ex. 36

a) VIOLETTA *(con entusiasmo)* Allegro *a tempo*

Più non e - si - ste Or amo Al - fre - do, e Dio lo can - cel - lò

allarg.

col pen - ti - men - to mi - o!

b) Andantino
VIOLETTA *(cantabile)*

Di - te al - la gio - - vi-ne sì bel - la e pu - - ra, ch'av-vi u - na

vit - ti - ma del - la sven - tu - - ra,

clarinet theme, though more prolonged and expressive. There follows the controlled hysteria prompted by Alfredo's unexpected entrance – 40 bars of steadily mounting tension that finds release in what could be called an apotheosis of Ex. 34 ('Amami Alfredo!'), the final bars doubled in length as if to tell us that everything lies in the cadence (so much for *Pia de'Tolomei*!)

In the finale (often performed as a separate act) Violetta's part is smaller but always telling. Three times during the card-game, set to an electric orchestral theme bristling with acciaccature, her voice rises and falls in a desolate phrase, scored slightly differently each time in a typically Verdian gradation. A touch of conventional Romantic opera marks the conclusion of the act. Alfredo's denunciation ('Ogni suo aver tal femmina') follows the tradition of Edgardo's 'Maledetto sia l'istante', the major key and the studied declamation bringing out the bitter irony of Alfredo's taunts. In the concertato that follows Germont's entrance the mood of each principal is caught in the contour and articulation of their lines: Germont's dignified reproof, which gathers warmth as it proceeds; Alfredo's babbled excuses; Violetta's heart-break. Hers is the music that generates that sad-sweet cantilena with which the Italian Romantics like to pour balm on a tragic situation and which gathers up the ensemble in a final burst of lyricism. Even here the Parisian waltz is not altogether forgotten.

229

The mortally sick Violetta of the final act is portrayed in a prelude whose point of departure is the sequence of violin chords that began the prelude to Act I; but here they launch a deeply expressive cantilena beginning in C minor, then wandering into D flat and finally returning to the home key and a coda full of sighs stressed off the beat. It is one of Verdi's least formal melodies with the freedom of a Chopin nocturne; and it forms a thematic backcloth to the conversation that follows. The aria 'Addio del passato' is the valedictory conterpoise to 'Ah, fors' è lui'. Both share the same couplet design of minor key strophes leading to a major key refrain. But here the consolatory effect of the major is immediately dispersed in a return to the original mode. For the last time the outside world obtrudes in the form of a noisy carnival chorus ('Largo al quadru-pede'); then a palpitating allegro heralds the arrival of Alfredo; and for a brief moment the lovers enjoy unclouded happiness in the simple tenderness of 'Parigi o cara'; yet even here we are reminded of the heroine's frail condition by the transparent texture of divisi violins that accompany her replies to Alfredo. In the following transition the music captures every detail – her failure to rise, her feigned cheerfulness, the chill realisation that not even her lover's return can save her and her outburst of grief at having to die so young. In the cabaletta 'Gran Dio! morir si giovine' jagged intervals in the melodic line compensate the lack of expressive harmony. The end is soon reached. The cabaletta runs without a pause to the entry of Germont which in turn leads to the final ensemble – one of Verdi's shortest and simplest. It is dominated throughout by Violetta, second-ed by those fatal tattoos on the full orchestra that in Italian opera connote the imminence of death. After the last swelling cadence comes the collapse, preceded by a brief illusion of well-being – a detail which Bernard Shaw carried over into *The Doctor's Dilemma*. The final exclamations of the bystanders are usually omitted.

For the revival of 1854 Verdi made certain changes whose importance he strove to minimise; but all are for the better and all passed into the definitive score. Some were clearly designed to accommodate the part of Germont to the average baritone who lacked the height of Varesi. Some improve the general shape of a number, others sharpen a local effect. Thus in Violetta's violent protest at having to renounce Alfredo ('Non sapete . . .') what was originally expressed through vocal contour alone is now conveyed through harmony and increased orchestral participation. As well as that, the rising inner line of the revised version forges a link with 'Addio del passato' in the following act.

When asked a few years later which was his favourite among his own operas he is said to have replied 'Speaking as an amateur, *La traviata*, as a professional, *Rigoletto*'.[3] Today *La traviata* is the best-loved opera in the Verdian canon. Not that it is the most flawless. In its world of private relationships the problem of the cabaletta is not entirely solved; while much of the public music from the brindisi onwards seems deliberately charmless. The bogus gipsies and toreros of Act II are mere tuneful interludes. The greatest moments of *La traviata* have the simplicity that is an attribute not of naiveté but of extreme refinement, the exclusion of everything superfluous. In numbers such as 'Ah, fors' è lui', 'Dite alla giovine', 'Addio del passato', 'Parigi o cara' the Italian lyric tradition of the time is pared down to its finest. The way of self-renewal would lie in a different direction.

[3] MV, p. 146.

16

Towards grand opera

For all their conspicuous differences *Rigoletto, Il trovatore* and *La traviata* all share a common idiom: the language of Italian Romantic opera purged of all that is inessential to dramatic expression; a heart-on-sleeve manner in which, though the formal reach may be long, the component units are short since the singers come quickly to the point (Verdi, like Mozart, has the ability to say in a handful of bars what others can barely express in a whole aria). The rhythmic schemes are plain, the accompaniments unencumbered. The emphasis is all on the individual − lit fiercely, as in *Il trovatore* or gently, as in *La traviata*; but the ambience barely impinges. (The Parisian waltz of *La traviata* is the subtlest of odours.) Verdi now aspired to wider and more varied canvasses. Over the next few years his sources would be many; but the most immediate was Paris and the world of Meyerbeer.

Les vêpres siciliennes, concerning the uprising of the Sicilians against their French conquerors in 1282, is an eminently conventional subject for a grand opera. It differs from *Guillaume Tell* and *Les Huguenots* only in that the two lovers are on the same side and the hero's divided loyalty springs from his discovery that the oppressor of his people is his own father. Yet it gave Verdi an opportunity to try his hand at a more complex genre whose measure he had scarcely taken in *Jérusalem*.

The overture, Verdi's last in the post-Rossinian style with its roots in sonata form, conveys the opera's 'tinta' with admirable succinctness. The menace of death that hangs over the action like a sword of Damocles, is embodied in a persistent 'rat-a-tat' that dominates the slow introduction. The second theme of the allegro, taken from the tenor/baritone duet ('Pour moi, pour moi quelle ivresse inconnue') typifies the lyrical aspects of the opera with a melody broader and more varied in its articulation than anything in *Il trovatore* (Ex. 37a). But the main motif of Meyerbeer's *L'étoile du nord* is not far off (Ex. 37b).

Ex. 37

Les vêpres siciliennes is an opera of dramatic tableaux, of grandiose spectacle against which the principals move, often in a somewhat diminished perspective.

The curtain rises on a double chorus ('Beau pays de France') in which Verdi for the first time makes a musical distinction between the two choral groups – major key and proud swaggering gait for the French, a subdued minor-key muttering for the Sicilians. With a few deft rhythmic touches he depicts the drunken Robert, unsteady on his feet, and the graceful bearing of the two officers Vaudemont and Béthune. The great cabaletta with chorus ('Courage, courage') with which the Duchess Hélène lashes the Sicilians into a spirit of revolt recalls Lady Macbeth's 'Or tutti sorgete' but it has a more spacious design, with episodes that serve to increase the music's momentum. There is a similar scene in the first act of *Le Prophète*; but while Meyerbeer relies on a multiplicity of ideas for his effect, Verdi sweeps to the climax on a single breath.

The theatrical highlight of Act II is the 'rape of the Sabine women' carried out during the Feast of Santa Rosalia. Here is the world of Auber's *La muette de Portici* enriched by a greater musical imagination: the lively tarantella, the graceful barcarolle ('Jour d'ivresse et de délice') against which the Sicilians' impotent rage, fanned by Hélène and Procida, dashes itself in a succession of death tattoos. Act III culminates in the attempted assassination of Montfort, thwarted at the last moment by Henri. The rather Offenbachian party music is brought to a halt; and a succession of abrupt gestures in Verdi's most sensational vein resolves itself into a broad cantilena on the lines of Ex. 37a but harmonised, as often in Meyerbeer, by a single line of stalking quavers in the bass. In Act IV other deaths are prepared – those of Hélène, Procida and the conspirators, to be suspended if only Henri will acknowledge Montfort as his father. While the monks chant a *De profundis*, the female bystanders plead for mercy and the side drum beats out a death signal, muted violins sing a poignant melody full of anguished sobs and displaced accents. As two monks hand Hélène over to the headsman, Henri can bear it no longer and cries out 'Mon père!' The act ends with a cheerful stretta disturbed only by the vengeful mutterings of Procida and his men. The final massacre is preceded by a terzetto of unbearable suspense during which Hélène tries to put off her wedding, Procida threatens and Henri cries out in bitter reproach. Montfort's arrival resolves the situation. He gives the couple his blessing ('Soyez unis, o nobles fiancés'), Procida echoes him mockingly; and the curtain falls on a scene of carnage.

In an opera where historical events, genuine or imagined, take pride of place the problem arises of giving depth and consistency to the principals. If Verdi had failed to solve it in *La battaglia di Legnano*, he is far more successful here. The Henri who proudly defies Montfort in the Gounodesque duetto finale of Act I is manifestly the Henri who courts Hélène in the duo of the next act – one who, like Lovelace's hero, could not love her so much loved he not honour more. But with the discovery that he is Montfort's son he becomes fatally uncertain; and his state of mind – unusual for a Verdian tenor – is beautifully captured in the strophic romance 'O jour de peine' and its agitated allegro coda. During the subsequent duo with Hélène he regains his serenity to become the poet of his Act V 'Mélodie'. Hélène herself develops in the opposite direction to Violetta. A female Tyrtaeus in Act I, by Act V she is a happy young bride looking forward to her wedding (her famous Sicilienne 'Merci, jeunes amies' is a worthy counterpart to Elvira's polacca in *I puritani*). But the gradation is beautifully managed. Already in the central movement of her Act II duo ('Près du tombeau') with its strangely hollow harmonies we can sense kindlier feelings encroaching upon her grim determination to avenge her brother. True, in Act IV she begins by treating her lover coldly. She flings back at him his excuse ('Malheureux et non coupable') in irony and scorn – until in an impressive paragraph of melodic declamation he reveals his paternity. Again Hélène repeats his plea, but at a lower pitch and in a tone of compassion. In this way an identical passage of words and

music is given three different emotional shadings. The central movement of the duet is a solo for Hélène, full of sorrow and tenderness;
for she is sure that they are both doomed; but at least they will die
assured of each other's love. The codetta illustrates Verdi's new-
found richness of harmonic vocabulary.

Ex. 38

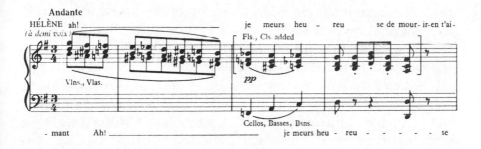

The final cabaletta is all lightness and charm. Hélène is already
rejuvenated.

Montfort is the first of Verdi's lonely figures of authority, a
precursor of Simon Boccanegra and King Philip. In the first act he is
little more than the governor whom everyone fears except Henri.
Not until Act III do we see the man behind the office. His aria ('Au
sein de la puissance') again shows Verdi forsaking the path of easy
lyricism for unexplored regions of musical expression – witness the
middle episode where the rhythm dissolves into irregularity and even
the F sharp minor tonality seems uprooted as Montfort contemplates
the void about him. The major key brings its usual sense of comfort,
but of the most austere kind with many a question mark. In the grand
duet which follows, once again a dialectical scheme of short contrasted movements, it is Montfort's warmth that dominates, expressed in
Ex. 37a. Henri reacts with horror which gives way to despair. For the
final movement Verdi decided to replace the original cabaletta with a
reprise of Ex. 37a, this time sung by Henri to different words ('Ombre
sainte que je révère') which makes a far more satisfactory conclusion
to a duet in which nothing has been resolved. Nor is the music so
unsuited to Henri as might appear. 'Je veux courir en vos bras', he
has said, 'Je ne peux pas'. From now on Montfort commands all our
sympathy. Nothing can be more moving than the Sarastro-like phrase

235

with which he proclaims the marriage of the lovers ('Soyez unis, o nobles fiancés'). The butcher of Palermo has become a father-figure in every sense of the word.

Procida, however, provided a problem. Verdi complained that Scribe had made of him 'a commonplace conspirator with a dagger in his hand'. The real trouble is that unlike Guillaume Tell or Masaniello he has no personal or family wrongs to avenge. He is a political animal and nothing else. Verdi redresses the balance against him with the beautiful 'Et toi Palerme', one of the great favourites of the bass repertoire. Preceded by a barcarolle-like introduction of the most delicate workmanship, it is a French ternary design with a middle episode that incorporates the death-tattoo to the words 'Levez vous'. Procida also has the leading part in the quartet of Act IV ('Adieu mon pays, je succombe'). The musical high point of the act, as Verdi intended that it should be, it is a quartet of pure contemplation; therefore the characters are distinguished less obviously than usual; but in harmonic and rhythmic freedom (the climax is preceded by a bar of 5/4) as in breadth and sweetness of melody it is unsurpassed among Verdian ensembles. But it is not enough to put Procida into our good graces. His Act II cabaletta ('Dans l'ombre et le silence') follows the pattern of Luna's 'Per me l'ora fatal' with a spezzato chorus protesting their departure and refusing to go; but it is far less spontaneous. By the Act V terzetto Procida has become the blackest of villains.

It is in the nature of Meyerbeerian grand opera to include genre pieces of a purely decorative or episodic nature. There is nothing of this in *Les vêpres siciliennes* until the fifth act. The opening chorus in the Spanish style never rises above the level of prettiness; while the two solos for bride and bridegroom, with all their charm and refinement merely mark time dramatically. The ballet 'Les Quatre Saisons' is vastly better than that of *Jérusalem* since presumably Verdi had more time to give to it; but it falls some way short of Delibes or Tchaikovsky. The classical ballet had not yet come of age. Flashily scored little waltzes, mazurkas and polkas were the order of the day. So far Parisian ballet could boast no score more distinguished than Adam's *Giselle*. In *Les vêpres siciliennes* Verdi produced one gem in the 'siciliano' movement danced by the nymphs of summer as they gather the corn – a haunting melody that has been compared to Mussorgsky's 'vecchio castello'. An adagio for 'Autumn' shows an ability to bend the rhythmic scheme so as to underline a choreographic flourish; and there is some ingenious mime music for the transition between each season. Yet Verdi himself authorised the omission of the ballet; and this is usually done except at festival performances.

Les vêpres siciliennes has never been a repertory piece. The necessity of coming to grips with new, more sophisticated techniques sometimes results in a muting of Verdi's artistic voice; and a concern with craftsmanship may result in a loss of spontaneity, as in the Act I quartet ('Quelle horreur m'environne'), a mere exercise in vocal part-writing. Yet the opera has qualities not to be found elsewhere in the canon. Berlioz was not far wrong in talking about a sense of power, impassioned but slow to deploy itself, which 'stamps the work with a grandeur, a sovereign majesty more marked than in the composer's previous creations'.[1]

Simon Boccanegra is for its time a far bolder venture. The original play, by Gutiérrez, has all the complexity, the vastness of time scale of *El trovador*; but its central figure is historical – the fourteenth-century Genoese freebooter who rose to become Doge of his native city and who died poisoned by one of his own faction. The plot is full of intrigue and melodramatic incident, including the recovery of a long-lost daughter. All this Verdi reduces to a basic theme – the conflict and reconciliation between Boccanegra and his political adversary, Jacopo Fiesco, the first a baritono nobile, despite his humble origins, the second a basso profondo as hard and unyielding as the basalt rocks of his native Liguria. The lynch-pin of the action is Amelia, daughter of Boccanegra and grand-daughter of Fiesco, who remains ignorant of her origins right up to the final act. There is a conventional love interest, but it takes second place. Gabriele Adorno, Amelia's suitor, is the least interesting of the four principals.

For Verdi the fourteenth century was an age of blood and iron. Accordingly he aimed here at an austerity of line and texture in which moments of tenderness occur like fitful gleams. 'If there aren't any melismata', he wrote to Leone Giraldoni, the first Boccanegra, 'there's no need to clutch at your hair and throw a mad fit.'[2] 1857

[1] Quoted in *La France Musicale*, 7.10.1855.
[2] Letter to L. Giraldoni (unpublished), 9.12.1857, in the archives of the Istituto di Studi Verdiani 48/50.

was the year in which Mercadante wrote *Pelagio* which contains one of the most florid baritone parts; what is more, its creator, Filippo Coletti, would sing Boccanegra under Verdi's direction. To a star baritone of the day it must have seemed an unrewarding part. Not only is the word setting syllabic and much of it on a single note, the Doge has not a single aria to himself; his part is mostly dialogue and declamation. Even the cabaletta-theme of Boccanegra's duet with his new found daughter ('Figlia! a tal nome io palpito') which provides the opera's chief recurring motif has, especially in the 1857 version, a somewhat martial ring:

Ex. 39

Where Boccanegra reveals to his would-be assassin, Gabriele, that Amelia is his daughter, not, as the young man had supposed, his mistress, the line is almost without expression, neither recitative nor arioso, yet all the more moving for its bleak restraint (Ex. 40).

Not until his final duet of reconciliation with Fiesco does Boccanegra's voice join with another's in what an Italian of the 1850s could regard as truly lyrical. 'At last', Basevi remarked in 1859, 'real passion and not just a dull combination of notes.' And he added, 'It was high time.'[3] The subsequent concertato lights up the last pages of the opera in a sunset glow.

In Jacopo Fiesco Verdi first brought to a principal basso profondo the qualities previously associated with comprimarii such as

---

[3] BSV, p. 278.

Ex. 40

Pope Leo, Pastor Moser and Jorg: an authority, a power of pregnant utterance out of all proportion to its length. His cavatina 'Il lacerato spirito', a lament for his dead daughter whom he had kept a prisoner in his palace, is remarkable not only for its craggy sombreness (it does not need a beautiful voice, only intelligence and good low notes) but also for its concision: a minor/major romanza reduced to its smallest proportions, its concentration facilitated by an elliptical use of the 6/4 chord in the maggiore section. The pentatonic contour of the melody is an important element in the opera's tinta (Ex. 41).

Such is the pressure of banked emotional fires that it seems to generate a long consolatory postlude. Throughout the opera Fiesco's appearances are brief but always telling: and nowhere more than in the last act where with his one line of dialogue ('Era meglio per te') he holds Boccanegra fascinated like a snake. At the start of their duet ('Delle faci festanti al barlume') Fiesco thunders at his old adversary like an Old Testament prophet, only to collapse during the following

239

Ex. 41

allegro – a movement with something of the dynamism of Beethoven's *Egmont* overture – into musical sighs and groans when he discovers Amelia's identity. It is the fall of a colossus.

Novelties of the 1857 score include two scènes-à-faire in which the musical argument falls to the orchestra: the gathering of the plebeian voters for the election of Simone as Doge, and Boccanegra's exploration of the Fiesco palace to the accompaniment of mime-music; a prelude to Act I evoking moonlight on the bay of Genoa; an aria-movement for the heroine ('Come in quest'ora bruna') on grand-opera scale with a modulating central episode and full reprise – an aria moreover which offers a perfect instance of the three-limbed melodic design that will become more and more frequent in the operas to come. But not all that was new in the first version passed over into the second. The fierce 'giuramento' between Gabriele and Fiesco was replaced by a solemn duettino with modal overtones ('Vieni a me, ti benedico') in which the old man blesses the future bridegroom of his ward. The Act I finale was startlingly original for its time. The concertato, a reaction to the sudden appearance of Amelia after her kidnap, is built on naturalistic lines: the words 'Ella è salva' are tossed from one choral group to another like an exclamation (compare 'Der Schwan! Der Schwan' in *Lohengrin*) and answered by two caressing cadences like sighs of relief ('Alfin,

alfin respiro'). Then, as the principals add their comments, the lyrical fragments come together and so wind up the ensemble in a blaze of sonority. There is a free 'racconto' in which Amelia describes her abduction but refuses to name her abductor except to the Doge. By this time the general excitement has risen to such a pitch that the music topples straight over into the stretta – no ordinary example of its type but a turmoil of rugged counterpoint, occasionally interrupted by calls of 'Giustizia' supported only by harp arpeggios, sustaining strings and upper woodwind. It is a long way from the conventional finales that were still being written by Pacini and Mercadante. But in the end it too was superseded.

In making his revision of 1881 Verdi was concerned firstly to soften the opera's harshness without altering its character or tinta. But he also wished to give depth and idealism to what is otherwise a drama of political intrigue. Hence the notion of a scene in the Council Chamber in which the Doge would call for unity amongst the Italian peoples; but under Boito's stimulus he went much further. A brief debate is followed by a full 'sommossa' of the people built on two developing themes in Verdi's maturest manner (remember that the revision was made on the threshold of *Otello*) and culminates in the Doge's address ('Plebe! Patrizi! Popolo!') in which he calls for peace between Genoa's warring factions, nobles and populace, Guelph and Ghibelline. It is just what the original opera so conspicuously lacked – a solo in which the protagonist could put forth the whole of his moral and spiritual strength to stand revealed as the noblest of all Verdian baritoni nobili. Appropriately the melodic climax preserves the pentatonic contour of the opera's tinta. All this gives rise to a new and freer concertato with Amelia and Fiesco standing out in relief, the old man's gloomy despair becoming submerged beneath the general sense of reconciliation, just as Count Almaviva's anger is outweighed by the strength of family affection in the sextet from *Figaro*. There is no stretta but a powerful scene in which the Doge forces Paolo to pronounce a curse upon himself. Needless to say it was Boito, with his penchant for creating Satanic figures, who was responsible for turning Paolo from a mere self-interested intriguer into the most melodramatic of villains. But even in 1857 Verdi had insisted that the part needed a good actor. His only solo in the opera remains his 'racconto' in the Prologue ('L'atra magion vedete?'), a nimbler, more concise conterpart to Ferrando's 'Abbietta zingara' which likewise causes its listeners to scatter in terror. The rest of his music, neutral in 1857, is re-inforced in 1881 here and there with the blackest of colours. Again it was Boito, with his sure instinct for an effective stage picture, who found him a suitable exit in Act III. While behind the scenes a female chorus is singing a wedding-hymn for Gabriele and Amelia, Paolo being escorted to prison is confronted by Fiesco who has just been released (in the original version he had never been confined). Verdi set this as a kind of funeral march with a sinuous line clearly deriving from the music of the self-imposed anathema, and a motif associated with poison woven into the accompaniment. The bridal chorus functions as a major-key trio; after which the initial theme resumes as Paolo is led away.

Many of the finest touches in the revision occurred to Verdi quite independently of Boito. The text of the Prologue was left unaltered. But Verdi discarded the original prelude based on themes from the opera; instead he supplied an entirely new melody to use as backcloth to the opening scene of dialogue between Paolo, Pietro and Boccanegra as he had used the prelude to the third act of *La traviata*, but with the difference that the melodic fragments are not merely repeated but developed. The melody itself makes for one of the most beautiful openings of any opera (Ex. 42a). Likewise the recognition duet is enlarged by a short episode in which a new freedom of harmonic vocabulary yields phrase after phrase of the purest poetry (Ex. 42b).

In 1881 acts were expected to be continuous unless there were a change of scene. Therefore as well as removing the weaker numbers of 1857 (a commonplace Hymn to the Doge, a cabaletta for Amelia, two undistinguished 'ballabili') Verdi was also careful to take away the full stops from the numbers that remained. A cabaletta for Amelia and Gabriele is shortened and made to finish on a half-close. Ex. 39 ends in the form of an orchestral peroration that passes straight into the conspiratorial dialogue between Paolo and Pietro. There are other local improvements too numerous to name; but one of the most striking is the re-elaboration of the final concertato. Here the original material is welded into still longer phrases; the melodic contours so graded as to increase the sense of scale, the texture diversified by a cross-rhythm in the bass and the climax enhanced by a typically Verdian 6/4 in a remote key just before the final cadence.

Describing to his friend Count Arrivabene the première of 1881, Verdi remarked that the second act drew less applause than the

Ex. 42

others; he added that with different singers it might have been
otherwise. In fact the second act is the least revised of all. Indeed the
orchestral reminiscence of Ex. 39, which occurs where the Doge falls
asleep, quotes the original 1857 cadence; while Gabriele's aria
('Sento avvampar nell'anima'), cast in the manner of 'Cortigiani, vil
razza' doubtless due to the similarity of situation (real in Rigoletto's
case, imagined in Gabriele's) is allowed to retain its cadenza –
an extraordinary anachronism for the 1880s. The explanation is
probably that the act belongs essentially to Gabriele for whom Verdi
felt little sympathy; compared to those of Fiesco and Boccanegra the
problems of that aristocratic young hot-head seem uninteresting.
True, at several points Verdi lifted his line for the benefit of Tamagno
and always with musical gain (the duet in Act I 'Vieni a mirar la cer-
ula' is a case in point). Yet despite the new scene for Paolo in which

we see him preparing the Doge's poison; despite the new music for the Doge in which we see him drinking it and despite the happy touches brought to the duet and final terzetto it is difficult not to feel a slight drop in the musical level after the glories of the Council Chamber scene. As in all Verdi's revisions, the better is the enemy of the good.

Simon Boccanegra is now a repertory work more loved perhaps by the connoisseur than the general public. Not so *Aroldo* (1857). This is undoubtedly the least successful of Verdi's revisions, forced on him by the censors of 1850. Here the dramatic thesis is fatally compromised since the procedures that befit a Protestant minister of the nineteenth century will not apply to an English crusader of the thirteenth; so that much of what was daring in *Stiffelio* is replaced by the conventional. A drinking chorus – the most hackneyed of all devices for opening an opera – cannot, however well written, compensate for a recitative as rich in nuance as that of Jorg (Ex. 24). This is not to deny that certain of the re-written numbers surpass their originals both in force of expression and in musical craftsmanship. Mina's Prayer ('Salvami, tu gran Dio') is nobler and more concentrated than Lina's ('A te ascenda, O Dio clemente'). The 'masked' cabaletta of Aroldo's aria ('Sotto il sol di Siria') with its controlled irony delays the outbursts of his anger to a more effective moment, unlike Stiffelio's rather petulant 'Ah v'appare in fronte scritto'. The dance music in the Act I finale is better organised; and Mina has a vastly improved cabaletta in Act II. All these changes affect only their immediate context. The impact of the opera as a whole is far weaker than that of *Stiffelio*. The new last act, however, deserves some attention. Here again most of the elements are the merest romantic stock-in-trade – choruses of shepherds, huntsmen, female reapers; an evening prayer; a storm; the arrival of Mina and Egberto in penitential mood and a quartet finale. But his essay in pictorialism, not admittedly one of Verdi's most distinguished, will have a bearing on future works. Hitherto he has not been over-concerned with filling in a scenic background except where the surroundings reflect the singer's mood. The evening's activities by the bonny banks of Loch Lomond are quite incidental to the drama; they impinge on the feelings of Aroldo and his fellow hermit only by contrast. But they pave the way for such episodes as the encampment scene of *La forza del destino* and the bonfire choruses of *Otello*. The presence of Mariani as conductor emboldened Verdi to try effects that he would never otherwise have risked. 'Angiol di Dio' is a far more ambitious essay in unaccompanied vocal writing than anything he had yet attempted; while the storm that lashes the Highland loch already prefigures the one which will rage outside the harbour in Cyprus. Nor is the quartet finale to be despised – a plain, pared-down version of a formula that has served Verdi for many an earlier opera's ending, each phrase just long enough to make its point without undue repetition and extension. Little known in its true context, it is familiar to ballet-lovers as the finale to Charles Mackerras's Verdian ballet *The lady and the fool.*

Un ballo in maschera has been called Verdi's *Don Giovanni* by some, his *Tristan und Isolde* by others. There is a certain truth in both descriptions. None of his love duets has the blazing intensity of that in Act II. Hero and heroine are devoted to no common cause like Foresto and Odabella, Henri and Hélène; it is a case of 'all for love'; hence the Wagnerian comparison. Yet *Un ballo in maschera* is less a romantic tragedy than a comedy with black edges; hence the comparison with Mozart. Wholly Mozartean too is the ease with which the composer embraces extremes of mood within a polished almost-classical framework, passing from one to the other without any sense of the incongruous. The subject is neither new or promising: Eugène Scribe's fictional account of the historical death at a masked ball of Gustavus III, King of Sweden in 1792. The true facts are obscure to this day. But to Scribe it was a case of 'cherchez la femme' – the wife of his private secretary; her husband being the assassin and the murder itself prophesied by a soothsayer. It had been set by Auber in 1833 and in Cammarano's Italian adaptation as *Il reggente* by Mercadante without much distinction. Verdi makes of it a drama of light and darkness, of reality and make-believe. Throughout the opera the two forces react upon each other always in a subtle and unexpected way. A sense of impending danger may be built up only to dissolve into mocking laughter, as at the end of Act II. In the final scene lightning strikes from a clear sky; the stage band continue their elegant mazurka for a while after Riccardo's murder, unaware that anything untoward has happened. The love duet takes place at the gallows foot.

Unlike *Il reggente* and *Gustave III*, *Un ballo in maschera* is a genuinely human and therefore moving drama; but the characters do not develop. Riccardo, Conte di Warwick and governor of Boston, remains to the end the frank, reckless pleasure-loving ruler that he was at the beginning. His love for Amelia is epitomised in the phrase which opens his cavatina ('La rivedrà nell'estasi') with its rising fifth suggestive of outstretched arms (Ex. 43a). The agents of darkness are summed up in the fugato theme of the conspirators Samuel and Tom (Ex. 43b). Both themes are heard in the prelude and will recur at various points in the opera, at one point being combined in a kind of impressionistic counterpoint.

Ex. 43

Together with Riccardo on the side of light, projecting his master's character into the soprano range, is the page Oscar. A French importation (Italians traditionally prefer their travesti roles mezzo), he adds brilliance to every scene in which he appears, sometimes with superbly ironical effect as in the stretta following the drawing of the lots. Both his arias are in French 'couplet' form. In 'Volta la terrea', in which he extols the powers of the soothsayer Ulrica, each refrain is preceded by an orchestral shout of laughter; in the teasing 'Saper vorreste' he carols away happily like a Viennese soubrette of twenty years later. A sophisticated ambience for Riccardo's court was something on which Verdi insisted from the first. Second Empire Paris could not therefore be far away. The courtiers echo the refrain of Riccardo's parody of a seafaring song (also, be it noted, in couplet form) strictly in the manner of a French operetta chorus. Together with Riccardo and Oscar they wind up the 'introduzione' with a superbly Offenbachian high kick (Ex. 44).

Amelia, curiously, is entirely on the dark side of the drama. From the start she is a Donna Anna, consumed with feelings of guilt – witness the turbulent motif to which she makes her entrance incognita into Ulrica's cave (Ex. 45).

Both her arias are in a minor key. In the first ('Ma dall'arido stelo divulsa') each strophe, after a brief moment of major-key consola-

Ex. 44

Ex. 45

tion, ends in the same mode as it began: not until the coda is a terrifying hallucination followed by the same consolatory phrase turned into a prayer ('Deh! mi regga, m'aita, O Signor'). The second ('Morrò, ma prima in grazia'), where Amelia begs for a last look at her infant son, is still more devoid of hope. Here the form is ternary, both the central and outer themes beginning and ending in the minor key. The middle episode has an obbligato for that most mournful of all instruments, the cello; and the final cadence is re-inforced by a Neapolitan depression ('che mai più').

Here a distinction should be made between the real darkness that surrounds Amelia and the artificial gloom generated by Ulrica, who is merely putting on a charade. Samuel and Tom, too, for all their inky bass resonance and malevolent mutterings, are harmless, even comic figures until joined by Renato. The opening of Act II re-calls the horror of the introduction to the graveyard scene in *Stiffelio* raised to a higher power. In the terzetto in Act I ('Della città all'occaso') Ulrica's insinuating tones and swiftly changing harmonies contrast with Amelia's long-drawn out phrases over tense string tremolandos. At such moments one realises why Amelia is often cast as a dramatic soprano rather than the usual lirico spinto.

Renato on the other hand has all the ambivalence of the Verdian baritone. It is he who brings the darkest shadows into the brilliance

247

of the introduzione with his warning to Riccardo about the plots against his life. Even his cavatina ('Alla vita che t'arride') – like Riccardo's in one movement with the gait of a cabaletta – is faintly clouded, a prominent horn in the second phrase, even though it signifies no more than a tender concern for his master's safety. Very remarkable is the terzettino movement in Act II ('Odi tu come fremono') in which he is the moving spirit in more senses than one. Sometimes unkindly compared to the Lord Chancellor's dream in *Iolanthe* it has a demonic insistence suggesting an infernal hunt with Riccardo as the quarry. Its perfect symmetry of form has already been the subject of an essay by Dallapiccola. But what is its purpose in the drama? To suggest, surely, that the forces which are hounding Riccardo are those of his own nature; and that Nemesis is already present in the figure of Renato even though he has not yet discovered Amelia's identity. Faced with danger, Riccardo remains fascinated by it, unable to move till too late. A modulation of Schubertian poignancy in his final romanza ('Ma se m'è forza a perderti') hints that Riccardo might have learned from experience; but no; the final scene shows him once more dancing on the edge of a precipice, with fatal consequences.

The turning point of the drama is embodied in Renato's 'Eri tu', justly one of the most famous arias in the baritone repertory, in which he turns the full force of his rage on the absent Riccardo. Never before have two sections been more strongly contrasted within a single movement. The Italian convention whereby a minor-key movement is allowed to end in the relative major is here exploited for all its inherent nostalgia. 'O dolcezze perdute', introduced by flutes and harp, is a deeply moving lament for a lost Eden. From now on Renato is heart and soul with the conspirators.

The forms of *Un ballo in maschera* are both freer in relation to the post-Rossinian tradition than usual yet at the same time more balanced and tightly knit. The opening 'introduzione' embraces three cavatinas within an opening and closing ensemble. The two movements of Ulrica's cavatina ('Re dell'abisso, affrettati') are based on the same theme, minor in the first, major in the second. The following complex scène-à-faire which sees the arrival first of Silvano the sailor then of Amelia's servant is held together by varied repetitions of a single cadential phrase (one thinks of the quartet 'Non ti fidar' from *Don Giovanni*). Ulrica's grim prophecy detonates the expected concertato; but it is as far removed from the customary massive ensemble as can be imagined. As light as a soufflé, it is based on two themes, the first stated by Riccardo ('E scherzo od è follia') the second by Oscar ('E tal fia dunque il fato') each in a different key to begin with, then recapitulated sonata-fashion in the original tonic. There are characteristic interventions for Ulrica and the two conspirators and a neat modulatory epigram to finish. More surprising still the two themes of the martial stretta ('O figlio d'Inghilterra') are thinly disguised versions of those of the concertato. By a final stroke of bravura Verdi combines them vertically in the reprise.

The final ensemble of Act II is a rondo based on a theme that derives quite logically from the previous scena material ('Ve', se di notte'). Here there is a deliberate sense of anti-climax. Ever since the love duet a sense of imminent danger has been piling up. But with the unmasking of Amelia it melts into hilarity. A husband having a moonlit tryst with his own wife – what a story that will make! The insistent laughter aggravates Renato's bitterness and sense of betrayal; but for the moment both his and Amelia's episodes are muted. Not until the beginning of the next act does he vent his feelings in a harrowing scene with his wife. The 'congiura' which follows the entrance of Samuel and Tom is organised on the polarity of two themes, one conversational, developing and confined to the orchestra with 'parlanti' interventions, the other static, regular and vocal ('Dunque l'onta di tutti sol una') and despite its dark scoring of thrumming harps, cellos and basses perhaps a trifle idealistic in tone for three people who are actuated solely by personal vengeance. It is the first theme which supplies the arpeggio motif that accompanies the casting and drawing of the lots, musically the most terrifying moment in the opera, to which Verdi brings all the resources of a by now sophisticated orchestral technique. As in *Simon Boccanegra* the grandiose slow ensemble is reserved for the hero's death scene.

The centre-piece of the score is the love-duet of Act II. It is cast in the traditional three movements; but the first two shade into one another, while the second proceeds in a constant crescendo of emotion which finally carries the music away from its tonal base into a realm of dreaming ecstasy. Here the singers lose coherence and it is left to the orchestra to vent their feelings (Ex. 46).

The same theme, now sung by both parties, intrudes into the cabaletta ('Oh, qual soave brivido') thus totally upsetting the usual formal emphasis – a wonderfully effective way of depicting two people swept off their feet. And is it significant that the violin shivers

Ex. 46

that mark the buoyant cabaletta melody are the same as those that punctuated Ulrica's welcoming of Beelzebub?

Like all Verdi's works of consolidation *Un ballo in maschera* evinces a notable progress in sheer musical technique. In the prelude we find violin harmonics used for the first time. The party music of the last act is far more elegant than any that the composer had written so far; and in general the score achieves a formal equilibrium not to be regained until *Aida*.

If Riccardo's fate is a natural consequence of his own temperament, that which pursues the hero and heroine of *La forza del destino* (1862, revised 1869) comes from without. Its dramatic premise is what might be called the millionth chance. Human beings are not consistent; they do not regularly adhere to the code that they profess. For a Spanish nobleman of the eighteenth century the pollution of his family's honour through a misalliance is a sin beyond all possibilities of foregiveness. When Leonora de Vargas decides to elope with the handsome Don Alvaro of whose origins nothing is known, she is aware that in theory at least her father is bound to cast her off. But she relies on illogical good will and commonsense to come to her aid. As her maid Curra puts it in the original play, her father will at first run complaining to the mayor about the stain on his family's escutcheon; he will have search parties out for them throughout the length and breadth of Spain; but he will soon calm down. And by the time Leonora has presented him with a grandchild he will be only too glad to welcome the fugitives home. As for Leonora's two brothers, Carlos and Alfonso, they will soon be boasting about their rich brother-in-law who gives them expensive presents and pays off their debts. But that is not how it happens. The lovers are caught in the act of eloping. Alvaro throws away his pistol, which accidentally fires, wounding Leonora's father fatally: and he dies cursing his daughter. She and Alvaro become separated. But Fate hounds them, figuratively, to the ends of the earth in the form of the avenging brothers. Not even in the arms of the Church can Alvaro avoid his destiny, which is to cause the death of the entire Calatrava family, including Leonora. At the end he goes mad and hurls himself from a precipice shrieking curses on mankind. Rivas' drama is a vast canvas of variegated humanity. Alvaro, Leonora, Alfonso move in spiritual isolation in a world of muleteers, soldiers, peasants, gipsies and monks whose down-to-earth normality makes a vivid contrast with their own obsessive behaviour. Inevitably the operatic version is subject to theatrical economy. Carlos, the soldier, Alfonso the student and his friend Pereda had to be amalgamated into the single figure of Carlo, who thus takes on a Protean character for which the baritone voice is eminently suited. By the same token three of the smaller roles – the gipsy girl Presiosilla, the muleteer Trabuco and the lay priest Fra Melitone – are expanded sufficiently to establish themselves musically and dramatically. In order to fill out the background still further Verdi devised an encampment scene on the lines of Schiller's *Wallensteins Lager* and even borrowed the punning sermon of Schiller's comic monk to put into the mouth of Fra Melitone. In all this he moved far beyond the scope of Rivas' drama, rounding his lesser characters in the manner of a Shakespearean chronicle play; and just as Rivas and Shakespeare distinguish between the nobles and the people by making the first talk verse and the second prose, so Verdi diversifies his musical language according to the status, real or pretended, or of his characters. Preziosilla, whether drumming up recruits for the war in Spain ('Al suon del tamburo'), telling fortunes at Velletri ('Venite all'indovina'), jollying the homesick recruits or leading the assembled soldiery in a Rat-a-plan chorus, is always a woman of the people. Trabuco, a tetchy comedian in the tavern in

Hornachuelos, takes on a curiously Jewish character when he turns pedlar at Velletri. His 'A buon mercato' is much in the idiom of Isacco's 'Stringhe e ferri' from Rossini's *La gazza ladra*. Fra Melitone is conceived wholly in comic terms; but they are a long way from those of conventional opera buffa. His interventions in the duet between Leonora and the Father Superior have an almost Haydnesque wit, as does his scene with the poor of the parish in Act IV (see Ex. 3b); while the punning sermon ('Toh, toh! Poffare il mondo!') offers a splendid example of that declaimed melody, free, varied, but never formless, that Verdi will later put into the mouth of Falstaff. The Padre Guardiano has all the authority of a high church dignitary. Don Carlo alters his character according to whom he happens to be addressing. As Pereda he is all high spirits, with just a hint of the cloven hoof in the final episode of his ballata ('Son Pereda, son ricco di onore'). As with so many Verdian baritones his is the pivotal aria which determines the outcome of the drama. The cantabile 'Urna fatale' has such breadth and nobility as to make us believe that Carlo's better nature will win the day. But unlike his great namesake in *Ernani* he lets personal feelings run away with him. 'Egli è salvo', in 1869 Verdi's last remaining solo cabaletta, suggests a bloodhound hot on the trail of his victim. At the start of his following scene with Alvaro he has no difficulty in adjusting the mask of kindly concern.

But it is the two lovers, Leonora and Alvaro, who dominate the canvas; and it is with them that the three recurring motifs are associated. Two belong to Leonora: the motto theme that symbolises the Fate of the title (Ex. 47a), and an expansive gesture denoting religious aspiration (Ex. 47b). The first with its Beethovenian drive develops and generates new ideas; the second remains unaltered at every appearance. Both form the pillars on which the prelude of 1862 and the overture of 1869 are supported. Ex. 47a furnishes the thematic basis for the scene of the accidental murder.

Alvaro's theme makes use of those overlapping fourths that so often carry overtones of piety (he has after all described his love as 'pure and holy') (Ex. 48).

Both characters develop during the action, their music becoming more inward under the growing weight of their memories. Even at the beginning Leonora is a more complex and imaginative person than her namesake in *Il trovatore*. The opening scene finds her in a state of growing indecision. Her aria ('Me pellegrina ed orfana') to

Ex. 47

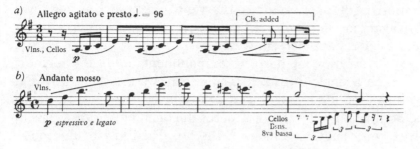

Ex. 48

words originally intended for Cordelia in the unwritten *Re Lear* is a
three-part design that oscillates between major and minor; its line is
full of convulsive accents and tormented contours. Eloquent use is
made of a solo cello, no longer as a concertato instrument but as part
of the orchestral fabric, springing into prominence only at certain
moments. With the arrival of Alvaro her state of mind becomes
desperate. She loves him, she is weeping tears of joy – but could they
not put off their elopement till to-morrow? Here the widely arching
phrases of 1862 were replaced in 1869 with an almost naturalistic
declamation which gradually falters into incoherence. Not until
Alvaro is about to leave her forever does she regain the will to act.

By the second scene of Act II Leonora has taken on a certain
grandeur in her resolve to escape from the world. First we hear the
pursuing Ex. 47a, then her aria ('Madre, pietosa Vergine') of which
Ex. 47b forms the climax and major key resolution, the distant
chanting of the monks adding to its spaciousness. In the course of her
duet with the Padre Guardiano she gradually attains a mood of calm,
disturbed only by the desperate eagerness – much enhanced in the
1869 version – with which she begs to be allowed to live out her life
as a hermit. In the final ensemble of the act ('La Vergine degli Angeli')
Leonora seems to have become absorbed into the tranquil faith of the
Church. But as the last cadence dies away an ominous figure in the
bass reminds us that she has not escaped her fate.

A whole act passes before we meet her again. Her aria ('Pace, pace, mio Dio'), scored with the utmost delicacy, is one of the inspirations of the opera: a long ternary movement such as Verdi will employ again in *Don Carlos* where the singer summons up remembrance of things past. Here, however, there are no changes of tempo; a steady undulation of harp accompaniment holds the melodic discourse on a single thread. It is sung beneath the shadow of Ex. 47a, which precedes it and obtrudes into the central episode. But to all the doubts and fears that it arouses the opening phrase seems to supply a consoling answer (see Ex. 49a). Then just as the music appears about to subside into a calm if somewhat pathetic coda, sounds of intrusion are heard and Leonora with rising screams of 'maledizione!' retreats terrified into her cave.

One of the strongest reasons for preferring the revised denouement despite its violation of the dramatic premise is that in 1862 Leonora's stature becomes diminished: a brief moment of lovers' re-union over a typical throbbing dominant pedal, and a somewhat commonplace death scene ('Vedi destin! Io muoio') which swells and fades. In 1869 Verdi reverts to the realism of the revised Act I. Leonora staggers in mortally wounded to an orchestral motif of unparalleled brutality, more daring than anything he or anyone else would write for years to come (Ex. 49b).

Thereafter she melts into the ethereal atmosphere of the final terzetto, ('Non imprecare; umiliati'); the last string tremolandos are her apotheosis.

Alvaro's character traces a similar trajectory. His duet with Leonora ('Ah per sempre') is designed to reveal all those qualities that the play only makes clear through the conversation of others. Youthful ardour propels the opening allegro in which Ex. 48 makes its first appearance as an episode. 'Pronti destrieri' is full of grace and tenderness, an idealised version of the Duke of Mantua's 'E il sol dell'anima', which opens out like a flower where Alvaro mentions the sun, the god of his ancestors. But fatalistic gloom descends upon him in the face of Leonora's persistent irresolution, to be instantly dispelled when finally she makes up her mind to elope. The Alvaro whom we meet at the beginning of Act III is already changed. A prelude with concertante clarinet in the form of a meditation on Ex. 48 recalls what has clearly become a distant memory, since the theme is slow to take shape. There follows a scena in which Alvaro describes – not perhaps as clearly as the average listener might wish – his 'life

Ex. 49

and miracles'. The son of the Spanish Viceroy of Peru and an Inca princess, he has come to Spain to plead for his father's release from prison to which he had been condemned after an unsuccessful rebellion. Then, with two oblique references to Ex. 48, Alvaro slips, as it were, sideways into his aria ('O tu che in seno agli angeli') in which the tonality declares itself only at the first cadence. The aria itself ranges through a succession of different ideas in which the rising sixth, whether soh to mi or doh to la, remains a constant. It bears the same connotation of romantic love as in *Ernani* and as such provides a link between the language of Leonora and Alvaro. But there is nothing here of the white-hot passions of the earlier opera. 'O tu che in seno agli angeli' perfectly illustrates Wordsworth's 'emotion recollected in tranquillity'. Here Verdi explores the 'inward' aspects of Romanticism – perhaps all the more easily for having segregated the extravert element into the scenes of everyday life.

In the duets Verdi followed the contemporary pattern of a series of alternating solos with the voices joining only in the final cabaletta. That for the lovers in Act I ('Seguirti fin agli ultimi') was criticised at the time for its resemblance to Donizetti's 'Il suon dell'arpe angeliche'. But the swiftly moving bass gives it an urgency beyond the reach of Donizetti's simple tonic and dominant harmonies. For Verdi the form with its built-in repetitions remained until the 1870s the perfect vehicle for lovers who outstay their own safety. Here the repetitions, far from easing the action to a halt, serve to increase the dramatic tension.

Leonora's duet with Padre Guardiano is unique in Verdi in that the singers stand in no personal relationship with one another. The Father Superior is Leonora's confessor and nothing else. Its brief movements – some of them no more than a few phrases – succeed or melt into one another without any of the usual sense of urgency and are even interspersed with snatches of recitative; yet a sure sense of direction is maintained. In the final cabaletta ('Sull'alba il pied'all' eremo') both singers have different themes.

Of the great duets between Carlo and Alvaro, 'Solenne in quest'ora', rendered famous on disc by generations of tenors and baritones, is essentially a minor-major romanza for two voices and at the same time an action piece, in which the wounded Alvaro gives his comrade the fatal locket. By contrast 'Voi che si larghe cure', often regrettably omitted, is remarkable for its range of style as well as expression. It begins as a 'parlante' in Verdi's most up-to-date sophisticated vein, flexible and lightly scored. The suavity is blown apart with the revelation that Carlo knows his fellow officer's identity. Tension grows with the cut and thrust of the dialogue until Alvaro learns that Leonora is still alive. 'Yes', Carlo replies, 'but soon she will die'; and while his own line is so encrusted with chromaticisms that two writers have described it as Verdi's most daring flight to date, Alvaro reacts with a lyrical effusion reminiscent of the composer's early heroes. 'No, d'un imen il vincolo' recalls Foresto's 'Ella in poter del barbaro' — harmonically more sensitive, but with the same broad articulation and accompaniment of string triplets. It is as though Alvaro has momentarily become a poetical Zamoro. Such is his absorption in a vision of a happy future that it takes him some time to realise the malignant force of Carlo's 'Stolto! fra noi dischiudesi' — for like most Italian baritones Carlo is a sneering rather than a barking villain. The incredulous boiling up of Alvaro's fury that follows explodes into a cabaletta, 'Morte! ov'io non cada', which Verdi cut short in 1869 and for a good reason. In the 1862 version it resulted in a duel in which Carlo was to all appearance mortally wounded. In the play he does indeed die at that point; and it is left to the younger brother, Alfonso, to take up the trail of vengeance. In the opera there is no Alfonso; and Carlo must live to fight another day. Originally Alvaro came to the footlights for a grand aria ('Qual sangue sparsi'). The andante, like so many numbers in the opera, is in minor-major form. Its opening is declaimed over an elaborate accompaniment of unusual, almost independent musical interest and it finishes with a prayer ('Miserere di me'). Trumpets sound; and, following a well-worn formula, Alvaro leads his men to battle in a stirring cabaletta ('S'incontri la morte') ending with one of those high Cs which Tamberlick was so proud of having introduced into 'Di quella pira'. By comparison with earlier caba-lettas, however, it is a mere rump: one statement and a coda with a tiny episode in which the bolero rhythm ceases and Alvaro declares that should he be spared, he will end his life in a monastery.

Seven years later Verdi decided that it was better to show the combatants being separated; at least Carlo would not have to explain to the audience his presence in the last act.

The final encounter ('Col sangue sol cancellasi') opens with a brusque 'parlante' with Carlo in the ascendant, and the vocal phrases draped asymmetrically over the orchestral theme with propulsive effect. The pith of the duet however resides in the andante ('Le minaccce, i fieri accenti') based on an oboe melody first heard in the overture (and prelude). Here for the first and only time (in 1869 but not in 1862) Carlo takes over the rising sixth from Alvaro as he hurls his propitiatory phrases in his teeth. The ebb and flow of Alvaro's resolution not to fight makes this a movement of rare excitement. At last he gives way and in the shortest of allegros the two retire for a duel. It remains to mention the little duettino between Melitone and the Father Superior ('Del mondo i disinganni') in which each preserves his own character – the Father's music austere with modal inflexions, the lay-brother's pert and good-humoured.

What could be called crowd scenes in *La forza del destino* are many and varied. That in the inn at Hornachuelos may appear somewhat episodic, but every incident is relevant to the drama. Even Preziosilla's 'E bella la guerra', like Carlo's ballata, incorporates into its final episode her penetration of 'Pereda's' imposture. In the great ensemble ('Su noi prostrati e supplici') a company of pilgrims passing by causes all present to fall on their knees with the result that Leonora, disguised as a boy, can make her escape without being recognised by her brother. Based on a simple melody like a popular hymn, it is the opera's nearest approach to a concertato with the voice of Leonora standing out in relief. The scene of Leonora's 'induction' is wonderfully solemn and strong, suggesting perhaps the church militant rather than the otherworldly piety of an ancient order. 'La Vergine degli Angeli' once more suggests a popular hymn, transfigured, however, by a tranquil sweetness.

The encampment scene is a kaleidoscope of tiny vignettes unique in Italian opera of the time. Carousing soldiers, *vivandières*, impoverished peasants, homesick recruits – all are planted with a characteristic musical idea. There is a tarantella richer in tunes and more inventively scored than that of *Les vêpres siciliennes* and a rataplan chorus to bring down the curtain. No single number in *La forza del destino* has come in for more abuse than this harmless piece of frippery – an ingenious essay in vocal instrumentation and onomatopoeia. It seems to call in question the seriousness of the encampment scene; they are all just playing at soldiers. Likewise one hears much condemnation of Preziosilla as one who likes to send young men to their death. But this is an anachronistic view. In an age when fighting was done mostly by regulars and wars were few the tradition persisted that a soldier's life was pleasant enough and that you could be sure of survival if you were brave. (Phrases like 'Bella vita militar', 'Quel plaisir d'être soldat' can be found in many a nineteenth-century opera.) Preziosilla is a cheerful hoyden, first cousin to Donizetti's Marie. She too, it may be remembered, leads a rataplan chorus; but without the excuse of Preziosilla, whose purpose is to rescue a lay-brother from being beaten up by the infuriated soldiery. Certainly Verdi's gypsy girl is intended to be on the side of kindliness, humour and sanity.

Yet it is possible to feel that the artistic problem has not been fully solved. That the 1869 version improves musically on the original is undeniable. The grand duets of Acts I and II are given stronger definition. Melitone's scene with the poor gains in charm and fluency. Some of the most memorable passages are late additions – the overture, that magnificent and far from formless 'trailer'; Alvaro's brief soliloquy before the first of the quarrel duets; the 'ronda' for the dawn patrol with its haunting Borodin-like intro- duction. Then, too, by changing one note of 'Povere madri' Verdi gives it something of the flavour of a Russian folk-melody, as though the experiences absorbed in St. Petersburg in 1862 were being worked out seven years later. But by altering the placing of the encampment scene Verdi blunted its dramatic point. As a prelude, and therefore a background to the grand duet of Act III, it is most effective; occurring afterwards, it leads nowhere. Likewise the 1869 ending can be seen as a compromise – a concession to the religious susceptibilities of nineteenth-century audiences. Certainly the original denouement, with its rising storm, its chanting of terrified monks and its demented hero, worked out in a series of mounting sequences is one of Verdi's most powerful conceptions, and its message of stark atheism makes it a favourite with East European managements today. The new con- clusion presents Alvaro as a kind of Job; its musical coherence is guaranteed by the derivation of the terzetto's main theme from the cadence of Ex. 49a. And surely there is no harm in a shaft of human warmth to penetrate a drama which threatens to become a theorem.

Despite the fluency of its musical discourse, compared to *Un ballo in maschera, La forza del destino* is a sprawling affair. Yet, given its thesis, it can hardly be anything else. The greater the variety of its episodes the more powerful appears the hand of fate in achieving its purpose. To Verdi himself it was an opera of ideas; and he withheld it when possible from managements which he thought incapable of doing it justice. Significantly this was the work which launched the Verdi renaissance in Germany in the 1920s; and it was with an unforgettable production of it that Fritz Busch ended his career as music director at Glyndebourne. When properly performed it reveals an epic quality which can hardly have been lost on the composer of *Boris Godunov*.

Don Carlos is Verdi's most ambitious essay in grand opera. In the entirely unhistorical tragedy of Carlos, Infante of Spain and champion of the oppressed, and his ill-starred love for his young stepmother he confronted for the first time a drama by Schiller in all its complexity and richness of characterisation. No other work cost him so much trouble in the effort to reduce it to manageable proportions. To this day managements differ as to the ideal way of presenting it, whether in the version of 1867, with or without the music cut before the première; the four-act version of 1884; the scissors-and-paste amalgam of 1886; or some permutation and combination of all three.

'Of the music that never reached the Parisian stage three pieces stand out. The first is a twelve-minute choral introduction to Act I, set in the forest of Fontainebleau and portraying a group of wood-cutters and their wives impoverished by the war and tormented by the winter cold. To sounds of the royal hunt Elisabeth de Valois appears in their midst, presents a golden chain to an old woman and promises better times to come. Stark, grim, thematically well-developed, it makes a very strong start to the opera as well as furnishing a good reason why Elisabeth should sacrifice her personal happiness to the welfare of her people. In Act IV there was a duet for Elisabeth and the Princess Eboli, notable for its economy and restraint – rare commodities in opera where two women are in love with the same man – and another for Carlos and his father with chorus of grandees, whose main theme was later adapted for the 'Lachrymosa' of the *Requiem*. The second, one of Verdi's most moving laments, is nowadays often re-instated in the edition of Ursula Günther.

The original Act I has nothing to do with Schiller; it seems to have been based on *Philippe II, Roi d'Espagne*, a play by Eugène Cormon, in the prologue to which Don Carlos pays a secret visit to Paris disguised as a student in order to catch a glimpse of his bride-to-be. As in *Les vêpres siciliennes* Verdi takes advantage of the narrower timbre of the French voice to create a tenor of a different sort. Carlos is neither a ranter nor an open-hearted lyric poet like Alvaro; he is more controlled and inward in his expression, with a morbid sensibility which becomes more apparent as the opera proceeds. For the present he is all boyish happiness, having seen Elisabeth and found her to his liking. Love at first sight is the burden of his 'cavatine'. 'Je l'ai vue' breathes a serene contentment with no emotional gushings.

Ex. 50

Elegance and lightness mark the opening of his scene with Elisabeth, who at first has no idea who he is. Only when he produces a miniature of himself does she recognise her betrothed. The cabaletta ('De quels transports poignants et doux') has the complex articulation of Meyerbeerian melody together with a spontaneous lifting of the heart:

Ex. 51

It is also a courtly melody; and the emotional climax is reserved for a moment of ecstatic declamation in a remote key ('Bois dépouillés) after which both singers return decorously to Ex. 51. Neither are prepared to let their feelings run away with them.

Long before Verdi made his revision of 1884 it had become the custom to omit the Fontainebleau act. Yet no sooner had the opera been re-fashioned without it than people began to clamour for its return. True, Verdi found a place for the cavatine near the start of the new act; and he rewrote it in such a way as to reflect the altered mood of the singer, enriching the preceding scena with many a reminiscence of the excised duet; but these mean very little if they recall music that has not been heard before. Moreover the later scenes between Carlos and Elisabeth gain vastly in their effect if we have witnessed the destruction of their idyll. Hence no doubt Verdi's agreement to the restoration of the Fontainebleau act in the edition of 1886.

The second duet of the lovers (the first in the 1884 version) is in a very different vein. Months have passed; yet Carlos is unable to reconcile himself to the loss of his fiancée. The music throughout is governed by a pattern of structure precisely attuned to the psychology of the participants. Both are moved by feelings that they are trying to

261

restrain: the result is a succession of mainly irregular phrases in which the same idea is repeated then followed by a much longer one where the emotion spills over. Whereas in the corresponding scene in Schiller Carlos's impetuosity reveals itself at the outset and is overcome in the course of the dialogue, here he progresses from the desolate unaccompanied 'Je viens solliciter de la Reine une grâce' through a brief oasis of delirious calm, to the cabaletta 'Que sous mes pieds se déchire la terre'. To his outburst in C minor Elisabeth responds with a no less emphatic E flat minor ('Eh bien frappez donc votre père'); and when Carlos has rushed out in horror she brings the duet to a radiant conclusion in E flat major with a single phrase ('Sur nous le Seigneur a veillé').

Between this and the final scene for Carlos and Elisabeth much has happened: Eboli's discovery of their love, her adultery with Philippe, remorse and banishment; Carlos's defiance of his father and imprisonment and subsequent release as a result of Rodrigue's self-sacrifice. He is about to set forth for Flanders to fight for the oppressed; Elisabeth has come to the monastery to wish him Godspeed. Here she is in the ascendant from the start; and just as the Fontainebleau duet had been preceded by an aria for Carlos, so their final encounter is prefaced by a grand aria for Elisabeth – a huge ternary design in the course of which she surveys with the aid of musical reminiscences her life of suffering and blighted hopes. The long prelude surrounds her with the gloom of the monastery; yet amid all the doubt, amounting at times to despair, she can still achieve what the music tells us to be an affirmation of faith (Ex. 52b), a radiant major-key reply to her opening apostrophe to the spirit of Charles V ('Toi qui sus le néant') (Ex. 52a).

Ex. 52

In this aria Elisabeth reaches her full spiritual stature; and if her aria of consolation to the Princess Aremberg in Act II – a minor-major strophic romance – is just too short to draw applause for all but the finest singers, it is a poor Elisabeth who fails to get an ovation here.

The 'scène et duo' that follows was re-thought more than once. Where Carlos talks of a fair dream of love that faded before a vision of a land laid waste by fire, Verdi originally took his cue from the word 'incendie' to produce an ingenious pattern of spreading sonorotities. In 1884 he removed this musical image altogether replacing it with a reminiscence of the duet in Act II (the 'beau rêve') which almost immediately sinks beneath a wave of brutal triplets. The next passage gave him even more trouble. Elisabeth, who has now taken on the mantle of Rodrigue, rallies Carlos's spirits with a rousing *marziale* ('Oui, violà, l'héroisme'); proudly he embraces her as a son without trembling. Only then does a tide of infinite sadness rise in both of them ('Lorsque tout est fini') to be quelled by the thought that they may meet in a better world. In 1872 Verdi removed the *marziale*, possibly finding it, as many critics have done, out of keeping with Elisabeth's regal character. Realising that its sequel would be ineffective without it and unable to think of anything better, he re-instated the marziale with improved scoring. The final cabaletta ('Au revoir dans un monde') is calm and poised, all passion spent; and once again it is too long for the singers' safety. For in the meantime Philippe, the Grand Inquisitor and their officers have surprised them. In 1867 a ritual trial followed with Carlos three times accused and three times condemned in a fine blaze of orchestral sonority. By 1884 Verdi found this otiose – he had already managed a similar scene much better in *Aida* – and preferred to move swiftly towards the final curtain where Carlos fighting for his life retreats towards the monastery, the Monk steps forward and covers him with his cloak and all present fall on their knees in terror at what they believe to be the apparition of Charles V. There is one further change. In 1867, after the din of the trial, the conclusion of the opera had been hushed, almost dreamlike. In the revision it is blared out fortissimo.

Two other duets are of central importance to the opera and both were incorporated at Verdi's own insistence. The first is between Philippe and Rodrigue in Act II and is nothing less than a political argument about the value of freedom. Hardly a natural subject for an opera, it gave Verdi more trouble than any other single number. Originally he conceived it as chain of lyrical ideas permeated by the march-like rhythms of French grand opera. But even before the première he had doubts about the moment near the end where the King proposes to confide his private troubles to Rodrigue; and he decided to cut the King's confession by several bars of dialogue. In 1872 he re-wrote part of the duet in freer style, loosening up the four-square phrase-structure and re-designing the end entirely. Unfortunately Ghislanzoni's Italian text to which the revision was made contains references to Schiller's play which makes no sense in the context of the opera. Finally in 1883–4 Verdi composed the duet anew as what he called a 'dramatic dialogue' to lines by Du Locle which at the composer's instance kept much closer to Schiller. All sense of the closed period has now gone; the phrases extend themselves freely, reflecting every nuance of the text with occasional excursions into stark brutality. The duet is crowned by a tight, almost motivically organised cabaletta ('Ah quelle aurore') by way of counterpoise to the freedom of what has gone before; and twice before the fall of the curtain Philippe gives his sinister warning against the Inquisitor. That the definitive version surpasses the other three is beyond question. If it does not always make the effect it deserves, the reason is that it comes at the end of a very long act, most of which is written in a simpler and less demanding style. It is *Otello* in the context of *Don Carlos*.

Wholly successful from the start was the duet between Philippe and the Grand Inquisitor – again a dramatic dialogue, but in one movement only and carried on a single flight of inspiration. The argument is no less intellectual than in the previous duet; but here the Inquisitor dominates throughout, now with a slow crescendo of anger, now wheedling with false suavity, now parrying Philippe's words with a chill indifference. The orchestral theme from which the piece starts and to which it returns aptly conveys the Inquisitor's all-embracing authority with its serpentine coils and gloomy bass resonance – the only passage in which Verdi uses the contra-bassoon. Well may Philippe exclaim that the pride of kings must always yield to that of the Church.

Philippe remains the most strongly drawn portrait in the opera; and his grand aria ('Elle ne m'aime pas') sets the first tableau of Act IV on a plane from which it never descends. The music is of one into whose soul the iron has entered but who retains sufficient vulnerable humanity to hold our sympathy. Formally it achieves the perfect integration of 'scena' and 'aria' through the placing of that recurring phrase that sums up the whole of Philippe's sadness:

Ex. 53

Philippe's is the commanding voice in the 'scène et quatuor' that follows his duet with the Inquisitor. The scène was altered in 1884 to allow Elisabeth to reply less submissively to her husband's accusations; while the quartet ('Maudit sois le soupçon infâme') was shortened and tightened, without however the sacrifice of one of those transfiguring phrases that Verdi sometimes brings to the tensest of situations. The only difference is that in 1867 it was sung by Philippe: in the revision it was given to the cellos with subdued declamation by Eboli and Philippe; at the same time its apex was lowered by a tone with a musical gain that is difficult to account for (Ex. 54).

In a letter to Faccio about a revival of *Don Carlos* Verdi regretted that the parts of Eboli and Rodrigue had stood out since both were dramatically marginal. This is rather hard on Eboli. True, her Veil song in Act II with its Spanish rhythm and 'cante hondo' cadenzas is no more than decorative; and her gallant exchanges with Rodrigue a mere backcloth to the serious business that follows; true also, her resolve to liberate Carlos at the end of Act IV, scene 1 is irrelevant

since by the time that she has carried it out by raising a 'sommossa' (which became shorter with each revision) Carlos had already been set at liberty. None the less in her grand aria ('O don fatal et détesté') a vain, rather shallow character is nobly redeemed. Beginning in remorseful agitation, it ends in heroic resolve. The still centre ('Adieu Reine'), poised between two 6/4 chords a semitone apart, explores the velvety sonority of the contralto range as Verdi had never done before; while the final movement is a fine example of the 'cabaletta surrogate' – a handful of phrases culminating in a melodic sweep of four and a half bars with an accelerating harmonic rhythm.

One problem which neither Verdi nor his librettists ever solved was that of her adultery with Philippe. Undoubtedly they had landed themselves in a difficulty by making Philippe genuinely in love with his young wife. Schiller's monarch makes no such claim; therefore it is natural that he should look elsewhere for female attention, and why not to Eboli? Scorned by the Infante and determined to be revenged upon her (as she thinks) hypocritical mistress, she yields to Philip's importunities and makes use of her position to steal the Queen's jewel-box containing the portrait of Carlos. But if all this were made clear to the audience Philippe would forfeit much of the sympathy his aria has won him. Verdi's first solution was to have Eboli make her confession in two stages. She admits her unrequited love for Carlos and in the course of a somewhat constrained duet Elisabeth pardons her. Then she mentions her adultery but leaves the occasion conveniently vague so that the audience can imagine that it occurred before Philippe's marriage to Elisabeth. At this Elisabeth leaves in horror and it is left to the Comte de Lerme to pronounce Eboli's sentence – exile or the veil. But since the two prima donnas disliked one another even more heartily than is normally the case, the duet was dropped at an early stage and with it all mention of adultery. Now it is the knowledge that Eboli loved Carlos that causes Elisabeth's horrified retreat – which does her no credit whatever. In the revision of 1884 Elisabeth forgives the milder confession in an almost offhand manner. The second, delivered by Eboli with an almost veristic hysteria, elicits a response of stern dignity. It is now the Queen herself who takes back Eboli's cross and offers her the choice between exile and the veil. She has understood the implication of Eboli's words even if the audience has not.

Rodrigue, both in play and opera is an anachronism, an idealist of the 'enlightenment', who would hardly have lasted a day at Philippe's court, and at the same time a Pylades to Carlos's Orestes. His opening duet with Carlos was progressively reduced. Originally it contained a solo for Rodrigue himself in which he described the

267

sufferings of the Netherlands, but this was dropped before the première. In 1867 it was still a two-movement duet with an intervening scena in which Carlos confessed his love for his stepmother. But in 1884 the lyrical first movement ('Mon compagnon, mon ami, mon frère') was removed and with it the charming touch whereby Rodrigue, about to be greeted affectionately by Carlos, quickly addresses him with frigid politeness and is answered in the same manner; only when the attendant monk has left do the friends embrace. But the scene that remains is far from formless, falling as it does into two large paragraphs, the first ending with Carlos's confession, the second with Rodrigue's word of comfort. Their voices join in a cabaletta which has left most commentators less than enthusiastic; but its main theme will function as a reminiscence motif in later scenes. It is the music of comrades-in-arms:

Ex. 55

As a component in a variegated ensemble Rodrigue never fails in his effect; on his own he is much less interesting. His strophic romance in Act II ('L'Infant Carlos, notre espérance') is no more than a vocal plum for a 'Cavalierbaryton'. Likewise the two movements of his final aria ('C'est mon jour suprême') are bland and heroic in the stately manner of the Paris Opéra but somewhat monochrome. Between them however, where Rodrigue falls wounded, there is a very striking *parlante* with cornets elegiac in thirds, an accacciatura sob on bassoon and a death figure on the timpani. Needless to say, Ex. 55 does not fail to put in a last, subdued appearance.

Of the smaller ensembles, besides the quartet mentioned above, the Act III terzetto is outstanding – pure musical gold minted as so often from the conflicting emotions of the participants. The opening movement, for Carlos and Eboli alone, is densely packed with lyrical ideas that open out into one another. The climax ('Ah vous aimez la Reine!') co-incides with Rodrigue's entrance so as to spark off the second movement, in the course of which Carlos's voice rises in pathetic dismay over the tense exchanges of the other two. The stretta uses to fine effect the unison of negative emotion, with Eboli showing all the malignity of a female Iago.

The 'grand' scenes and those that evoke an ambience are more variable, the second markedly superior to the first. The monastery of St. Just is wonderfully 'planted' at the start of Act II: a prelude for four horns, the distant voices of monks chanting prayers for the soul of Charles V, an old monk kneeling beside the Emperor's tomb (the Emperor himself or his ghost?). The theme of the prelude furnishes one of the basic motifs of the opera and an important element in its 'tinta'. It is recalled in the terzetto of Act III, the *Auto-da-fè* scene, Eboli's 'O don fatal' and in Elisabeth's grand aria of Act V:

Ex. 56

The monks oscillate between major and minor common chords; while their imperial brother, a sonorous basso profondo, speaks the idiom of Fiesco with short but pregnant utterances of such intensity as to generate a long melodic postlude. No less masterly is the conclusion of the scene with Philippe, Elisabeth and their suite entering the cloister to a ceremonial march which, as they kneel before the Emperor's tomb, dwindles into the chanting of the monks. Carlos cries out in pain. Again the Monk's voice is heard; Rodrigue exhorts his friend to take heart; and the scene ends with a triumphant thundering out of Ex. 55.

The Fontainebleau forest, Carlos's prison cell, the gardens outside the monastery are all conjured up with a few deft strokes, the women's chorus in the last ('Sous ces bois au feuillage immense') being especially charming. The finale of the Fontainebleau act is neatly constructed over a march with two themes in minor and major respectively; the first reflecting the apprehension of Carlos and Elisabeth, the second the people's joy at the prospect of peace. In an oasis of quiet Elisabeth consents to marry Philippe instead of Carlos;

whereupon the gratitude of the people rises like incense in a crescendo of overlapping phrases that bear witness to Verdi's admiration for the opening of *Norma*. The march is resumed, the disconsolate cry of the lovers forming a descant and the stage empties leaving a lamenting Carlos. The 'sommossa' that ends Act IV is not especially remarkable apart from the splendid curtain provided by the sudden appearance of the Inquisitor ('A genoux! . . . A genoux!').

The *auto-da-fè*, laid out with an unerring sense of scale and proportion, is compromised from the start by its opening chorus, a particularly brash variant of Ex. 56, which touches of harmonic sophistication do nothing to improve. The short 'march to the stake' with its muffled scoring, minatory trombone unisons, its consolatory cello tune later taken up by the Heavenly Voice adds contrasting threads to the tapestry; but it is all external with no depth; and there is a more than usually disagreeable march for the stage band to follow. Only with the entry of the Flemish deputies and the resulting 'pezzo concertato' does the scene regain the musical level of its predecessor. Their melody ('La dernière heure à-t-elle déjà sonné?') with its restless Meyerbeerian bass has warmth and dignity; and the varied reactions of their audience are precisely portrayed. Philippe seems to shake an angry fist, the monks to pronounce an anathema, Carlos, the populace and the female principals to plead for mercy. As the voices all join, the heightened emotion is expressed in rapidly changing harmonies. Not one of Verdi's longest *concertati*, it is certainly one of his most concentrated.

The quarrel between Carlos and his father, brought forward from an earlier scene of the play, may be explained by Verdi's long cherished idea of including a scene that would correspond to that in *Le Prophète* in which at the moment of his coronation Jean denies his own mother in the presence of the populace of Munster ('one of those scenes which draw tears from the eyes . . .'[4]). Posa's apparent betrayal of his friend, followed by a crestfallen recurrence of Ex. 55, was the nearest that could be managed. How much store the composer set by this passage may be seen from his letters to Mazzucato, who conducted the first performance at La Scala, Milan. It would have made a fine 'curtain' did not considerations of musical architecture require a reprise of the opening themes.

[4] See above LCC, p. 158.

The ballet 'La Peregrina' is the only one of Verdi's to contain a narrative: the story of a fisherman who discovers a cave where all the finest gems of the ocean are gathered; the finest of them all however is required by King Philippe whose page interrupts the proceedings to carry out his master's orders. The music is brilliantly scored and at times witty; the action passages are apt, especially those that feature a solo violin, which is treated with a flexibility worthy of Tchaikovsky. But some of the ideas are disappointingly commonplace; nor are there any of those gems like the Dance of Summer that lights up the 'Four Seasons' from *Les vêpres siciliennes*; which is no doubt why, along with that of *Jérusalem*, 'La Peregrina' remains the least performed of Verdi's ballet scores.

Its omission, however, posed yet another problem for the revision. The original Act III started with a *scène-à-faire* in the Spanish style, where to the background of an offstage chorus Elisabeth persuades Eboli to take her place in the evening's entertainment. Accordingly Eboli takes the royal mask, mantilla and necklace and declares that she will 'intoxicate the prince with love'. For the Queen herself has a part in the ballet; she is 'La Peregrina' who appears in a final tableau mounted on a golden chariot and receiving the homage of all the dancers. Eboli has no doubt that Carlos, whom she believes to be in love with her anyway, will become still more besotted when he sees her thus gorgeously attired. But once the ballet is removed the scene loses its point. Therefore Verdi replaced it in 1884 with the richly yet delicately woven prelude based on Ex. 51 in its revised form that we know today. But he also instructed Ricordi to restore the original scene in its place should the ballet be given. Many performances of to-day include both prelude and *scène-à-faire*, while omitting the ballet. Eboli's words then suggest that Carlos will love her in mistake for the Queen. That he actually does so is no part of her plan. Eboli, it seems, is destined to be misunderstood.

The best of Don Carlos remains unsurpassed by Verdi or anyone else; and for many people today it remains their favourite in the canon. It is the most wide ranging of all in the emotions explored and in its wealth of sharply drawn characters. It is certainly not his most perfect. Certain problems remain unsolved no matter which version is performed. Many Germans criticise the ending as an insult to Schiller; and even Verdi himself had his doubts about the ambiguity of the Monk-Emperor. But Du Locle's answer is surely conclusive. Firstly Schiller's play makes no claim to historical truth; then if the monk is to be a monk like any other, the first scene by the monastery of St. Juste loses all its grandeur and significance since its purpose is to prepare the final curtain as originally planned. And who would wish to sacrifice a character as rich in mysterious resonance as the Monk-Emperor?

When asked by Ferdinand Hiller which of the two operas, *Aida* and *Don Carlos*, Verdi himself preferred he replied: 'In *Don Carlos* there is perhaps a passage here or a piece there which surpasses anything in *Aida*; but in *Aida* there's more bite and (if you'll forgive the word) more *theatricality*.'[5] Fifty years ago such a statement would have seemed obvious. For the liberal Westerner of today history has somewhat devalued *Aida* with its swaggering parades and war-like sentiments, its implicit acceptance of the closed society; while the struggle of youthful idealism against the tyranny of the old that informs *Don Carlos* finds a much readier response. (Significantly, in Eastern Europe *Aida* is still much preferred.) Yet once its dramatic premise can be accepted, *Aida* is certainly the more perfect opera of the two. Here all the problems of length and proportion which had eluded Verdi in his two previous works are triumphantly resolved. All the panoply of grand opera is there but it never weighs the opera down. It has been said that *Aida* is the only grand opera (in the Meyerbeerian sense) from which it is impossible to cut a single note.

The plot is classically simple and even familiar: a tale of love and patriotism, with a heroine torn between allegiance to her father and to her lover. The musical forms are more symmetrical than in *Don Carlos* with an almost mathematical use of repetition. For the first time since *I due Foscari* Verdi returns to labelling themes, as distinct from thematic reminiscence: wistful and vaguely yearning for *Aida* (Ex. 57a), proud and stately for her rival Amneris (Ex. 57b), and stern, with a tendency to contrapuntal proliferation for the priests of Isis (Ex. 57c). The prelude, a finely-spun tone-poem, is compounded from (a) and (c). (b) first appears in the Act I terzetto, as does a fourth motif representing Amneris' jealous fury (Ex. 57d).

Inevitably the leading figures of *Aida* incline to the generic. They merge with the background of that public, formal life of which they are part. Radames appears to us as patriot in his recitative and as

[5] Letter to F. Hiller (unpublished), 7.1.1884, in the archives of the New York Philharmonic Society.

Ex. 57

lover in his aria 'Celeste Aida' – a typical instance of Verdian three-limbed melody fashioned into a French ternary design. But as yet there is no conflict between the two roles. The lover can express himself in terms of the purest classical poetry. Likewise he and Amneris can take part in the battle hymn ('Su! del Nilo') – a far more acceptable piece of public music than anything in the *auto-da-fè* scene, with a genuinely vigorous bass and no contrapuntal trimmings – without any loss of character. The final words, 'Ritorna vincitor!', first declaimed by Amneris, then echoed by the chorus, and finally taken up by Aida (note the mathematical procedure by threes) makes for the smoothest of transitions to Aida's own solo – a nucleus of brief contrasted movements in which her inner conflict is laid bare. It ends with a prayer of heartfelt simplicity.

Ex. 58

Two ritual scenes stand out in which Radames and the high priest

Ramphis have pride of place. The first is concerned with the consecration of Radames as captain of the Egyptian armies. Three times a soprano solo (Ex. 59) is answered by a solemn male chorus. A dance of priestesses follows; like the soprano solo, it is in Verdi's own Egyptian style with flattened supertonic.

Ex. 59

The ensemble that ends the scene ('Nume, custode e vindice') is led by Ramphis then Radames to a strain that anticipates the solemnity of the 'Oro supplex' of the *Requiem*. The theme develops, puts out contrapuntal shoots and is finally yoked with Ex. 59 in a series of dynamic contrasts. It is curious that Verdi's first truly successful expression of religious awe should relate to the worship of Isis. By comparison even the grandest choruses of *La forza del destino* seem purely external.

In the scene of Radames' trial, the iron rule of three – a symbol of officialdom or even the Greek 'ananke' – is asserted in all its relentless authority. There is a triple invocation to the Gods. Radames' name is called three times. Three charges are laid against him, each set out in Dantesque tercets. There are three reactions to his silence: 'Ramfis' 'Egli tace', the priests' 'Traditor!', and Amneris' despairing 'Ah, pietà, egli è innocente!'. The trial gains in sinister force from being conducted beneath the stage like a medieval 'Vehmgericht'. As Radames is led away to immurement, the frantic reproaches of Amneris break on the retreating priests like waves on a rocky shore.

The architectural pinnacle of *Aida* is of course the Triumph scene. If it moves us less than the more intimate moments, it should be remembered that public music in nineteenth-century opera is rarely very compelling unless nationalistically inspired. Where this scene scores immeasurably over its counterpart in *Don Carlos* is in the fact that the elements belong together and follow each other naturally. The final cadence of the grand chorus that began with 'Gloria all'Egitto', unmistakably prepares us for the trumpet march

– one of those pieces that instantly take root in the memory due to the inspired use of just a few notes. The march in turn discharges the ballet like an arrow from a bow – a kaleidoscope of brilliantly scored themes each preserving the exotic flavour which *L'Africaine* had brought into vogue. A sharp ear will detect the point at which in 1880 Verdi added two fresh ideas, more piquant and less straight-forwardly melodic than the others; so by means of a reprise with the opening theme placed at the end he was able to make the ballet more than twice its original length. So much is mere pageantry. Drama returns with the appearance of Amonasro, not, as some maintain, a villain but a man of infinite cunning whose character is limned in the course of two contrasted themes, the first formidable with the suggestion of savagery held in check (Ex. 60a), the second falsely placatory, as the singer pleads for a clemency of which he intends to take full advantage (Ex. 60b). The more idealistic side of his nature will be revealed in the following act (Ex. 60c).

Ex. 60b forms the basis of the central concertato, the populace evidently taking the honeyed progressions at their face value. As in *Don Carlos* there is a tug of war, the priests countering with a demand for severity. The ensemble proceeds through a wide tonal orbit, so creating a sense of scale quite out of proportion to its length. Once more the sequel to the concertato is not a stretta but a varied reprise of the opening music of the scene here concentrated into three and a half minutes. 'Gloria all'Egitto' is followed by two variations each sounding like a new idea. After a brief but telling exchange between Amonasro and his daughter, all three tunes are vertically combined with an ease that Meyerbeer might have envied. The opening strain of the trumpet march brings down the curtain.

If the second scene of Act II is the opera's climax in terms of sheer sound, its poetic heart is the entire third act, which Verdi had wished to have printed without subdivisions of any sort. From the garish brightness of a high holiday we are transported to the magic of a subtropical night. The tapestry of pulsating strings, the circling flute motif, the distant chant of the priests all form the backcloth to Aida's desolate romanza ('O patria mia, mai più ti rivedrò!'). Each of its strophes is preceded by an oboe melody with modal inflexions that seems to have strayed in from the world of Massenet and Godard (Ex. 61). Through textual repetition and an ambiguous tonal scheme (F major alternating with the false tonic of A minor) it merges into the surrounding material much as an 'English' garden is

Ex. 60

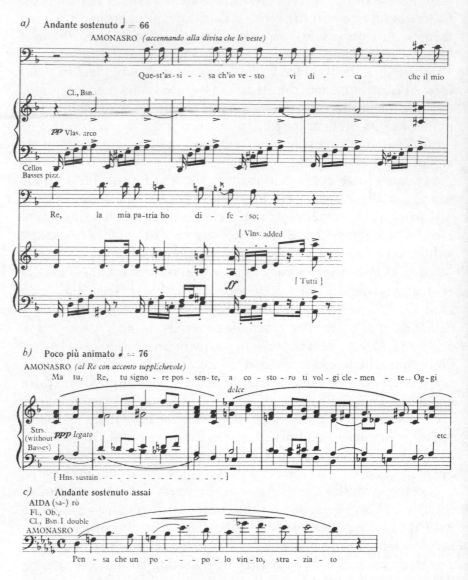

made to melt into the landscape that stretches beyond it. But the romanza is remarkable in other ways as well. Here is a new kind of strophic variation in which the second verse no longer retains the proportions of the first (it is three bars shorter). The same is true, but in reverse, of the first movement of Aida's duet with Radames '(Là tra foreste vergini'). Here too is the same idiom, the same ambiguity of key conveying seductiveness rather than nostalagia. Also in this

276

Ex. 61

act we can see the fruits of Verdi's experiments in his songs with the eleven-syllable metre without caesura as a means of melodic self renewal. The romanza is one example; the duet-movement for Aida and Amonasro ('Rivedrai le foreste imbalsamate') is another. Here the unusual cut of the opening phrase generates a chain of ideas each more captivating than the last, as Amonasro tries to re-awaken his daughter's longing for home. His subsequent outburst ('Su, dunque sorgete') makes its effect also through a calculated blend of metres but more especially through an ever widening circle of keys reaching its climax in the taunt 'Dei Faraoni tu sci la schiava!'. Rapid harmonic movement gives way to complete harmonic stasis. The repeated A flats of the violins with their off-the-beat throbbings lie like an iron bar over the prostrate Aida. The gloom is lightened by Amonasro's 'Pensa che un popolo' – a transfiguring phrase in the tradition of Macbeth's 'Come angeli d'ira' – only to settle again as Aida reflects how dearly her fatherland has cost her. Regularity of pace returns with the appearance of Radames. For the last time Verdi employs a cabaletta for runaway lovers ('Si, fuggiam da queste mura'); but it is not they who delay too long; it is Amonasro who wastes valuable time with his reassurances to Radames that he is not to blame for betraying his country's secrets. Where once an elaborate ensemble would have been needed, now Radames' 'Sacerdote, io resto a te' is sufficient to conclude an act which is a masterly blend of formality and freedom.

If Aida is the heroine, Amneris is the more interesting character. In her the seeds of rebellion are present from the start; and her music gains in power from her constant vigilance in keeping her feelings under control. At first she is all graciousness; but from the moment she suspects Radames of loving someone else Ex. 57d begins to rampage in the orchestra. In the terzetto of Act I she is like a repressed Eboli in the terzetto in *Don Carlos*; but this time it is the soprano Aida whose voice soars melodically above the muttered soliloquies of Radames and Amneris. As usual in the later opera the design is pithier and the craftsmanship more skilled; also the internal contrast gains tension from its faster tempo.

The first scene of Act II belongs mainly to Amneris. At first we see her framed within her regal surroundings. Female attendants sing a chorus of two quatrains; she replies in a third ('O vieni, vieni, amor mio') like the refrain to a minor-major couplet. The pattern is twice repeated, the second time in shortened form and preceded by a dance of Moorish slave-boys; and since musical ideas are comprehended not simultaneously but down a perspective of time, the effect is one of balanced symmetry. The subsequent duet ('Fu la sorte dell'armi') proceeds in a musical prose densely packed with lyrical motifs that sometimes burgeon into full periods. Here Ex. 57a for the first and only time reaches its fullest extension ('Amore, amore, gaudio, tormento'). Within this framework, half free, half formal, every emotional nuance is reflected, from Amneris' false suavity to Aida's wildly fluctuating moods. But with the betrayal of her secret the music moves into a more orthodox duet cantabile, since the respective attitudes are now fixed – Amneris fuming with jealous rage, Aida abjectly humble. At the first performance in Cairo the scene ended with a cabaletta modelled loosely on the battle hymn of the returning army. For Milan in 1872 Verdi devised the more varied scheme that we know today, finishing with a reprise of Ex. 58 with harmonic enhancement. If only, Ponchielli wrote to Giulio Ricordi, he himself could have thought of such an ending for his duet between Barnaba and Enzo!

The start of Act IV finds Amneris and Radames like figures in a classical tragedy, poised and irremovable in their respective positions. So a fundamentally Rossinian pattern with cantabile and cabaletta is not out of place. The opening is simple and stark with sinister colouring from trumpet and bass clarinet; but soon emotion breaks the icy surface in Amneris' sweeping cantilena ('Morire! . . . ah! tu dei vivere'), in Radames' apostrophe to Aida ('Gli Dei l'adducano salva alle patrie mura') and his reply to Amneris in the cabaletta ('È la morte un ben supremo'). But Amneris' theme ('Chi ti salva, sciagurato') already betrays that all engulfing despair that will remain with her to the end. Througout, however, she holds our sympathy without sacrificing a tithe of her dignity. Indeed many an Amneris has been known to steal the show from her rival on the basis of her brief intervention near the beginning of Act III ('Io pregherò') where unconsciously she betrays the vulnerable young girl beneath the trappings of a princess.

The final scene has something of the character of an epilogue, as it moves from a cold, almost numb opening to an idyllic close through a succession of lyrical ideas each simpler and more diaphanously scored than the last. The lovers' farewell to life ('O terra, addio') is a miracle of imagination in which the unbroken eleven-syllable metre is extended over wide melodic arches:

Ex. 62

The melody is restated in the form of the most repetitive cabaletta with only a brief 'cutaway' to the temple music and Amneris' prayer. Moreover of the melody's five limbs three are identical. Not even Bellini, who never failed to work a good tune for all that it was worth, risked stating a single phrase twelve times. Yet did ever opera end more magically than this?

For Verdi *Aida* was the final word on grand opera. Not however for his contemporaries. Indeed it remained the prevailing form of opera in Italy throughout the 1870s and much of the '80s. Yet of the various grand operas by Marchetti, Gomes, Ponchielli and Catalani only *La gioconda* survives. Lively, theatrical, full of spontaneous melody, by comparison with *Aida* it seems an absurd, exaggerated affair (who has ever been able to take the last scene seriously?). The aged Rossini was surely right when he observed in a letter to Tito Ricordi '. . . may my colleagues forgive me for saying so, but Verdi is the only man capable of writing grand operas'.[6]

---

[6] Letter from Rossini to Tito Ricordi, 18.4.1868, L. Rognoni, *Rossini* (Parma, 1956), pp. 264–5.

17

The final masterpieces

From *Aida* to *Otello* is a huge step, even if certain pages of the *Requiem* and the revised *Simon Boccanegra* have prepared us for it. The intervening years had seen a gradual change of taste among Italian audiences. Wagner was no longer a stranger, though his mature works had yet to be appreciated. *Lohengrin* had become an honorary Italian opera. The reform of the conservatories in 1870 was now bearing fruit in a revival of interest in instrumental music under the leadership of Martucci and Sgambati, so that even in opera a more symphonic approach was expected. Acts proceeded from beginning to end without interruption, unless there were a change of scene. The ideals preached by Boito in the 1860s in vague, rhapsodic fashion were now beginning fitfully to be realised, partly under his own guidance, not as composer or propagandist, but rather as poet.

Much has been said in recent years about the harmful effect of his sophistication on the simple, direct vision of Verdi. The truth is that Boito understood composers' requirements better than any librettist since Felice Romani; which is why he helped many of them to their most successful work (Ponchielli's *La gioconda* is an obvious instance). He had a sure instinct not only for the pacing of a music drama but also for a stage picture. His idea it was to insert a chorus of Cypriots paying homage to Desdemona in Act II of *Otello* though there is no precedent for it in Shakespeare. 'At this fateful moment', he wrote to Verdi, referring to the 'green-eyed monster' speech,

> it will be like a pure, sweet apotheosis of songs and flowers encircling the beautiful figure of Desdemona. Throughout the scene it is desirable that the chorus and Desdemona remain framed within the arch of the central aperture . . . The moment Desdemona pronounces the name of Cassio the memory of the chorus which still haunts Othello's soul ceases and the drama resumes its inexorable course.'[1]

[1] MCVB, pp. 51–7.

To Boito must go the credit of clearing Verdi's mind on the subject of the Act III curtain (see p. 126). His intellectual subtlety was a continual source of stimulus to the older composer, for which his preciosity of language was a small price to pay.

To expect Verdi in his seventies to write in the style of *Macbeth* or *Il trovatore* is like expecting the Beethoven of the 1820s to write in the style of his septet. Yet alongside those Germanophiles for whom *Otello* and *Falstaff* constitute Verdi's patent of respectability, there have always been those for whom his last two operas represent a false trail: the writer Antonio Fogazzaro in Verdi's own time, Bruno Barilli a generation later, even Stravinsky for whom '*Falstaff*, if not Wagner's best work, certainly isn't Verdi's'[2] (later however he was to change his mind). There exists also a middle view, held by, amongst others, the late Gabriele Baldini, which accepts *Falstaff* but rates *Otello* far below *Macbeth* as a musical realisation of Shakespeare. The real reason, one suspects, is that *Otello* demands far more of its audience than any of Verdi's previous operas. Also it is a difficult work to place. Written at a time when 'grand opera' was still the norm, though younger composers such as Catalani and Puccini were trying to escape from it, *Otello* employs all the resources of the genre except the ballet. The score calls for four bassoons, three flutes, two cornets as well as trumpets, two harps, a cornamusa, two mandolines, two guitars and a boys' chorus. The brass bass is for the first time specified as a bass trombone. Only the use of trombones with valves instead of slides harks back to an earlier time and renders certain effects, notably in the storm, impossible to achieve with modern instruments. But of routine grandiosity – of the pageantry and processions of *Aida* and *Don Carlos* – there is not a trace. Everything is directed towards the realisation of the drama.

Though the range of harmony is extraordinarily wide, the music bears little relation to what was being written at the time. There are no intimations of 'verismo', no Wagnerian echoes, except in part of the love-duet where the use of a similar metre set to a similar rhythm recalls that of *Lohengrin* (though Verdi is more successful than the Wagner of 1848 in avoiding excessive regularity). Likewise the modal inflexions of the Willow Song owe something to the example of Frenchmen such as Massenet, Lalo and Godard. But where can

[2] J. B. Janin, *Poètique Musicale de I. Stravinsky* (Paris, 1945), pp. 93–4.

one find a precedent for the chord of piled-up thirds that opens the opera (Ex. 63) and of which variants recur later in the storm and in the bonfire chorus?

Ex. 63

To call Ex. 63 a dominant eleventh is surely to miss the point, since it nowhere resolves, and is thus a good deal harder to analyse harmonically than the opening of *Tristan und Isolde*. In his preface to the opera Boito stressed the importance of Iago's first mention of the word 'jealousy' in bringing about the change in the Moor's character. Accordingly Verdi underlines the moment with a grinding succession of parallel common chords (Ex. 64).

Be it noted, however, that no matter how bold the progression at certain key-points of the drama, the basic idiom is markedly consonant. Chains of suspensions and appoggiature resolving on one another as in the overture to *Die Meistersinger* or the Prologue to *Mefistofele* were not for Verdi. His chief complaint about Mascagni's *L'amico Fritz* and Bruneau's *La rêve* was of their pointless use of dissonance for the mildest of situations – in effect that the extreme medicine of the dramatic constitution was becoming its daily bread.

Ex. 64

Characteristically he draws together the jumble of heterogeneous, often dissonant motifs that make up the storm in a plain, A minor melody of thirty-two bars placed, as in *Rigoletto*, at the climax ('Dio fulgor della bufera').

Precisely because he uses it so sparingly, Verdi is able to extract full sweetness from Romantic harmony without risk of cloying. The descending ninths of the four muted cellos preceding the love duet, Desdemona's melting cadence where she first makes her ill-timed plea on behalf of Cassio, the orchestral motif of the kiss (Ex. 65) attain a radiant sublimity through means which in lesser hands would result in mere mawkishness.

Ex. 65

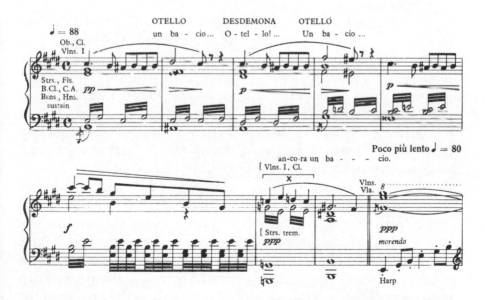

Never has that Verdian device of a 6/4 chord in a remote key (x) been used to such superb effect. Indeed it is through an extension of certain procedures long familiar as finger-prints of his idiom that Verdi often seems to reach towards the future. In Iago's dream a succession of typical seventh inversion chords gives a foretaste of Debussyan impressionism:

Ex. 66

Elsewhere the reach is backward as well as forward to those classics on which Verdi had been educated and in which he had begun to show a new, creative interest. The central section of the handkerchief terzetto ('Essa t'avvince con vaghi rai') takes Domenico Scarlatti as its point of departure. There is a touch of eighteenth-century grace about the introduction to the duet in Act III ('Dio ti giocondi, o sposo') out of which the fearful irony of Otello will emerge with all the greater intensity. *Otello* is a summing up of a lifetime's experience in more ways than one.

It is strictly contemporary to the '80s in that it was conceived from the start in terms of whole acts that proceed from beginning to end without interruption. There was no question of welding existing joins as in the revision of *Simon Boccanegra*. The drama no longer jolts from situation to situation but moves by smooth transition from one event to the next. The affray caused by Cassio's drunkenness is followed by a stretch of thirty-nine bars during which the tension relaxes and the mood changes to one of tranquil happiness in preparation for the love duet. Two ideas are used, the first a *parlante*, the second purely instrumental and followed by the passage for muted cellos mentioned above. Both rise and fall over a tonic pedal inducing a sense of languorous repose. Inevitably the aim towards continuity is reflected in the form of the arias and ensembles. Where once Otello might have been given a two-movement cavatina for his entrance, a mere handful of phrases starting from C sharp major to a powerful cadence in E plants his triumph with all the finality of the Alphorn theme in the finale of Brahms's First Symphony. Unlike the drinking song in *Macbeth*, Iago's 'Innaffia l'ugola!' is not a static piece embedded in a scene of action; rather it carries the action within itself. For this purpose Verdi uses a type of bar-form with refrain already adumbrated in *Un ballo in maschera* and *La forza del destino*, in which there is room for Cassio's stammering, his growing intoxication, Iago's asides to Roderigo and the amused reactions of the crowd, and always from the steady development of one idea into another, the recurrence of the refrain 'Chi all'esca ha morso' giving unity to the design. A similar form is used for the Willow Song, where we are never allowed to forget that Desdemona is preparing for bed. The duettino for Iago and Cassio that begins Act II offers an example of a melody which realised its full shape only at its second repetition (compare 'Quid sum miser' from the *Requiem*). Then by a master-stroke the triplet figure that punctuates the orchestral texture is transformed into a brutal gesture in preparation for Iago's Credo of evil. This, his only soliloquy, takes the form of a declaimed melody that could be said to originate in Fra Melitone's comic sermon. Built on two instrumental themes, one a savage unison on the full orchestra, the other dancing with echoes of Liszt's Mephisto, it is one of the most powerful expressions of negative emotion in all music. For Otello's monologue ('Dio! mi potevi scagliar'), as it moves from spiritual prostration through poignant regret to an uncontrollable outburst of fury, Verdi uses a variant of the minor-major romanza so transformed that the listener is aware not of the form but only of the emotional graph that it traces. A close examination of the love duet will discover traces of the old tri-partite duet, though most listeners will be happy to hear a 'string of exquisite tunes which meander through one unlikely key after another in the most unexpected but unchallengeably logical manner'.[3] The extreme freedom of Otello's duet with Iago in Act II is wound up with a disguised cabaletta ('Si, per ciel marmoreo giuro!') More obvious echoes of the past can be heard in Otello's 'Ora e per sempre addio', like a broken recollection of Renato's 'Dunque l'onta di tutti sol una', and Iago's three-limbed 'É un idra fosca livida' reminding us of King Philip's confidences to Posa. But in general the old foundations remain buried beneath the ebb and flow of a powerful and infinitely various music drama.

The characters are rounded as never before. Iago is Protean,

[3] HVFO, p. 440.

suiting his personality to whomever he addresses; mocking with Roderigo, respectful and insinuating with Otello, brutal with Emilia. Otello's music is that of a man who has passed the zenith of youth; his love-duet proceeds in a glow of tranquil recollection. A few significant phrases here and there are sufficient to plant Cassio's attractive candour. Yet Verdi's greatest feat is surely to have sustained interest in the passive Desdemona by lavishing upon her a never-ending stream of lyrical poetry, whether in the quartet ('Dammi la dolce e lieta parola'), the harrowing duet from Act III or the entire fourth act.

Yet for all that it remains a singer's opera, *Otello* shows a rare orchestral imagination, whether in the text-book passage for muted double basses where Otello enters Desdemona's bedroom, the prelude to Act IV for cor anglais solo, woodwind and horns, the transition to the pezzo concertato with its Wagnerian voicing of wind and strings, the horn pedal at the start of 'Dio! mi potevi scaglair', the expertly varied harp-writing in the love duet, or the pretty blend of popular and orchestral instruments in the serenade to Desdemona. In two passages we can sense a conscious putting forth of strength. The opening storm is a concentrated six minutes of musical turbulence packed with themes and gestures of every conceivable rhythmic variety. Among its percussive effects is the novel use of a cluster of organ pedal notes that creates a feeling of tension without impinging on the listener's consciousness. The *pezzo concertato* in Act III ('A terra! . . . sì . . . nel livido fango') is the most massive that Verdi ever wrote, with no less than five constituent ideas, three of them associated with Desdemona. That static ensembles of this kind were becoming anachronistic Verdi himself was well aware; and just as he had given motion to the Act II quartet, turning it into an action piece for Iago and Emilia, so he sought to galvanise the concertato through the intriguing of Iago. 'I would group the chorus close together,' he wrote to Ricordi in 1889, 'in isolation and very distant, so that Iago can dominate and hold the attention with his movements, his actions, his infamous words to Otello and Roderigo without being disturbed by the muffled din of the orchestra.'[4] But in practice this generally proves impossible. For the French version, therefore, Verdi re-wrote the entire ensemble in a reduced form, thinning out the texture so

---

[4] AGV, IV, pp. 371–2.

that Iago can be clearly seen and heard. He did not however reinstate this version in subsequent Italian editions of the score. Nor, once heard, is it difficult to see why. The music suffers a loss of motive power just when it needs to press on towards its first climax. The freezing of the drama is a trivial price to pay for the towering magnificence of the ensemble as Verdi first wrote it.

The ballet is as distinguished as one would expect from the man who had already composed *Falstaff*, though it weakens rather than strengthens the drama and is never performed in context. The opening 'danse turque' is an amusing piece of orientalism à la française using augmented intervals within a minor tonality. Its major-key complement is a 'danse arabe' in the form of a steady crescendo culminating in a quotation of the Muezzin's Call from Félicien David's *Le Désert*, which had so impressed Verdi in 1845. The 'danse grèque' is limpid and gracious, a musical evocation of Keats's Grecian Urn; while for the Venetian dances Verdi returns to a popular idiom, vigorous and brilliantly scored but without a trace of vulgarity. Altogether a worthy, if untimely tribute to the ambassador of La Serenissima.

The title role lies well beyond the scope of the average operatic tenor. He is not the barnstorming titan that certain singers make of him, and no tenor part of Verdi's is encrusted with more nuances. It is not only in phrases such as 'Esultate' that he makes an impact. Toye is not far wrong in saying of the passage beginning 'E tu . . . come sei pallida!' from his final solo, 'In this phrase half sung, half sobbed, without accompaniment of any kind, lies the kernel of the entire tragedy.'[5] (Ex. 67).

Verdi declared more than once during the composition of *Falstaff* that he was writing it for his own amusement, as a way of passing the time. This is sometimes regarded as the disclaimer of a man too old to be tied down to deadlines and who was afraid he might not live to finish his work. It is true that for one of Verdi's upbringing an opera without a public to enjoy it is a contradiction in terms and that he was never above making concessions to an outstanding performer (witness the late addition to Act II, scene 2 of an extended solo for the Quickly of Giuseppina Pasqua). Yet there is a sense in which *Falstaff* touches a plane of musical idealism through

[5] TGV, p. 426.

Ex. 67

an independence of those factors which had conditioned the output of every composer for the theatre. Unlike *Otello* it is not a singers' opera but one of ensemble, of give and take between voices and instruments. The grand vocal gesture occurs only by way of parody as in Ford's monologue or where the wives read aloud the flowery conclusion of Falstaff's letter. The singers are expected to pick up the melodic threads from each other and quickly pass them on. Of the four women all except Meg Page could be accounted principals; yet Verdi hurls them all onto the stage at once in airy conversation. The qualities that he requires for his artists are purity of tone and that combined accuracy of verbal and musical attack known as 'accento'. If *Falstaff* finds little favour amongst the groundlings, it has scarcely more appeal for the star singer. It is an opera for the connoisseur.

In drawing up the libretto Boito defined the opera's terms of reference. His aim, he said, was to 'squeeze all the juice from that Shakespearean orange without letting any of the useless pips fall into the glass . . . It is very very difficult and it must seem very very easy.'[6] He was aware that the Falstaff of *The Merry Wives of Windsor* lacked the panache of Prince Hal's drinking companion; so he padded

6 MCVB, pp. 153–5.

him out with suitable passages from the chronicle plays with the same skill with which he had recouped part of the omitted Venetian act of *Otello*. In declaring to his friend Bellaigue that 'L'éclatante farce de Shakespeare a été reconduite par le miracle des sons à sa claire source Tuscane de Ser Giovanni Fiorentino,'[7] Boito was clearly alluding to what had been his aim from the start; for the libretto is full of Tuscan words and phrases. The refrain of the love duettino in Act I ('Bocca baciata non perde ventura, Anzi rinnova come fa la luna') is lifted directly from Boccaccio, where it has a different, more ribald significance. It was also Boito's idea that there should be no grand duet for Fenton and Nannetta (see p. 133).

Boito had already infected Verdi with his love of conundrums and ingenious word-play, with the result that in *Falstaff* music and text reflect each other in subtle and unexpected ways. In its opening bars *Falstaff* appears to plunge more immediately into the action than any of its predecessors with a thrusting accent off the main beat. Examine the music more closely and you will find that the entire scene with Dr Caius forms a built-in overture with the first subject (Ex. 68a) portraying Caius' anger, the second Falstaff's lordly phlegm (Ex. 68b).

Overtures generally draw to a full cadence at the end of the exposition, but they do not finish there. Accordingly 'Non è finito!' Caius cries at that point. But the genuine finality of his 'I'll never be drunk again while I live but in honest, civil and godly company' is marked by Bardolph and Pistol with a prolonged 'Amen' in two-part counterpoint. It is also possible that the expansive phrase that embodies Falstaff's maxim 'rubar con garbo e a tempo' is meant to serve as an illustration of 'tempo rubato'.

Thereafter the musical organisation of *Falstaff* is very difficult to classify. In general it continues that progress towards a seamless continuity that can be observed throughout Verdi's career, not through any predetermined forms but rather through ways that arise from the dramatic situation. The periodic melody is not banished – indeed the two most obvious examples of it, the women's E major quartet in Act I and Falstaff's 'Quand' ero paggio' were regularly encored in Verdi's day. Fenton's sonetto and Nannetta's 'Sul fil d'un

---

[7] C. Bellaigue, 'A. Boito: Lettres et Souvenirs', in *Revue des deux Mondes* lxxxviii/48 (Paris 1918), p. 906.

Ex. 68

soffio etesio' are variants of aria forms that Verdi had used before: the 'tempo di minuetto' that bursts on the audience with miraculous freshness just when the important business of the score might be thought to be over is as strict in its ternary design as any movement from the eighteenth century; while the final fugue is in every respect – a fugue (Verdi's final tribute to *Don Giovanni*?). In three cases motival development is used and in each the motif derives from a vocal phrase. In Falstaff's 'Honour' speech in Act I the phrase of the central section, 'Può l'onore riempirvi la pancia?' (Ex 69a), is transformed into a pattern which draws the musical design together and rounds it off with a superb, blaring tutti. The same structural importance is given to the phrase 'Dalle due alle tre' in Falstaff's duet with Mistress Quickly (Ex. 69b); while the figure of 'Te lo cornefico' (Ex. 69c) not only links Ford's solo with the preceding duet, but provides the unifying element of the monologue itself buzzing about like an angry wasp between the soloist's swelling phrases. Elsewhere Verdi's methods are more elusive. Themes will be stated then broken into sequences then transformed into new ideas; what first appears as an episode will turn into a main subject; the end of

Ex. 69

one period will change into the beginning of another. An apparently inconsequent transition whose only purpose seems to be to give an appropriate outline to a verbal phrase will be found to be riveted to what has gone before by some linking figure that develops through it, often in an inner part. The binding agent may be a figure of two notes as in the scene in which Bardolph and Pistol tell Ford of Falstaff's designs upon his wife. The texture may thin down almost to vanishing point, as at the start of Act II, scene 2, where Alice is laying her trap, or in the first scene of Act III, where she is giving instructions for the masquerade in Windsor Forest. Yet though the material is on paper often the merest small change of academic figuration, the effect is sparkingly alive. Wagner's celebrated remark about Beethoven comes to mind – that he could create whole worlds out of nothing.

Indeed out of the various influences which impinge upon the score musicians from Charles Stanford to Massimo Mila have recognised Beethoven as among the most prominent, especially the Beethoven of the 'Pastoral' symphony, the violin sonatas and the string quartets. Mendlessohn and Weber can be glimpsed in the fairy music of Act III, Delibes' *Coppélia*, transfigured by delicacy and the subtlest of development, in the rough and tumble preceding the concertato of Act II, and, more remotely, Don José's Flower Song in Fenton's sonetto, though without any echoes of the Parisian salon. As for the end of Act I, with its tenor solo rising above a vocal mêlée of conflicting rhythms, it is not hard to find a precedent in the ensemble that concludes Act I of *Die Meistersinger*, whose Italian première in 1889 at La Scala, Milan, Verdi is unlikely to have missed. Reminiscences of Verdi's own past are there, too, but in small doses. The ritual drubbing of Falstaff in Act III follows the time-honoured triple pattern with a theme derived partly from the Hostias and partly from the Ingemisco of the *Requiem*; and it concludes with what is almost a quotation from the judgement scene towards the end of the 1867 version of *Don Carlos*

The harmonic style of *Falstaff* is as fresh and limpid as

Mediterranean sunlight but it is far from naive. The familiar seventh inversions are in evidence, so too the elliptical progressions. Nor is Verdi afraid of modern procedures where the occasion requires. The opening of Ford's monologue '(È sogno? o realtà) draws on the dream-like associations of the whole-tone scale. The twelve chords under-lining the chimes of midnight are a tour de force of ingenuity and have inspired at least one modern composer to a set of variations. Does all this indicate a drying up of the melodic well, as some have suggested? The answer is rather that in *Falstaff* the entire texture is pervaded by melody, much of it instinct with the implications of physical gesture and nuances of verbal intonation. 'Reverenza!' says Mistress Quickly as she greets Falstaff; and the musical phrase has a deep curtsey built into it. 'Alice è mia!' cries Falstaff triumphantly; and the full orches-tra responds with a melodic snatch of belly-laugh. Then, too, the melodic units vary widely in length. Falstaff's 'Quand'ero paggio' lasts a mere thirty seconds. The reading of Falstaff's letter by contrast forms a huge paragraph of forty-four bars. Beginning with the cor anglais solo before 'Fulgida Alice', it gathers strength and continuity as it proceeds, finishing in an outrageous bloom of romantic harmony followed by a burst of merry laughter (Ex. 70).

Yet the most astonishing feat of *Falstaff* is surely this: that while much of the score stands the clichés of Romanticism on their head, the third act can enter the world of 'faerie' without a hint of caricature. The poetry that Shakespeare cannot resist bestowing on his 'moon-shine revellers' is far surpassed by Verdi's. With Nannetta's 'Ninfe! Elfi' we seem to be back in the Romantic dawn of the 1820s and '30s with Berlioz' Queen Mab, the fairies of Mendelssohn's Midsummer Night's Dream overture and Weber's *Oberon*, all composed by young men: yet the Verdi of *Falstaff* seems younger than any of them.

The balance between fantasy and comedy, the transition from one plane to the other and back, was not achieved as easily as the finished result might lead us to expect. The end of scene 1 of the third act was written after the première, the thematic organisation being changed and the rhythmic design varied and improved. A still more substantial alteration was made in the ensemble that ends Act II. It was the old problem of the pezzo concertato: how to develop the music satisfactorily without allowing the drama to freeze and the audience's attention to wander. Averse to mere cuts as the most brutal type of surgery, Verdi re-wrote six bars and removed sixteen. But the earlier version exists in the first printed vocal scores; and

Ex. 70

although the relevant pages were as usual torn out of the autograph, it is possible to reconstruct the scoring quite plausibly; and indeed both scenes have been given in their original form in America in an edition by James Hepokoski.

Has the character of Falstaff a tragic dimension? Some would say that is has and would point to the monologue at the start of Act III ('Mondo ladro! mondo rubaldo!') for confirmation (and is there not a virtual quotation of Klingsor's motif before the words 'che giorna-taccia nera'?):

Ex. 71

But to most of us Falstaff's ill-humour is as funny as his roguery; it is the Falstaff of *King Henry IV* who sees 'lime in the sack' as a symbol of the age's depravity. Besides, his mood is short-lived; a glass of mulled wine 'mixed with the waters of the Thames' – and here he hums a snatch which might have come from an English glee – is enough to restore his spirits. The charm of Verdi's Falstaff lies in his boundless effrontery. To Boito he was one of nature's incorrigible subversives. In the preface to *Mefistofele* he is coupled with Goethe's demon as one who says 'no!' to everything. The link between 'Son lo spirito che nega' and 'L'onore! Ladri!' is thus explained.

It is easier to find an element of tragedy in Ford, whose sufferings as a self-imagined cuckold might be presumed genuine enough – except that they are never designed to appear other than totally ridiculous: his play-acting as 'Signor Fontana', the ferocious pantomime in the monologue ('Prima li accoppio e poi li colgo'), the overturning of the household in his search of the guilty pair even to the extent of searching in drawers. If a certain passage for horns in the monologue recalls the loneliness of King Philip, and the final phrase ('Laudata sempre sia in fondo del mio cor la gelosia') the heartbreak of *Otello*, it is only by way of parody. It is as though the greatest outrage that can befall a husband has given Ford a mighty sense of self-importance; indeed we could even imagine that Ford welcomes such a discovery as the opportunity for getting the moral ascendancy over a wife who is so much cleverer than he. True, there is room here for a more serious interpretation, as in any play by Chekhov; and Charles Stanford could not understand why the first-night audience found Ford's plight so amusing. But surely if Verdi and Boito had intended a tragic impersonation, they would not have chosen Italy's leading comic baritone, Antonio Pini-Corsi, to create the role.

If we look for that element of seriousness, the *lacrimae rerurm* without which no work of art can achieve sublimity, we shall find it more plausibly in the music of the lovers. In setting their lyrical encounters to a fast tempo Verdi gives them a sense of transience, of moments of happiness snatched from 'devouring time' in the last scene in Windsor Forest – in the sonetto, Nannetta's solo, and the minuet – a sense of autumnal melancholy persists along with the pranking. It is here that Verdi joins hands with the Mozart of *Le Nozze di Figaro*.

The work of a composer's eightieth year might be expected to sum up the experience of a lifetime. What is astonishing about *Falstaff* is that it looks forward as well as back. Alfredo Casella described it as the point of departure for modern Italian music; and today it appears far less dated than the veristic works which were to remain in fashion for the next twenty years. To have inaugurated a new way of musical thinking at so advanced an age is no mean feat. Verdi himself put the matter neatly when he wrote to Giulio Ricordi about his failure to appreciate Mascagni's *L'Amico Fritz*. 'But', he finished apologetically, 'I'm just an old fogey [*codino*]; well, old, certainly; perhaps not such a fogey as all that.'[8]

[8] AGV, IV, pp. 426–7.

18

Miscellaneous operatic compositions

The practice of writing extra numbers for insertion into one's own and other people's scores has a history that goes back into the eighteenth century. Unprotected by copyright, operas once performed passed out of their composers' hands to be at the mercy of anyone who chose to perform them. The leading parts would be adapted to the means of the new singers partly by transposition partly by 'puntatura' – i.e. by raising or lowering the pitch of the line without disturbing the harmony. But it would also happen that a singer might decide that this or that aria did not do justice to his or her qualities and would insist on substituting one that did. Many singers carried about with them a collection of 'arie di baule' (suitcase arias) each suitable to a different stock situation which they would insert at will into any opera in which they took part. The more intelligent would apply to the original composer for something new; or, if he were unavailable, to another of high repute. Many of Mozart's so-called concert arias were written at the request of individual singers for insertion into the operas of his contemporaries. For the Viennese première of *Don Giovanni* he wrote fresh arias for Don Ottavio and Donna Elvira; for the 1789 revival of *Figaro* he did the same for Susanna. At the height of his fame he was not too proud to submit to this custom. Even when the copyright laws of 1840 onwards combined with Ricordi's practice of printing full vocal scores to make the substitution of arias increasingly rare, it took a long time to die out. In his last years Pacini continued to provide new arias on request for his one enduring opera, *Saffo*. Verdi, though opposed to the practice on principle, was obliged to submit to it in his youth. In most of his substitute-arias he is careful to preserve the 'tinta' of the opera for which they were destined; and several of them show a degree of melodic craftsmanship that equals or even surpasses that of the original number. But they fit their context less easily; nor do they add anything to the work as a whole. Verdi never succeeded in writing an equivalent of 'Dalla sua pace' which modern performances of *Don Giovanni* exclude at their peril.

Verdi's earliest known operatic number is the aria *con pertichini* for tenor 'Io la vidi', text from Giuseppe Persiani's *Il solitario ed Elodia*. Its pre-Rossinian form suggests that it was written as an exercise for Lavigna rather than for insertion into a performance of that opera. Likewise the duet for Leonora and Cuniza to be found in an appendix to the autograph of *Oberto*, 'Pria che scende sull'indegno', was probably cut from the original score before publication (indeed I take it to be the one referred to in a letter from Verdi to Massini written in 1838). But the cavatina for Cuniza and the duet for her and Riccardo, also in the appendix, are undoubtedly later additions. The original Cuniza, Mary Shaw, was a deep contralto and one whose inexperience made an opening cavatina inadvisable. Accordingly when Luigia Abbadia undertook the role in Turin a few weeks after the Milan première she inserted an 'aria di baule' by Mercadante and omitted the original duet. For the 1840 revival at La Scala which took place under his own supervision Verdi wrote for her the cavatina 'D'innocenza i cari inganni' of no distinction whatever. The duet 'Ah Riccardo, a mia ragione' is musically more impressive than what it replaces, having three fully extended movements where the original had only two and a transition. But Cuniza's aria at the start of Act II contains a reminiscence of the latter which is lost if the new duet is used. For Naples in 1841 Verdi wrote a brief two-movement duet for the first encounter between Leonora and her father ('Dove corri, o sciagurata?') in which Oberto's opening words are neatly illustrated by a cursive figure in the orchestra; the cabaletta ('Vieni, pietosa è il ciel') has an agreeable lilt, Bellinian rather than Verdian. The music of a new chorus for Cuniza's attendants ('Sorge un canto') is found only in a poor piano transcription.

In *Nabucco* it seems that the low range of Fenena's romanza ('Oh dischiuso è il firmamento') posed a problem. For a revival in the autumn of 1842 Verdi provided a 'puntatura' for Giuseppina Zecchini in which the melodic line is raised in certain phrases by a third. Later, for the Venetian première on 26 December 1842 he would write an entirely new romanza to the same words for the soprano Almerinda Granchi. Very much in the broad 'Risorgimentale' style, it suggests a sketch for the famous chorus 'O Signore, dal tetto natio' from *I Lombardi* and is hardly appropriate to the prayer of a young princess about to be put to death.

The original cabaletta of Oronte's cavatina in *I Lombardi*

('Come poteva un angelo') was slow and soulful, rather like those of Bellini's *La straniera*. For a revival at the Senigallia fair with the tenor Antonio Poggi Verdi provided a fleeter, pithier alternative in the rhythm of Donizetti's 'O luce di quest'anima'. Both appear in the printed score, so giving the singer a choice; though the fact that at one point Verdi recommended the former to Mario to sing in *I due Foscari* suggests that he considered it superseded. Nowadays either may be heard. If the original is less lively than its successor, it fits the character of the singer much better.

It was at Rossini's request that Verdi wrote a new grand aria for the Russian tenor Nicola Ivanoff to sing at the end of Act II of *Ernani* instead of the duet with Silva. Having arrived at Silva's castle alone and in disguise he is unaccountably joined by a body of his followers and proposes to lead them against the King of Spain – a disregard for the dramatic proprieties that was all too common at the time. The andante 'Odi il voto, O grande Iddio' is a fine piece of writing, both heroic and tender. The cabaletta 'Sprezzo la vita' is unusually spacious both in form and tonal lay-out but altogether of coarser fibre. Nor was this the only compromise that Verdi was induced to make to ensure the opera's continued success. *Ernani* ideally demands four principal singers; the Teatro la Fenice had no principal bass on their roster. Consequently Silva was designed as a comprimario role. Star basses such as Derivis preferred to essay the part of Don Carlos, making the transpositions and 'puntature' necessary to bring it within their range. Marini had a better solution. He tacked on to the cantabile 'Infelice, e tuo credevi' a cabaletta of a new cavatina that Verdi had written for him to sing in a revival of *Oberto* given in Barcelona in 1841 ('Infin che un brando vindice'). As both Oberto and Silva are old men bent on vengeance, the addition is not inappropriate but its effect in performance is awkward since it implies an exit which does not take place; it is also rather vigorous for Silva's character – indeed the codetta reappears note for note in Nabucco's cabaletta of regained strength ('Cadran, cadranno i perfidi'). The cabaletta, being Marini's property, does not figure in any vocal score before Boosey's of 1851.[1]

At the request of Prince Poniatowski Verdi reluctantly agreed to

---

[1] The source of this cabaletta, which has puzzled scholars for many years, was recently traced by Professor Roger Parker of Cornell University. The original title was 'Ma fin che un brando vindice'.

compose a new cabaletta for Mario to sing in *I due Foscari* in place of the fierce 'Odio solo ed odio atroce' with its vocal syncopations and rapping trumpets. ('Make it a powerful one', Verdi had written to Piave, 'because we're writing for Roppa.')[2] Mario however was a gentle, sensitive singer who still cultivated the falsetto range. Accordingly in 'Si, lo sento, Iddio mi chiama' Verdi takes him up to high f in little bursts of fioritura. The result is one of the least Verdian pieces of music ever written by Verdi.

Nothing beyond the text exists of the cavatina ('Potrei lasciar il margine') written for Sofia Loewe to sing in a revival of *Giovanna d'Arco* in 1845; nor yet of another solo ('Sventurato! alla mia vita') composed – again at Rossini's instance – for Ivanoff as a replacement for the romanza 'Chi non avrebbe il misero' in the last act of *Attila*. (The autograph surfaced briefly in the catalogue of an antiquarian bookseller some years ago only to disappear into the hands of a private collector before anyone had the chance to examine it.) Another romanza intended for the same context has survived since Napoleone Moriani, for whom it was written, decided most unusually to sell it to a publisher. 'Oh dolore! ed io vivea' adapts the *Attila* tinta – strong, bow-shaped melodic lines with carefully graded pinnacles – to the means of the 'tenor of the beautiful death'. The scoring is refined and subtle, the harp adding a delicate bloom at the lines beginning 'Ah beato fui in quell'amore'. But this too is heard to best advantage in the concert hall.

From the time of *Macbeth* onwards Verdi began to demand that in his contracts with the various theatres Ricordi should make it a condition of hire that the music of his operas should not be tampered with in any way. Nothing was to be omitted apart from the ballet, nothing transposed. By the same token he ceased to write substitute arias to suit individual singers. When Teresa De Giuli-Borsi's husband asked for an aria with which to replace 'Caro nome' in *Rigoletto* Verdi humorously replied that the only place for another aria for Gilda would be in the Duke's bedroom – and then it would have to be a duet. However he did subsequently make one exception to his rule. In 1863 the Paris Opéra revived *Les vêpres siciliennes* with a new tenor, Villaret, for whom Verdi wrote 'O toi que j'ai chérie', a splendid specimen of the minor-major romance with a *Traviata*-like

[2] LCC, p. 426.

spread of strings in the central part and in the major-key denouement one of those sweeping, lyrical cadential phrases that we find in the revised *Macbeth* and *Don Carlos*. What is missing, however, is that sense of emotional twilight, that uncertainty that pervades the original 'O jour de peine', and which suits it so admirably to Henri's character and situation.

This is perhaps also the place in which to mention two overtures unpublished during the composer's life. The first is a Sinfonia in D, a manuscript score of which is preserved in the Scala Museum in Milan. True, the handwriting is not instantly identifiable as Verdi's; but in form and style this is very much the kind of work that one would expect from the apprentice composer whether at Busseto or Milan. There is a short introduction, a Mannheim rocket for a first theme and a second subject dominated by perky Rossinian triplets; no crescendo, however, and a reprise of the second subject group only, in conformity with Verdi's usual practice. The scoring is heavy with some particularly busy writing for a second clarinet. The musical personality is still unformed, the melodic ideas being the merest small-change of the 1830s. In a word there is nothing here to merit a revival.

Of very different calibre is the overture to *Aida* which Verdi wrote for the Milan première and then withdrew after hearing it in rehearsal. The conductor's score however remained in the possession of Ricordi. It was examined in 1912 by a group of musicians including Toscanini with a view to performance; but in the end it was decided to respect Verdi's wishes and return it to the shelves. However Toscanini must in the meantime have made his own copy since in 1942 he was able to give a performance of it in America, a recording of which has for some years been available on pirate disc. It begins with the prelude as we know it, which breaks off towards the end into an allegro compounded of 'Numi pietà' (Ex. 58) and the four thematic lables (Ex. 57) in various permutations and combinations. As an orchestral piece in its own right it is highly entertaining and has moments of real imagination; but as an introduction to a drama as straightforward as that of *Aida* it is far too complex. The existing prelude could not be bettered.

19
Chamber compositions

If the majority of Verdi's chamber works are of marginal interest only, the fault lies not so much in his lack of aptitude for the medium as in the musical tradition of his time and place. In Italy, since the beginning of the century, only opera was considered to have any importance. The few remaining practitioners of instrumental music pursued their activity abroad – Cherubini in France, Boccherini in Spain, Clementi in England. The last descendant of the great violin school of Corelli and Tartini was Niccolò Paganini whose art was of a very different kind: taut, memorable themes extended with a maximum of technical display and a minimum of musical thought. Liszt, his pianistic counterpart, who had no such melodic fertility, made far more of Paganini's themes than Paganini himself.

By the eighteen-thirties instrumental music in Italy was represented by a host of virtuosi of every conceivable instrument, the summit of whose ambition was to play intricate variations on 'Le Carnaval de Venise'. For their occasional appearances in a theatre orchestra composers were careful to provide them with showy solos in an act prelude. The quartet, quintet, trio or duo sonata was virtually unknown in nineteenth-century Italy before the cultural initiative of Abramo Basevi in Florence in the 1850s.

Likewise for a long time piano music meant florid transcriptions of opera. Baron Ertmann, husband of the amateur pianist to whom Beethoven dedicated his Sonata op. 101, complained that in all the time he had spent in Milan he had not found a single pianist able or willing to play a Beethoven sonata. Indeed the only 'home' music of any vitality was the 'arietta' or 'romanza' for voice and piano, which varied in character from the miniature operatic scena to the popular or pseudo-folksong with dialect words. Such pieces were highly fashionable in Verdi's youth. Usually they were published in groups of six with picturesque titles such as 'Nuits à Pausilippe' or 'Soirées de Vienne' (Schubert's publishers were not alone in counting on the snob value of a French title). But one would search them in vain for the qualities of a Schubert Lied, if only because there was no classical tradition of pianism to nourish the accompaniments, which merely reproduce the most elementary of orchestral thrummings. Nor was there an Italian Goethe or Heine to initiate a school of lyrical poetry which could suggest to the musician a multitude of shades of feeling. The serious texts are mostly conventional, built up on those weary clichés that only in the context of an opera are capable of a certain grandeur. Thwarted love is still the favourite theme; and the strongest stylistic influence is that of Bellini, whose 'Ariette' of 1829 are among the least unworthy specimens of the genre. As always, Donizetti's range is wider, his Neapolitan songs having a particular charm. To the same category belong Rossini's 'Soirées Musicales', which have a polish and refinement all their own.

It was with a collection of 'Sei Romanze', published in 1838 by Canti in Milan, that Verdi first came before the public; and it is clear from their nature that he was determined to present himself as a composer of tragic operas *in posse*. In the first, 'Non t'accostare all' urna', by Vittorelli, a lover warns his faithless sweetheart not to approach his funeral urn with floral tributes but to let his bruised spirit rest in peace. Menacing dominant minor ninths over a left-hand tremolando suggestive of rolling drums (a device repeated in no.4) introduce the brooding C minor vocal theme. The first paragraph proceeds with a certain repetitive emphasis to its final cadence, only to change direction at the last moment. The voice then breaks into a kind of declamatory recitative ('Empia! Empia!'). The vocal line becomes irregular and convulsive; the accompaniment throbs and sighs in the approved tragic manner. For the reprise Verdi sets the last two lines only of the third strophe, having used the first two for an extension of the central episode. So what was expanded in the first statement reappears compressed in the second and enhanced by more powerful harmonies – a technique that Verdi was regularly to apply in his operas. The second romanza, 'More, Elisa, lo stanco poeta', is a more modest affair – a simple, strophic setting in slow 6/8 of a dying poet's farewell to his beloved; in the minor key as before but with a caressing excursion into the relative major (with increased motion in the accompaniment) from which it seems reluctant to return. In contrast to its predecessor, it finishes with a slightly unconvincing *tierce de Picardie*. In Vittorelli's 'In solitaria stanza' it is the loved one that is dying – a fact which evidently merits the more restrained wistfulness of the major key. Much about it pre-echoes the more conventional features of the early operas – the triplet-based accompaniment, the regular phrase-lengths with their use of double dots, the predictable cadences. But note the unusual design in sixteen rather than eight-bar paragraphs; also that the second is identical with the first only up to its mid-point; thereafter the music takes on greater urgency with an anticipation of 'Tacea la notte' from *Il trovatore*.

Ex. 72

With Angiolini's 'Nell'orror di notte oscura' we are back with the deserted lover who in the still watches of the night broods on his betrayal: four double strophes, the first two in the minor, the second in the tonic major, without, it must be said, the slightest textual justification. But the piano part is more varied than in most of the set and suggests an acquaintance with Schubert's 'Der Neugierige' (Verdi's brook flows in an entirely pianistic manner). Eminently operatic, however, are the accents on the semiquavers that set the words 'Di colei che lo tradia'. Already we seem to be hearing Don Carlo belabouring Silva in *Ernani*. Schubertian associations are all too ready to hand in 'Perduta ho la pace', a translation by Balestra of 'Gretchen am Spinnrade'. While making no attempt to imitate the turning of the spinning wheel, Verdi follows Schubert in designing the piece as a rondo – the only possible solution. The D minor opening catches the mood of the poem and the episodes contain inventive touches, but the piece ends in a repetitive abundance of F major which not even the unexpected modulation on the word 'bacio' can redeem. There is more interest in the last of the set, 'Deh, pietoso, oh Addolorata', again a translation from Goethe by Balestra. In the large-scale ternary design, Verdi is depicting Gretchen's distraction in the language which comes naturally to him. The opening ten-bar melody leads into an ordered chaos of ideas similar to those in which the madness of Nabucco will be expressed, even down to the pleading phrases in thirds. Alas, the final section is a typical major key release at total variance with the text and with the fatal suggestion of a cabaletta about it. Verdi the artist had a long way to

303

go; yet considering his inexperience (he had not yet produced a single opera) his first set of romances augured well. Clearly his visit to Milan in the late summer of 1838 had not been wasted.

The following year the same firm published a *Notturno a 3 voci* for soprano, tenor, bass, piano and concertante flute. Here the world of Rossini's *Soirées Musicales* is suffused with romantic pathos: the silver moon, the calm sea, the gentle night breezes, the nightingale singing to his mate, who replies with sweet affection – so unlike the poet's beloved. A gently swaying accompaniment, a bland progress of the three voices, mostly in close harmony, convey the soothing nocturnal atmosphere; the flute is the nightingale with a showy introduction of fourteen bars (doubtless here Verdi had his eye on the first flute of the Busseto Philharmonic Society, to wit his own father-in-law). Formally it is one of those indeterminate pieces which proceed mainly by repeated phrases without a long-range reprise; except that the final melodic idea is an enhanced variant of the opening – an inspired touch that more than redeems the crude parallel fifths between tenor and bass which make the initial phrase look like the work of an amateur.

Two more songs belong to the year of *Oberto*. 'L'esule', to words by Solera, is nothing less than a full-length *scena ed aria*, the solo part marked merely 'canto', though the tessitura seems to indicate baritone or mezzo soprano. Again the scene is nocturnal with a 'bianca luna'; and throughout the 'scena' the accompaniment ripples pianistically; but from the cantabile onwards the sound is strictly orchestral with imaginary string figuration and wind doublings. The exile remembers the happy hours spend beneath his native sky to a slow melody moving between D minor and F major in which we can discern faint traces of the Risorgimentale laments of *Nabucco* and *I Lombardi* with their decasyllabic meter. Finally the singer longs for death, which will leave his spirit free to fly back to the land he loves, a sentiment which finds expression in the brashest of Verdian cabalettas. Less pretentious and more sympathetic is Luigi Balestra's 'La seduzione', his story of an Italian Fanny Robin. Here all is simple pathos with a touch of unforced drama in the A minor episode where the girl dies in giving birth.

Between these and the next set of published 'romanze' Frank Walker unearthed an Italian setting of Goethe's 'Erster Verlust' 'Chi i bei di m'adduce ancora', translation presumably by Balestra. It was written for the Marchesa Sofia De'Medici evidently on the crest of popularity that followed the première of *Nabucco*. Beginning in simple E minor 6/8, this regret for the innocent sorrows of childhood develops into a highly operatic climax in the major with agonized syncopations, repeated high Bs and a cadenza. Alfredo's 'Di quell'amor' is intimated in the strain of 'O i bei dì chi mi ritorna' just as Azucena's 'Giorni poveri vivea' is hinted at in the opening phrase. An agreeable piece, despite a disproportion of means to ends.

The six romanze of 1845 are very different from those of seven years earlier. They are lighter, more popular, at the same time more mondaine – in a word, more Donizettian, alternating grave and gay. Yet the former show a longer melodic span than the songs of 1838 while being entirely free from their operatic pretensions. The forms too are freer and follow more strictly the sense of the poetry. Maffei's 'Il tramonto', a kind of *Abendempfindung* in which the setting sun induces thoughts of mortality, is a spacious binary structure whose second paragraph introduces a new idea just when we expect a reprise of the opening. To begin with the accompaniment is admirably pianistic even if the spread chords in the right hand occasionally obstruct the triplet movement in the left; but soon orchestral habits of thought assert themselves, until at the words 'al desio di quell'aureo sentiero' we can hear in our mind's ear the entry of the harp. Maggioni's 'La zingara' in conventional bolero rhythm and modified rondo form is a light hearted piece for soprano leggiero of no great distinction; but the moment where the gipsy girl thinks of an uncertain future is appropriately matched by a sudden turn into the minor key, reverting to the major when she returns to the joys of the moment. The third, 'Ad una stella', with poetry again by Maffei is the gem of the set, its melody showing that little touch of the unexpected which occurs all too rarely in Verdi's salon pieces (Ex. 73).

The poem is nebulous enough – an ode to the evening star as the refuge of a careworn spirit; but Verdi weaves it into a spacious three-part design with a particularly well developed central episode. Better known, though far less substantial, 'Lo spazzacamino' figures in the programme of many a soprano recital. More mudlark than the chimney-sweep of Hans Andersen's tales, the singer chirrups his, or her way through three melodically different verses in 2/4, each followed by the same waltz-like refrain. 'Il mistero', words by Romani, offers another fine example of Verdi's growing melodic craftsmanship: a freely extended binary structure with carefully judged high points and vivid word painting where the singer com-

Ex. 73

pares his mood to a lake, calm on the surface but in turmoil below.
The final 'Brindisi' exists in two versions, that of the autograph and
that of the printed edition, the difference however being confined to
the first melodic phrase and its recurrence at the end. The second
with its contrasts of dynamic, its momentary minor inflexion, is so
manifestly superior to the first as to put it out of court. For the rest it
presents an amiable succession of ideas as conventional as the sentiments they accompany.

Two years later Lucca published a single romanza to words by
Maggioni which Verdi probably composed during his visit to London
in the summer of 1847, where Maggioni was resident poet at the
Royal Italian Opera. 'Il poveretto' concerns a soldier crippled in the
service of his country and constrained to beg from passers by. The
setting is distinguished from Verdi's earlier serious romanze by a
short expressive piano preamble full of wistful suspensions. Though
hardly up to the best of the 1845 set, 'Il poveretto' has a curious
history. In 1858 *Rigoletto* was given in French at the Théâtre de la
Monnaie in Brussels. The Maddalena insisted on having an aria to
herself; accordingly Verdi's French publisher, Escudier, adapted the
music of 'Il poveretto' to a French text, in which Maddalena begs her

brother to spare the Duke's life ('Prends pitié de sa jeunesse'). He even had it published in this form as a separate 'Mélodie'. Neither he nor Verdi could have foreseen that the 'newly discovered aria for Maddalena' would one day prove a red herring to be drawn across the path of Verdian scholars.

In 1849 Léon Escudier advertised a romance by Verdi entitled 'L'abandonnée' to words by L.M.E. of which there is no mention in standard Verdian literature. It took Frank Walker to run a copy to earth, to identify the initials as standing for Léon and Marie Escudier and the figure on the cover as Giuseppina Strepponi, with whom Verdi was now living. Apart from noticing certain anticipations of *La traviata* Walker made no great claims for it as music; and indeed a glance at the vocal line would suggest that it was intended as an exercise for Giuseppina's singing pupils. The range extends over two octaves and a third from low A to high C; the phrases are full of the standard technical devices – roulades, staccato and legato, *note picchettate*, turns and portamenti over wide intervals. There is nothing to suggest that the composer took the abandoned lady's plight very seriously.

The birth of a son to the Triestine tenor Giovanni Severi called forth a tribute from Verdi in the form of a *Barcarola* 'Fiorellin che sorge appena' – a pleasant trifle of 19 bars in A1–A2–B–A3 form in which, characteristically, the climax first introduced in A2 is heightened in A3. Never published in the composer's lifetime, it is printed in facsimile in Giuseppe Steffani's book *Verdi e Trieste* of 1951.

Of even less consequence is 'La preghiera del poeta', apparently jotted down after an agreeable walk with the Neapolitan poet Nicola Sole in the autumn of 1858. At the time Verdi had seriously considered setting a libretto by Sole based on a subject by Byron; while Sole for his part was eager that Verdi should set one of his 'Canti'. But the poet died in 1859 and all that was left of their collaboration were these sixteen bars of dignified commonplace for bass and piano, harmonised by Verdi in spread chords that presumably take their cue from the words 'fede ed arpa'. One feature alone is of interest; the text is in eleven-syllable verse, from now on Verdi's favourite metre for solo song.

Though it too was never published in Verdi's lifetime, 'Il Brigidino' is of very different quality. It appears to have been written during intervals between sessions of the Italian Parliament in 1861 and given as a present to the daughter of his fellow deputy Piroli. Clearly, however, it must have enjoyed a few private performances amongst Verdi's friends; otherwise Ferrarini, director of the Parma Conservatoire, would hardly have asked for a copy for a forthcoming concert. Finally it was performed publicly by the soprano Isabella Gianetti-Galli in Parma in 1863. Why it should have been withheld from publication is a mystery.

The poem by the patriot Francesco Dall'Ongaro is in the form of a Tuscan *stornello*. The singer is a peasant girl whose lover has brought her from Siena a *brigidino* (a local 'sweet' or 'pudding'). To its colours of red and white she has added a sprig of verbena, so forming the Italian 'tricolore', whose virtues she extols in the rest of the poem. The two strophes of six lines apiece of hendecasyllabic verse are as far from operatic 'versi lirici' as can be imagined; and Verdi sets them in an intimate conversational style, each pair ending in a particularly graceful cadence. Gone are the measured triplets and the taut double dots. If there is any operatic comparison here it is with the opening scene of *La forza del destino*, already on the stocks.

Ex. 74

But what astonishes chiefly is the total mastery of keyboard style. There is not a trace here of orchestral figuration. For the first time

Verdi avails himself of the nuances afforded by the horizontal disposition of chords with intervening chromatic passing notes, and of
the delicate effect produced by subsuming the fundamental note
before it is sounded. Had he proceeded further along that path how
much richer the treasury of Italian song might have been.

Verdi's last song was occasioned by sadder circumstances – the
stroke that laid Piave low for eight years and brought his family to
the point of destitution. Verdi's own contribution to the Album-
Piave took the form of another Stornello ('Tu dici che non m'ami')
this time a genuine piece of folk-poetry such as we find in Wolf's
Italian Song Book. The singer snaps her fingers at the man who has
ceased to love her. She too is as inconstant as the wind – everyone's
mistress including her own. It is a brisk, splendidly economical little
piece in which the hendecasyllabic verse is handled with rare flexibility and aplomb. Less specifically pianistic than that of 'Il Brigidino'
the accompaniment is witty and pointed with that vigorous movement of the bass and inner parts that marks so much of Verdi's later
music. As early as 1868 the style of *Falstaff* is already in sight.

In general, then, the romanze follow much the same line of
development as the operatic arias, acquiring over the years greater
flexibility of rhythm and structure, more variety and subtlety of
expression. It could even be said that Verdi's technique for handling
eleven-syllable verse in his operas was forged in the later songs.

The instrumental category consists of two curiosities and one minor
masterpiece. In 1865 under the title of 'Gioie e Sospiri' Canti brought
out an album of piano pieces by fashionable composers of the time
(Arditi, Cagnoni, Pedrotti and others). Doubtless as a kindly gesture
towards his first publisher, Verdi contributed a 'Romanza senza
parole' as the last item: a Bellini-ish melody of twenty-four bars with
a twelve-bar coda and much tinkling at the top of the keyboard.
There is so little here of Verdi's mature style as to make one wonder
whether he had merely exhumed one of the compositions of his
youth. Evidently the publication sold badly; for today the only copy
known to have survived is in the Library of the Milan Conservatory.

Far more intriguing, and of indubitable authenticity, is a little
'Valzer' for 'cembalo' discovered by the composer Nino Rota and
the producer Luchino Visconti and included by them in the film 'Il
Gattopardo'. The authograph is printed in facsimile in the *Discoteca* together with an article by Gioacchino Lanza Tommasi, who somewhat

arbitrarily ascribes it to the year 1859. It is a pleasant little trifle a main melody of sixteen bars with two episodes – having something of the 'slancio' of the party music in *La traviata*. For whom or what purpose it was composed remains to be discovered.

The Quartet in E minor of 1873 is unique in quite a different way. It was three years before he considered publishing it at all. To all appearance he set very little store by it musically ('I don't know whether it is good or bad, only that it is quartet').[1] Curiously it is precisely this claim, modest enough it would seem, that today's high priests of chamber music are disposed to contest; indeed Verdi himself has fuelled their argument by welcoming the plan to perform the quartet in London with twenty players to a part 'since there are certain passages which require a fuller sonority than a mere quartet can furnish'.[2] Clearly those refinements of texture characteristic of the great nineteenth-century quartet-writers find no place in Verdi's work; but to disparage it on that account is like finding fault with the piano pieces of Schubert for not exploiting the full range of piano sonority in the manner of Chopin and Liszt. A more vulnerable feature is the absence of a closely worked symphonic argument in miniature such as redeems the somewhat awkwardly written quartets of Brahms. Verdi was first and foremost a lyrical composer to whom the wider dimensions of thematic development were foreign; which is not to say that his quartet lacks either counterpoint or motivic working; rather that it never feels the weight of its classical heritage. Therein lies its appeal – it is a work which knows its own limitations, and is content to explore the implications of its own material. Had Verdi gone about his task in a spirit of greater reverence he might have produced the equivalent of a symphony by Rubinstein: instead he has given us something like a symphony by Borodin.

One criticism the quartet (unlike the *Requiem*) has fortunately been spared: namely that of being an opera in disguise; which is not to deny that certain thematic affinities with the operas exist. The opening subject of the first movement is clearly derived from one of the principal motifs of *Aida* (Ex. 75a). Other than that, if the opening twenty-six-bar paragraph has a model, it is more probably the beginning of Mozart's G minor quintet. A second germinating motif appears on the cello at the eleventh bar (Ex. 75b) to undergo several

[1] AVI, pp. 156–8.
[2] Ibid., p. 199–201.

transformations in the course of the movement. First, it serves to launch the transition with a succession of imitative entries; then it re-appears as a pounding background to a new theme, lyrical but modulating (Ex. 75c). So through workings of previous material, as well as some free figuration, to the Mendelssohnian second subject (Ex. 75d). A final idea combines simplicity with a humorous insistence worthy of Beethoven (Ex. 75e).

Ex. 75

Anticipating Brahms's symphony in the same key, Verdi begins the development with a restatement of his first subject in its original tonality, though with a characteristic elaboration of the accompaniment. Thereafter Ex. 75a and b proliferate into closely worked counterpoint, until the stream of sound broadens out into a series of sequences alternating Ex. 75a on cello and viola. Polythematic yet strongly developed, a shifting kaleidoscope of ideas, this movement more than any other work of Verdi's allows a glimpse of the *Falstaff* to come.

The second movement is the most obviously original. The form is one that is especially associated with Brahms: ternary, with a central episode that wanders freely through a variety of keys. But there is nothing here of Brahms's inward discourse; rather the quirky, non-slow movements of Beethoven's middle years come to mind. Note the coyness with which the mazurka-like main theme hesitates to reveal its tonality.

Ex. 76

Two ideas stand out in the central section: a theme in plain crotchets and minims stated first in the minor then varied and transformed into the major; and a pattern of rapping semiquavers. Between them occurs a short, modified reprise of Ex. 76 in the remote key of G flat, giving to the movement the suggestion of a rondo. A coda of 29 bars gathers up the separate threads.

The third movement recalls the *Macbeth* ballet music – a whirling prestissimo with the quality of a Danse Infernale. The trio, however, is a delicate serenade sung by cello, then first violin over the other strings pizzicati. The finale, marked 'scherzo-fuga' is a tour de force of counterpoint – a light-hearted Grosse Fuge. The subject (Ex. 77a) is bizarre, the tonality remaining unstable up till the fourth bar; the counter subject (Ex. 77b) is nondescript. Yet the variety that Verdi distils from both is astonishing.

Ex. 77

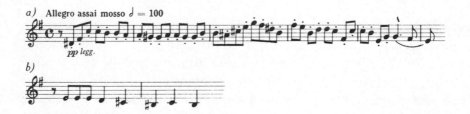

All the scholastic devices are there – canon, stretta, pedal-point – as well as much that owes nothing to precedent. Sometimes the texture is rich and full, at others a mere wisp of sound. As in all vital music, logic and surprise combine. Somewhere beyond the mid-point a short figure first on viola, then cello prepares for a statement of the subject in inversion. A false exposition follows in which both forms of the subject are combined and then broken down into spiralling sequences in contrary motion, once again recalling Beethoven. The three repeated notes of Ex. 77b then yield a succession of powerful unisons. A high trill ushers in a shortened version of Ex. 77a, now in

312

E major. The fugal texture remains to the end but nourished now by suave harmonies and cadences in the composer's ripest manner.

That this was the most difficult movement to perform Verdi himself was well aware. 'If during the rehearsal', he told Giulio Ricordi, 'you hear a passage which sounds rather messy, tell them that though they may be playing it well they are interpreting it badly. Everything should emerge clearly and precisely, even in the most complex counterpoint; and that is achieved by playing very lightly and staccato so that the subject stands out whether straight or inverted.'[3]

If not on the level of the greatest classical quartets, Verdi's is a fine and original contribution to the repertoire, in which only the occasional lapse into frieze-like figuration betrays the writer of operatic accompaniments.

[3] AGV, IV, p. 22.

20

Choral and religious works

All Italian composers of the last century had at some time to write religious music, whether as part of their training or for performance by their local community. But by the time of Verdi's youth the great liturgical traditions of the seventeenth and eighteenth centuries had long since declined. Masses consisted mostly of arid counterpoint in the choruses and operatic brilliance or sentimentality in the arias. Even those of Donizetti and Bellini barely rise above this level. Solemn beginnings too often decline into sugary ends.

Of Verdi's early church music only one piece has survived[1] and that because the singer for whom it was written took care to keep a copy. What surprises about the *Tantum Ergo* of 1836 for tenor and orchestra is its academic correctness. The man who would perpetrate many a crudity on the stage of La Scala or La Fenice has not put a fifth out of place. True there is little trace here of devotional spirit. The opening andante has a gavotte-like rhythm embellished here and there with semiquaver triplets in Rossini's manner; the allegro suggests an inhibited bravura aria. Nowhere is the future composer of the *Requiem* in evidence.

More in tune with Verdi's personal convictions is the war hymn 'Suona la tromba' of 1848 for three-part men's chorus and orchestra. Yet it is good neither as music nor for the purpose for which it was intended. Clearly Verdi had aimed at an Italian Marseillaise with something of the same rough freedom of design; but he never achieves the spontaneous combustion of Rouget De Lisle's hymn, in which all the ideas cohere without the need for repetition. One reason for this is that whereas all the phrase lengths of the French anthem are regular, 'Suona la tromba' starts with a phrase of five bars which

---

[1] The duets for Good Friday entitled *Gesù morì* once ascribed to Verdi, are now known to be the work of Bellini. See D. Stivender, 'The Composer of *Gesù morì*', AIVS newsletter no. 2, Dec. 1976, pp. 6–7.

gives it a 'list' which is never corrected. For want of a counter-weight the various strains fail to buttress one another. As usual Verdi is not at a loss for a powerful concluding phrase, but it comes too late. No wonder the Italian troops preferred Novaro's 'Fratelli d'Italia' with its elementary conjugation of a single rhythmic motif. This is at least music to march to.

And indeed, ennobled as Italy's national anthem, 'Fratelli d'Italia' turns up again in Verdi's next choral piece, the *Inno delle nazioni* composed for London's Great Exhibition of 1862. Boito's text is a lesser *Ode to Joy* with specific references to the participating nations – England, France and Italy. An orchestral introduction presents two of the principal themes, which are taken up in due course by the chorus. The first ('In questo dì giocondo') faintly pre-figures Amneris; the second, sung by men only, the priests of Isis. In a long *scena* a tenor bard welcomes the hordes that are flocking to the new temple of peace, recollects the horrors of war with the aid of a few graphic orchestral figures and in a noble phrase ('Ma di oggi un soffio di serena dea'), perhaps the most distinguished moment of the score, prepares for the centrepiece, the choral hymn 'Signor che sulla terra' with rippling harp accompaniment. Again there are pre-echoes of *Aida* in the unexpected progression at the end of the third phrase (x):

Ex. 78

A parade of national anthems follows, chorus representing England, orchestra France, and the tenor soloist Italy. It goes without saying that the Marseillaise, on account of its length, is merely topped and tailed, though its first phrase is allowed to generate a fugato. There follows a bizarre attempt to combine all three melodies. 'God Save the Queen' is forced into 4/4 time, while the other two undergo varieties of Procrustean treatment. There is a final, full-blooded restatement of Ex. 78, a dying echo of 'God Save the Queen' that suggests an acquaintance with Beethoven's *Battle Symphony*, and a noisy coda. A *hymn of nations* in this manner is an ingenious idea –

315

and it was Verdi's own – but it founders on the incompatibility of the three anthems; while the nationally neutral idiom of the intervening material, with no dramatic context to set it off, falls too often into well-mannered dullness. The only merit of the *Inno delle nazioni* is to have served as a preliminary exercise for the Act II finale of *Aida*.

In choosing to set the 'Libera me' as his contribution to the Rossini *Requiem* Verdi declared a particular fondness for that prayer dating from his organ-playing days. It is also possible that he already had in mind to complete the *Requiem* on his own at some future date, since two of the most important moments are recalled in the course of the prayer – the 'Requiem aeternam' and the 'Dies irae'. In the context of the Rossini mass there could be no question of a musical reminiscence since the original settings by Buzzola and Bazzini respectively would be quite different. In fact the 'Libera me' of the composite Mass and that of the Manzoni *Requiem* are essentially the same. Such discrepancies as exist are due partly to the greater range and power of Teresa Stolz, the soloist of 1874, as compared to that of Antonina Fricci for whom the original version was written, and partly to those improvements that were the fruit of five years reflection. The *Dies Irae* shows how a strong idea of 1869 has flowered into an overwhelming one in 1874 (Ex. 79).

The *Requiem* stands with Beethoven's *Missa Solemnis* and the late Haydn masses at the summit of nineteenth century liturgical music. Not that there is much competition. The age of Romanticism was the age of the individual, for whom religion is a private matter;

Ex. 79

c) Allegro agitato lo stesso movimento col tempo raddoppiato (♩ = 144)

its most characteristic product is Fauré's *Requiem* of 1888 and the Masses of Bruckner – an intimate communication between one man and his God. Collective religious sentiment was more often channelled into nationalism – logically since the nation is merely the individual writ large. A more genuinely religious spirit informs the secular music of Smetana or Mussorgsky than all the masses and oratorios of their contemporaries; and how preferable is Dvořák's folksy 'Jubilate' to his consciously classical *Stabat Mater*. Mendelssohn's *St. Paul* and *Elijah* are not free from a certain spiritual passivity; even less so such fashionable works as Gounod's *Redemption* and *Mors et Vita*. By the end of the century religiosity rather than religion had become the order of the day.

The decline of religious music in Italy has already been noted. It was France that provided the venue for Cherubini's austerely impressive Masses. Where there was no story to tell, no confrontations of character, no moments of dramatic suspense, it seems that composers wrote with less commitment. Donizetti's *Requiem in memory of Bellini* draws upon the same idiom that served him in his operas. Rossini's *Stabat Mater* and *Petite Messe Solonnelle* are also couched in an essentially operatic language, refined and uplifted by that natural taste and musicianship that never deserted him and also by a resurgence of creative energy that everyone had believed to be extinct. Both works reveal an essentially pre-Romantic outlook, in their formal character as well as in their spiritual optimism and in their acceptance of the mortal condition as a temporary stage (one thinks of those innocent tenor marches, the *Cujus animam* and the *Domine Deus*). 'Allegro cristiano' is for once in Rossini not a joke. But for a conception such as Verdi's, only one model could serve: the *Grande Messe des Morts*. In 1869 Berlioz too had died, a year after Rossini; if Verdi knew his Grande Messe of 1837 (and there is no proof that he did), it must surely have been near the surface of his mind when he composed the original 'Libera me'.

The question, 'which is Verdi's supreme masterpiece?', is as difficult to answer as in the case of any great artist. But if it be changed to 'which work shows his genius at its most concentrated?' then the answer must surely be the *Requiem*. Into it he poured all the purely musical resources that he had developed in the course of twenty six operas, and which he could here exploit to the full without having to take into account the special *données* which a stage action inevitably imposes. Like Beethoven he deeply admired the choral works of Handel; but there is a limit to what an operatic chorus is able to memorise for performance in a theatre. Only in a work such as the *Requiem* was it possible to attain that choral dimension that sets Handel's oratorios apart from his operas in scale and variety of musical thought.

Yet any comparison with Handel must be with *Messiah* rather than with the dramatic oratorios if only to refute the familiar charge, first laid by Bülow, that the *Requiem* is an opera in ecclesiastical garb. In both works the four soloists are depersonalised, though one or other may represent at one remove a figure in the text, like the tenor who utters the prophecy of Isaiah or the soprano who suggests a vision of St. Michael. Nothing in the *Requiem* is more operatic than 'Why do the nations' or 'The trumpet shall sound'. The truth is that from the Renaissance to the early nineteenth century few composers have made a conscious distinction between sacred and secular styles. Handel drew upon a chamber duet for 'For unto us a child is born'. It is as well for Bach's reputation for piety that he never wrote an opera; but he filled his *Christmas Oratorio* with arias and duets torn unaltered from secular cantatas (how many admirers of 'Schäfe können sicher weiden' realise that it was intended to celebrate the birthday of a German princeling?). Nobody complains that the Benedictus of Beethoven's *Missa Solemnis* quarries the same vein as the slow movement of his Quartet opus 127, or that the violin solo is too emotional for a religious work. It may still be argued that certain moments in Verdi's composition, by the force and vividness of their expression, violate the proprieties in the way that the occasional incursion of a slow waltz rhythm into Brahms's *Requiem* does not. This merely serves to illustrate Verdi's isolation in a world in which a vital tradition of religious music no longer obtained.

The orchestra is that which he had used for *Don Carlos* with four bassoons and four trumpets,[2] three flutes and an ophicleide for the brass bass. Modest by comparison with the monster forces of Wagner and Bruckner, it provides the composer with all the grandeur of sound that he needed.

Indeed the manner in which Verdi manages to establish a vast sense of scale within the first ten minutes is worth considering. Like *Das Rheingold* the *Requiem* opens in utter quietness. From a line of

[2] In Paris the second pair of trumpets were in fact cornets-à-pistons.

muted cellos only just within the threshold of audibility there evolves a large paragraph of twenty-seven bars for chorus and muted strings in which three motifs are prominent (Ex. 80a, b and c).

Ex. 80

The effect is beautifully described by Ildebrando Pizzetti in his preface to the published facsimile: '. . . In that Requiem aeternam murmured by an invisible crowd over the slow swaying of a few simple chords you straightaway sense the fear and sadness of a vast multitude before the mystery of death. In the change that follows into the 'et lux perpetuam' the melody spreads its wings up to an F sharp before falling back upon itself and coming to rest on an E more than an octave below, you hear a sigh for consolation and eternal peace. You see first a shadow, then a general radiance. In the darkness are human beings bowed down by fear and sorrow, and in the light they reach out their arms towards Heaven to invoke mercy and forgiveness. Far from being merely lyrical the music portrays sadness and hope.'[3]

Here a brief digression is in order on the subject of motivic analysis, to which of all Verdi's compositions the *Requiem* should most readily lend itself. Yet once again the primacy of the vocal period renders this as difficult as in the operas. It is possible to regard Ex. 80 (a), (b) and (c) as germinating cells to which everything in the score is related. But since one is an arpeggio, the second part of a diatonic and the third of a chromatic scale, this is not very illuminating, as between them they account for every conceivable melodic variant. Not until (a) flowers into (d) do we find an important pattern in the total design – a descending arpeggio based on two triads usually linked as a seventh. This will recur throughout the

---

[3] I. Pizzetti, *Preface to published facsimile of the Requiem* (Milan, 1941).

Requiem and always at points of high relief. At the same time (c) can be said to form the paradigm for a number of short melodic ideas that proceed by conjunct motion and then fall back on themselves. Equally there are many melodic ideas in the *Requiem* that cannot significantly be related to either figure yet whose existence in no way impairs the unity of the whole. Once again for a unifying principle it is difficult to go beyond the Basevian *tinta*.

A brief episode in F major ('Te decet hymnus') allows the chorus to show its paces in flights of imitative *a cappella* counterpoint, while at the same time setting the reprise of Ex. 80 (shorn of its first five bars) in a new perspective. Already the backcloth has been withdrawn, hinting at vast interior spaces. But it is in the Kyrie, the major-key complement to what has gone before, that the full dimensions of the edifice begin to disclose themselves. First there is an increase of motion in the orchestra. Over a descending pattern of cello and bassoon, clearly derived from (b), the four soloists successively launch their rockets.

Ex. 81

The sense of a continually widening vista is conveyed partly by the contrary motion between voice and orchestra, partly by an adroit combination of pitch and tonality in the soloists' entries (note the emphatic dominant cadence in that of the tenor, a sure device for enhancing the height of an upward phrase). A further stage is reached at bar ninety-six where the orchestral movement breaks into semiquavers. By now soloists and chorus are on equal terms; but any hint of a formal *concertato* is dispelled by Verdi's mastery in re-shaping his material, dissolving it into ever new and unexpected combinations. But this is no exercise in hedonistic sonority. Behind the

321

harmonic shiftings, with their varying pace, the orchestra after a while establishes a two-bar tramp; the music thrusts forward into D minor urged by 'fatal' rat-tat-at-at-ats from the timpani. At the climax the music breaks off; a few spezzati chords follow like faltering questions, answered in turn by a melting, but not cloying cadence in A major. A coda re-assumes the previous material in much the same sense, doubt and anxiety being quelled by a still richer cadential phrase. A harmonic epigram (Γ—B flat—E—A), typical of the mature works, brings the movement to its hushed close. Upon this the 'Dies Irae' bursts with a volcanic force intensified by the tonal non sequitur (A major — G minor). This is the longest and most elaborate of the seven pieces that make up the *Requiem*. The unusual cut of the verses in rhymed ottonario tercets is reflected in many of the movements, whether as simple three-fold repetition, variants of bar-form or in procedures less easily classified. The principal section is conceived as an unearthly storm: four tutti thunderclaps, later separated by powerful blows on the bass drum, the skin tightened so as to give a hard, dry sound (the Shakespearean 'crack of doom'?); rapid scales in contrary motion: peremptory calls to attention on the brass, and a chromatic choral line collapsing into those slow triplets that Verdi will use again for the real storm in *Otello*. An answering phrase in D minor ('Solvet saeclum in favilla') hints at the outline of the plainsong 'Dies Irae', by the 1870s a commonplace of romantic *diablerie* of which Verdi saw no reason to avail himself directly. Over the next seventeen bars the rhythmic symmetry is indeed 'dissolved' as a new idea takes shape, is developed in irregular sequences and finally crystallises into an emphatic consequent to Ex. 79b based on the anguished dominant minor ninth (see Ex. 82) both themes standing as bastions to this massive opening block.

The music subsides into anxious mutterings ('Quantus tremor est futurus') as all await the Second Coming. Here the tercets allow a characteristic 'ritual' formula: three unison staments on a single note, each a tone higher than the last, accompanied by the traditional apparatus of terror – shuddering strings, acciaccatura 'laments' on the winds, fatal 'rat-at-ats' on the timpani. The Trump sounds not as in Berlioz with a peal of brass from the four quarters of the earth, but as a single note played softly and extended by the familiar anapaest of death. To suggest the approach from a vast distance Verdi makes use of four extra trumpets behind the scenes, a modest enough addition to basic resources but it serves him far better than the

Ex. 82

Frenchman's lavishness. For the effect of quadrophonic interplay,
bright splashes of major tonality, modulations and changes of
rhythm, is merely to astonish. Verdi by contrast keeps to the dark
ambience of A flat minor throughout and generates his entire passage from one cell, expanding the semiquavers into triplets where
appropriate. Thus rhythmic insistence, a prevalence of dominant
harmony all add to the growing sense of menace.

When the long-awaited tonic chord is reached full brass, bassoons and timpani weigh in giving the music an almost thematic
substance (Ex. 83).

Ex. 83

The bass soloist rejoins with 'Tuba mirum spargens sonum' over a full orchestral chord to which chromatically descending strings give the feeling of a universe falling apart. The chorus echo his words while the air resounds with brass fanfares. The pace quickens as the two blocks of sound – brass and tutti each with chorus – alternate and intermingle, until the music stops short with a terrified shriek. In the quietness that follows the bass contemplates as though peering into an abyss the amazement of Death and Nature as every creature is called to account. Strings repeat an obsessive ostinato of jagged contour (♪♫♪♩♪♩) punctuated by a beat on the bass drum, the skin now slackened to suggest infinite depth. On the last two syllables of 'responsura' there is a unison blast from lower woodwind and horns, the latter marked for once in Verdi 'frizzante' ('cuivré'), a device normally associated with terror. The canvas becomes increasingly empty, the bass unable to get beyond the word 'Mors', almost as though the composer were looking forward to Iago's 'La morte è il nulla'. Here is all the horror of the void; the equivalent of E.M. Forster's 'panic and emptiness'.

For the 'Liber scriptus' Verdi happily withdrew a very dull and academic choral fugue in favour of a solo for the mezzo-soprano, as emblem of the recording angel. It is a superb example of declamatory melody articulated in three massive periods each following the tercet design of the poem. The first ('Liber scriptus proferetur') is a typical instance of late Verdian three-limbed melody such as we encounter in the second duet between hero and heroine in the five-act *Don*

Carlos, the first two phrases identical, both featuring the rising fifth like a finger raised in warning, followed by a menacing death-figure on the timpani:

Ex. 84

The third is equal in length to the other two combined yet it evolves so freely that all sense of regularity is obliterated. The effect is not, as in *Don Carlos*, an involuntary spilling over of repressed emotion but rather of a lesson firmly driven home – witness the emphatic cadence in the low, dark register of the mezzo-soprano voice. The second period ('Judex ergo cum sedebit') is an expanded counterpart of the first. Introduced by blazing brass chords in the major – the search-light gaze of the Supreme Judge from whom nothing is hid – its first two phrases are similar but not identical, being of four and five bars respectively. The third proceeds for seven bars before merging into the corresponding phrase of the first period. The setting of the second strophe is thus half as long again as that of the first. One could make a comparison here with the two Stollen of Walter von

Stolzing's Preislied, the difference being that here it is the endings, not the beginnings that are the same. Thereafter the analogy breaks down. In the third period Verdi resumes the text of both the preceding strophes in a kind of coda; the first is sung over a pounding harmonic pedal that breaks off on a fortissimo diminished seventh. The second is muttered over shifting harmonies that seem to give way beneath our feet, the soloist trailing into incoherence and repeating 'Nil' as the bass had repeated 'Mors' with a growing sense of emptiness. But here the device has another purpose; that of lulling the listener into a state of unpreparedness for the thunderbolt of the final phrase (Ex. 84b). Based on one of those secondary sevenths that are only recently a part of Verdi's vocabulary, it is the dark equivalent of Desdemona's outburst 'Ah Emilia addio!'

Throughout this movement the chorus have contributed no more than an occasional murmured 'Dies irae'. Now they combine with the orchestra in a furious crescendo leading to a restatement of Ex. 82. After it has subsided as before, our attention is turned to the individual sinner in a trio for soprano, mezzo soprano and tenor ('Quid sum miser'). Where can the poor supplicant look for help when even the righteous are hardly safe? Two clarinets and a bassoon open the musical discourse with a cadential figure like an idiogram of grief that recurs like a refrain:

Ex. 85

But as so often with Verdi it does not reveal its full identity at the outset. Not till the third occurrence does it acquire that F sharp that gives it its unique poignancy. So too with the intervening vocal entries. The mezzo-soprano's first phrase, a setting of the first line of the tercet, is brought to a cadence after four bars. When she resumes it to the remaining two lines it flowers into something like a theme. Next the tenor takes it up the other two voices joining in, to produce a still longer variant. A third and final period begins an unaccompanied trio in the relative major but like the preceding two returns inexorably to the same cadential phrase (Ex. 85) as the preceding two. In this way a tentative opening has solidified into a species of bar-form with refrain. Another binding element is the purling bassoon pattern which forms the instrumental bass throughout – a wholly original use of that instrument adumbrated as early as *Luisa Miller*. The coda alternates major and minor with a sweetness worthy of Schubert; but the sense of consolation is precarious, and the soloists are left repeating one by one the three questions on rising levels of pitch. To these the next episode ('Rex tremendae majestatis') brings a brutal answer: a descending arpeggio from the chorus basses in Verdi's best 'maledizione' manner, backed by the lower instruments in unison and a tremolando of upper strings (Ex. 86a). Tenors divisi repeat the words in a subdued mutter. But the suppliants will not be silenced. The bass launches a contrasting idea ('Salva me fons pietatis'), Ex. 86b, featuring the rising sixth from soh to mi, whose association with the concept of love would seem to be Mozart's legacy to the Romantic age.

Ex. 86

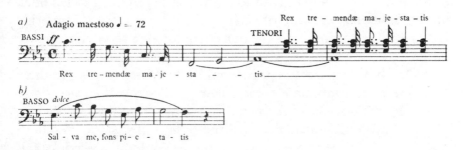

The two themes engage in conflict. At first the soloists' phrases are isolated each in a different key, linked only by the soprano's 'Salva me'; subsequently they join together, one answering the other. Finally, just when it seems that the battle is lost, a fragmented statement of Ex. 86b rises like a cloud of incense from the chorus basses to culminate in a cadential variant over wonderfully rich and mellow harmonies – surely a case of the perfect love that casteth out fear.

The 'Dies Irae' now enters on a calmer phrase. The 'Ricordare', a duettino for the two women discourses gently on a swaying 4/4 melody announced by the mezzo-soprano over a velvet cushion of sustaining horns, flute and clarinet and a murmur of lower strings. Only a dotted figure in the upper woodwind remains to remind us of the soprano's insistent 'salva me' from the preceding prayer. There are two episodes, neither of which depart very far from the main theme, and a tranquil coda, with some imaginative two-part writing for the voices. Next it is the tenor's turn with 'Ingemisco tamquam reus'; and indeed what voice could be more suitable to suggest a helpless groan? His introductory arioso recalls the desolate utterances of Don Carlos; but he takes heart with the beginning of the movement proper, ('Qui Mariam absolvisti') – a rare case in Verdi of a compressed sonata design with two distinct themes in tonic and dominant respectively. The reason for this becomes clear when we reach the second of them ('Inter oves locum praesta').

Ex. 87

It is a remarkably direct evocation of a shepherd piping to his flock on a mountainside. If the oboe suggests the pipe, the shimmering violins rarified atmosphere, the dominant tonality serves to enhance the sense of height.

Clearly an orthodox reprise would ruin the effect. Instead there is a mere orchestral reminiscence beneath the tenor's closing lines, which in turn dovetails neatly into a cadence from the first theme.

In the 'Confutatis maledictis' the bass soloist stands for both priest and suppliant, so embracing the two poles of sternness and entreaty on which the movement rests. Two themes alternate. The first epitomizes the internal conflict. Beginning 'con forza' it consigns the accursed to their doom with octave leaps and abrupt orchestral gestures; then softens into a plea to be called among the blessed. The second ('Oro supplex et acclinis') is purely lyrical, moving on a typical Verdian axis of C sharp minor – E minor and coming meltingly to rest in E major. But what first strikes the academically minded listener is the blatant chain of parallel fifths with which it opens (Ex. 88). Tovey took this to be a way of indicating total abjection – as though in an excess of humility the bass had forgotten the first rules of musical grammar. But in that case

Ex. 88

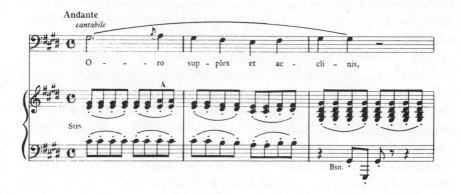

why should the same device occur in the Consecration scene of *Aida*? More probably Verdi was aiming in both cases at an antique organum-like solemnity that antedates the rules of part-writing. The conflict continues, using elements of both themes. Then Ex. 88 returns unaltered save for a prolongation of the final bars. A codetta moves away towards E minor; but the bass's last note is covered by a final irruption of the 'Dies Irae' theme (Ex. 79b) leaping out, as it were, from behind a harmonic corner. It is only a partial reprise; for before Ex. 82 is reached it has already swung away towards the region of B flat minor, approaching the next movement with Wagnerian foreboding.

The melody of the 'Lachrymosa' has its origins in a discarded duet for tenor and bass with male chorus from *Don Carlos* following the death of Posa (see Ex. 89). With its sombre scoring and disposition of voices, its B flat minor tonality, it is one of the most moving

Ex. 89

operatic laments ever written, which is why, now that modern research has enabled its reconstruction, several recent revivals of the
opera have restored it. By comparison the 'Lachrymosa' is simpler in
outline and more complex in detail. Just as Verdi had concluded
Aida with a slow cabaletta of the utmost plainness and regularity so
he rounds off this most wide-ranging and tempestuous prayer of the
Requiem with a movement whose main theme forms a period of
thirty-two bars with a phrase pattern A—A—B—A (the melody had
evolved very differently in the duet). But with each successive phrase
the tapestry becomes richer, embellished with counterpoint and an
abundance of lamenting figures entrusted to voices as well as instruments – the sighs and groans of a universe in torment. The last cadence
is interrupted so as to lead into a twelve-bar coda in the course of
which the theme is broken down over a descending bass, then rises to
a climax taking the solo soprano over a high B flat. But this is not the
end. A new pleading melody in G flat is sung by the four soloists to
the lines 'Pie Jesu, Domine, dona eis requiem'. It is the palest shaft of
light soon to vanish as fragments of the opening melody treated in
imitation take over the rest of the movement; but somehow the
darkness has been softened. For the final bars Verdi makes telling use
of the full orchestra hushed, including bass drum ('le corde molto
allentate'). The 'Amen' yields a cadence unknown to ecclesiastical
rules: a chord of G major, swelling and dying answered by orchestra
alone with one of B flat. Verdi concludes the 'Dies Irae' as impressively as he has begun it.

Despite a text which speaks of delivery from the lion's mouth
and from the lake of Tartarus, the Offertorio for soloists without
choir preserves a mood of almost unclouded serenity, its movements
forming a five-part pattern (A—B—C—B—A). The opening andante
('Domine Jesu Christe') is a miracle of thematic economy and also a
convincing demonstration of how a theme can alter its sense according to context, like the first line of a medieval rondeau or a modern
triolet. The entire movement is based on a motif announced by the
solo cello (Ex. 90a). When it first appears as the culmination of a
flowing pattern of quavers that alternate with the gentle cadences of
flute, oboe and clarinet, its function is clearly to bring the paragraph
to a close. But with the entry of mezzo-soprano and tenor soloists the
close is delayed. Ex. 90a is twice repeated, the second time leading to
the dominant where the long awaited cadence occurs. But a paragraph which ends in the dominant requires a complement if only to

point the way home. This is done in the most natural way possible by
a restatement of Ex. 90a but with modified harmony. From then to
the end of the movement there is not a single phrase or figure that is
not derived from it. St Michael the standard bearer makes an unobtrusively dramatic appearance in the form of a prolonged 'messa di
voce' while high divisi violins carry Ex. 90a through a magical
harmonic side-slip, already anticipated in the final duet of *Rigoletto*
(Ex. 90b). The souls of the departed are carried upward in a series of

Ex. 90

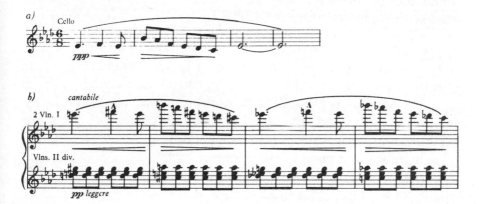

modulations into a radiant sonority – sustained chords for voices
and brass, celestial arpeggios for flutes, piccolo and clarinet and
sparkling pizzicato patterns for divided violins.

It was traditional to set the reminder 'Quam olim Abrahae
promisisti et semini ejus' as a fugue. Verdi begins imitatively but
soon slips into homophony of a truly fugal vigour with a whirlwind
rapidity of harmonic rhythm. In total contrast the central movement,
'Hostias et preces tibi, Domine', is one of the still oases. The irregularity of the ten-bar theme (2+4+4) far from being propulsive,
enhances the sense of timelessless; while the note E in the tenor voice,
constantly recurring, is as important to the colour of the melody as in
Donizetti's 'Spirto gentil'. Again the design is A–A–B–A with the
unusual tonal scheme of C major—F major—C minor—C major.
Tenor and bass alternate the cantilena with lyrical counterpoints
from the other soloists, the bass's heavy sound lightened by an
accompaniment of divisi violins. A conclusive episode in C minor,

331

dominated by the soprano, restores an abbreviated Ex. 89 high on the flute over violin harmonics and acciaccature on flute and horn and tonic pedal harmony while below the singers murmur their prayer that the dead may pass to eternal life. 'Quam olim Abrahae' is repeated with a more emphatic ending which in turn ushers in a shortened reprise of Ex. 90a – shortened literally since the autograph shows that it was originally several pages longer. The reason is clear enough. The musical equivalent of bilateral symmetry in the visual arts does not strictly speaking exist since each successive statement of a musical idea is apprehended through a perspective of time, so that the last always bulks the largest in the listener's mind. Ernest Newman once observed that in the prelude to *Lohengrin* the grail takes twice as long to descend as to ascend; yet the hearer is left with the impression of an unvarying motion. In the same way a few repetitions at close range of Ex. 90a with arrestingly varied harmony and scoring are sufficient to balance the opening movement.

The 'Sanctus' is a tour de force from every aspect: a double fugue for double chorus and orchestra with a cursive accompanying figure on the violins. From the opening trumpet calls and cries of 'Sanctus' all is lightness and vigour. The progress by four bars may give it a dance like character but, as Tovey beautifully put it, the dance is that of the Sons of the Morning.[4] The entire text from 'Sanctus' to 'Benedictus' and 'Hosanna' is set as a continuous movement – a transparent tapestry of counterpoint, settling at the eightieth bar into lyrical homophony pervaded by that calm radiance that Verdi so often distils from the key of F major. In a final burst of energy the orchestral quavers get the upper hand and drive the movement to a brilliant conclusion.

Timelessness again prevails in the 'Agnus Dei'. The thirteen-bar melody begins as a kind of diatonic plainchant for the two women an octave apart – a unique vocal effect – even if the cadence (x) has been encountered as early as Giselda's death scene in *I Lombardi* (Ex. 91).

This is now subjected to variation *à la Russe*, the melody remaining unaltered save for one change of mode and the sonorous palette altering with every repetition. Twice we are given the second part of the theme only. The texture is calculated down to the minutest detail.

---

[4] D. F. Tovey, *Essays in Musical Analysis*, 2 vols (Oxford 1981), Concertos and Choral Works, p. 417.

Ex. 91

Clarinets, bassoons, violins on the G string, violas, cellos and one bass double the unison chorus. The minor version, again for female soloists, is harmonised by violas and cellos and embellished with a pattern of quavers on flute and clarinet. A counterpoint of three flutes envelops the two voices at their final statement – a passage quoted in every textbook on orchestration. The movement ends with repetitions of the cadence to the words 'Dona, dona eis requiem sempiternam'.

The 'Lux Aeterna', a trio for mezzo-soprano, tenor and bass, sees a return of conflict: B flat and G flat major against a sombre B flat minor. The mezzo-soprano's prayer ('Lux aeterna luceat eis, Domine, cum sanctis tuis in aeternum qui pius es'), surrounded by ethereal divisi strings, betrays anxiety in its tonal instability within the prevailing B flat major – witness those characteristic side-slipping chords of the sixth. The bass launches an inexorable reply ('Requiem aeternam dona eis') in B flat minor over low chords on bassoons, trombones and ophicleide with timpani rolling in fifths. In a trio a cappella based on G flat the three soloists resume their pleading, to be answered as before, tremolando strings and woodwind doublings replacing the brass chords. But it is the mezzo soprano who finds the soft answer that turneth away wrath with a commonplace of consolation which becomes new-minted in Verdi's hands, supported only by violins, flute and glinting piccolo (Ex. 92).

Developed in imitation and aided by a succession of melting cadences, it ensures a peaceful end to the movement, even though the

333

Ex. 92

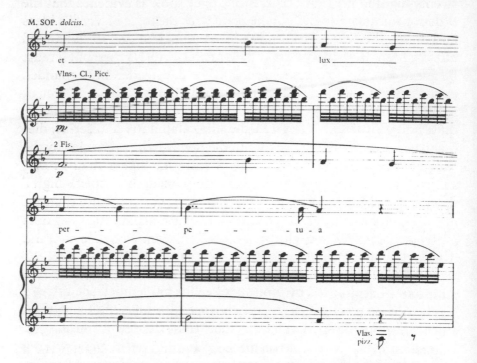

lower brass can be heard growling beneath the celestial arabesques of flute and piccolo – the mortal remains contrasted with the immortal soul.

It is in the 'Libera me' that the *Requiem* comes closest to the world of opera, not, to be sure, in its musical form but rather in the sense of personal anxiety conveyed by the soprano – it might be Leonora di Vargas in her lonely cave. An opening 'scena' of eighteen bars proceeds through free declamation on a single note, a reminiscence of Ex. 92, and a sinister clucking and purring of the four bassoons before reaching its first C minor cadence (one would suspect the influence of Brahms's First Symphony were it not two years in the future). Too broken in its utterance to be called a theme, the soprano's 'Tremens factus' is a two-limbed statement, the second delayed by a five-bar extension in the region of the dominant. The swift harmonic rhythm recalls the 'Quam olim Abrahae'; strings and low flute account for most of the agitated figuration. A cadential swoop from G in alt hints at the subject of the fugue to come and the singer falters into silence. There follows the final and most substantial statement of the 'Dies Irae' (Ex. 79b and its related ideas). That the diminuendo from Ex. 82 runs to forty-two bars as against twenty-eight in the first occurrence Tovey took as evidence that the order of composition did not interfere with the logic of Verdi's ideas and that in the heat of inspiration he could hold in reserve what had already been designed for the end. In principle this is true; but it must be added that in the definitive version Verdi considerably expanded the passage in question with elements from the introductory 'scena'. An extra turn of the screw is given by the altered, more powerful and quite unmetrical text ('Dies irae, dies illa calamitatis et miseriae, dies magna et amara valde'). The tumult dies away to be succeeded by the 'Requiem aeternam' (Ex. 80), now a semitone higher than before, sung by the soprano and chorus unaccompanied, the soloist's high F magically anticipated by oboe and horn. Ampler in texture than the opening statement, it gives the effect of a finished painting as against a preparatory sketch. Eight bars of declamation from the soprano over tremolando strings introduce the fugue.

No more orthodox than the 'Sanctus' (what classical fugue ever closed each entry in the exposition with a tutti cadence?), it remains a marvel of contrapuntal and architectonic skill. The subject is inverted, treated in canon, broken down and developed in sequences: augmentation is reserved for the solo soprano's first entry over a temporary lull in the contrapuntal movement. The climax is unashamedly chordal with the soprano carried up to a C in altissimo. But there is no subsequent lightening of the gloom, no winding up in a triumphant C major. The E natural that marks the repeated final cadences has the quality of a *tierce de Picardie*; and at the end the soprano is left murmuring in an anxious monotone 'Libera me Domine, de morte acterna in die illa tremenda' joined by the chorus in a final 'Libera me . . . libera me.'

In the early years of the century when the composer's reputation was at its nadir even the sympathetic Bernard Shaw expressed a doubt as to whether any of his works would prove immortal except for the *Requiem*; the operas could well pass into oblivion, not because their music was bad but because their style of dramatic expression would not be acceptable to a generation reared once and for all on Wagnerian principles.[5] If time has disproved Shaw's pessimism regarding the stage works, it has confirmed the place of honour he assigned to the *Requiem*. No longer the victim of false notions of

[5] Shaw, op. cit., Vol. III, p. 583.

piety, it is seen to stand in the front rank of the world's choral masterpieces.

The *Pater Noster* and *Ave Maria*, composed for a benefit concert directed by Faccio in 1880 at La Scala, Milan, are works of less commitment, though each is noble in thought and refined in craft. Both prayers are set in the vernacular versions attributed to Dante, again bearing witness to Verdi's continuing fondness for that freest of all lyrical metres, the hendecasyllabic.

The *Ave Maria* for voice and string orchestra, equally suited to soprano or mezzo-soprano, is a variant of the minor—major 'romanza', both elements being epitomised in a substantial introduction for strings alone. For her first ten bars the singer remains, figuratively speaking, on her knees declaiming in a monotone over shifting chords. Thereafter the part takes on increasing melodic interest, opening out into the lyricism of 'Vergine benedetta', which forms the major key 'release'. Well before the final cadence, however, the singer has retreated into the opening B minor; and it is left to the strings to supply the final words of comfort in an eight-bar coda.

The *Pater Noster* is Verdi's first act of homage to Palestrina, whom he considered the father of Italian music just as Bach was the father of German. Written for unaccompanied mixed chorus in five parts, it has something of the texture of a Renaissance motet; but the form is entirely modern. Like certain of the later operatic scenes, it is based on two contrasted themes, the first ('Sanctificata') subjected to imitation, the second ('Dà oggi a noi pane') a recurring moment of lyrical repose bearing a strong resemblance to the final lines in Giselda's 'Salve Maria' from *I Lombardi*. Modern too is the harmony: the powerful dissonances at 'Dell' infernal nemico' ('And deliver us from evil'); the wealth of 'expectant' 6/4s that follow, and miraculous ellipsis of the final 'Amen' (Ex. 93).

Nearer to the Palestrina motet in form are the *Laudi alla Vergine* a setting for four solo female voices from the final canto of Dante's *Paradiso* and the first to be composed of the so-called Four Sacred Pieces. Here each tercet begins with a new motif, sometimes stated in block harmony, sometimes in unison, sometimes developed in imitation. The effect however is essentially homophonic. There are none of those intertwining melismata to be found in, say, Palestrina's 'Hodie Christus natus est' for the same vocal combination. But as a balanced composition that succeeds in illustrating Dante's text with the subtlest of harmonic and rhythmic inflexions, unashamedly

Ex. 93

modern in character, it far outweighs the most skilful attempts at polyphonic archaizing. An F major triad on the word 'umile' within a G major context is sufficient to suggest the 'lowliness' of the Virgin. The greatness of the Creator ('Fattore') is conveyed by an emphatic jump to the chord of flattened 'La'; yet the same line ends, without the slightest incongruity, in the tenderest of pianissimo cadences drawn out with a slow triplet calling to mind the arms of the Madonna cradling the Christ child. The plight of those who try to fly without wings is embodied in a succession of repeated block chords that only just avoid a sense of stasis. The final cantabile ('La tua benignità') with its nineteenth-century suspensions is saved by Verdi's refinement of taste from any hint of sentimentality. The *Laudi* is certainly not the greatest of the Four Sacred Pieces; but one can understand why it was invariably encored.

The *Ave Maria sulla scala enigmatica* stands apart from its fellows. Verdi never attached any artistic importance to it; for him it was a *sciarada*, a rebus, a mere conundrum. As far as he was concerned the Sacred Pieces were three, not four. However once the *Ave Maria* was in print he had no control over its circulation; and a concert given by the Gesellschaft der Musikfreunde in Vienna under Richard Perger initiated the by now universal practice of giving it along with the *Stabat Mater, Laudi* and *Te Deum.*

Were Verdi's doubts justified? Certain scholars, including Mila and Hussey believe that they were; that a *donnée* as arbitrary as Crescentini's 'scala sgangherata' (Verdi's term) could only result in a triumph of ingenuity. To Hermann Scherchen on the other hand the scale is not arbitrary at all but a perceptive blend of the four scales on which all modern music is based – the minor, the major, the whole-tone and the chromatic. This would apply to the upward scale only; in its descending form the F sharp is modified to F natural so as to permit an easier and more conclusive return to base (Ex. 94).

The average listener will probably find such relationships difficult

Ex. 94

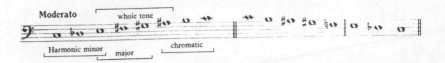

to bear in mind, given the slow pace of the *cantus fermus* and the kaleidoscopic change of harmonic perspectives, the climax of the phrase never coinciding with that of the scale. Indeed much of the piece's charm lies in those lyrical blooms that burgeon and fade with the inexorable march of the semibreves; in the new and unexpected vistas opened up by each transition and above all in the endless variety of harmony and texture thrown up by the four placings of the *scala enigmatica*.

Of the two versions the reconstructed one of 1896 is predictably the better. The differences, such as they are, affect mainly the second half of the piece, where the text is better distributed and the polyphony freer and more adventurous. The final Amen is broadened out by the equivalent of two bars, thereby providing a far more satisfactory bridge from the B flat major to the original tonic of C.

The remarkable density of Verdi's musical thought in his last years is impressively illustrated by his 'Pietà Signor' of 1894 for solo voice and piano accompaniment to a text adapted by Boito from the *De profundis*. A mere twenty-one bars long, it forms a complete statement, a lapidary expression of spiritual longing, every chord charged with emotional significance. Has even Webern said so much with so few notes?

So to the two last and greatest of the Four Sacred Pieces, the *Te Deum* and *Stabat Mater*, both written for large turn-of-the-century orchestra with triple woodwind, three trumpets, a fourth bassoon and in the case of the *Stabat Mater*, a harp. But the *Te Deum* has a more massive sonority, since it features a double choir as against the single one of the *Stabat* (for each choir Verdi stipulated voices in the ratio of 12.12.12.14.) The *Te Deum* seems to have been the earlier of the two; the *Stabat* following a year or so later. But from the start there was never any doubt in the composer's mind in which order they should be performed. The *Te Deum* is the only possible conclusion to the set.

Pietà, Signor! (1894)

For once Verdi launches his composition with a snatch of plainchant (Ex. 95a).

Ex. 95

It was a bold device; and Verdi, fearful of faulty intonation, wrote to Boito in Paris suggesting an improvised organ prelude to establish the tonality firmly in the minds of the choir. But the point becomes clear when we find as the piece proceeds that almost all of its themes derive from Ex. 95a. Verdi never wrote a more thematically organised work than this. Different groups of voices, one of them marked 'in the distance', respond with chordal mutterings (note once again the organum-like consecutives at 'omnis terra veneratur' – surely not an expression of spiritual abasement); then at the word 'Sanctus' full choirs and orchestra peal forth, like a multitude of the heavenly host, in divine praises. 'Pleni sunt coeli et terra' brings the second main motif of the piece, sequential in its nature and forming the third limb of the musical paragraph (Ex. 96).

The climatic cadence which follows is interrupted with a powerful affirmation of G flat, a tonality which will dominate the next fifty-four bars; the music sinks to pianissimo; and the praises are now

Ex. 96

those of men rather than angels. But an intuition of divine grace can be sensed in the first derivative of Ex. 95a on the woodwind ensemble (Ex. 95b). The singers proliferate in simple, counter-themes one of which ('Te Martyrum candidatus'), also derived from the plainchant opening, will assume great importance later on (Ex. 95c). As the tally of praises proceeds Ex. 95b takes on various structural and harmonic guises in relation to intervening material until at the mention of the Paraclete it develops into what will strike the listener as a new theme altogether (Ex. 95d). The G flat gravitational pull weakens and fades to make way for what Verdi, according to his letters, regarded as one of the great moments of the score – the transformation of Ex. 95c into a 'canto liturgico grandioso':

Ex. 97

Taken up by the choirs it develops into a closely worked contrapuntal discourse during which Ex. 95b, embellished with new counter themes, is not forgotten. Then as the text passes from a hymn of praise to prayer we find one of those poised periodic melodies with which Verdi loved to crown his most elaborately busy passages (Ex. 98a)

In the first bar of the third strain (Ex. 98b), with its subdominant triad over a dominant pedal, we can recognise a favourite chord of

Ex. 98

Franz Liszt, whose influence on Italian composers during the late
nineteenth century should not be underestimated. During the
sequential combinations of Exx. 96 and 98b that follow, this same
bitter-sweet chord works as a propulsive agent until we reach the
hushed episode 'Dignare, Domine die isto sine peccato nos custo-
dire', with its muffled bass drum-beats and stark two-part writing – a
chill breath from the world of *Don Carlos* and the *auto-da-fè*.
'Miserere' the chorus chant in isolated groups, gathering together for
their final prayer, 'Fiat misericordia tua, Domine, super nos'. This
turns out to be Ex. 98a sung by both choirs supported by a luminous
voicing of the full orchestra. As the notion of hope breaks in the
melody changes course, swells to a climax ('In te speravi'), then
plunges into torbid depths ('Non confondar in aeternum'). Out of
the horrified silence Ex. 96 emerges, now pleading where it had once
been triumphant. A solo trumpet answers and with it the voice of
suppliant humanity embodied, as in the 'Libera me', in a soprano;
not however a prima donna with all her capacity for fluttering
emotion, but the small steady tone of a chorister. Chorus and orchestra join for the last 'In te speravi'; and while low orchestral chords
drag themselves up to a plagal cadence, a long held e' ' ' on first
violins, shines like the faintest of stars in the night sky.

Of the four pieces the *Te Deum* was Verdi's favourite; he is even
said to have wanted the score to be buried with him. But not all
writers have shared his view. At the first performance in Paris the

Stabat Mater was more highly praised. Stanford, who was present, with a view to conducting the English première, asked Boito for permission to place it last. Tovey maintained that 'Of the Four Sacred Pieces . . . the *Stabat Mater* is the most important and the most perfect.' More consistent in style than the *Te Deum* and more beautiful in conception, it recalled for him Palestrina's setting of the same poem, 'the purest cloud-scape in the world of harmony, without even a flight of birds to show the scale of its mighty perspective'. What both works have in common is a total lack of textual repetition, so that (Tovey again) 'the lines of the poem roll on in their groups of three like a planet in its orbit'.[6] A marked contrast, this, to the multi-movement settings of Pergolesi, Rossini and Dvořák where the immediacy of the words is stifled by the musical development, and in Rossini's case occasionally contradicted by it. Not that this is in itself wrong (it happens in most settings of the Mass); it is just that Verdi's procedure, like Palestrina's, is different. Rather than take the text of Jacopo da Todi as the basis of a large musical structure, he treats it as a piece of poetry, realising it in music with a Schubertian skill, but without the aid of Schubertian forms. Nor is the music thematically organised as with the *Te Deum*. All of which makes the *Stabat Mater* very difficult to analyse in conventional terms. The musical ideas are many and striking but they rarely repeat except at short range. An exception is the opening where after a succession of bare orchestral fifths recalling Otello's 'Niun mi tema' the chorus in unison launch a gaunt, jagged theme, the alpha as well as the omega of the composition (Ex. 99a).

Here more than in any other of the Sacred Pieces Verdi draws on the vocabulary of his operas, but always with the strictest economy: the sobbing violins at 'Cujus animam' are those of the exiles' chorus in the revised *Macbeth*; the baritone's line at 'Quae morebat' could have belonged to any of Verdi's mournful old men from Doge Foscari to King Philip, here intensified by the wonderfully expressive orchestral patterning. 'Quis est homo' brings the first major key melody, a gesture of sudden warmth and compassion all the more compelling for the austerity that has preceded it (Ex. 99b). But the tonality, like the mood, is far from stable; and no sooner has the paragraph moved to a half close than a tiny motif of alarm insinuates

[6] Tovey, op. cit, Concertos and Choral Works, p.421.

Ex. 99

itself into the texture (Ex. 99c). It is sufficient to generate a powerful diminished seventh climax evocative of Christ's suffering. The numb grief or 'Vidit suum dulcem natum' (compare 'Mors stupebit' from the *Requiem*) might seem unduly protracted had not Verdi pointed the end with a minor key reminiscence of Ex. 99b in the orchestra. A somewhat organ-like transition leads to the still heart of the piece: 'Eja Mater, fons amoris' in which two tercets are set in two perfectly balancing periods of seven bars each (Ex. 99d).

There is a brief return to the turbulence of Ex. 99c ('Crucifixi fige plagas cordi meo valide'). After which the words 'Tui nati vulnerati' the altos begin what seems like a long ascent towards faith and hope – two eight-bar strains like question and answer are repeated a fourth higher and with increasingly varied scoring. With 'Fac ut portem Christi mortem' the pace becomes more urgent, leading to a brief but terrifying vision of the fires of Hell where by an unusual phrasing Verdi achieves much the same effect as Brahms with alternating groups of strings in the introduction to the finale of his first symphony – a fluttering terror before some catastrophe. By 'Per te virgo sim defensus' the choir has sunk to a unison pianissimo, while insistent raps on the trumpet prepare us for another outburst ('in die judicii'). Yet these same 'rat-a-tats' with their traditional connotation of finality will close the next tercet as a triumphant D major flourish on trumpets and trombones to the word 'victoriae'. Horns raise a warning finger; a solemn funereal tramp ushers in the basses' 'Quando corpus moriretur'. The full choir join them in the hushed prayer 'Fac ut animae donetur'; while at the word 'paradisi' the gates of Heaven open with one of those miraculous entries of the harp that Verdi reserves for moments such as these. Tremolando flutes sustaining wind and a simple spacing of strings add to the ethereal effect. As the voices mount higher, crotchet pulsations give way to quaver, quaver to quaver triplet and finally to sextuplet, culminating in a blaze of G major glory. But that is not the end. The brightness dissolves; the texture dwindles to that of harp, flutes and strings; and the music winds down a final pianissimo 'Amen' which in turn brings back Ex. 99a and with it the implication of G minor and a doubt unresolved. Verdi's last word on the immortality of the soul? We shall never know.

Appendix A

Calendar

Year	Age	Life	Contemporary Events
1813		Giuseppe Fortunino Francesco Verdi born 9 Oct at Le Roncole, nr Busseto (Parma) son of Carlo, innkeeper, and Luigia Uttini.	Dargomizhsky born 2/14 Feb; Grétry (72) dies 24 Sept; Petrella born 1 Dec; Wagner born 22 May.
1814	1	Soldiers of the Holy Alliance pass through Le Roncole; Luigia hides with child in belfry.	Congress of Vienna.
1815	2		Battle of Waterloo.
1816	3		Rossini's *Barbiere di Siviglia* first given, Rome. Paisiello (75) dies 5 June.
1817	4	Begins elementary education under Don Pietro Baistrocchi.	
1818	5		Gounod born, 17 June.
1819	6		Offenbach born, 21 June.
1820	7	Carlo buys him an old spinet; V, begins to substitute as organist of S. Michele at Roncole.	
1821	8		Defeat and suppression of *Carbonari* in Naples. Death of Napoleon I, 5 May; Manzoni publishes ode *Il cinque maggio*, later set by V. Première Weber's *Der Freischütz*, Berlin, 18 June.
1822	9	Engaged as organist at church of Roncole.	Franck born, 10 Dec.
1823	10	Lives in Busseto, lodging with cobbler, Pugnatta; returns to Roncole to play for church services on Sundays and feast days. Admitted to Busseto *ginnasio*.	Lalo born, 27 Jan. *Semiramide*, Rossini's last Italian opera, 1st perf. Venice, 3 Feb.
1824	11		Bruckner born, 4 Sept; Smetana born, 2 Mar. Beethoven's

Year	Age	Life	Contemporary Events
			Choral Symphony 1st perf. Vienna, 7 May.
1825	12	Begins formal musical training with Ferdinando Provesi, organist of collegiate church S. Bartolomeo, municipal music master and director of Philharmonic Society.	J. Strauss II born, 25 Oct.
1826	13		Weber (40) dies, 5 June.
1827	14		Beethoven (57) dies, 26 Mar. Bellini's *Il Pirata* 1st perf. Milan, 27 Oct.
1828	15	Composes overture for Rossini's *Barbiere di Siviglia* and cantata *I deliri di Saul*.	Schubert (31) dies, 19 Nov.
1829	16	Applies for post of organist at Soragna but is rejected; becomes Provesi's assistant in Busseto; composes *Le lamentazioni di Geremia*.	*Guillaume Tell*, Rossini's last opera, 1st perf. Paris, 3 Aug.
1830	17		July revolution in France; revolution in Belgium occasioned by Auber's *La Muette de Portici*, 25 Aug.
1831	18	Moves to home of Antonio Barezzi, merchant and President of Philharmonic Society; gives lessons to daughter, Margherita, his future wife. Carlo applies for grant from Monte di Pietà to send V. to study in Milan.	Bellini's *Norma* 1st perf. Milan, 26 Dec. Meyerbeer's *Robert le Diable* 1st perf. Paris, 21 Nov. Abortive uprisings in Parma, Modena and Piedmont.
1832	19	Travels to Milan, lodges with Giuseppe Seletti; his application for admission to the Conservatory is turned down; Rolla, composer and violinist, advises private study in Milan. Begins lessons with Vincenzo Lavigna, composer and former *maestro al cembalo* at La Scala.	Clementi (80) dies, 20 Mar. Donizetti's *L'elisir d'amore* 1st perf. Milan, 12 May.
1833	20	Provesi dies; Giovanni Ferrari applies for post; Lavigna writes to Monte di Pietà that V. needs	Brahms born, 7 May. Donizetti's *Lucrezia Borgia* 1st perf. Milan, 26 Dec.

Year	Age	Life	Contemporary Events
		a further year of study. V.'s sister, Giuseppa Francesca, dies.	
1834	21	Directs Haydn's *Creation* at Casino de 'Nobili; is invited by Pietro Massini, director of Filodrammatici to compose an opera. Ferrari appointed organist at Busseto, 18 June. V. returns to Busseto to apply for post and remains for rest of the year.	Borodin born, 30 Oct/12 Nov; Ponchielli born, 2 Sept. Mazzini's failed attempt to provoke an uprising in Piedmont.
1835	22	Completes studies with Lavigna; returns to Busseto. Lavigna recommends him for organist at Monza cathedral; but V. declines because of public opinion.	Bellini (34) dies, 24 Sept; Saint-Saens born, 9 Oct. Première of Bellini's *I Puritani*, Paris, 25 Jan, and Donizetti's *Lucia di Lammermoor*, Naples, 26 Sept.
1836	23	Begins opera, *Rocester*, to text by Antonio Piazza. Examined for post of municipal music master of Busseto by Giuseppe Alinovi, court organist at Parma; and later nominated. Weds Margherita Barezzi, 4 May; after honeymoon in Milan takes up duties in Busseto; composes *Il cinque maggio* and a *Tantum ergo* and completes *Rocester*.	Balakirev born, 30 Dec. Première of Meyerbeer's *Les Huguenots*, Paris, 29 Feb.
1837	24	Birth of a daughter, Virginia, 26 Mar. Attempts without success to get *Rocester* performed at Parma or Milan.	Field (55) dies, 11 Jan. Berlioz' *Grande Messe des Morts* 1st perf. 5 Dec.
1838	25	Birth of a son, Icilio Romano, 11 July; death of Virginia, 12 Aug. Visits Milan to arrange for performance of *Rocester*, Sept–Oct. Publication of *Sei romanze* by Canti of Milan. Submits resignation as municipal music master.	Bizet born, 25 Oct. Première of Berlioz' *Benvenuto Cellini*, Paris, 10 Sept.
1839	26	Leaves Busseto with family; settles in Milan, Via S. Simone. Canti publishes two songs,	Mussorgsky born, 9/21 Mar. Paer (68) dies, 3 May.

Year	Age	Life	Contemporary Events
		L'esule and *La seduzione* and *Notturno a 3* which is well-reviewed. Icilio Romano dies, 22 Oct. Première of *Oberto, conte di S. Bonifacio* (probably revised *Rocester*) at La Scala, Milan, 17 Nov. Accepts contract for 3 more operas.	
1840	27	During composition of *Un giorno di regno* Margherita dies of encephalitis, 18 June; V. returns to Busseto to complete opera. Première of *Un giorno di regno* at La Scala, Milan, 5 Sept, a total failure; all further performances cancelled; *Oberto* revived, 17 Oct.	Faccio born, 8 Mar; Tchaikovsky born, 25 Apr/7 May. Première of Donizetti's *La favorite*, Paris, 2 Dec. Publication of Manzoni's novel *I promessi sposi* in its definitive form.
1841	28	Attends revival (with revisions) of *Oberto* at the Teatro Carlo Felice, Genoa. Receives libretto of *Nabucco* from impresario, Merelli, Jan, and completes composition by Oct. Meets Giuseppina Strepponi and enlists her support in having it performed the following season.	Chabrier born, 18 Jan; Dvořák born, 8 Sept.
1842	29	Première of *Nabucco* at La Scala, Milan, 9 March. Success gains V. entrée to Milanese high society; salons of Clarina Maffei, Emilia Morosini, Giuseppina Appiani. Composes *Chi i bei dì m'adduce ancora* for album of Sofia de' Medici. Visits Rossini in Bologna, June. Writes new preghiera for Granchi to sing in Venice revival of *Nabucco*.	Boito born, 24 Feb; Cherubini (82) dies, 15 Mar; Massenet born, 12 May.
1843	30	Première of *I Lombardi alla prima crociata*, 11 Feb. Goes to Vienna for revival of *Nabucco*, Mar. Begins negotiations with La Fenice, Venice, for what will	Grieg born, 15 June. Premières of Donizetti's *Don Pasquale*, Paris, 3 Jan; and Wagner's *Der fliegende Holländer*, Dresden, 2 Jan.

349

Year	Age	Life	Contemporary Events
		be *Ernani*. Goes to Parma for *Nabucco* with Strepponi, Apr, and to Senigallia for revival of *I Lombardi*; writes new cabaletta for Poggi.	
1844	31	Première of *Ernani* at La Fenice, Venice, 9 Mar. Muzio comes to study with him in Milan, 15 Apr. Directs *Ernani* with Strepponi at Bergamo, Aug. Première of *I due Foscari* at Teatro Argentina, Rome. Friendship with poet Ferretti and sculptor, Luccardi. At Rossini's request writes new aria for Ivanoff to sing in *Ernani*.	Rimsky-Korsakov born, 6/18 Mar. Uprising in Cosenza put down. Fratelli Bandiera face firing squad in Naples singing chorus from Mercadante's *Donna Caritea*.
1845	32	Première of *Giovanna d'Arco* at La Scala, Milan, 15 Feb. *Sei romanze* for voice and piano published by Lucca. Première of *Alzira* at San Carlo Theatre, Naples. Buys Palazzo Dordoni in Busseto, 6 Oct. Léon Escudier acquires Verdi's French rights, Oct.	Fauré born, 13 May. Mayr (82) dies. Première of Wagner's *Tannhäuser*, Dresden, 19 Oct.
1846	33	Première of *Attila* at La Fenice, Venice, 17 Mar. V.'s health breaks down; he cancels commitments and spends July at spa, Recoaro, with poets Andrea Maffei and Giulio Carcano; witnesses separation of Andrea and Clarina Maffei. At work on *Macbeth* during autumn. Writes alternative romanze for Moriani and Ivanoff to sing in *Attila*; also new cabaletta for Mario to sing in *Foscari*.	Mendelssohn's *Elijah* at Birmingham, 26 Aug. Berlioz' *La Damnation de Faust*, Paris, 6 Dec.
1847	34	In Florence for première of *Macbeth* at the Teatro della Pergola, 14 Mar. Acquaintance with sculptor Dupré, Baron	Mendelssohn (38) dies.

Year	Age	Life	Contemporary Events
		Ricasoli and poet Giusti. Departs for London with Muzio via Switzerland, Rhine valley and Paris. Meets Mazzini and Louis Bonaparte in London. Première of *I masnadieri* at Her Majesty's Theatre, 22 July. Composes *Il poveretto*. To Paris for première of *Jérusalem* at the Opéra, 26 Nov. Begins life with Giuseppina Strepponi.	
1848	35	Completes *Il corsaro* and sends it to Lucca. In Milan, then Busseto (May) to buy estate at S. Agata. Returns to Paris, June, to begin work on *La battaglia di Legnano*. Signs appeal to General Cavaignac to intervene in war on Italy's behalf, sends setting of *Suona la tromba* to Mazzini. Première of *Il corsaro*, Teatro Grande, Trieste, 25 Oct, in V.'s absence.	Abdication of Louis-Philippe in France, Feb; uprising of Cinque Giornate in Milan, Mar; Austrians retreat; Carlo Alberto of Piedmont invades Lombardy but is defeated at Battle of Custozza, July, and forced to make peace. Revolutions in Vienna, Warsaw and German cities. Wagner forced into exile. Donizetti (51) dies, 8 Apr. Pope Pio Nono flees from Rome, Nov.
1849	36	*L'abandonnée*, song, published in French periodical. Première of *La battaglia di Legnano*, Teatro Argentina, Rome, 27 Jan. Leaves Rome for Paris, Feb. Returns with Giuseppina Strepponi to Palazzo Dordoni, Aug–Sept. Works on *Luisa Miller*; travels with Barezzi to Naples for première at Teatro San Carlo, 8 Dec. Friendship with Cesare De Sanctis, business man.	Rome declared a republic, 9 Feb. Carlo Alberto denounces amnesty and is defeated at Novara by Radetzky (23 Mar). Rome, besieged, holds out under Garibaldi till July. French troops restore Pope. Garibaldi retreats into the mountains, eventually flees to America. Status quo restored throughout the peninsula. Chopin (40) dies, 17 Oct; Nicolai (39) dies, 11 May. Première of Meyerbeer's *Le Prophète*, Paris, 16 Apr.
1850	37	Plans a *Re Lear* with Cammarano; sends him a synopsis. Suggests to Piave	Wagner's *Lohengrin* first perf. at Weimar under Liszt, 28 Aug.

		Hugo's *Le roi s'amuse* as subject for Venice. In Bologna to direct revival of *Macbeth*, Sept–Oct. To Trieste for première of *Stiffelio*, Teatro Grande, 16 Nov; composes barcarole *Fiorellin* in Trieste for Giovanni Severi, Nov. Has difficulties with censorship over *Le roi s'amuse* (*Rigoletto*).	
1851	38	Première of *Rigoletto*, Teatro La Fenice, Venice, 11 Mar. Settles parents at Vidalenzo and moves with Giuseppina to S. Agata. Death of Luigia Verdi, 28 June. In Bologna for revivals of *Macbeth* and *Luisa Miller*, Sept–Oct. Leaves Busseto for Paris, Dec.	D'Indy born, 27 Mar. Lortzing (48) dies, 21 Jan; Spontini (77) dies, 14 Jan.
1852	39	Signs contract with director of Opéra, Feb. Returns to Busseto, Mar. Signs contract with La Fenice, May. Cammarano dies, July; libretto of *Il trovatore* completed by Bardare. Nominated Chevalier de la Légion d'Honneur by Louis Bonaparte, Aug. Signs contract with Teatro Apollo, Rome, Oct.	Première of Dumas's *La dame aux camélias*.
1853	40	Première of *Il trovatore*, Teatro Apollo, Rome, 19 Jan; unsuccessful première of *La traviata*, Teatro la Fenice, Venice, 6 Mar. Returns to Busseto, Mar; leaves for Paris, Oct. Corresponds with Antonio Somma, playwright, about a *Re Lear*.	Abortive uprising in Milan inspired by Mazzini, Feb. Ecclesiastical courts abolished in Piedmont. Cavour becomes Prime Minister.
1854	41	Begins *Les vêpres siciliennes* at Mandres and Paris. To London to secure rights of *Il trovatore*, Mar. Première of revised *Traviata* at Teatro Gallo,	Assassination of Duke Carlo III of Parma (Mar). By Law of Convents Piedmont becomes a secular state. Vittorio Emanuele is

Year	Age	Life	Contemporary Events
		Venice in V.'s absence. Rehearsals of *Vêpres* interrupted by flight of Cruvelli. Directs *Il trovatore* at Théâtre des Italiens, Paris, 26 Dec.	excommunicated. Catalani born, 19 June, Humperdinck born, 1 Sept; Janáček born, 4 July.
1855	42	Rehearsals resumed, director of Opéra replaced. Première of *Les vêpres siciliennes*, Opéra, 13 June. Remains in Paris to work on Italian translation of *Vêpres* and French translation of *Trovatore* with Emilien Pacini. In London to secure rights of *Vêpres*. Returns to Busseto, Dec.	Piedmont despatches expeditionary force to Crimean War on the side of Britain, France and Austria; it fights with distinction at Battle of Chernaya. Chausson born, 21 Jan. Première of Offenbach's *Les deux aveugles*, Paris, 5 July.
1856	43	In Parma to urge signing of international treaty to safeguard performing rights. Receives from Vittorio Emanuele title of 'Cavaliere dell'Ordine di S.S. Maurizio e Lazzaro, Feb. Signs contract for opera at La Fenice, May. Works with Piave on revision of *Stiffelio*. In Venice with Giuseppina for sea-bathing, June–July. Leaves for Paris to prosecute Calzado, director of Théâtre des Italiens, for using pirated versions of his works. Fails; but signs contract for *Le trouvère* at Opéra, Sept.	Martucci born, 6 Jan; Schumann (46) dies. Cavour takes part in Congress of Nations following Crimean War. Enlists support of Republicans such as Manin and Garibaldi for House of Savoy.
1857	44	Première of *Le trouvère* at Opéra, 12 Jan. Enlists help of exiled patriot Montanelli for adjustments to Piave's libretto of *Simon Boccanegra*. Returns to Busseto, Jan. Signs contract with S. Carlo Theatre, Naples. Première of *Simon Boccanegra*, Teatro La Fenice, 12 Mar. Revived in Reggio Emilia, May. Première of *Aroldo* (revised *Stiffelio*) at Teatro Nuovo, Rimini,	Elgar born, 2 June; Glinka (54) dies, 15 Feb. Attempt on the life of Ferdinand I of Naples.

Verdi

		conducted by Mariani. Encounters trouble with Neapolitan censors over plot of *Un ballo in maschera*.	
1858	45	Censors return libretto altered into *Adelia degli Adimari*. Verdi refuses it, Feb. Arranges for opera to be produced in Rome, Mar. Wins suit to withdraw opera from Naples, on condition of reviving *Simon Boccanegra* in Nov. Works on modifications to *Un ballo in maschera*. Writes song, *La preghiera d'un poeta*.	Leoncavallo born, 8 Mar; Puccini born, 22 June. Attempt by Felice Orsini to assassinate Napoleon III, 14 Jan.
1859	46	In Naples witnesses first use of slogan 'Viva V.E.R.D.I. To Rome for première of *Un ballo maschera*, Teatro Apollo, 17 Feb. Elected honorary member of Accademia Filarmonica Romana, Feb. Marries Giuseppina Strepponi at Collonges-sous-Salèves (Savoy), 29 Aug. Elected to represent Busseto in assembly of Parma provinces; goes to Turin to present petition for annexation to Piedmont, Sept; is made honorary citizen of Turin and meets Cavour.	L. Ricci (54) dies, 31 Dec; Spohr (75) dies, 22 Oct. Austria invades Piedmont, 29 Apr. Battles of Magenta, 4 June, and Solferino, 23 June. Peace of Villafranca. Mob murder Anviti, police chief of Parma, Oct. Première of Gounod's *Faust*, Théâtre Lyrique, 19 Mar.
1860	47	Manages estates at Busseto; late winter in Genoa; high summer at Tabbiano spa. Buys rifles for the Busseto militia.	Albeniz born, 29 May; Charpentier born, 25 June; Franchetti born, 18 Sept; Mahler born, 7 July; Wolf born 13 Mar. Nice and Savoy annexed to France, 24 Mar; Garibaldi invades Kingdom of Two Sicilies, May; Cialdini marches into Eastern Papal States, Sept.
1861	48	Elected Deputy for Borgo S. Donnino, Jan; attends opening of Italian Parliament, Feb. Signs contract for St. Petersburg	Marschner (66) dies, 14 Dec; Cavour dies, 6 June. Première of Wagner's revised *Tannhäuser*, Opéra, 13 Mar.

Year	Age	Life	Contemporary Events
		opera; leaves for Russia, Nov; but première is postponed, Dec. Friendship with Piroli and Arrivabene.	
1862	49	Leaves Russia for Paris, Feb; receives text of *Inno delle nazioni*, performed at Her Majesty's Theatre, 24 May. Spends summer between Busseto and Turin. To St. Petersburg for première of *La forza del destino*, at Italian Imperial Theatre, 10 Nov; receives Cross of Imperial and Royal Order of S. Stanislas.	Debussy born, 22 Aug; Delius born, 29 Jan; Halévy (63) dies, 17 Mar.
1863	50	Revival of *La forza* at Teatro Real, Madrid, 21 Feb; composes new romance for Villaret to sing in revival of *Les vêpres siciliennes*, Opéra, 20 July. Summer in Busseto and composes song *Il brigidino* for niece of Piroli.	Mascagni born, 7 Dec. Berlioz' *Les Troyens à Carthage*, Théâtre Lyrique, Paris, 4 Nov. Première of Faccio's *I profughi fiamminghi*, Milan, 11 Nov. Boito's offending 'Ode to Italian Art'. Pio Nono issues Syllabus of Errors, Dec.
1864	51	Between Genoa and Busseto; with visits to Turin. Begins revision of *Macbeth* for Paris. Elected member of the French Académie des Beaux-Arts, June.	Meyerbeer (73) dies, 2 May; R. Strauss born, 11 June. Florence becomes capital of Italy, 11 Dec.
1865	52	Première of revised *Macbeth*, Théâtre Lyrique, Paris, 1 April in V.'s absence. Dispute with Busseto authorities over new theatre; agrees to let it be named after him but refuses to set foot inside it. Stands down from Parliament, Sept. Signs contract in Paris for *Don Carlos* to be given at the Opéra, Dec.	Dukas born, 1 Oct; Glazunov born, 29 July; Sibelius born, 8 Dec. Posthumous première of Meyerbeer's *L'Africaine* at Opéra, 28 Apr; and of Faccio's *Amleto*, Genoa, 30 May with libretto by Boito. Wagner's *Tristan und Isolde* first given in Munich, 10 June, under Bülow.
1866	53	Composes *Don Carlos* at Busseto, Paris and Cauterets. Arranges to rent apartment in Genoa, in Palazzo Sauli in which to spend winter months, July.	Busoni born, 1 April; Cilea born, 26 July. Italy declares war on Austria, June; suffers defeats at Custozza, 24 June, and Lissa, 20 July. Garibaldi captures

Year	Age	Life	Contemporary Events
			Trentino with volunteer army including Faccio and Boito. Prussians defeat Austria at Königgratz, 3 July; Austria make peace ceding Veneto to France who hands it to Italy. Première of Smetana's *The bartered bride*, Prague, 30 May.
1867	54	Carlo Verdi dies, 14 Jan. Première of *Don Carlos*, Opéra, 11 Mar. Takes possession of apartment in Genoa, Mar. Is made an honorary citizen of Genoa, April. Assumes guardianship of Filomena Verdi, *aet.* 7. Antonio Barezzi dies, (21 July). In Paris with Giuseppina and Mariani to see Great Exhibition. Mariani conducts Italian première of *Don Carlos* in V.'s absence at Teatro Comunale, Bologna (27 Oct).	Giordano born, 27 Aug; Granados born, 29 July; Pacini (71) dies, 6 Dec. Garibaldi attempts to march on. Defeated at Mentana, arrested and kept under surveillance at Caprera (autumn).
1868	55	Refuses Cross of the Crown of Italy because of Minister Broglio's attack on all Italian music since Rossini, May. Meets Manzoni in Milan, June. Plans composite Mass to commemorate death of Rossini, Nov. In Genoa begins work on revision of *La forza del destino*, Dec.	Rossini (76) dies, 13 Nov. Première of Wagner's *Die Meistersinger*, Munich, 21 June, and Boito's *Mefistofele*, La Scala, Milan, 5 Mar. Bruckner's Symphony no. 1 first given, Linz, 9 May.
1869	56	Première of revised *La forza del destino*, La Scala, Milan, 27 Feb. Agrees to compose *Libera me* for Rossini-Requiem, June. Nominated Cavaliere dell'ordine del Merito Civile di Savoia, July. Publication of 'Album Piave' to which V. contributes *Stornello*, Dec.	Berlioz (66) dies, 8 March; Dargomizhsky (56) dies, 17 Jan; Pfitzner born, 5 May; Roussel born, 5 May. Opening of Suez Canal; new Cairo Opera House inaugurated with *Rigoletto*.
1870	57	Applies to Du Locle for French translations of Wagner's prose works, Jan; searches for	Mercadante (75) dies. Pio Nono proclaims Papal infallibility as official dogma,

Year	Age	Life	Contemporary Events
		operatic subject, Mar–April; agrees to compose *Aida* for Khedive's opera house, May. Works with Ghislanzoni as versifier, July–Dec. Declines directorship of Naples Conservatory in succession to Mercadante, Dec.	July. Outbreak of Franco-Prussian War, Aug. French defeated at Sedan; Italian troops march into Rome, Sept. Siege of Paris begins.
1871	58	Appointed honorary member of Società Filarmonica of Naples, Jan. Forms part of committee in Florence to decide on reform of Conservatories, Mar. Concerns himself with casting and production of Egyptian and European premières of *Aida*. Attends *Lohengrin* at Bologna, conducted by Mariani, 19 Nov. Première of *Aida*, Cairo Opera House, 24 Dec, in V.'s absence.	Auber (89) dies, 12 May. Scriabin born, 25 Dec. German Empire proclaimed at Versailles, Jan. Paris capitulates. Rome becomes capital of Italy, Feb. Commune and second siege of Paris, Mar; ends May with massacre of Communards.
1872	59	Italian première of *Aida*, La Scala, Milan, 8 Feb. Directs revival in Parma, 20 Apr; to Naples for revivals of *Don Carlos* and *Aida*. Performance of partially revised *Don Carlos*, San Carlo, Dec.	Carafa (85) dies, 26 July; Vaughan-Williams born, 12 Oct.
1873	60	Revival of *Aida* at San Carlo, 30 Mar. Private performance of String Quartet in E minor. Manzoni dies, 22 May; V. proposes to Mayor of Milan a *Requiem* in commemoration, June.	Rakhmaninov born, 20 Mar; Reger born, 19 Mar.
1874	61	Conducts première of *Requiem* at Church of San Marco, Milan, 22 May; and at La Scala, 25 May; at Opéra Comique, Paris, 9 June. In London to arrange for performance following year, June. Moves into new apartment in Genoa in Palazzo Doria. Nominated Senator, Nov.	Cornelius (50) dies, 26 Oct; Schoenberg born, 13 Sept. Première of Mussorgsky's *Boris Godunov*, St. Petersburg, 8 Feb; Johann Strauss's *Die Fledermaus*, Vienna, 5 Apr.

Year	Age	Life	Contemporary Events
1875	62	Conducts *Requiem* at Opéra Comique, Paris, 19 Apr; receives Cross of Légion d'Honneur; conducts *Requiem* (revised) at Royal Albert Hall, London, 15 May, Hofoperntheater, Vienna, 11 June, followed by *Aida*, 19 June. Sworn in as Senator in Rome, 15 Nov.	Bizet (37) dies, 3 June; Montemezzi born, 31 May; Ravel born, 7 Mar. Première of Bizet's *Carmen*, Paris, 1 Mar; Boito's revised *Mefistofele*, Bologna, 4 Oct. Opening of Palais Garnier (Opéra) Paris.
1876	63	Conducts *Aida* at Théâtre des Italiens, Paris, 22 April, and *Requiem*. String Quartet performed privately in Hotel de Bade, 1 June; V. decides to publish. Attends graduation of Maria Filomena from school in Turin, Aug; her engagement to Alberto Carrara announced.	Alfano born, 8 Mar; Falla born, 23 Nov; Wolf-Ferrari born, 12 Jan. First Bayreuth Festival, première of Wagner's *Ring*, 13–17 Aug. Ponchielli's *La gioconda*, Milan, 8 Apr; Brahms's Symphony no. 1, Karlsruhe, 4 Nov.
1877	64	Conducts *Requiem* at Lower Rhine Festival, 21 May. Friendship with Ferdinand Hiller. Visits Holland, May.	Dohnanyì born, 27 July; Petrella (64) dies, 7 Apr; F. Ricci (68) dies, 10 Dec. Première of Tchaikovsky's *Eugene Onegin*, Moscow, 29 Mar.
1878	65	Visits Monte Carlo, Mar; Paris, Apr and Nov. Maria Filomena marries Alberto Carrara, 11 Oct. Elected honorary member of Modena's Accademia di Scienze, Lettere e Arti, Dec.	Vittorio Emanuele II dies; Umberto I succeeds, Jan. Pio Nono dies, Feb.
1879	66	In Milan with Giulio Ricordi and Boito conceives idea for *Otello*; conducts *Requiem* in benefit concert for flood victims. Maria Filomena gives birth to daughter, Giuseppina. Boito sends synopsis of *Otello* libretto, Sept.	Medtner born, 25 July; Ireland born, 13 Aug; Respighi born, 7 July.
1880	67	Elected honorary member of Gesellschaft der Musikfreunde of Vienna, Jan. Directs *Aida* in French with definitive ballet at Opéra, 22 Mar. Nominated	Bloch born, 24 July; Offenbach (61) dies, 4 Oct; Pizzetti born, 20 Sept.

Year	Age	Life	Contemporary Events
		Grand Officer of the Foreign Legion, Mar, Cavaliere of the Great Cross of Italy, 11 Apr. Attends Performance of *Ave Maria* and *Pater Noster* at benefit concert in Milan, 18 Apr. Receives revised libretto of *Otello*, Aug; begins revision of *Simon Boccanegra*, Dec.	
1881	68	Première of revised *Simon Boccanegra*, La Scala, Milan, 24 Mar. Further work on libretto of *Otello*.	Bartók born, 25 Mar; Mussorgsky (42) dies, 16 Mar. Posthmous première of Offenbach's *Les Contes d'Hoffmann*, Paris, 10 Feb.
1882	69	In Paris to ensure copyright interests after death of Léon Escudier. Plans 4-act *Don Carlos*. Begins revision of *Don Carlos*, Sept.	Kodály born, 16 Dec; Malipiero born, 18 Mar; Raff (60) dies; Stravinsky born, 5 June. Second Bayreuth Festival; première of Wagner's *Parsifal*, 26 July. Triple Alliance formed, May.
1883	70	Complete revision of *Don Carlos*, Mar.	Bax born, 6 Nov; Casella born 25 July; Szymanowski born, 21 Sept; Wagner (69) dies, 13 Feb; Webern born, 3 Dec; Zandonai born, 18 May. Deaths of Hugo and Garibaldi.
1884	71	Première of revised *Don Carlos*, La Scala, Milan, 10 Jan. Begins *Otello*, Mar.	Smetana (60) dies. Première of Massenet's *Manon*, Paris, 19 Jan. Puccini's *Le Villi*, Teatro Dal Verme, Milan, 31 May.
1885	72	Resumes composition of *Otello*, Sept.	Berg born, 7 Feb.
1886	73	Completes *Otello*, Nov. Première of final version of *Don Carlos* with Fontainebleau act restored, Teatro Municipale, Modena, 26 Dec.	Liszt (75) dies, 31 July; Ponchielli (52) dies, 16 Jan.
1887	74	Receives Great Cross of the Order of SS. Maurizio e Lazzaro. Première of *Otello*, La Scala, Milan, 5 Feb. Awarded honorary citizenship of Milan, 8 Feb.	Borodin (53) dies, 16 Feb.

Year	Age	Life	Contemporary Events
1888	75	Composes *Laudi alla Vergine*. Inauguration of hospital at Villanova sull'Arda, 6 Nov.	Italian première of Wagner's *Tristan und Isolde* conducted by Martucci, Bologna, 2 June.
1889	76	Composes *Ave Maria sulla scala enigmatica*, Mar. Decides to write *Falstaff*, July. Acquires site in Milan for musicians' Casa di Riposo.	Wagner's *Die Meistersinger* first given in Italian, La Scala, Milan, 26 Dec. Mahler's Symphony no. 1 first given, Budapest, 20 Nov.
1890	77	Completes Act I of *Falstaff*.	Franck (68) dies. Première of Mascagni's *Cavalleria Rusticana*, Rome, 17 May.
1891	78	Works slowly on composition of *Falstaff*.	Bliss born, 2 Aug; Delibes (55) dies, 16 Jan; Faccio (51) dies, 23 July; Prokofiev born, 11 Apr. Wagner's *Die Walküre* in Italian, Turin, 22 Dec.
1892	79	Conducts prayer from *Mosè* as part of Rossini centenary celebrations in Milan, 10 Apr. Finishes *Falstaff*, Dec.	Honegger born, 10 Mar; Lalo (69) dies, 22 Apr; Milhaud born, 4 Sept. Premières of Leoncavallo's *Pagliacci*, 21 Mar, Catalani's *La Wally*, Milan, 20 Jan. Publication of Debussy's Prélude à l'après-midi d'un faune.
1893	80	Première of *Falstaff*, La Scala, Milan, 9 Feb; made honorary citizen of Rome, 14 Apr; attends *Falstaff* in Rome with definitive alterations, 15 Apr.	Catalani (39) dies, 7 Aug; Gounod (75) dies, 18 Oct; Tchaikovsky (53) dies, 25 Oct. Première of Puccini's *Manon Lescaut*, Turin, 2 Feb. Humperdinck's *Hansel and Gretel*, Weimar, 23 Dec.
1894	81	Attends *Falstaff* at Opéra Comique, Paris, 18 Apr. Composes ballet for French *Otello* (summer). Attends première of French *Otello* at Opéra; receives Grand Cross of Legion of Honour, 12 Oct. Song *Pietà, Signor* published in periodical *Fata Morgana* for benefit of earthquake victims in Sicily and Calabria.	Chabrier (53) dies, 13 Sept; A. Rubinstein (64) dies, 8 Nov.
1895	82	Plans the construction of Casa di Riposo in Milan. Begins	Castelnuovo-Tedesco born, 3 Apr; Hindemith born, 16 Nov.

Year	Age	Life	Contemporary Events
		composition of *Te Deum*. Performance of *Ave Maria sulla scala enigmatica* by students of Parma Conservatory, June.	
1896	83	Works on *Te Daum* and *Stabat Mater*.	Bruckner (72) dies, 11 Oct; Cagnoni (68) dies, 30 Apr. Italian defeat at Battle of Adowa. Première of Puccini's *La Bohème*, Turin, 1 Feb.
1897	84	Sends *Quattro pezzi sacri* to Ricordi for publication, Oct. Giuseppina Verdi dies, 14 Nov.	Brahms dies, 3 Apr.
1898	85	*Stabat Mater*, *Laudi* and *Te Deum* performed in Paris in V.'s absence, 7 Apr; also at Turin Exhibition under Toscanini, May.	
1899	86	Founds Casa di Riposo, Dec.	Poulenc born, 7 Jan; J. Strauss II (74) dies, 3 June.
1900	87	Sketches composition of Queen Margherita's prayer.	Krenek born, 23 Aug. Assassination of Umberto I.
1901		Has fatal stroke, 21 Jan; dies 27 Jan.	

Appendix B
List of Works

I OPERAS

Oberto, Conte di San Bonifacio, opera in 2 acts by Temistocle Solera (probably adapted from *Rocester* by Antonio Piazza). Milan, Scala, 17.11.1839.

Un giorno di regno (later *Il finto Stanislao*), melodramma giocoso in 2 acts by Felice Romani (after *Le faux Stanislas*, comedy by Alexandre Vincent Pineu-Duval). Milan, Scala, 3.9.1840.

Nabucodonosor (later *Nabucco*), opera in 4 parts by Temistocle Solera (after *Nabucodonosor*, play by Anicet-Bourgeois and Francis Cornue). Milan, Scala, 9.3.1842.

I Lombardi alla prima crociata, opera in 4 acts by Temistocle Solera (after poem of the same title by Tommaso Grossi). Milan, Scala, 11.2.1843.

Ernani, opera in 4 acts by Francesco Maria Piave (after *Hernani*, play by Victor Hugo). Venice, Fenice, 9.3.1844.

I due Foscari, opera in 3 acts by Francesco Maria Piave (after *The two Foscari*, play by Lord Byron). Rome, Argentina, 3.11.1844.

Giovanna d'Arco, opera in a prologue and 3 acts by Temistocle Solera (after *Die Jungfrau von Orleans*, play by Schiller). Milan, Scala, 15.2.1845.

Alzira, opera in a prologue and 2 acts by Salvatore Cammarano (after *Alzire, ou les Américains*, tragedy by Voltaire). Naples, San Carlo, 12.8.1845.

Attila, opera in a prologue and 3 acts by Temistocle Solera, additions by Piave (after *Attila, König der Hunnen*, play by Zacharias Werner). Venice, Fenice, 17.3.1846.

Macbeth, opera in 4 acts by Francesco Maria Piave, with additions by Andrea Maffei (after Shakespeare). Florence, Pergola, 14.3.1847; revised version Paris, Théâtre Lyrique, 19.4.1865.

I masnadieri, opera in 4 acts by Andrea Maffei (after *Die Räuber*, play by Schiller). London, Her Majesty's, 22.7.1847.

Jérusalem opera in 4 acts by Alphonse Royer and Gustave Vaëz (adapted from *I Lombardi*). Paris, Opéra, 22.11.1847.

Il corsaro, opera in 3 acts by Francesco Maria Piave (after *The corsair*, poem by Lord Byron); Trieste, Teatro Grande, 25.10.1848.

La battaglia di Legnano, opera in 4 acts by Salvatore Cammarano (after *La battaille de Toulouse*, play by Joseph Méry). Rome, Argentina, 27.1.1849.

Luisa Miller, opera in 3 acts by Salvatore Cammarano (after *Kabale und Liebe*, play by Schiller). Naples, San Carlo, 8.12.1849.

Stiffelio, opera in 3 acts by Francesco Maria Piave (after *Le pasteur, ou L'évangile et le foyer*, play by Emile Silvestre and Eugène Bourgeois). Trieste, Teatro Grande, 16.10.1850.

Rigoletto, opera in 3 acts by Francesco Maria Piave (after *Le roi s'amuse*, play by Victor Hugo) Venice, Fenice, 11.3.1851.

Il trovatore, opera in four parts by Salvatore Cammarano, with additions by Leone Emanuele Bardare (after *El trovador*, play by Antonio Garcia Gutiérrez). Rome, Apollo, 19.1.1853.

La traviata, opera in 3 acts by Francesco Maria Piave (after *La dame aux camélias*, play by Alexandre Dumas, fils). Venice, Fenice, 6.3.1853.

Les vêpres siciliennes, opera in 5 acts by Eugène Scribe and Charles Duveyrier (after *Le Duc d'Albe*, libretto by the same authors). Paris, Opéra, 13.6.1855.

Simon Boccanegra, opera in a prologue and 3 acts by Francesco Maria Piave, with additions by Giuseppe Montanelli (after *Simon Bocanegra*, play by Antonio Garcia Gutiérrez). Venice, Fenice, 12.3.1857; revised version with additions by Arrigo Boito, Milan, Scala, 24.3.1881.

Aroldo, opera in 4 acts by Francesco Maria Piave (adapted from *Stiffelio*). Rimini, Teatro Nuovo, 18.8.1857.

Un ballo in maschera, opera in 3 acts by Antonio Somma (after *Gustave III ou le bal masqué*, libretto by Eugène Scribe) Rome, Apollo 17.2.1859.

La forza del destino, opera in 4 acts by Francesco Maria Piave (after *Don Alvaro o La fuerza del sin*, play by Angel de Saavedra, Duke of Rivas, with a scene added from Schiller's *Wallensteins Lager*, translated by Andrea Maffei). St. Petersburg, Bolshoi, 10.11.1862; revised version with additions by Antonio Ghislanzoni, Milan, Scala 27.2.1869.

Don Carlos, opera in 5 acts by Joseph Méry and Camille Du Locle (after *Don Carlos, Infant von Spanien*, play by Friedrich Schiller). Paris, Opéra 11.3.1867; revised version in 4 acts, additions to French text by Du Locle, Italian translation by Angelo Zanardini based on that of original version by Achille De Lauzières, Milan, Scala 10.1.1884.

Aida, opera in 4 acts by Antonio Ghislanzoni (after scenario by Auguste Mariette). Cairo, Opera House, 24.12.1871.

Otello, opera in 4 acts by Arrigo Boito (after Shakespeare). Milan, Scala, 5.2.1887.

Falstaff, opera in 3 acts by Arrigo Boito (after Shakespeare). Milan; Scala, 9.2.1893.

II MISCELLANEOUS OPERATIC COMPOSITIONS

Io la vidi for tenor and orchestra, text from *Il Solitario ed Elodia* by Giuseppe Persiani, comp. 1832–5(?).

Pria che scende sull'indegno, duet for Leonora and Cuniza in *Oberto*, probably a relic from *Rocester* and removed before first performance; composed *c*.1837(?).

D'innocenza i cari inganni, cavatina for Cuniza in *Oberto*, composed 1840 for Luigia Ábbadia, text by Solera (?).

Ah Riccardo, a mia ragione, duet for Cuniza and Riccardo in *Oberto* composed 1840 for Luigia Abbadia and Lorenzo Salvi, text by Solera (?).

Dove corri, o sciagurata?, duet for Leonora and Oberto in *Oberto*, composed 1841 for Antonietta Rainieri-Marini and Ignazio Marini. Text unknown.

Ma fin che un brando vindice, cabaletta for Oberto in *Oberto* composed summer 1841 for Ignazio Marini, text by Solera (?). (pub. in vocal score of *Ernani* as *Infin che un brando vindice*.)

Oh, dischius' è il firmamento, alternative setting of Fenena's prayer from *Nabucco* composed late 1842 for Almerinda Granchi, text by Solera.

Come poteva un angelo, alternative setting of Oronte's cabaletta from *I Lombardi* composed summer 1843 for Antonio Poggi, text by Solera. (pub. in vocal score).

Odi il voto, O grande Iddio, aria for title role in *Ernani* composed late summer-autumn 1844 for Nicola Ivanoff, text by Piave (?) pub. Suvini Zerboni.

Potrei lasciar la margine, cavatina for Giovanna in *Giovanna d'Arco* composed winter 1845–6 for Sofia Loewe, text unknown, music lost.

Si, lo sento, Iddio mi chiama, cabaletta for Jacopo in *I due Foscari* composed summer 1846 for Giovanni Mario, text by Piave (?).

Sventurato! alla mia vita, romanza for Foresto in *Attila* composed late summer 1846 for Nicola Ivanoff, text by Piave, (music inaccessible).

Oh dolore! ed io vivea, romanza for Foresto in *Attila* composed autumn 1846 for Napoleone Moriani, text by Piave (?).

O toi que j'ai chérie, romance for Henri in *Les vêpres siciliennes* composed 1863 for Villaret, text unknown.

Overture: Aida: composed 1872 then withdrawn; pub. Suvini Zerboni.

Prends pitié de sa jeunesse mélodie for Maddalena in *Rigoletto* adapted from romanza, *Il poveretto* (1847).

III CHORAL AND RELIGIOUS WORKS

Tantum Ergo for tenor and orchestra, composed 1836 for Luigi Machiavelli.

Suona la tromba for 3-part male chorus and orchestra, composed summer 1849, text by Goffredo Mameli.

Inno delle nazioni for tenor, chorus and orchestra, composed 1862 for London's Great Exhibition, text by Arrigo Boito.

Libera me for soprano, chorus and orchestra composed 1869 for composite requiem in memory of Rossini.

Messa da Requiem for SATB soloists, chorus and orchestra composed 1873–4 to commemorate anniversary of death of Alessandro Manzoni.

Ave Maria for soprano and string orchestra, composed 1879–80 for benefit concert, text attributed to Dante.

Pater Noster, for 5-part unaccompanied chorus composed 1879–80 for benefit concert, text attributed to Dante.

Laudi alla Vergine Maria for 4-part female voices composed 1887–8, pub. 1898 as no. 3 of *Quattro pezzi sacri*; text by Dante from final canto of *Paradiso*.

Ave Maria sulla scala enigmatica for 4-part unaccompanied chorus composed 1889, pub. as no. 1 of the *Quattro pezzi sacri*.

Pietà, Signor! for tenor and piano composed 1894 and pub. in periodical *Fata Morgana* for victims of earthquakes in Sicily and Calabria, text adapted from *De profundis* by Arrigo Boito.

Te Deum for double chorus and orchestra composed 1895–6, pub. 1898 as no. 4 of *Quattro pezzi sacri*.

Stabat Mater for chorus and orchestra, composed 1896–7 (?), pub. 1898 as no. 2 for *Quattro pezzi sacri*.

IV VOCAL CHAMBER MUSIC

Sei romanze (pub.1838)
  Non t'accostare all'urna, poem by Jacopo Vittorelli
  More, Elisa, lo stanco poeta, poem by Tommaso Bianchi
  In solitaria stanza, poem by Jacopo Vittorelli
  Nell'orror di notte oscura, poem by Carlo Angiolini
  Perduta ho la pace, poem by Goethe, translated Luigi Balestra
  Deh, pietoso, oh Addolorata, poem by Goethe, translated Luigi Balestra
Guarda che bianca luna, notturno for STB, flute and piano, poem by Jacopo Vittorelli (pub. 1839)
L'esule (pub. ?1839), poem by Temistocle Solera
La seduzione (pub. ?1839), poem by Luigi Balestra
Chi i bei dì m'adduce ancora, poem by Goethe translated Luigi Balestra (?), composed 1842 for autograph album of Sofia De'Medici, Marchesa di Marignano, pub. Frank Walker in *The Music Review*, Vol. 9 no. 1, Feb. 1948.

Sei romanze (pub. 1845)
  Il tramonto, poem by Andrea Maffei
  La zingara, poem by Manfredo Maggioni
  Ad una stella, poem by Andrea Maffei
  Lo spazzacamino, poem by Manfredo Maggioni
  Il mistero, poem by Felice Romani
  Brindisi, poem by Andrea Maffei (earlier version 'according to the autograph' pub. by Ricordi as no. 16 in their *Composizioni di camera* 1935, reprinted 1948).
Il poveretto (pub. 1847), poem by Manfredo Maggioni (see also (II) *Prends pitié de sa jeunesse*).

365

L'abandonnée (pub. 1849), poem by Marie and Léon Escudier (reprinted 1882 by Heugel).

Fiorellin che sorgi appena, baracarola, poem by Francesco Maria Piave (comp. Nov 1850 for Giovanni Severi.; pub. in fascimile in G. Steffani *Verdi e Trieste* (Trieste 1951).

La preghiera del poeta, poem by Nicola Sole (comp. 1858; pub. in *Rivista Musicale Italiana*. vol XLV, anno 1941).

Il Brigidino, poem by Francesco Dall'Ongaro (comp. 1863 for niece of Piroli; pub. by Sonzogno, 1948).

Stornello, poem anon. (contribution to *Album Piave*, pub. 1869).

V INSTRUMENTAL MUSIC

Sinfonia in D
Valzer
Romanza senza parole for piano (pub. 1865 in *Gioie e sospiri* by Canti)
String Quartet in E minor (comp. 1873, pub. 1876).

Appendix C
Personalia

Appiani, Giuseppina (*c*.1797–?). Born Countess Strigelli. Maintained salon in Borgo Monforte, Milan. Close friend of Bellini, Donizetti and Verdi.

Arditi, Luigi (1822–1903). Italian conductor, composer and violinist. Friend of Verdi. Conducted première of *Inno delle nazioni* London 1862 and numerous U.S. and British Verdi premières.

Arrivabene, Count Opprandino (1805–87). Italian newspaper correspondent; editor of *Gazzetta di Torino* during first Italian parliament. Close friend and frequent correspondent of Verdi's.

Balestra, Luigi (1808–63). Italian lawyer and poet from Busseto; provided text for a revival of *Oberto* in Genoa. Verdi set his translations of poems by Goethe.

Barbieri–Nini, Marianna (1820–87). Italian soprano, one of the finest interpreters of early Verdi. Created Lucrezia in *I due Foscari* (1844), Lady Macbeth (1847) Gulnara in *Il corsaro* (1848); left an entertaining account of Verdi's methods of rehearsal at Florence in 1847.

Bardare, Leone Emanuele (b. 1820). Neapolitan librettist. Director of teacher training schools in Naples. Completed libretto of *Il trovatore* after death of Cammarano.

Barezzi, Antonio (1798–1867). Busseto merchant and music lover. Verdi's patron and father-in-law – his 'second father' (Verdi's words). *Macbeth* is dedicated to him.

Basevi, Abramo (1818–95). Doctor, author and music critic. Founded the *Società del Quartetto* in Florence. Published an analysis of Beethoven's Quartets opus 18; author of the first serious work on Verdi's music, *Studio sulle opere di Giuseppe Verdi* (Florence 1859).

Basily, Francesco (1767–1850). Italian musician and educator. Headed the examining board at Milan Conservatory which rejected Verdi's application for entrance, but recognised his talent.

Bellaigue, Camille (1858–1930). French critic and author; wrote for *Revue des deux mondes* and other periodicals. A friend of Boito; corresponded with Verdi and published a monograph on the composer, 1912.

Boito, Arrigo (1842–1918). Italian poet, composer and Verdi's last librettist; wrote text for *Inno delle nazioni* (1862); collaborated on the revision of *Simon Boccanegra* (1881); provided libretti of *Otello* (1887) and *Falstaff* (1893) also, under a pseudonym, of Ponchielli's *La Gioconda* (1876). In his youth a leading member of the 'Scapigliatura Milanese' his own operas are *Mefistofele* (1868 rev. 1875) and *Nerone* (posth. 1918).

Bottesini, Giovanni (1821–89). Italian composer, conductor and double-bass virtuoso. Conducted première of *Aida* in Cairo (1871). Appointed director of Parma Conservatory shortly before death, due to Verdi's recommendation.

Brenna, Guglielmo. Secretary of the managing committee of the Teatro la Fenice, Venice. Introduced Verdi to the work of Piave and proved a valuable go-between in the composer's dealings with the theatre.

Bülow, Hans Guido, Baron von (1830–94). German conductor and pianist. First husband of Wagner's second wife, Cosima; much associated with Wagner in Munich in the 1860s; settled in Florence after break-up of marriage; moved to Meiningen to become noted exponent of Brahms. Wrote attacking Verdi's *Requiem* but recanted in 1892.

Calzado, Torrivro (b.1805). Manager of the Théâtre des Italiens, Paris, in the 1850s. Presented *Trovatore* under Verdi's direction 1854–5. Sued unsuccessfully by Verdi for refusing to pay rights on *Rigoletto* and *La traviata* (1856).

Cammarano, Salvatore (1801–52). Italian librettist, member of a large theatrical Neapolitan family. Wrote libretti of *Alzira, La battaglia di Legnano, Luisa Miller, Il trovatore*. Verdi's first choice for *Re Lear*. Also librettist of Donizetti's *Lucia di Lammermoor*, and several other operas by him and Mercadante.

Carcano, Giulio (1812–84). Italian poet and translator of Shakespeare. Suggested to Verdi a libretto on *Hamlet*.

Carrara, Alberto (1854–1925). Italian lawyer. Married Verdi's ward, Filomena Maria, in 1878.

Carvalho, Léon (1825–97). French impresario. Managed Théâtre Lyrique, Paris (1856–60, 1862–68). Premièred Gounod's *Faust* (1859), Berlioz' *Les Troyens à Carthage* (1863); a French *La traviata* under the title of *Violetta* (1864) and the revised *Macbeth* (1865).

Coletti, Filippo (1811–94). Italian baritone, notable exponent of Verdian roles. Created Gusman in *Alzira*, Francesco in *I masnadieri* and Germont in the revised *Traviata*.

Corticelli, Mauro. Italian theatrical agent and friend of Giuseppina Verdi. Managed tours of actress Adelaide Ristori. Installed as 'fattore' at S.Agata 1867–9 until dismissed for financial misconduct.

Cruvelli, Sofia (1826–1907). German soprano. Created Hélène in *Les vêpres siciliennes*; caused trouble during rehearsals by departing on a pre-marital honeymoon with her future husband, Baron Vigier.

De Bassini, Achille (1819–81). Italian baritone, known as the 'Ronconi of the South'. Created Francesco in *I due Foscari*, Seid in *Il Corsaro* and Miller in *Luisa Miller*; was chosen by Verdi to create Fra Melitone in *La forza del destino* due to a natural gift for comedy.

Delfico, Melchiorre (1825–95). Italian caricaturist and writer. Left a set of cartoons of Verdi and the musical world or Naples in 1858 and another in connection with the première of *Otello* in Milan, 1887.

Demaldé, Giuseppe ('Finola') (b.1795). Italian writer and friend of the

young Verdi. Left a series of notes for an unwritten biography of Verdi
c.1842 (*Cenni biografici*).

De Sanctis, Cesare (d.1881). Italian business man. Verdi's chief contact with
Naples from 1849. He and Giuseppina stood as godparents to his son.

Draneht, Paul (1815–94). Greek Cypriot (real name Pavlidis). Intendant of
the Cairo theatre at the time of *Aida*.

Du Locle, Camille (1832–1903). French librettist and theatre manager.
Son-in-law of Emile Perrin (*q.v.*). Librettist of *Don Carlos* with Joseph
Méry. Translator with Nuitter of *La forza del destino* and *Aida*; responsible for revised text of *Don Carlos* (1884). Managed the Opéra Comique
1870–5; premièred Bizet's *Carmen* (1875).

Dupré, Giovanni (1817–82). Italian sculptor; made a cast of Verdi's right
hand in Florence 1847 and left an affectionate memoir of the composer.

Escudier, Léon (1821–81). French publisher, later impresario. Verdi's publisher in France; together with his brother, Marie, founded *La France
Musicale*. Managed the Théâtre des Italiens, 1874–6. Mounted French
première of *Aida*. Left an account of Verdi in his Memoirs.

Faccio, Franco (1840–91). Italian composer and conductor. Italy's leading
conductor after death of Mariani in 1873. Close friend of Boito and
fellow-'scapigliato'. Composed *I profughi fiamminghi* (1863) and *Amleto*
(1865). Conducted Italian première of *Aida*; of revised *Simon Boccanegra*
and *Don Carlos* and *Otello*.

Ferretti, Jacopo (1784–1852). Italian librettist; member of Arcadian Society.
Wrote libretto of Rossini's *La cenerentola* and Donizetti's *Torquato
Tasso*. Met Verdi at première of *I due Foscari*; recited a poem in his
honour.

Filippi, Filippo (1830–87). Italian music critic. Wrote for *La Gazzetta
Musicale di Milano* and *La Perseveranza*. His sympathies were modern
and Wagnerian.

Florimo, Francesco (1800–88). Italian writer and librarian. Friend and
fellow student of Bellini at the Naples Conservatory. Wrote books on
Bellini and music in Naples. His looks and gentlemanly manners earned
him the nickname of Lord Palmerston. Attempted unsuccessfully to persuade Verdi to accept directorship of Naples Conservatory in 1870.

Fraschini, Gaetano (1816–87). Italian tenor much admired by Verdi. Created Zamoro in *Alzira*, Corrado in *Il corsaro*, Arrigo in *La battaglia di
Legnano*, title role in *Stiffelio* and Riccardo in *Un ballo in maschera*. Verdi
had him in mind as late as 1870 for Radames in *Aida*. Known as the 'tenore
della maledizione' from the force with which he delivered Edgardo's curse
in *Lucia di Lammermoor*.

Frezzolini-Poggi, Erminia (1818–84). Italian soprano, admired by Verdi as
exponent of modern, expressive style of singing. Created Giselda in *I
Lombardi* and title role of *Giovanna d'Arco*. Daughter of a famous basso
buffo, she was engaged to Otto Nicolai before marrying the tenor Antonio
Poggi.

Gallo, Antonio. Italian impresario, violinist and bookseller. One of Verdi's

supporters in Naples; mounted the revised *La traviata* at his theatre in
1854.

Gemito, Vincenzo (1852–1929). Italian sculptor. Verdi bought his exemp-
tion from military service in return for busts of himself and Giuseppina.

Ghislanzoni, Antonio (1824–93). Italian baritone, writer and one of the
most skilled librettists of the 1870s and '80s. Provided additional text for
the revised *Forza del destino* (1869) and the 'intermediate' *Don Carlos* of
1872. Wrote the libretto of *Aida*. An entertaining writer on contemporary
Italian events, he left a valuable account of a visit to S.Agata in his *Libro
serio*.

Giusti, Giuseppe (1809–50). Italian poet and patriot. Referred to Verdi in
one of his most famous poems. Met the composer at Florence during
rehearsals for *Macbeth* and wrote him a well-known letter urging him to
keep to Italian subjects.

Hiller, Ferdinand (1811–85). German composer and pianist. As Director of
the Lower Rhine Festival he invited Verdi to conduct his *Requiem* there in
1877. They corresponded cordially until Hiller's death.

Ivanoff, Nicola (1810–77). Russian tenor who came to Italy with Glinka and
settled there. At Rossini's request Verdi wrote two insert-arias for him to
sing in *Ernani* and *Attila* respectively.

Jacovacci, Vincenzo (1811–81). Italian impresario active in Rome. Presented
premières of *Il trovatore* and *Un ballo in maschera*. Renowned for unwill-
ingness to spend.

Lanari, Alessandro (1790–1862). Italian impresario, one of the most famous
of his day. Managed Giuseppina Strepponi in her professional career.
Presented *Macbeth* at the Teatro della Pergola, Florence.

Lucca, Francesco (1802–72) and Giovannina Strazza (1814–94). Italian
music publishers. The firm shared rights in *Nabucco* with Ricordi. Published *Attila, I masnadieri, Il corsaro*. Ricordi's chief rivals, they acquired
Italian rights of Gounod, Thomas, Meyerbeer and Wagner. Giovannina
sold out to Ricordi in 1888.

Luccardi, Vincenzo (1811–76). Italian sculptor, professor at the Accademia
di San Luca, Rome. Close friend and correspondent of Verdi from 1844.

Lumley, Benjamin (1811–75). English impresario. Managed Her Majesty's
Theatre London at various times 1841–59; mounted première of *I masnadieri*. Left a valuable set of memoirs.

Maffei, Andrea (1798–1885). Italian poet and translator. Close friend of
Verdi, who set three of his poems. Provided libretto of *I masnadieri* and
modifications to libretto of *Macbeth*. Verdi borrowed his translation of
Schiller's *Wallensteins Lager* for comic sermon of Fra Melitone in *La
forza del destino*.

Maffei, Clara (1814–86) wife of the above, legally separated from him 1846.
Maintained salon in Milan, frequented by artists, musicians and writers of
a patriotic persuasion. Corresponded with Verdi from 1840s till her death;
introduced him to Manzoni. Extended patronage to 'scapigliati'.

Manzoni, Alessandro (1785–1873). Italian poet, novelist and patriot of liberal Catholic views. Verdi, a life-long admirer, met him in June 1868 and wrote *Requiem* commemorating his death.

Mariani, Angelo (1822–73). Italian conductor, violinist and composer. Conducted premières of *Aroldo* and the revised *Forza del destino*; gave much lauded first Italian performance of the original *Don Carlos*, also of Wagner's *Lohengrin* and *Tannhäuser*. A close friend of Verdi's from 1857 to 1869.

Mariette, Auguste-Edouard (1821–81). French Egyptologist; established Boulaq in 1863. Provided the plot of *Aida*.

Marini, Ignazio (1811–73). Italian bass; created title roles of *Oberto* and *Attila*. Verdi wrote for him the cabaletta 'Infin che un brando vindice' to sing in a revival of *Oberto*. He transferred it to *Ernani*.

Mario, Giovanni Matteo di Candia (1810–83). Italian tenor, Rubini's successor in the so-called 'Puritani quartet'. Lived with soprano Giulia Grisi. Verdi wrote for him the cabaletta 'Sento Iddio che mi chiama' to sing in *I due Foscari*. One of the few remaining stars to use 'falsetto'.

Massini, Pietro. Italian amateur musician; directed the Filodrammatici of Milan. Did much to promote Verdi's early career.

Maurel, Victor (1848–1923). French baritone of outstanding intelligence and dramatic ability. Created title role of revised *Simon Boccanegra*, Iago in *Otello* and title role of *Falstaff*; also Tonio in Leoncavallo's *Pagliacci*. His book *Dix ans de carrière* contains valuable chapter on the mounting of *Otello*.

Mazzucato, Alberto (1813–77). Italian composer, teacher and conductor. From 1839 taught at Milan Conservatory; his pupils included Boito. Conducted first Milan performance of *Don Carlos*. Became director of Conservatory in 1872.

Merelli, Bartolomeo (1795–1879). Italian impresario. Commissioned and mounted *Oberto*, *Un giorno di regno*, *Nabucco*, *I Lombardi* and *Giovanna d'Arco*; fell out of favour with Verdi due to parsimonious and inefficient management of La Scala, Milan.

Méry, François Joseph (1797–1865). French playwright of Bonapartist sympathies. Author of *La bataille de Toulouse* which furnished basis of *La battaglia di Legnano*. Part-author with Du Locle of libretto of *Don Carlos*

Mocenigo, Count Alvise. Italian nobleman. Presidente agli Spettacoli, Teatro La Fenice, Venice, during the 1840s. Helpful to Verdi over the première of *Ernani*. Also president of the company that opened Italy's first railway line from Milan to Venice.

Morelli, Domenico (1826–1901). Italian painter. One of Verdi's Neapolitan circle of friends, he painted the composer's portrait and corresponded with him over the figure of Iago.

Moriani, Napoleone (1806–78). Italian tenor, known as 'il tenore della bella morte' from his romantic portrayal of Edgardo's death in *Lucia di Lammermoor*. Verdi wrote a romanza for him to sing in *Attila*. Most probable father of Giuseppina Strepponi's third illegitimate child.

Morosini, Countess Emilia (d.*c*.1848). Italian noblewoman. Maintained a salon in Milan during the 1840s. Verdi was a friend of the countess and her family.

Muzio, Emanuele (1825–90). Italian composer and conductor, Verdi's only pupil, also a protegé of Barezzi. Accompanied Verdi to London in 1847. Composed operas; *Claudia* and *Giovanna la pazza*; thereafter confined his career to conducting. Gave foreign premières of several Verdi operas. Resident conductor of the Théâtre des Italiens, Paris, 1870–6.

Nuitter, Charles-Louis-Etienne (1828–99). French librettist, translator and archivist. Collaborated with Beaumont on French translation of *Macbeth* and with Du Locle on translations of *Aida*, *La forza del destino* and *Simon Boccanegra*. As archivist of the Paris Opéra, he kept valuable records relating to *Don Carlos* and acted as intermediary between Verdi and Du Locle over the opera's revision 1882–3.

Pantaleone, Romilda (1847–1917). Italian soprano. Created Desdemona in *Otello*, not to Verdi's satisfaction; but on his recommendation was cast for Tigrana in Puccini's *Edgar*. Mistress of the conductor Faccio.

Pasqua, Giuseppina (1855–1930). Italian contralto. Cast by Verdi for Mistress Quickly; he added for her the solo at start of Act II scene 2 of *Falstaff*.

Perrin, Emile-César-Victor (1814–85). French painter and administrator. Directed Opéra Comique 1848–57; Théâtre Lyrique 1854–5; and Opéra 1862–73, during which time he commissioned *Don Carlos*. Father-in-law of Du Locle.

Piave, Francesco Maria (1810–76). Italian librettist. Author of *Ernani, I due Foscari, Macbeth, Il corsaro, Stiffelio, Rigoletto, La traviata, Simon Boccanegra, Aroldo, La forza del destino* and the last act of *Attila*; resident poet and stage manager at La Fenice, Venice 1844–60; moved to La Scala, Milan 1861 at Verdi's recommendation. Suffered a stroke in 1867 and remained paralysed until his death.

Piazza, Antonio. Italian journalist. Author of libretto which was subsequently fashioned by Solera into *Oberto*.

Piroli, Giuseppe (1815–90). Italian lawyer and parliamentarian. Professor of law at Parma University and deputy for the city in the first Italian parliament. A member of the Liberal party he was made a Senator in 1884. A close friend and correspondent of Verdi.

Poggi, Antonio (1808–75). Italian tenor. Created Carlo in *Giovanna d'Arco*. Verdi wrote new cabaletta for him to sing in *I Lombardi*. Husband of Erminia Frezzolini and lover of Countess Samoyloff.

Pougin, Arthur (1834–1921). French writer. Wrote a life of Verdi 1881 which was translated into Italian and amplified by Folchetto with an account, not always reliable, of the composer's early years authorised by Verdi himself.

Provesi, Ferdinando (*c*.1770–1833). Italian organist and teacher. Municipal music master, organist at the church of S.Bartolomeo and director of the Philharmonic Society at Busseto during Verdi's youth. Verdi was his pupil, then his assistant and finally his successor as municipal music master.

Ranieri-Marini, Antonietta. Italian mezzo-soprano. Created Leonora in *Oberto*, appearing in most contemporary revivals of the opera, and the Marchesa in *Un giorno di regno*.

Ricordi, Giovanni (1785–1853). Founded in 1808 the publishing house that bears his name; published most of the operas of Rossini, Bellini, Donizetti and Verdi. Founded the *Gazzetta Musicale di Milano* which continued to appear until 1902.

Ricordi, Giulio (1840–1912). Son and successor of Tito. A friend of Boito and Faccio, he took an increasingly active part in the firm's affairs from 1868 onwards. Established cordial relations with Verdi and was responsible for mounting all his Italian premières from the revised *Forza del destino*. A powerful force in Italy's musical life, he was among the first to recognise Puccini's talent and to give him material help before he made his name. He was also a writer, painter and – under the pseudonym of Burgmein – a composer.

Ricordi, Tito (1811–88). Son of Giovanni, whom he succeeded as head of the firm. An intimate friend of Verdi, who addressed him with 'tu' but frequently complained of his laziness and inefficiency.

Rivas, Angel de Saavedra, Duque de (1791–1865). Spanish dramatist and patriot of Liberal sympathies. Author of *Don Alvaro o la fuerza del sin* on which *La forza del destino* is based.

Romani, Felice (1788–1865). Italian librettist, the most accomplished of his generation. Author of all but two of Bellini's librettos. Wrote *Il finto Stanislao* for Adalbert Gyrowetz, later set as *Un giorno di regno* by Verdi.

Ronconi, Giorgio (1810–90). Italian baritone. Created several leading roles for Donizetti as well as the title role in *Nabucco*. The prototype of the high dramatic baritone.

Roqueplan, Nestor (1804–70). French administrator. Managed Paris Opéra at the time of *Jérusalem*. Commissioned *Les vêpres siciliennes*, but forced to resign in 1854 after flight of Cruvelli.

Royer, Alphonse (1803–75). French librettist. Co-author with Gustave Vaez of *Jérusalem* and Donizetti's *La favorite*.

Salvini-Donatelli, Fanny (1815–91). Italian soprano. Created Violetta in *La traviata*, in which she sang well but her matronly figure carried little dramatic conviction.

Sasse, Marie-Constance (1838–1907). Belgian soprano. Star of the Paris Opéra during the 1860s; created Elisabeth in *Don Carlos*, Selika in Meyerbeer's *L'Africaine* and Elisabeth in the Paris première of *Tannhäuser*.

Scribe, Augustin Eugène (1791–1861). French dramatist and librettist, author of innumerable plays, vaudevilles, libretti and ballet scenarios including *Gustave III* on which *Un ballo in maschera* is based. With Charles Duveyrier he wrote *Le Duc d'Albe*, later transformed, with many modifications, into *Les vêpres siciliennes*.

Severi, Giovanni. Italian tenor. Created Prior of Milan in *I Lombardi*; later retired to Trieste as businessman. Verdi and Piave wrote the barcarola 'Fiorellin che sorgi appena' for the birth of his son.

Sole, Nicola (1827–59). Italian lawyer and poet, a member of Verdi's Neapolitan circle. Verdi set his 'La preghiera del poeta'; his death put an end to future plans for collaboration.

Solera, Temistocle (1815–78). Italian librettist and jack-of-all-trades. Resident poet at La Scala, *c*.1839–45. Author of *Nabucco, I Lombardi, Giovanna d'Arco* and *Attila,* which he failed to complete; re-fashioned *Oberto* from a previous libretto. Pursued an adventurous but mostly ill-fated career.

Somma, Antonio (1809–65). Italian lawyer and playwright. Wrote tragedies performed by the famous actress Ristori; librettist of *King Lear,* which Verdi commissioned but never set, and of *Un ballo in maschera.*

Stolz, Teresa (1834–1902). Austrian soprano. Sang Leonora in the revised *Forza del destino,* the title role in the Italian première of *Aida* and the soprano solo in the first performance of the *Requiem* as well as in many revivals. Together with Maria Waldmann (*q.v.*) appeared in many Verdi revivals. Rumoured to be Verdi's mistress; but it is difficult to prove that she was more than a close friend of husband and wife.

Strepponi, Giuseppina (1815–97). Italian soprano. Verdi's second wife. A star in the late 1830s, her voice rapidly declined; she created Abigaille in *Nabucco* in poor vocal condition. After retiring from the stage she taught singing in Paris, where Verdi first lived with her in 1847. They were married in 1859. Left much interesting and lively correspondence.

Tamagno, Francesco (1850–1905). Italian tenor. Created Gabriele in the revised *Simon Boccanegra* and title role of *Otello,* whose death scene he recorded twice.

Tamberlick, Enrico (1820–89). Italian 'tenor di forza' renowned for being the first to sing a C sharp 'di petto'. Created Alvaro in the original *La forza del destino.* The tenor solo in the 'Inno delle nazioni' was also written for him. Believed to have obtained Verdi's permission to introduce the high C into 'Di quella pira' (*Il trovatore*) 'provided it is a good one'.

Vaez, Gustave (1812–62). Belgian librettist and administrator. Co-author with Royer of *Jérusalem* and Donizetti's *La favorite.*

Varesi, Felice (1813–89). Italian dramatic baritone. Created title roles of *Macbeth* and *Rigoletto* and Germont in *La traviata.* Valued by Verdi for his intelligence and acting ability.

Vasselli, Antonio (*c*.1795–1870). Italian lawyer, brother-in-law of Donizetti. Helpful to Verdi in steering *Un ballo in maschera* through the Roman censorship.

Vigna, Cesare (1814–1912). Italian alienist. A pioneer in the field of mental illness. Venetian correspondent of the *Gazzetta Musicale di Milano* he was a strong supporter of Verdi and a close friend.

Waldmann, Maria (1844–1920). Austrian mezzo-soprano; sang Amneris in the Italian première of *Aida* and the mezzo-soprano solo in the first performance of the *Requiem* and in many revivals. Together with Teresa Stolz often appeared in *Don Carlos* and *Aida.* Retired early from the stage to marry into the aristocracy.

Appendix D
Select bibliography

List of abbreviations of principal periodicals

AcM	Acta Musicologica
AMw	Archiv für Musikwissenschaft
AnMc	Analecta Musicologica
JAMS	Journal of the American Musicological Society
ML	Music and Letters
MQ	Musical Quarterly
MR	Music Review
MT	Musical Times
NRMI	Nuova Rivista Musicale Italiana
NZM	Neue Zeitschrift für Musik
PRMA	Proceedings of the Royal Musical Association
RaM	Rassegna Musicale
RdM	Revue de Musicologie
ReM	Revue Musicale
RIM	Rivista Italiana di Musicologia
RMI	Rivista Musicale Italiana

MUSICAL STUDIES

A. Basevi: *Studio sulle opere di Giuseppe Verdi* (Florence, 1859)

G.B. Shaw: 'A Word More about Verdi', *Anglo-Saxon Review* (1901, March); repr. in *London Music in 1888–89* (London, 1937, 2/1950) 405

A. Soffredini: *Le opere di Verdi: studio critico analitico* (Milan, 1901)

G. Roncaglia: *L'ascensione creatrice di Giuseppe Verdi* (Florence, 1940) *Verdi: studi e memorie* (Rome, 1941)

G. Roncaglia: 'Il "tema-cardine" nell'opera di Giuseppe Verdi', *RMI*, xlvii (1943), 220

A. Della Corte: *Le sei più belle opere di Giuseppe Verdi: Rigoletto. Il trovatore, La traviata, Aida, Otello, Falstaff* (Milan, 1946; pubd separately, 1923–43)

M. Mila: 'Verdi e Hanslick', *RaM*, xxi (1951), 212

I. Pizzetti: 'Contrappunto ed armonia nell'opera di Verdi', *RaM*, xxi (1951), 189

U. Rolandi: *Il libretto per musica attraverso i tempi* (Rome, 1951), 126

R. Vlad: 'Anticipazioni nel linguaggio armonico verdiano', *RaM*, xxi (1951), 237

Verdi

F.I. Travis: *Verdi's Orchestration* (Zurich, 1956)

G. Roncaglia: *Galleria verdiana: studi e figure* (Milan, 1959)

L. Dallapiccola: 'Parole e musica nel melodramma', *Quaderni della Rassegna musicale*, ii (1965), 117; Eng. trans. as 'Words and Music in Italian XIX Century Opera', *Quaderni dell'Istituto italiano di cultura* (Dublin, 1964), no.3; repr. in *PNM*, v/1 (1966), 121. See also *The Verdi Companion*, 193–215

F. Lippmann: 'Verdi e Bellini', *I° congresso internazionale di studi verdiani: Venezia 1966*, 184; Ger. version in *Beiträge zur Geschichte der Oper*, ed. H. Becker (Regensburg, 1969), 77

J. Kovács: 'Zum Spätstil Verdis', *I° congresso internazionale di studi verdiani: Venezia 1966*, 132

P. P. Várnai: 'Contributo per uno studio della tipizzazione negativa nelle opera verdiane: personaggi e situazioni', *I° congresso internazionale di studi verdiani: Venezia 1966*, 268

L. K. Gerhartz: *Die Auseinandersetzungen des jungen Giuseppe Verdi mit dem literärischen Drama: ein Beitrag zur szenischen Strukturbestimmung der Oper*, Berliner Studien zur Musikwissenschaft, xv (Berlin, 1968)

S. Hughes: *Famous Verdi Operas* (London, 1968)

J. Kerman: 'Verdi's Use of Recurring Themes', *Studies in Music History: Essays for Oliver Strunk* (Princeton, 1968), 495

Colloquium Verdi-Wagner: Rom 1969 [*AnMc*, no. 11 (1972)]

C. Osborne: *The Complete Operas of Verdi* (London, 1969)

G. Baldini: *Abitare la battaglia: la storia di Giuseppe Verdi* (Milan, 1970); Eng. trans. by R. Parker as *The Story of Giuseppe Verdi* (Cambridge 1980)

P. Petrobelli: 'Osservazioni sul processo compositivo in Verdi', *AcM*, xliii (1971), 125 [incl. sketches]

W. Dean: 'Some Echoes of Donizetti in Verdi's Operas', *3° congresso internazionale di studi verdiani: Milano 1972*, 122

J. Budden: *The Operas of Verdi: from Oberto to Rigoletto* (London 1973); from *Il trovatore* to *La forza del destino* (1978); from *Don Carlos* to *Otello* (1981)

D. Lawton: *Tonality and Drama in Verdi's Early Operas* (diss., U. of California, Berkeley, 1973).

F. Lippmann: 'Der italienische Vers und der musikalische Rhythmus: zum Verhältnis von Vers und Musik in der italienischen Oper des 19. Jahrhunderts, mit einem Rückblick auf die 2. Hälfte des 18. Jahrhunderts', *AnMc*, no. 12 (1973), 253–369; no. 14 (1974), 324–410; no. 15 (1975). 298–333

M. Mila: *La giovinezza di Verdi* (Turin, 1974)

F. Lippmann: 'Verdi und Donizetti', *Opernstudien: Anna Amalie Abert zum 65. Geburtstag* (Tutzing, 1975), 153

V. Godefroy: *The Dramatic Genius of Verdi: Studies of Selected Operas*, i: 'Nabucco' to 'La traviata' (London, 1975); ii: 'I vespri siciliani' to 'Falstaff' (London, 1977)

F. Noske: *The Signifier and the Signified: Studies in the Operas of Mozart and Verdi* (The Hague, 1977)

W. Weaver and M. Chusid, eds.: *The Verdi Companion* (New York, 1979)

M. Mila: *L'arte di Verdi* (Turin, 1980)

D. Kimbell: *Verdi in the Age of Italian Romanticism* (Cambridge, 1981)

J. Nicolaisen: *Italian Opera in Transition, 1871–1893*, (Ann Arbor, Michigan, UMI Research Press, 1981 *Musicology*, 31)

P. Weiss: 'Verdi and the fusion of genres', *JAMS* xxxv/1 (1982) 138

G. De Van: *Verdi: Un Théâtre en Musique* (Paris, 1992)

M. Engelhardt: *Verdi und andere* (Parma, 1992)

BIOGRAPHY, LIFE AND WORKS

G. Demaldè: *Cenni biografici* (MS, archives of Monte di Pietà, Busseto, c1953); pubd in *Newsletter of the American Institute for Verdi Studies* (1976–7), nos. 1–3

M. Lessona: 'Parma: Giuseppe Verdi', *Volere è potere* (Milan, 1869), 287

A. Pougin: *Giuseppe Verdi: vita aneddotica* (Milan, 1881 [trans. and annotated by Folchetto (pseud. of J. Caponi) from biographical articles in *Le ménestrel*, 1878]; Fr. orig., incorporating Caponi's additions, 1886; Eng. trans., 1887)

G. Monaldi: *Verdi* (Turin, 1899, 4/1951)

F. Bonavia: *Verdi* (London 1930)

C. Gatti: *Verdi* (Milan, 1931, 2/1951; Eng. trans., much abbreviated, 1955, as *Verdi: the Man and his Music*)

F. Toye: *Giuseppe Verdi: his Life and Works* (London, 1931)

H. Gerigk: *Giuseppe Verdi* (Potsdam, 1932)

D. Hussey: *Verdi* (London, 1940, 5/1973)

G. Cenzato: *Itinerari verdiani* (Parma, 1949, 2/1955)

F. Walker: 'Vincenzo Gemito and his Bust of Verdi', *ML*, xxx (1949), 44

M. Mila: *Giuseppe Verdi* (Bari, 1958)

F. Abbiati: *Giuseppe Verdi* (Milan, 1959)

F. Walker: *The Man Verdi* (London, 1962); new ed. Chicago, 1982

G. Martin: *Verdi* (New York, 1963), rev. 2/1964)

M. J. Matz: 'The Verdi Family of Sant'Agata and Roncole: Legend and Truth', *I° congresso internazionale di studi verdiani: Venezia 1966*, 216

—: 'Verdi: the Roots of the Tree', *Verdi: Bollettino dell'Istituto di studi verdiani*, iii (1969–73), 333

W. Weaver: 'Verdi the Playgoer', *Musical Newsletter*, vi/1 (1976), 3

G. Marchesi: *Verdi, Merli e Cucù* (Busseto, 1979)

M. Conati: *Interviste e incontri con Verdi*, (Milan, 1980); Eng. trans. as *Interviews and Encounters with Verdi* (London, 1984)

G. Marchesi: *Giuseppe Verdi: l'uomo, il genio, l'artista*, (Milan, 1981)

A. Porter: *The New Grove Masters of Italian Opera* (London, 1983), 193.

J. Rosselli: 'Verdi e la storia della retribuzione del compositore italiano', *Studi verdiani*, ii (1983)

—: *The Opera Industry in Italy from Cimarosa to Verdi: The Role of the Impresario* (Cambridge, 1984)

Verdi

C. Osborne: *Verdi: a life in the theatre* (London, 1987)
G. Martin: *Aspects of Verdi* (New York, 1988)

LETTERS AND DOCUMENTS

I. Pizzi: *Ricordi verdiani inediti* (Turin, 1901)
A. Pascolato: *Re Lear e Ballo in maschera: lettere di Giuseppe Verdi ad Antonio Somma* (Città di Castello, 1902)
G. Cesari and A. Luzio: *I copialettere di Giuseppe Verdi* (Milan, 1913/*R*1973; Eng. trans., abridged, 1971, as *Letters of Giuseppe Verdi*, ed C. Osborne)
J. G. Prod'homme: 'Unpublished Letters from Verdi to Camille du Locle', *MQ*, vii (1921), 73–103; Fr. orig., *ReM*, x (1928–9), no. 5, p.97; no. 7. p.25
—: 'Verdi's Letters to Léon Escudier', *ML*, iv (1923), 62, 184, 375; Fr. trans., *Bulletin de la société Union musicologique*, v (1925), 7; It. orig., *RMI*, xxxv (1928), 1, 171, 519–52
F. Werfel and P. Stefan: *Das Bildnis Giuseppe Verdis* (Vienna, 1926; Eng. trans., enlarged, 1942, as *Verdi: the Man in his Letters*)
A. Luzio: 'Il carteggio di Giuseppe Verdi con la contessa Maffei, *Profili biografici e bozzetti storici*, ii (Milan, 1927), 505–62
A. Alberti: *Verdi intimo: carteggio di Giuseppe Verdi con il conte Opprandino Arrivabene (1861–1886)* (Verona, 1931)
L. A. Garibaldi: *Giuseppe Verdi nelle lettere di Emanuele Muzio ad Antonio Barezzi* (Milan, 1931)
R. De Rensis: *Franco Faccio e Verdi, carteggio e documenti inediti* (Milan, 1934)
A. Luzio: *Carteggi verdiani, i—ii (Rome, 1935), iii—iv (Rome, 1947)*
C. Bongiovanni: *Dal carteggio inedito Verdi-Vigna* (Rome, 1941)
A. Oberdorfer: *Giuseppe Verdi: autobiografia dalle lettere* (Verona, 1941 [under pseud. C. Graziani and censored]; complete Milan 2/1951); new ed. by M. Conati (Milan, 1981)
F. Walker: 'Verdi and Francesco Florimo: some Unpublished Letters', *ML*, xxvi (1945), 201
—: 'Four Unpublished Verdi Letters', *ML*, xxix (1948), 44
—: 'Cinque lettere verdiane', *RaM*, xxi (1951), 256
F. Schlitzer: 'Inediti verdiani nella collezione dell'Accademia musicale chigiana', *Giuseppe Verdi*, Chigiana, viii (1951), 30: pubd separately, enlarged as *Inediti verdiani nell'archivio dell'Accademia chigiana* (Siena, 1953)
F. Walker: 'Verdi and Vienna: with Some Unpublished Letters', *MT*, xcii (1951), 403, 451
—: 'Verdian Forgeries', *MR*, xix (1958), 273: xx (1959), 28: It. trans., *RaM*, xxx (1960), 338
T. Jauner: *Fünf Jahre Wiener Operntheater, 1875–1880: Franz Jauner und seine Zeit* (Vienna, 1963)
E. Zanetti: 'La corrispondenza di Verdi conservata a S Cecilia', *Verdi: Bollettino dell'Istituto di studi verdiani*, iii (1969–73), 1131

U. Günther: 'Documents inconnus concernant les relations de Verdi avec l'Opéra de Paris', *3°congresso internazionale di studi verdiani: Milano 1972*, 564

M. Conati: 'Saggio di critiche e cronache verdiane dalla *Allgemeine musikalische Zeitung* di Lipsia (1840–48). *Il melodramma italiano dell'ottocento: studi e ricerche per Massimo Mila* (Turin, 1977), 13

W. Weaver: *Verdi: a Documentary Study* (London, 1977)

M. Medici & M. Conati: *Carteggio Verdi/Boito*, 2 vols (Parma 1978)

E. Baker: 'Lettere di Giuseppe Verdi a Francesco Maria Piave', *Studi verdiani* iv (1986–7), 136

C.M. Mossa: 'Le lettere di Emanuele Muzio alla Casa Ricordi', *Studi verdiani*, iv (1986–7), 167

P. Petrobelli, M. Di Gregorio Casati and C.M. Mossa (eds): *Carteggio Verdi-Ricordi 1880–1881* (Parma, 1988)

L. Sartoris: *Nuovi inediti verdiani* (Genoa, 1990)

CATALOGUES

D. Lawton and D. Rosen: 'Verdi's Non-definitive Revisions: the Early Operas', *3° congresso internazionale di studi verdiani: Milano 1972*, 189

C. Hopkinson: *A Bibliography of the Works of Giuseppe Verdi, 1813–1901*, i (New York, 1973) [vocal and inst works excluding operas]; ii (New York, 1978) [operas]

M. Chusid: *A Catalog of Verdi's Operas* (Hackensack, 1974)

M. Chusid, L. Jensen, D. Day: *The Verdi Archive at New York University: Part II (A List of Verdi's Music, Librettos, Production Materials, Nineteenth-Century Italian Periodicals, and other Research Materials)*, in *Verdi Newsletter*, 9–10, 1981–2

ICONOGRAPHICAL

G. Bocca: 'Verdi e la caricatura', *RMI*, viii (1901), 326

C. Gatti: *Verdi nelle immagini* (Milan, 1941) [incl. sketches, pp. 64f, 184, 186f]

M. T. Muraro: 'Le scenografie delle cinque "prime assolute" di Verdi alla Fenice di Venezia', *I° congresso di studi verdiani: Venezia 1966*, 328

W. Weaver: *Verdi: a documentary study* (London, 1977)

BIBLIOGRAPHICAL

C. Hopkinson: 'Bibliographical Problems concerned with Verdi and his Publishers', *I° congresso internazionale di studi verdiani: Venezia 1966*, 431

D. Lawton: 'Per una bibliografia ragionata verdiana', *I° congresso internazionale di studi verdiani: Venezia 1966*, 437

Verdi

M. Pavarani: 'Per una bibliografia e documentazione verdiana', *I° congresso internazionale di studi verdiani: Venezia 1966*, 446

G. Tintori: 'Bibliografia verdiana in Russia', *I° congresso internazionale di studi verdiani: Venezia 1966*, 458

M. Mila: *La giovinezza di Verdi* (Turin, 1974), 501ff

Newsletter of the American Institute for Verdi Studies (1976–) [incl. detailed lists of publications, 1975–]

E. Surian: 'Lo stato attuale degli studi verdiani: appunti e bibliografia ragionata', *RIM*, xii (1977), 305

A. Porter: 'A select bibliography', *The Verdi Companion* (London, 1979), 239

M. Conati: 'Bibliografia verdiana', *Studi verdiani* i (1982), 129
           'Bibliografia verdiana' (1980–2), *Studi verdiani*, ii (1983), 150

LOCATIVE STUDIES

U. Dauth, *Verdis Opern im Spiegel der Wiener Presse von 1843 bis 1859. Ein Beitrag zur Rezeptionsgeschichte* (Munich, 1981)

G. M. Ciampelli: *Le opere verdiane al Teatro alla Scala (1839–1929)* (Milan, 1929)

Verdi e Roma (Rome, 1951)

G. Steffani: *Verdi e Trieste* (Trieste, 1951)

Verdi e Firenze (Florence, 1951)

M. Conati: *La bottega della musica: Verdi e La Fenice* (Milan, 1983)

PUBLICATIONS OF THE ISTITUTO DI STUDI VERDIANI, PARMA

Verdi: Bollettino dell'Istituto di studi verdiani, I/1–3 (1960) [mainly on *Un ballo in maschera*]

Verdi: Bollettino dell'Istituto di studi verdiani, II/4–6 (1961–6) [mainly on *La forza del destino*]

Verdi: Bollettino dell'Istituto di studi verdiani, III/7–9 (1969–82) [mainly on *Rigoletto*]

Verdi: Bollettino dell'Istituto di studi verdiani, X *Ernani Ieri e Oggi* (1987)

[*Atti del*] 1° *congresso internazionale di studi verdiani: Venezia 1966* (1969)

[*Atti del*] 2° *congresso internazionale di studi verdiani: Verona 1969* (1971)

[*Atti del*] 3° *congresso internazionale di studi verdiani: Milano 1972* (1974)

Quaderni dell'Istituto di studi verdiani, i *Il Corsaro* (1963), ii: *Gerusalemme* (1963), iii: *Stiffelio* (1968), iv: *Genesi dell'Aida* (1971) v: *Messa per Rossini. La storia, il testo, la musica*, M. Girardi and P. Petrobelli (eds) (1988)

Studi verdiani i (1982), ii (1983), iii (1985), iv (1986–7), v (1988–91), vi (1990) [Miscellaneous articles]

SPECIAL PERIODICAL NUMBERS

(*article titles listed in M. Mila: *La giovinezza di Verdi* (Turin, 1974), 514f)
* *Gazzetta musicale di Milano*, lvi (1901, March)
Natura ed arte (1901)
* *RMI*, viii/2 (1901)
Die Musik, xiii (1913–14) [incl. articles by A. Weissmann, E. Istel, R. Specht]
* *Nuova antologia*, clxvii (16 Oct 1913)
* *Aurea Parma*, xxv (1941), Jan–Feb
Illustrazione italiana (26 Jan 1941)
* *La regione Emilia-Romagna* (1950), nos. 9–12
* *ZfM*, Jg. 112 (1951), Jan
* *Das Musikleben*, iv (1951), Feb
* *Il diapason* (1951), Feb
* *Melos*, xviii (1951), Feb
* *Opera*, ii/2 (1951)
* *La fièra letteraria* (22 April 1951)
* *RaM*, xxi (1951), July
Verdiana: bollettino di notizie (1950–51) [12 issues]
HMYB, vii (1952) 494
High Fidelity, xiii (1963). Oct [incl. articles by A. Moravia, W. Weaver, and
  on early New York productions]
19th Century Music, ii/2 (1978–9)

INDIVIDUAL WORKS

OBERTO

C. Sartori: 'Rocester, la prima opera di Verdi', *RMI*, xliii (1939), 97
M. Conati: 'L'Oberto, conte di San Bonifacio in due recensioni straniere
  poco note e in una lettera inedita di Verdi', *1° congresso internazionale di
  studi verdiani: Venezia 1966*, 67
D. R. B. Kimbell: 'Poi ... diventò l'Oberto', *ML*, lii (1971), 1
P.D. Giovanelli: 'La storia e la favola dell'Oberto', *Studi verdiani*, ii (1983),
  29

UN GIORNO DI REGNO

R. Parker: 'Un giorno di regno; from Romani's libretto to Verdi's opera',
  Studi verdiani, ii (1983), 38
M. Engelhardt, 'Nuovi dati sulla nascita dell'opera giovanile di Verdi *Un
  giorno di regno*', *Studi verdiani*, iv (1986–7), 11

NABUCCO

P. Petrobelli: 'Nabucco', *Conference 1966–67: Associazione Amici della
  Scala*, 17
D. Lawton: 'Analytical Observations on the *Nabucco* Revisions', *3° con-
  gresso internazionale di studi verdiani: Milano 1972*, 208

I Lombardi alla prima crociata (see Jérusalem)

ERNANI

L. K. Gerhartz: *Die Auseinandersetzungen des jungen Giuseppe Verdi mit dem literärischen Drama: ein Beitrag zur szenischen Strukturbestimmung der Oper*, Berliner Studien zur Musikwissenschaft, xv (Berlin, 1968), 30–82, 453ff

J. Kerman: 'Notes on an Early Verdi Opera', *Soundings*, iii (1973), 56

R. Parker: 'Levels of motivic definition in Verdi's *Ernani*', *19th Century Music*, vi/2 (1982), 141

Verdi: Bollettino dell'Istituto di studi verdiani, X *Ernani Ieri e Oggi* (1987)

I DUE FOSCARI

C. Simone: 'Lettere al tenore Mario de Candia sulla cabaletta de *I due Foscari*', *Nuova antologia*, lxix (1934), 327

G. Biddlecombe: 'The revision of "No, non morrai, che i perfidi"; Verdi's compositional process in *I due Foscari*', *Studi verdiani* (1983), ii, 59

ALZIRA

M. Mila: 'Lettura dell'*Alzira*', *RIM*, i (1966), 246

ATTILA

M. Noiray and R. Parker: 'La composition d'*Attila*: étude de quelques variantes', *RdM*, lxii (1976), 104

M. Mila: 'Lettura dell' *Attila*', *NRMI*, ii (1983), 247

MACBETH

G. C. Varesi: 'L'interpretazione del *Macbeth*', *Nuova antologia*, cclxxxi (1932), 433

L. K. Gerhartz: *Die Auseinandersetzungen des jungen Giuseppe Verdi mit dem literärischen Drama: ein Beitrag zur szenischen Strukturbestimmung der Oper*, Berliner Studien zur Musikwissenschaft, xv (Berlin, 1968), 82–193, 465ff

W. Osthoff: 'Die beiden Fassungen von Verdis *Macbeth*', *AMw*, xxix (1972), 17

F. Degrada: 'Lettura del *Macbeth* di Verdi', *Studi musicali*, vi (1977), 207

D. Goldin: 'Il *Macbeth* verdiano: genesi e linguaggio di un libretto', *AnMc*, no. 19 (1979), 336

M. Conati: 'Aspetti della messinscena del *Macbeth* di Verdi', *NRMI*, xv/ (1981), 374

see also 'Shakespeare operas'

Verdi's 'Macbeth': a sourcebook, ed. D. Rosen and A. Porter (London, 1984)

N. John (ed.): *Macbeth*, English National Opera Guide, 41 (London, 199)

Select bibliography

JÉRUSALEM

'Gerusalemme', *Quaderni dell'Istituto di studi verdiani*, ii (1963)

D. Kimbell: 'Verdi's first rifacimento: *I Lombardi* and *Jerusalem*', *ML*, lx/1 (1969), 1

IL CORSARO

'Il corsaro', *Quaderni dell'Istituto di studi verdiani*, i (1963)

M. Mila: 'Lettura del *Corsaro*', *NRMI*, i/1971, 40

D. Lawton 'The Corsair reaches port', *Opera News*, xlvi/20, 1982, 16

LUISA MILLER

L. K. Gerhartz: *Die Auseinandersetzungen des jungen Giuseppe Verdi mit dem literärischen Drama: ein Beitrag zur szenischen Strukturbestimmung der Oper*, Berliner Studien zur Musikwissenschaft, xv (Berlin, 1968), 193–270, 475ff

STIFFELIO

V. Levi: *'Stiffelio* e il suo rifacimento (*Aroldo*)', *1° congresso internazionale di studi verdiani: Venezia 1966*, 172

'Stiffelio', *Quaderni dell'Istituto di studi verdiani*, iii (1968)

G. Morelli (ed.): *Tornando a 'Stiffelio'. Popolarità, rifacimento, messinscena, effettismo et altre 'cure' nella drammaturgia del Verdi romantico* (Florence, 1987)

RIGOLETTO

C. Gatti: Introduction to *L'abbozzo del Rigoletto di Giuseppe Verdi* (Milan, 1941) [sketches]

G. Roncaglia: 'L'abbozzo del *Rigoletto* di Verdi', *RMI*, xlviii (1946), 112; repr. in G. Roncaglia: *Galleria verdiana* (Milan, 1959)

P. Petrobelli: 'Verdi e il *Don Giovanni*: osservazioni sulla scena iniziale del *Rigoletto*', *1° congresso internazionale di studi verdiani: Venezia 1966*, 232

Verdi: Bollettino dell'Istituto di studi verdiani, iii (1969–82)

N. John (ed.): *Rigoletto*, English National Opera Guide, 15 (London, 1982)

IL TROVATORE

P. Petrobelli: 'Per un'esegesi della struttura drammatica del *Trovatore*', *3° congresso internazionale di studi verdiani: Milano 1972*, 387

D. Rosen: *'Le trouvère*: Comparing Verdi's French Version with his Original', *Opera News*, xli/22 (1977), 16

W. Drabkin: 'Characters, key relations and tonal structure in *Il trovatore*', *Music Analysis*, i/2 (1982), 143

R. Parker: 'The dramatic structure of *Il trovatore*', *Musical Analysis*, i/2 (1982), 155

J. Black: 'Salvadore Cammarano's programma for *Il trovatore* and the problems of the finale', *Studi verdiani*, ii (1983), 78

N. John (ed.): *Il trovatore*, English National Opera Guide, 20 (London, 1983)

LA TRAVIATA

M. Chusid: 'Drama and the Key of F major in *La traviata*', *3° congresso internazionale di studi verdiani: Milano 1972*, 89

J. Budden: 'The Two *Traviatas*', *PRMA*, xcix (1972–3), 43

D. Rosen: 'Virtue restored', *Opera News*, xlii/9 (1977–8), 36

N. John (ed.): *La Traviata*, English National Opera Guide, (London, 1981)

F. Della Seta: 'Il tempo della festa; su due scene della *Traviata* e su altri luoghi verdiani', *Studi verdiani*, ii (1983), 108

J.A. Hepokoski: 'Genre and content in mid-century Verdi: "Addio, del passato" (*La traviata*, Act III)', *Cambridge Opera Journal*, I (1989), 249

LES VÊPRES SICILIENNES

P. Bonnefon: 'Les metamorphoses d'un opéra', *Revue des deux mondes*, xli (1917), 877

J. Budden: 'Varianti nei Vespri siciliani', *NRMI*, vi (1972), 155

M. Mila, R. Celletti and G. Gualerzi: *Opera: collana di guide musicali* 1st ser., 1 (Turin 1973) essays with Fr./It. libretto

A. Porter: '*Les vêpres siciliennes*; New Letters from Verdi to Scribe', *19th Century Music*, ii (1978–9), 95

F. Noske: 'Melodia e struttura in *Les vêpres siciliennes* di Verdi', *Ricerche musicali*, iv (1980), 3

J. Budden: 'Verdi and Meyerbeer in relation to *Les vêpres siciliennes*' *Studi verdiani*, i (1982), 11

M. Conati: 'Ballabili nei *Vespri*; con alcune osservazioni su Verdi e la musica popolare', *Studi verdiani*, i (1982), 21

SIMON BOCCANEGRA

F. Walker: 'Verdi, Giuseppe Montanelli and the libretto of *Simon Boccanegra*', *Verdi: Bollettino dell' Istituto di studi verdiani*, i (1960), 1373

W. Osthoff: 'Die beiden *Boccanegra*-Fassungen und der Beginn von Verdis Spätwerk, *AnMc*, no. 1 (1963), 70

J. Kerman: 'Lyric Form and Flexibility in *Simon Boccanegra*', *Studi verdiani*, i (1982), 47

P.P. Varnai: 'Paolo Albiani. Il cammino di un personaggio', *Studi verdiani*, i (1982), 63

E. T. Cone: 'On the road to *Otello*. Tonality and Structure in *Simon Boccanegra*', *Studi verdiani*, i (1982), 72

N. John (ed.): *Simon Boccanegra*, English National Opera Guide, 32 (London, 1985)

H. Busch: *Verdi's 'Otello' and 'Simon Boccanegra' (Revised Version) in Letters and Documents* (Oxford, 1988)

AROLDO (see STIFFELIO)

UN BALLO IN MASCHERA

A. Pascolato: *Re Lear e Ballo in maschera: lettere di Giuseppe Verdi ad Antonio Somma* (Città di Castello, 1902)

Verdi: Bollettino dell'Istituto di studi verdiani i (1960–1)

G. Salvetti and R. Celletti: *Opera: collana di guide musicali* 1st ser. ii (Turin, 1973) essays with lib.

S. Levarie: 'Key relationships in Verdi's *Un ballo in maschera*', *19th century music,* ii/2 (1978), 142

N. John (ed.): *Un ballo in maschera*, English National Opera Guide, 40 (London, 1990)

LA FORZA DEL DESTINO

Verdi: Bollettino dell'Istituto di studi verdiani, ii (1961–5)

E. Rescigno: *La Forza del destino di Verdi* (Milan 1981)

N. John (ed.): *The Force of Destiny*, English National Opera Guide, 25 (London, 1983)

W.C. Holmes: 'The earliest revisions of La forza del destino', *Studi verdiani,* vi (1990)

DON CARLOS

2° congresso internazionale di studi verdiani: Verona 1969

A. Porter: 'A Sketch for *Don Carlos*', *MT,* cxi (1970), 882

—: 'The Making of *Don Carlos*', *PRMA*, xcviii (1971–2), 73

U. Günther: 'La genèse de *Don Carlos*', *RdM,* lviii (1972), 16; lx (1974), 87

A. Porter: 'A Note on Princess Eboli', *MT,* cxiii (1972), 750

U. Günther and G. Carrara Verdi: 'Der Briefwechsel Verdi-Nuitter-Du Locle zur Revision des *Don Carlos*', *AnMc,* no. 14 (1974), 1; no. 15 (1975), 334

A. Porter: 'Preamble to a New *Don Carlos*', *Opera,* xxv (1974), 665

M. Clémeur: 'Eine neuentdeckte Quelle für das Libretto von Verdi's *Don Carlos*', *Melos/NZM,* iii (1977), 496

U. Günther: 'L'edizione integrale del *Don Carlos*'. Preface to complete edition of the opera (Milan, 1977)

—:'La genese du *Don Carlos* de Verdi: nouveaux documents', *RdM,* lxxii (1986), 104

N. John (ed.): *Don Carlos*, English National Opera Guide, 46 (London, 1992)

AIDA

A. Luzio: 'Come fu composta l'Aida', *Carteggi verdiani,* iv (Rome, 1947), 5

E. Lendvai: 'Verdis Formgeheimnisse', *1° congresso internazionale di studi verdiani: Venezia 1966,* 157

'Genesi di Aida', *Quaderni dell'Istituto di studi verdiani,* iv (1971)

U. Günther: 'Zur Entstehung von Verdis *Aida*', *Studi musicali,* ii (1973), 15–71

P. Gossett: 'Verdi, Ghislanzoni and *Aida:* the Uses of Convention', *Critical Inquiry,* i (1974), 291

J. Humbert: 'A propos de l'égyptomanie dans l'oeuvre de Verdi: attribution à

Auguste Mariette d'un scénario anonyme de l'opéra *Aïda*', *RdM*, lxii (1976), 229

L. Alberti: 'I progressi attuali [1872] del dramma musicale: note sulla *Disposizione scenica per l'opera "Aida"* ', *Il melodramma italiano dell'ottocento: studi e ricerche per Massimo Mila* (Turin, 1977) 125

H. Busch: *Verdi's Aida: the History of an Opera in Letters and Documents* (Minneapolis, 1978)

P. Petrobelli: 'Music in the theatre (a propos of *Aida*, act III)', *Themes in Drama, 3. Drama, Dance and Music* (Cambridge, 1980), 129

N. John (ed.): *Aida*, English National Opera Guide, 2 (London, 1980)

M. Conati, 'Aspetti di melodrammaturgia verdiana. A proposito di una sconosciuta versione del finale del duetto Aida–Amneris', *Studi verdiani*, iii (1985), 45

OTELLO

F. Busoni: 'Verdi's *Otello*: eine kritische Studie', *NZM*, liv (1887), 125

J. Kerman: 'Verdi's *Otello*, or Shakespeare explained' in J. Kerman: *Opera as Drama* (New York, 1956), 129

W. Dean: 'Verdi's *Otello*: A Shakespearean masterpiece', *Shakespeare Survey*, xxi (1968), 87

D. Lawton: 'On the 'bacio' theme in *Otello*', *19th Century Music*, i (1977–8), 211

J. Budden: 'Time stands still in *Otello*', *Opera*, xxxii/9 (1981), 888

N. John (ed.): *Otello*, English National Opera Guide, 7 (London, 1981)

J.A. Hepokoski, *Giuseppe Verdi: 'Otello'* (Cambridge, 1987)

H. Busch, *Verdi's 'Otello' and 'Simon Boccanegra' (Revised Version) in Letters and Documents* (Oxford, 1988)

FALSTAFF

H. Gal: 'A deleted episode in Verdi's *Falstaff*', *MR*, ii (1941), 266

E. T. Cone: 'The stature of *Falstaff*: Technique and content in Verdi's last opera', *Center*, i (1954), 17

G. Barblan: *Un prezioso spartito di Falstaff* (Milan, 1957)

D. Sabbeth: 'Dramatic and musical organisation in *Falstaff*', *3° congresso internazionale di studi verdiani: Milan, 1972*, 415

W. Osthoff: 'Il sonetto nel *Falstaff* di Verdi', *Il melodramma italiano dell'ottocento: studi e ricerche per Massimo Mila* (Turin, 1977), 157

D. Linthicum: 'Verdi's *Falstaff* and classical sonata form', *MR*, xxxviii/1 (1978), 39

J. Hepokoski: 'Verdi, Giuseppina Pasqua and the composition of *Falstaff*', *19th Century Music*, iii/3 (1980), 239

N. John (ed.): *Falstaff*, English National Opera Guide, 10 (London, 1982)

J. Hepokoski: *Giuseppe Verdi: Falstaff* (Cambridge, 1983)

IL RE LEAR

A. Pascolato: *Rè Lear e Ballo in maschera: lettere di Giuseppe Verdi ad Antonio Somma* (Città di Castello, 1902)

M. Medici: 'Lettere su Re Lear', *Verdi: Bollettino dell'Istituto di studi verdiani*, i (1960)

L.K. Gerhartz: 'Il *Re Lear* di Antonio Somma ed il modello melodrammatico dell'opera verdiana: principi per una definizione del libretto verdiano', *1° congresso internazionale di studi verdiani: Venezia* 1966, 110

—: *Die Auseinandersetzungen des jungen Giuseppe Verdi mit dem literarischen Drama: ein Beitrag zur szenischen Strukturbestimmung der Oper*, Berliner Studien zur Musikwissenschaft, xv (Berlin, 1968), 277ff, 497ff

G. Martin: 'Verdi, *King Lear* and Maria Piccolomini', *Columbia Library Columns*, xxi (1971), 12

see also 'Shakespeare operas'

SHAKESPEARE OPERAS

E. T. Cone: 'Verdis letzte Opern: di Spielzeuge eines alten Mannes: die Spätwerk Verdis im Lichte der modernen Kritik', *Perspektiven*, vi (1953), 127; Eng. orig., 'The Old Man's Toys', *Perspectives USA*, vi (1954), 114

W. Dean: 'Shakespeare and Opera', *Shakespeare in Music*, ed. P. Hartnoll (London, 1964), 89

—: 'Shakespeare in the Opera House', *Shakespeare Survey*, xviii (1965), 75

see also 'Macbeth', 'Otello', 'Falstaff', 'Il re Lear'

REQUIEM

I. Pizzetti: 'La religiosità di Verdi: introduzione alla Messa da Requiem', *Nuova antologia*, i (1941)

D. Rosen: 'Verdi's "Liber scriptus" Rewritten', *MQ*, lv (1969), 151

—: 'La *Messa* a Rossini e il *Requiem* per Manzoni', *RIM*, iv (1969), 127; v (1970), 216

—: *The Genesis of Verdi's Requiem* (diss., U. of California, Berkeley, 1976)

QUATTRO PEZZI SACRI ETC

H. Scherchen: 'I quattro pezzi sacri', *Il diapason* (1951), Feb

F. Walker: 'Verdi's *Four Sacred Pieces*', *Ricordiana*, vi/2 (1961), 1

D. Stivender: 'The Composer of *Gesù morì*' Newsletter of the American Institute for Verdi Studies (1976), no. 2, p. 6

M. Conati: 'Le *Ave Maria sulla scala enigmatica* di Verdi dalla prima alla seconda stesura (1889–1897)', *RIM*, xiii (1978), 280

DISPOSIZIONI SCENICHE

Contemporary production books. (Photocopies exist at the Istituto Nazionale di Studi Verdiani, Parma.)

Les Vêpres siciliennes, opéra à cinq actes, paroles de MM. E. Scribe et Ch. Duveyrier, musique de G. Verdi, représenté pour la première fois à Paris sur le Théâtre Impérial de l'Opéra le 13 juin 1855 (collection de mises-en-scène rédigés et publiés par M. L. Palianti) (Paris 1855)

Disposizione scenica per l'opera *Giovanna de Guzman* del maestro cavaliere Giuseppe Verdi ufficiale della Legion d'Onore compilata e regolata sulla mise-en-scène nel Teatro Imperiale dell'Opera di Parigi (Milan ?1855)

Disposizione scenica per l'opera *Un Ballo in Maschera* di G. Verdi sulla messa in scena del Teatro Apollo in Roma il carnevale del 1859, del direttore di scena del medesimo, Giuseppe Cencetti (Milan, 1859)

La Forza del Destino, opera del maestro Giuseppe Verdi, libretto di Francesco Maria Piave, ordinazioni e disposizione scenica (Milan ?1863)

Disposizione scenica per l'opera *Don Carlo* di Giuseppe Verdi compilata e regolata secondo la messa in scena del Teatro Imperiale dell'Opera di Parigi (1st ed. Milan 1867, 3rd ed. 1884)

Disposizione scenica per l'opera *Aida* versi di Antonio Ghislanzoni, musica di Giuseppe Verdi, compilata e regolata secondo la messa in scena del Teatro alla Scala da Giulio Ricordi (Milan 1872)

Disposizione scenica per l'opera *Simon Boccanegra* di Giuseppe Verdi compilata e regolata secondo la messa del Teatro alla Scala da Giulio Ricordi (Milan 1881)

Disposizione scenica per l'opera *Otello*, dramma lirico in quattro atti, versi di Arrigo Boito, musica di Giuseppe Verdi; compilata e regolata secondo la messa in scena del Teatro alla Scala da Giulio Ricordi (Milan 1887)

NOTE

A critical edition of Verdi's works is in process of publication by the Casa Ricordi in conjunction with the University of Chicago Press. Already in print:
Rigoletto (2 vols) ed. M. Chusid (1983)
Ernani (2 vols) ed. C. Gallico (1984)
Nabucco (2 vols) ed. R. Parker (1988)
Messa da Requiem (2 vols) ed. D. Rosen (1990)
Luisa Miller (2 vols) ed. Jeffrey Kallberg (1991)

For a comprehensive bibliography the reader is referred to the *New Grove Dictionary of Opera*, ed. S. Sadie (London, 1992).

Appendix E
Glossary of nineteenth-century operatic terms

ACCENTO	(1) Manner of simultaneous articulation of words and notes. (2) The final accent in a line of verse: *piano*, if it falls on the last syllable but one; *sdrucciolo* if on the last but two, so adding an extra syllable to the metre (see VERSO); *tronco* if on the last, so robbing the metre of a syllable.
APPALTATORE	A theatrical agent, usually an impresario as well.
ARIA	A large-scale solo usually in two contrasted movements and preceded by a scena (*q.v.*) (See also CANTABILE, CABALETTA, CAVATINA, RONDÒ-FINALE); *con pertichini* with interventions from one or more singers, which give it the character, though not the form, of a duet or ensemble; *di baule*, (lit. 'suitcase aria'), one suitable to a stock situation, which principal singers carried with them to interpolate into any opera in place of what the composer had written; *di sortita* (see CAVATINA).
ARIOSO	A lyrical passage with the character of an aria but in free form.
BALLABILE	Usual term for a sung dance.
CABALETTA	The concluding, usually fast movement of an aria or duet (see also STRETTA). From 1820–80 it connotes a form involving the repetition of a melodic period with ritornello (*q.v.*) and noisy, applause-provoking coda.
CADENZA	A passage of free vocalisation preceding the singer's final cadence in a cantabile.
CANTABILE	The first movement of an aria or the second of a three-movement duet; slow and expressive, usually ending with a cadenza.
CANTO FIORITO	Decorated vocal music of the type associated with the age of Rossini.
CARNEVALE-QUARESIMA	The main operatic season of the year running from 26 December until Easter.
CARTELLO	The playbill for a whole season. *Teatro di cartello*: leading opera house.
CAVATINA	Aria marking the singer's first appearance.
COMPARSA	Walking-on part.
COMPRIMARIO	Sub-principal singer, who qualifies for a 'romanza' (*q.v.*)

	or an important part in an ensemble, but never for a full aria in two movements.
CONVENIENZE	Rules of etiquette governing singers' rank (see PRIMO, COMPRIMARIO, SECONDO).
COUPLETS (Fr.)	A song consisting of two parallel strophes set to the same melody, of which the last lines, identical in each case form a refrain, sometimes echoed by chorus (e.g. 'Di tu se fedele' from *Un ballo in maschera*). Often minor-major in key structure.
DECASILLABO	see VERSO
ENDECASILLABO	see VERSO
FALSO CANONE	A slow ensemble in the form of a round proceeding as far as the entry of the last voice.
FIORITURA	Florid vocal decoration.
FINALE	Final ensemble of an act usually consisting of two formal, contrasted movements during which the action is frozen, alternating with two freer movements during which it is carried forward (see TEMPO D'ATTACCO, PEZZO CONCERTATO, TEMPO DI MEZZO, STRETTA).
INTRODUZIONE	A complex of chorus, scena material and one or more cavatine occurring at the beginning of an opera after the prelude or overture.
MAESTRO CONCERTATORE	A 'coach' or 'repetiteur' responsible not only for teaching the singers their notes but also for rehearsing the whole opera at the keyboard; hence the alternative title MAESTRO AL CEMBALO).
MELISMA	A group of notes sung to a single syllable.
OPERA DI OBBLIGO	Opera commissioned as one of the novelties of the season.
OPERA DI RIPIEGO	An opera held in reserve to be mounted when the scheduled novelty is delayed.
OTTONARIO	see VERSO
PARLANTE	An orchestral theme with which the voices engage intermittently either on the melodic line (*parlante melodico*) or on harmony notes (*parlante armonico*) or alternatively on both (*parlante misto*).
PEZZO CONCERTATO	A large-scale ensemble with elaborate part-writing forming the cantabile of a finale and often the musical pinnacle of the opera; not always balanced by a *stretta*. (see also FINALE).
PERTICHINO	See ARIA
PIANO	See ACCENTO
PREGHIERA	Prayer (see ROMANZA)
PRIMO (A)	Term denoting principal singer (e.g. 'prima donna, primo tenore').
PUNTATURA	See page 296

QUINARIO	See VERSO
RECITATIVO	The declamatory or conversational part of an opera where the vocal line follows the free rhythm and accentuation of ordinary speech.
RITORNELLO	Conventional term for a short repeated instrumental passage within a formal movement.
ROMANZA	A short, slow aria in one movement, often minor-major in key-structure; sometimes called 'Preghiera' where the context is appropriate.
RONDÒ-FINALE	A grand aria usually with choral interventions and pertichini occurring at the end of an act.
ROSALIA	The identical repetition of a melodic idea a tone higher, keeping the exact intervals of the notes. (Derived from an old song 'Rosalia, mia cara'.)
SCENA	(1) A 'scene', marked off by the entrance and exit of one or more characters but including sometimes a preparatory chorus. (2) Any part of an act during which the scene remains unchanged. (3) A complex of recitative, arioso, orchestral figuration and parlante preparatory to a formal number (as in 'scena ed aria', 'scena e duetto').
SCIOLTI	See VERSO
SDRUCCIOLO	See ACCENTO
SECONDO (A)	'Second'. Term denoting the lowest category of solo singer, confined to recitative and a harmonic part in a large ensemble (e.g. 'seconda donna, secondo tenore etc.')
SENARIO	See VERSO
SETTENARIO	See VERSO
SINFONIA	Overture
STRETTA	Fast, concluding movement of an ensemble, especially a finale, corresponding to the cabaletta of an aria or duet (often the terms are used interchangeably).
TEMPO D'ATTACCO	Fast first movement of a three-movement duet or ensemble.
TEMPO DI MEZZO	Free, transitional movement occurring between the cantabile and cabaletta of a duet or ensemble or the pezzo concertato and stretta of a finale.
TRONCO	See ACCENTO
VERSO	A line of verse, classified according to its metre e.g. *Verso decasillabo*: 10-syllable verse in anapaestic metre; *endecasillabo*, 11-syllable verse usually in iambic metre; *ottonario*: 8-syllable verse in trochaic metre; *quinario*: 5-syllable verse in iambic metre; *senario*: 6-syllable verse in broken anapaests; *settenario*: 7-syllable verse in iambic metre (see also ACCENTO). *Versi sciolti*; a free mingling of 7- and 11-syllable verse employed for recitatives.

Index

Verdi

Africaine, L', 93, 275
Étoile du Nord, L', 67, 232–3
Huguenots, Les, 69, 232
Prophète, Le, 69, 221, 233, 270
Robert le Diable, 69, 233
Mila, Massimo, 291, 337
Milanov, Zinka, 217
Mirate, Raffaele, 58
Mocenigo, Count Alvise, 22, 24
Montanelli, Giuseppe, 72–3, 82
Monteverdi, Claudio, 151, 162
Morelli, Domenico, 79, 127
Moriani, Napoleone, 15, 37, 46, 299
Morosini, Emilia, 21
Mozart, Wolfgang Amadeus, 1, 3, 90, 148, 151, 189, 232, 305, 310, 327
Don Giovanni, 133, 164, 166, 215, 245–6, 248, 290, 296–7
Nozze di Figaro, Le, 241, 295
Mugnone, Leopoldo, 141
Mussorgsky, Modeste, 236, 259, 318
Boris Godunov, 259
Muzio, Emanuele, 27–32, 34, 39, 41–5, 48, 63, 65, 105–6, 109, 119, 127, 131, 148

Napoleon Bonaparte, 2, 5, 158
Napoleon III, 44, 82–3
Negrini, Carlo, 73
Newman, Ernest, 332
Nicolai, Otto, 19, 26, 162
Templario, Il, 18
Novaro, Michele, 49, 315
Nuitter, Charles, 119, 127

Offenbach, Jacques, 225, 233

Pacini, Giovanni, 14, 24, 153–4, 160–1, 241, 296
Paganini, Niccolò, 11, 175, 218, 301
Paisiello, Giovanni, 8
Palestrina, Pierluigi da, 123, 132, 136, 151, 336, 343
Pantaleone, Romilda, 131
Parker, Roger, 298n
Pasqua, Giuseppina, 136, 287
Penco, Rosina, 62

Verdi

Choral and Religious

Miscellaneous operatic compositions

Operas